西方语言学教材名著系列

A COURSE IN PHONETICS

语音学教程

(Seventh Edition)

(第七版)

〔美〕Peter Ladefoged　著
　　　Keith Johnson

(影印本)

北京大学出版社
PEKING UNIVERSITY PRESS

著作权合同登记号 图字：01-2015-4540

图书在版编目（CIP）数据

语音学教程：第 7 版 = A COURSE IN PHONETICS (Seventh Edition)：英文／（美）赖福吉（Ladefoged, P.），（美）约翰逊（Johnson, K.）著. —影印本. —北京：北京大学出版社，2015.11
（西方语言学教材名著系列）
ISBN 978-7-301-23228-6

Ⅰ. ①语… Ⅱ. ①赖… ②约… Ⅲ. ①语音学－教材－英文 Ⅳ. ①H01

中国版本图书馆 CIP 数据核字(2015)第 219054 号

Copyright © [2015,2011,2006] by Cengage Learning.
Original edition published by Cengage Learning. All Rights reserved. 本书原版由圣智学习集团出版。版权所有，盗印必究。
Peking University Press is authorized by Cengage Learning to publish and distribute exclusively this reprint edition. This edition is authorized for sale in the People's Republic of China only (excluding Hong Kong, Macao SAR and Taiwan). Unauthorized export of this edition is a violation of the Copyright Act. No part of this publication may be reproduced or distributed by any means, or stored in a database or retrieval system, without the prior written permission of the publisher.
本书英文影印版由圣智学习集团授权北京大学出版社独家出版发行。此版本仅限在中华人民共和国境内（不包括中国香港、澳门特别行政区及中国台湾）销售。未经授权的本书出口将被视为违反版权法的行为。未经出版者预先书面许可，不得以任何方式复制或发行本书的任何部分。
Cengage Learning Asia Pte. Ltd.
151 Lorong Chuan, #020-08 New Tech Park, Singapore 556741

书　　　　名	语音学教程（第七版）（影印本） YUYINXUE JIAOCHENG (DI-QI BAN) (YINGYINBEN)
著作责任者	〔美〕Peter Ladefoged 〔美〕Keith Johnson 著
责 任 编 辑	孙　娴
标 准 书 号	ISBN 978-7-301-23228-6
出 版 发 行	北京大学出版社
地　　　　址	北京市海淀区成府路205号　100871
网　　　　址	http://www.pup.cn　新浪微博：@北京大学出版社
电 子 信 箱	zpup@pup.cn
电　　　　话	邮购部 62752015　发行部 62750672　编辑部 62753027
印 刷 者	河北滦县鑫华书刊印刷厂
经 销 者	新华书店
	720毫米×1020毫米　16开本　22.25印张　517千字 2015年11月第1版　2021年1月第2次印刷
定　　　　价	76.00元

未经许可，不得以任何方式复制或抄袭本书之部分或全部内容。
版权所有，侵权必究
举报电话：010-62752024　电子信箱：fd@pup.pku.edu.cn
图书如有印装质量问题，请与出版部联系，电话：010-62756370

导　读

　　先师林焘先生给我开的第一本参考书就是 *A Course in Phonetics*，因此我对这本教材较为熟悉，而且各版本也都读过，格外有些感情。记得第一版是向沈炯师借的，当时他对我说"你要像爱护自己的眼睛一样爱护它"；虽然他语带玩笑，我还是能感觉到他的认真以及他对这本书的重视。第二版是跟学长兼老师北京林业大学的史宝辉教授借阅的；第三版得北京师范大学许小颖博士之助，购于新加坡南洋理工大学；第四版借自北京语言大学图书馆；第五版（外研社版）购于北京；第六版是在网上浏览的。这最新的第七版为北大出版社王飙编审所赠，而且巧的是，在我拿到书的当日正好 Keith Johnson 教授来访！

　　见面时，Keith 提到好几次，说这本书是 Peter Ladefoged 的，不能说是他的。这话一半对，一半不对。自谦的成分重了点。

　　我们知道第五版是 Peter Ladefoged 生前做的最后一次修订。正如 Keith Johnson 在第六版序言中所说，通过前四次修订，*A Course in Phonetics* 几乎已经成为理想的语音学教程，因而在此基础上再作提升，殊属不易。可结果我们却看到，由 Keith Johnson 主笔修订的第六版在 2011 年出版后很快售罄。许多中国的语音学爱好者（包括我在内）几乎还没来得及品读，第七版又于 2015 年由同一家出版社 Cengage Learning 出版了。这既反映了 Peter Ladefoged 的遗孀和出版社慧眼识人（请 Keith Johnson 担纲），也说明 Keith 作为 Ladefoged 教授的得意门生青出于蓝，名不虚传。

　　第七版影印本由北京大学出版社引进，几乎与美国发行同步。从框架、目录来看，与以前诸版，尤其第五、六版差别不大。比如：全书主要由三部分组成，共 11 章——第一、二章是基本概念，第三、四、五章是英语语音学，第六至十一章是普通语音学。不过，稍加对比，不难发现还有如下一些变化：(1) 有些章节的内容及顺序作了调整；(2) 对一些小节的标题进行了修改；(3) 每章正文后——或者说练习前——都增加了一段"要点重述（Recap）"。

因(1)(2)两点实际都涉及对一些语音现象在认识上的进步或表述上的完善,所以我想在下面的"内容简介"中再提。此处先谈谈(3)"要点重述"。我认为它们是每一章的点睛之语。这部分内容可以说完全是 Keith 的匠心独运。"要点重述"——或者说 Keith Johnson 的 Recap——不同于我们所习见的提要(summary)。后者通常只是内容的梗概,而前者则近似于对全章内容的综述与理论观照。而且,Keith Johnson 每每能在这里用一两个精到的比喻,把从纷繁的语音现象和细节中提炼或归纳出来的关键理论观点说得清清楚楚,既易于理解,又使人印象深刻。例如,他在英语辅音一章(第三章)的"要点重述"中说,"也许从本章谈到的许多细节中,可以得出的最重要的观点就是:人们口中发出辅音并不像在电脑上键入字母……在我们为描写方便而使用的语音学字母之下,隐藏着更为基本的事实。"

某种意义上说,"要点重述"使读者得以用研究者的眼光来对待所阅读的材料,使教材内容的深度得以展现,价值得到提升。作为本版的导读撰写者,我强烈建议大家——即使是对本教材已很熟悉的同仁——认真阅读这个部分。

下面我对本版各章的内容作一简介,目的纯为给学习语音学的年轻学生一点儿引介,希望不至于把他们带到沟里。至于语音学界各种各样的"咖"们,敬请飘过、观望或指教。

上篇　基本概念

第一章　发音与声学

本章介绍发音与声学的基本知识。如果读者已经系统学过语音学,我认为这一章可以跳读,或者直接做后面的笔头练习和口头练习,遇到难题再寻找、回看有关内容。这样的话,一来效率高,二来印象深。

需要指出的是,自第五版以来,A Course in Phonetics 开始用过程、加工(process)的视角来解释言语产生机制(参见图 1.3)。这相较于常见的对发音器官的静态描写与分类来说,无疑是一种更新和进步。这使得发音过程的描述变得易于理解,而且不那么干巴和枯燥。此外,教程还用"发音姿态(articulation gestures)"或"姿态(gestures)"这样的说法来代替传统的术语"发音部位"。这至少有两个好处:第一,它能体现"发音是一个动态过程"这样的意涵;

第二,简洁、概括——既然叫"姿态",自然就会涉及"主动发音部位"和"被动发音部位",学界不时有人争论的话题"辅音要用主动发音部位还是被动发音部位命名"就变得无谓了。

如Keith在自序中所言,本版较以往适当增添了一些语图,一方面这是语音学发展所致,另一方面添加语图可以使有关现象多少变得直观可察,增加说服力。本章在"声波"一节也增加了部分内容,讲解声波、二维频谱和三维语图之间的关系(参见图1.5),讲得比较清楚,有助于读者理解。此外,在"辅音声学"一节,图1.12因在波形之外引入了三维语图,对有关音段的标注较之过去也更为简洁、明白。

第二章　音系/音位和语音学的标音

本章主要介绍了一些与音系学有关的最基本的概念,以及初步的国际音标知识,诸如:音系(phonology)、音位(phoneme)、分布(distributions)、变体(variation)、互补(complementary)、区别性/对立(distinctiveness/contrast)、宽式标音(broad transcription)、严式标音(narrow transcription)等等。同样,对于那些已经受过较为系统的语音学训练的读者来说,这一章似乎也可以跳读或挑读。

另外,还有一种学习法是挑选那些具体的例子来看。一般它们都会以斜体字的形式呈现。这样做一定能丰富大家的英语语音知识。

表2.1和2.2中一些国际音标的称说法(或者说"名称")过去常常被忽视,实际在教学中是很有用的。

图2.3是第七版新加的,用来说明音变的三种基本类型:对立、互补、自由变体。图中对送气塞音的标注有不一致的地方,白璧微瑕,请读者注意辨别。

中篇　英语语音学

第三章　英语的辅音

本章首先按不同的发音类型/方法,包括塞音、擦音、塞擦音、鼻音、通音等,对英语中每个辅音的发音姿态及标音进行了详细的介绍,随后用近三页的篇幅讲解了英语辅音发音涉及的音姿叠加(大体相当于协同发音)问题,最后讲的是英语辅音音位变体的规则以及几个相关的附加符号。

教程在"塞音"一节还介绍了一点语音调查的方法,并鼓励读者利用一些常见的语音软件,如 WaveSurfer、Praat、Audacity 等,对教材相关网络提供的语音材料进行观察、分析。

关注斜体举例的方法在本章的学习中仍然适用。通过本章的学习,相信读者对英语的辅音,包括英语方言的辅音,会有广泛而深入的了解,储备更细致的变体知识。教材作者提到,希望读者多多思考和比较,从而培养对语音的细致观察能力。比如通音的常态是浊音,但是当我们仔细琢磨 play,twice,cue 等词的发音时,就会发现这些词中的通音都不浊。严格地标音的话,它们应当是[pʰeɪ][tʰwaɪs] [kʰju]。其中的规律,相信读者不难看出。

第四章　英语的元音

本章的内容第六、七版相较于第五版有不少改进。其中,最明显的就是将"元音的音质"一节拆分、扩展出多个小节——元音音质、元音听觉空间、美语和英语中的元音、复元音、卷舌元音。此外,本章第七版还增加了"词汇集(Lexical Sets)"一节。

虽然扩展出的几个小节主要只是在原第五版的基础上增加了相关的标题,但这使得有关的内容变得条理清晰,有利于读者建立知识体系、把握重点。其中,"元音听觉空间"一节尤其如此。

自丹尼尔·琼斯提出"正则元音(Cardinal Vowels)说"以来,人们一直把元音舌位图与发音等同起来。后来,随着声学语音学的发展,人们又根据元音一、二共振峰数据做出声学元音图,而且经常把两种舌位图进行对应和关联。实际上,我们所熟知的元音舌位图真的不好说是发音舌位图。Ladefoged 提出"元音听觉空间"这一概念已经有十年,根据这一观点,所谓的元音舌位图只是听觉分布图。有了这样的认识,将元音舌位图与声学元音图作对比才是正确的。然而我们至今未对元音舌位图的性质作这样的厘清,我个人认为跟我们的教材中没有独立的一节有很大的关系。

至于新增的"词汇集"一节,我以为起到了一种"授人以渔"的作用。Keith 在教材中不只是传授英语方言发音(变体)的知识,也传授了英语方言发音的调查方法。

第五章 英语的词语和句子

这一章主要讲的是英语里的语流音变、轻重音和语调。个人认为这是最值得精读的一章。

一个句子或一段自然的话语不是由一系列离散的音姿简单地连起来就能发出的。换言之,一个语言成分或词语单说或单念时跟它在连续的语流和句子里是有所不同的。这里面既有音姿叠加、同化、异化等主要表现在音段层面的问题或现象,也有强弱、轻重、长短等超音段、韵律层面的问题或现象。本章对英语中的这些现象有清楚而翔实的介绍及讨论。例如对一般较难说清的句中音节的轻重、强弱、突显度之间的关系,书里用一张树形图(图5.2)很轻松地就说清楚了。

需要指出的是,Keith将本章原第五版的"句重音(Sentence Stress)"一节更名为"句子的节奏(Sentence Rhythm)",我认为这是一个非常恰当的修改。一方面,句重音的有关内容在"重音的等级(Degrees of Stress)"一节已作讲解,另一方面,英语句子的节奏(或曰"节拍")本就表现为句子里重音及强弱音的规律性分布。孔子说过,"必也正名乎"。此节标题的修改是概念的厘清,善莫大焉。当然,奥巴马胜选演说的47秒节拍图(图5.3)也使本节的内容更加丰富,标题更加名副其实。

"语调"一节在第七版也有值得称道的改进。其主要表现为给每个例句的音高曲线都"顺便"标上ToBI符号。ToBI全称是Tone and Boundry Indices,可译为"音调及边界标记"。自上世纪80年代诞生以来,ToBI已成为语调研究的一个常用工具暨标注体系。教程过去的几个版本或者未提,或者未能将之与调形结合起来进行展现。作为ToBI的主要发明人之一Mary Beckman的弟子和同事,Keith对ToBI的把握和理解无疑是相当准确的。这一点非常重要,他的顺便一标,大大方便了读者对英语语调及ToBI系统的学习与理解。说实话,我过去常常觉得教程对语调的描写有点"隔靴搔痒",如今这种感觉基本消除。可以说,新版这一点"小小的"改进,使这一节的价值得到"大大的"提高。至少我个人愿意把这一节的内容作为入门的知识推荐给有志于语调研究的读者。

下篇　普通语音学

在这一篇中，教程对语音知识的介绍进入了更广阔的背景：世界语言。一些我们平常没听说过的语言和语音现象会频繁出现在此篇中。

第六章　气流机制和发声类型

任何语言的发音都离不开气流。用肺中呼出的气流来发音可以称之为"肺部气流机制（pulmonic airstream mechanism）"。我们时常听到的一些语言，如汉语（普通话）、俄语、英语、法语、德语、西班牙语等等，一般都是用肺部气流机制来发音的。然而，还有一些语言，如豪萨语、拉科塔语、信德语、祖鲁语、那玛语、乍得语等等，它们除使用肺部气流机制来发音以外，还使用其他的气流机制，诸如"喉部气流机制（glottalic airstream mechanism）""软腭气流机制（velaric airstream mechanism）"来发音。另外，在英语的一些变体及病理性的发音中也能发现一些非肺部气流音。学习本章内容时，多听听教材提供的音例，了解并记住一些语言的名称和语音现象，那将对语音学习大有好处。

如前面的有关章节一样，Keith在本版本章也尽可能地增加了一些三维语图。这些语图对理解和观察相关的发音机制和结果十分有益。

表6.8是本章有关喉部发声类型部分的总结。发声类型、声带状态以及音例都言简意赅地集成在了一张表中，希望读者能够善加利用。

第七章　辅音的音姿

"音姿"这一术语主要适用于辅音。前面已经提到，"音姿"比起"发音部位"来更有概括性。事实上，由于"音姿"还涉及发音的过程，传统的"发音方法"这一术语所涉及的"成阻""持阻""除阻"等环节与"音姿"也就有了交叉。

实际上本章的内容完全可以视作是用世界语言的例子对国际音标（IPA）辅音表的详细解析。解析的线索为辅音表的行与列，只是"发音部位"（行）更名为"发音目标（articulatory targets）"，"发音方法"（列）更名为"音姿类型（types of articulatory gestures）"而已。

第八章　声学语音学

这一章的内容较之第五版有相当大的改动与深化。由于写过一本《声学及听觉语音学》,Keith 对本章的改动可谓驾轻就熟。表面上他舍弃了"共振峰(Formants)"一节而代之以三种理论/模型的介绍——声源/滤波理论、管道模型、扰动理论;实际上,这些理论/模型对共振峰的形成、预测及合成都有一定的解释力。

"辅音声学"一节,Keith 更换了原第五版中的两张语图(图8.7和图8.8)。原图的第二共振峰出现近乎断层式的移动,明显与例子单元音的性质不符。

"破译语图(Interpreting Spectrograms)"一节,我个人认为是本章最有意思的部分。声学语音学作为实验语音学的主体,读图及看图识音是学习者必须训练的一项基本功。本章通过几幅语图,详细介绍了识图的方法及推导出句子的过程。

第九章 元音和类元音的发音

本章详细介绍和讨论决定元音音质的诸特征,如舌位高低、舌位前后、唇形圆展以及卷舌、鼻化、舌根前伸等等。书中还对这些特征的声学关联物/现象作了归纳总结(参见表9.2)。此外,半元音、(硬)腭化、软腭化、咽音化和唇化现象在这里也得到了讨论。

本章的主要目标是使读者能够运用正则元音及其符号,对所听到的语言或言语中的元音进行准确的描写。

第十章 音节和超音段特征

本章主要分为两个部分。一个部分讨论音节的概念、一些已有的音节理论及其不足之处;另一部分介绍超音段特征在世界语言中的应用和表现,主要包括重音、时长、声调、语调等。

需要特别指出的是,书中对音节的分析既有与传统的汉语音韵学相似的地方——如把每个音节分成声(onset)韵(rhyme)两部分,韵又分为韵核(nucleus,相当于韵腹)、韵尾(coda);也有与我们的习惯看法不一致的地方——他们只把音节最后的辅音看作韵尾,而我们把 ai、ao 中的-i、-o/u 也看作韵尾。

此外,Keith 把原第五版本章超音段部分的"节奏(Rhythm)"一节更名为"计时性(Timing)"是又一个非常恰当的修改。无论是 syllable-timed、stress-timed,还是 mora-timed,归根到底都是在说计时的特点;而且,节奏固然跟时间有关,但是轻重的交替与往复起主要作用,即便有的语言常常利用时长来控制轻重。

第十一章　语言学的语音学

本章的重点在于探讨言语的风格如何影响语音学乃至语言学的描写，以及学习语音学需要掌握的相关知识。

与书里其他章节不同的是，本章有许多理论性的讨论内容。这就是为什么"国际音标"在全书的最后一章还以整节的形式出现。事实上，从第六版开始，Keith就对全章的内容进行了较大的修改。除了调整有关小节的顺序和内容以外，新版还增加了两个半小节：社会的语音学和个体的语音学、语言学解释中的一个难题、言语记忆——其中，"难题"一节因为使用了第五版"音系特征"一节中的表（表11.1），故而我称之为"半个"小节。而所谓社会的语音学主要讲某个群体能够分享的公众语音学知识（public phonetic knowledge），而个体语音学更多地是关注认知层面的东西。

本章中有许多观点说得非常到位和新颖，比如：

言语的生成是由许多音姿合作完成的，而这些音姿本质上又存在着对肌肉和声道控制权的竞争关系。(P. 291)

对每个语言的语音学描写都需要一套针对言语风格变体的补充规则。(P. 292)

如果两个对立的音有可能在某个词的相同位置出现，其感知上的距离就会有增加的趋势。(P. 295)

Keith在第七版的前言中说，该版全书经过了"彻底的更新与修订（thoroughly reviewed and updated）"。这一点在本章表现得淋漓尽致。

北京语言大学
曹文
2015.9.15

Contents

Preface I
About the Authors V

PART I INTRODUCTORY CONCEPTS 1

CHAPTER 1
Articulation and Acoustics 2

Speech Production 2
Sound Waves 6
Places of Articulatory Gestures 10
The Oro-Nasal Process 15
Manners of Articulation 15
  Stop 15
  Fricative 17
  Approximant 17
  Lateral (Approximant) 17
  Additional Consonantal Gestures 18
The Acoustics of Consonants 19
The Articulation of Vowel Sounds 20
The Sounds of Vowels 23
Suprasegmentals 24
Recap 26
Exercises 27

CHAPTER 2
Phonology and Phonetic Transcription 35

The Transcription of Consonants 37
The Transcription of Vowels 41
Consonant and Vowel Charts 45
Phonology 47
Recap 51
Exercises 52
Performance Exercises 56

PART II ENGLISH PHONETICS   59

CHAPTER 3
The Consonants of English   60

Stop Consonants   61
Fricatives   69
Affricates   71
Nasals   71
Approximants   72
Overlapping Gestures   73
English Consonant Allophones   76
Diacritics   80
Recap   81
Exercises   81
Performance Exercises   86

CHAPTER 4
English Vowels   89

Transcription and Phonetic Dictionaries   89
Vowel Quality   91
The Auditory Vowel Space   93
American and British Vowels   95
Diphthongs   97
Rhotic Vowels   99
Lexical Sets   101
Unstressed Syllables   104
Tense and Lax Vowels   105
English Vowel Allophones   107
Recap   109
Exercises   110
Performance Exercises   113

CHAPTER 5
English Words and Sentences   115

Words in Connected Speech   115
Stress   119
Degrees of Stress   121
Sentence Rhythm   124
Intonation   126

Target Tones   134
Recap   138
Exercises   139
Performance Exercises   142

PART III GENERAL PHONETICS   143

CHAPTER 6
Airstream Mechanisms and Phonation Types   144

Airstream Mechanisms   144
States of the Glottis   156
Voice Onset Time   159
Summary of Actions of the Glottis   164
Recap   165
Exercises   166
Performance Exercises   168

CHAPTER 7
Consonantal Gestures   173

Articulatory Targets   173
Types of Articulatory Gestures   183
  Stops   183
  Nasals   184
  Fricatives   185
  Trills, Taps, and Flaps   186
  Laterals   189
Summary of Manners of Articulation   191
Recap   192
Exercises   192
Performance Exercises   194

CHAPTER 8
Acoustic Phonetics   197

Source/Filter Theory   197
Tube Models   200
Perturbation Theory   202
Acoustic Analysis   203
Acoustics of Consonants   208
Interpreting Spectrograms   213

Individual Differences 221
Recap 224
Exercises 225

CHAPTER 9
Vowels and Vowel-Like Articulations 227

Cardinal Vowels 227
Secondary Cardinal Vowels 232
Vowels in Other Accents of English 234
Vowels in Other Languages 236
Advanced Tongue Root 238
Rhotacized Vowels 239
Nasalization 241
Summary of Vowel Quality 242
Semivowels 242
Secondary Articulatory Gestures 244
Recap 246
Exercises 247
Performance Exercises 249

CHAPTER 10
Syllables and Suprasegmental Features 253

Syllables 253
Stress 259
Length 260
Timing 261
Intonation and Tone 264
Stress, Tone, and Pitch Accent Languages 270
Recap 271
Exercises 272
Performance Exercises 274

CHAPTER 11
Linguistic Phonetics 277

Phonetics of the Community and of the Individual 277
The International Phonetic Alphabet 278
Feature Hierarchy 282
A Problem with Linguistic Explanations 287
Controlling Articulatory Movements 289
Memory for Speech 291

The Balance Between Phonetic Forces 294
Recap 296
Performance Exercises 296

Appendix A: Additional Material for Transcription 303
Appendix B: Guidelines for Contributors to the Journal of the International Phonetic Association 305
Notes 307
Glossary 313
Further Reading 321
Index 325

Preface

This book aims to help you (the student) become a knowledgeable user of phonetics. You may be (or become) a speech pathologist who diagnoses speech disorders and devises treatment plans for your clients. Or you may be an engineer who develops speech user-interface technology using automatic speech recognition or speech synthesis. Or you may be a language teacher showing your students how words and sentences are pronounced. Or you may be a student of English seeking to improve your pronunciation. Or you may be a cognitive scientist conducting studies on the neural response to spoken language. Or you may be an opera singer preparing to sing words in a language that you don't speak fluently. Or you may be an actor speaking a dialect you didn't grow up speaking. In each of these cases, you could use some knowledge of phonetics. This book, if you study it well, will help you do your job better.

Some of you start with phonetics out of general interest. Your program of study requires that you take some general education courses, and phonetics is one course that meets that requirement. This book will do that, but it will enrich your life, too. You will be a more knowledgeable person, which is the aim of general education. In this course, you will travel the world listening to people speak different languages. You will hear clicks and ejectives, implosives and glides. You will delve into anatomy and acoustics, motor control and aerodynamics, sometimes applying knowledge that you picked up in other courses, sometimes learning completely new things. And so we will develop a picture of a most interesting, complex, and fundamental human characteristic. We humans speak, and through our speech we form and maintain our relationships and communities, and we transmit our accumulated knowledge from one generation to the next.

Another aim of the book is to prepare some of you (those who are bitten by the phonetics bug) to be ready to contribute to phonetics research. This book is an authoritative account of phonetics by one of the greatest phoneticians of all time (I am speaking here not of myself but of Peter Ladefoged). It is a solid foundation for the new phonetician, and at points the book offers suggestions for research topics and indicates where further research is needed. If you study this book well, you should be ready to start making valuable research contributions right away (for example, see Appendix B) and you shouldn't shy away from doing so.

WHAT'S NEW IN THE SEVENTH EDITION

The seventh edition of *A Course in Phonetics* retains the chapter layout and most of the content of the sixth edition. All of it has been thoroughly reviewed and updated. I revised all of the chapters, sometimes in small ways and sometimes with a serious change in emphasis. For example, I revised the discussion of phonology extensively to bring this book into better alignment with current perspectives. Although there is no formal phonology in this book, the presentation will bring students into phonology with (one hopes) a pretty sophisticated conception of phonological patterning. I also introduce speech spectrograms in the first chapter and use spectrograms extensively on the course website and in several additional places in the text of the book. I include more MRI and x-ray images (again both in the text of the book and on the website). These additions encourage you to look at speech from several points of view: (1) auditory, as one would transcribe the utterance in the international phonetic alphabet, (2) articulatory, as one would see it in images of the moving vocal tract, and (3) acoustic, as revealed by waveforms and spectrograms.

I identify with what J. C. Wells (2000) said, "I remain a great admirer of the Daniel Jones tradition in phonetics (see Collins and Mees, 1999: 421–424). I continue to regard it as important for budding phoneticians to learn not only to recognize but also to perform all the sound-types of the world's languages." This book contains performance exercises in most chapters, and on the website you will find audio recordings of Peter Ladefoged demonstrating the exercises. This remains a distinctive and highly valuable component of *A Course in Phonetics*, which I hope you will employ. My own tendency is to look at spectrograms without listening to the speech that they show, or to look at articulatory movement traces without attempting to pronounce the speech they represent. So it is important for me (and perhaps also for others) to keep in mind that a part of phonetics is based on skill, and much of the practical work of the phonetician and practical utility of training in phonetics involves producing and recognizing sounds.

THE LINGUISTICS COURSEMATE

Jenny Ladefoged, with help from Peter, produced a CD for the fifth edition of *A Course in Phonetics*. This was based on the extensive work of Peter and generations of students and colleagues at UCLA that went into a HyperCard stack called *Sounds of the World's Languages*. I didn't do much with the CD for the sixth edition other than to update the format of the sound files and make sure that the links on the CD worked (an archive of the CD has been hosted by UCLA Linguistics for many years). For the seventh edition, with the generous help of the Department of Linguistics at the University of California, Berkeley (UCB), this material is now available via the Linguistics CourseMate for this book in the introductory section about Professor Keith Johnson on the UCB website.

The Linguistics CourseMate includes interactive learning, study and exam preparation tools that support the printed textbook. CourseMate includes an interactive eBook, as well as all of the audio files that were previously available on the CD, now embedded and linked to tables and buttons. For example, accompanying Chapter 8, on acoustic phonetics, is an update of a great little demo that Peter produced in 1971. The page lets you hear each formant individually and in combination by clicking on a button. You can also see a spectrogram of each audio file by right-clicking on the buttons. In fact, right-click will show you a spectrogram for any audio file anywhere on the site, and Alt-click will open the file in a separate window so you can save it locally for further analysis or use.

Chapter 8 - Speech synthesis demo

Speech sounds can be minimally specified in terms of a small set of parameters, each of which can be described in terms of how they are made (physiological characteristics), or their physical (acoustic) characteristics.

Some of these parameters are isolated in the synthesized speech tokens in this table. For example, token number 1 (linked in the column labeled "1") is composed of a monotone voice with only a first formant resonance frequency. When you look at the spectrogram of this utterance, there is only one formant. Token 4 combines the first three formants, token 5 is composed of only stop release burst noises and fricatives, and finally in token 7 the voice has normal fundamental frequency variation.

This speech was synthesized in 1971 by Peter Ladefoged on a synthesizer at UCLA. The values of the parameters were a modified version of a set provided by John Holmes.

	PHYSIOLOGICAL	ACOUSTIC	1	2	3	4	5	6	7
1	Rate of vibration of the vocal folds	Fundamental frequency							O
2	First resonance of the vocal tract	Formant 1 frequency	O						
3		Formant 1 amplitude	O						
4	Second resonance of the vocal tract	Formant 2 frequency				O			
5		Formant 2 amplitude				O			
6	Third resonance of the vocal tract	Formant 3 frequency				O			
7		Formant 3 amplitude				O			
8	Fricative and stop bursts	Center of noise frequency					O		
9		Amplitude of noise					O		

I also expanded the web materials by adding interactive versions of many of the homework exercises in the book. The exercises provide immediate feedback so that you know whether you got the right answer; if not, the correct answer is given. The exercises are not meant to be tests, given to evaluate students, but are rather designed to help you review the materials and evaluate your own level of retention and understanding. Some of my testers even describe these new exercises as "fun."

The textbook has marginal icons that direct you to material on the website that is related to the topic under discussion, such as auditory examples, so you can immediately hear the sounds you are reading about.

The site will also document that you have completed the exercises with a certificate that says at the bottom "save me, print me, show me to your teacher!"

> **A Course in Phonetics**
> This document certifies that you completed exercise 10A
> Completion time: Sat Aug 03 2013 22:29:54 GMT-0700 (PDT)
> (save me, print me, show me to your teacher!)

Collins, B., and I. Mees. (1999). *The Real Professor Higgins. The Life and Career of Daniel Jones.* Berlin: Mouton de Gruyter.

Wells, J. C. (2000). My personal history. Retrieved Aug 5, 2013, from http://www.phon.ucl.ac.uk/home/wells/philsoc-bio.htm.

ACKNOWLEDGMENTS

In the preface to the sixth edition of *A Course in Phonetics* I said, "When you start from such a high point, there is a lot of room to go down and not much room to go up." I am still trying to avoid doing harm to this marvelous textbook, and I really appreciate all the help that colleagues, students, and publishers have given me.

Natasha Warner (University of Arizona) wrote an incredibly detailed and helpful review of the sixth edition. I especially appreciate that feedback. I also appreciate the very helpful comments and suggestions that came from Susan Russell (Simon Fraser University), Christina Gildersleeve-Neumann (Portland State University), Lisa Davidson (New York University), Angela Carpenter (Wellesley College), Richard Wright (University of Washington), Pat Keating (UCLA), Ian Maddiesson (University of New Mexico), and Caroline Smith (University of New Mexico). Special mention to Mary Beckman (Ohio State University) and Sun-Ah Jun (UCLA) for help with the intonation section in Chapter 5. Also, much thanks to John Coleman (Oxford) for providing and guiding my use of the vowel MRIs in Chapter 4, and for the MRI movie on the website, and to Molly Babel (University of British Columbia) for feedback on many of the online exercises. Professor Babel also contributed audio as "American no. 2" in the online version of Figure 4.3 and as the voice of Minnesota for the online lexical set examples. Alice Gaby (Monash University) contributed audio clips for the website as the voice of Australia. John Sylak-Glassman (University of California, Berkeley) saved me from making mistakes in the web pages on languages of the Caucasus. I appreciate Shri Narayanan (University of Southern California,) for his contribution of an MRI movie for the website. Continuing thanks to Bruce Hayes (University of California, Los Angeles) for contributing his voice as the voice of General American on the website. I am also grateful to Jenny Ladefoged for her continued support and good humor as I change what she and Peter produced.

Several students at UC Berkeley offered feedback on the website and I really appreciate their help. Thank you, Sarah Bakst, Emily Cibelli, Greg Finley, Clara Cohen, Will Chang, Melinda Fricke, Grace Neveu, Ruofan Cai, and Taylor Hickok for feedback on the exercises.

The team at Cengage has been great. In particular, Joan Flaherty read every word of the revised manuscript and guided the process of producing the book. I am so grateful.

Keith Johnson
Berkeley, California
August 6, 2013

About the Authors

Peter Ladefoged (1925–2006) was preeminent in the field of phonetics. He received his Ph.D. from the University of Edinburgh, Scotland, in 1958. He founded the UCLA Phonetics Laboratory and was its director from 1962 to 1991, while he was also a professor in the Department of Linguistics. His contributions to the discipline of linguistics are enormous and have furthered our knowledge of language and languages in many ways. His phonetics fieldwork (pre-computers) took him around the globe, carrying equipment to record and document and describe little-known languages. He catalogued the sounds of thousands languages. Ladefoged also experimented with and encouraged development of better scientific research methods and equipment. He was instrumental in revising the IPA to include more sounds and advocated for preservation of endangered languages. In his spare time, he consulted on forensics cases and even served as a dialect advisor and lent his voice to the film *My Fair Lady*.

Peter will be remembered for his outstanding contributions to phonetics and linguistics, and also for his lively and impassioned teaching and his service as mentor to a great number of doctoral students and to his junior colleagues. Many careers have been built on his influence, enthusiasm, and encouragement.

Keith Johnson taught phonetics in the Department of Linguistics at Ohio State University from 1993 to 2005 and is now a professor in the Department of Linguistics at the University of California, Berkeley. He is the author of *Acoustic and Auditory Phonetics* and *Quantitative Methods in Linguistics*. His Ph.D. is from Ohio State University, and he held postdoctoral training fellowships at Indiana University (in Cognitive Psychology) and at UCLA (with Peter Ladefoged and Pat Keating).

PART I
INTRODUCTORY CONCEPTS

1

Articulation and Acoustics

Phonetics is concerned with describing speech. There are many different reasons for wanting to do this, which means that there are many kinds of phoneticians. Some are interested in the different sounds that occur in languages. Some study the cognitive processes involved in speaking and listening. Some are more concerned with pathological speech. Others are trying to help people speak a particular form of English. Still others are looking for ways to make computers talk more intelligibly or to get computers to recognize speech. For all these purposes, phoneticians need to find out what people are doing when they are talking and how the sounds of speech can be described.

SPEECH PRODUCTION

We will begin by describing how speech sounds are made. Most sounds are the result of movements of the tongue and the lips. We can think of these movements as gestures forming particular sounds. We can convey information by gestures of our hands that people can see, but in making speech that people can hear, humans have found a marvelously efficient way to impart information. The gestures of the tongue and lips are made audible so that they can be heard and recognized.

Making speech gestures audible involves pushing air out of the lungs while producing a noise in the throat or mouth. These basic noises are changed by the actions of the tongue and lips. Later, we will study how the tongue and lips make about twenty-five different gestures to form the sounds of English. We can see some of these gestures by looking at an x-ray movie (which you can watch on the book's website—http://linguistics.berkeley.edu/acip/). Figure 1.1 shows a series of frames from an x-ray movie of the phrase *on top of his deck*. In this sequence of twelve frames (one in every four frames of the movie), the tongue has been outlined to make it clearer. The lettering to the right of the frames shows, very roughly, the sounds being produced. The individual frames in the figure show that the tongue and lips move rapidly from one position to another. To appreciate how rapidly the gestures are being made, however, you should watch the movie.

Example 1.1 plays the sounds and shows the movements involved in the phrase *on top of his deck*. Even in this phrase, spoken at a normal speed, the

Speech Production 3

Figure 1.1 Frames from an x-ray movie of a speaker saying *on top of his deck*.

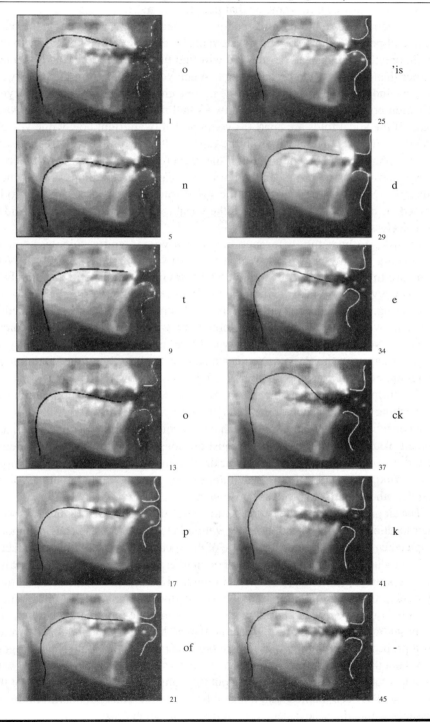

tongue is moving quickly. The actions of the tongue are among the fastest and most precise physical movements that people can make.

Producing any sound requires energy. In nearly all speech sounds, the basic source of power is the respiratory system pushing air out of the lungs. Try to talk while breathing in instead of out. You will find that you can do it, but it is much harder than talking when breathing out. When you talk, air from the lungs goes up the windpipe (the trachea, to use the more technical term) and into the larynx, at which point it must pass between two small muscular folds called the *vocal folds*. If the vocal folds are apart (as yours probably are right now while you are breathing in and out), the air from the lungs will have a relatively free passage into the pharynx and the mouth. But if the vocal folds are adjusted so that there is only a narrow passage between them, the airstream from the lungs will set them vibrating. Sounds produced when the vocal folds are vibrating are said to be **voiced**, as opposed to those in which the vocal folds are apart, which are said to be **voiceless**.

EXAMPLE 1.2

In order to hear the difference between a voiced and a voiceless sound, try saying a long 'v' sound, which we will symbolize as [vvvvv]. Now compare this with a long 'f' sound [fffff], saying each of them alternately— [fffffvvvvvfffffvvvvv]. (As indicated by the icon in the margin, an audio file illustrating this sequence is on the website.) Both of these sounds are formed in the same way in the mouth. The difference between them is that [v] is voiced and [f] is voiceless. You can feel the vocal fold vibrations in [v] if you put your fingertips against your larynx. You can also hear the buzzing of the vibrations in [v] more easily if you stop up your ears while contrasting [fffffvvvvv].

EXAMPLE 1.3

The difference between voiced and voiceless sounds is often important in distinguishing words. In each of the pairs of words *fat, vat*; *thigh, thy*; *Sue, zoo*, the first consonant in the first word of each pair is voiceless; in the second word, it is voiced. You can check this by saying just the consonant at the beginning of each of these words and try to feel and hear the voicing as suggested in the example. Try to find other pairs of words that are distinguished by one having a voiced and the other having a voiceless consonant.

The air passages above the larynx are known as the **vocal tract**. Figure 1.2 shows their location within the head (actually, within Peter Ladefoged's head, in a photograph taken many years ago). The shape of the vocal tract is a very important factor in the production of speech, and we will often refer to a diagram of the kind that has been superimposed on the photograph in Figure 1.2. Learn to draw the vocal tract by tracing the diagram in this figure. Note that the air passages that make up the vocal tract may be divided into the oral tract, within the mouth and pharynx, and the nasal tract, within the nose. When the flap at the back of the mouth is lowered (as it probably is for you now, if you are breathing with your mouth shut), air goes in and out through the nose. Speech sounds such as [m] and [n] are produced with the vocal folds vibrating and air going out through the nose. The upper limit of the nasal tract has been marked with a dotted line since the exact boundaries of the air passages within the nose depend on soft tissues of variable size.

Figure 1.2 The vocal tract.

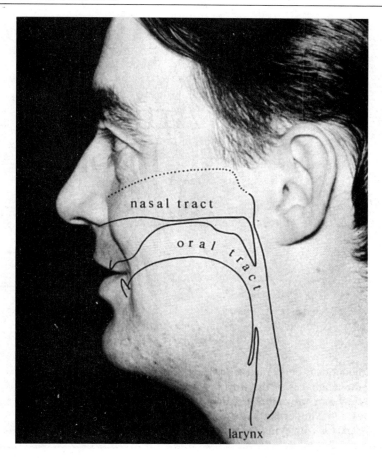

The parts of the vocal tract that can be used to form sounds, such as the tongue and the lips, are called *articulators*. Before we discuss them, let's summarize the speech production mechanism as a whole. Figure 1.3 (on page 6) shows the four main components—the airstream process, the phonation process, the oro-nasal process, and the articulatory process. The *airstream process* includes all the ways of pushing air out (and, as we will see later, of sucking it in) that provide the power for speech. For the moment, we have considered just the respiratory system, the lungs pushing out air, as the prime mover in this process. The *phonation process* is the name given to the actions of the vocal folds. Only two possibilities have been mentioned: voiced sounds in which the vocal folds are vibrating and voiceless sounds in which they are apart. The possibility of the airstream going out through the mouth, as in [v] or [z], or the nose, as in [m] and [n], is determined by the *oro-nasal process*. The movements of the tongue and lips interacting with the roof of the mouth and the pharynx are part of the *articulatory process*.

Figure 1.3 The four main components of the speech mechanism.

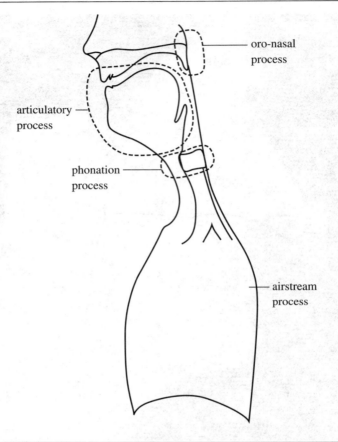

SOUND WAVES

So far, we have been describing speech sounds by stating how they are made, but it is also possible to describe them in terms of what we can hear. The way in which we hear a sound depends on its acoustic structure. We want to be able to describe the acoustics of speech for many reasons (for more on acoustic phonetics, see Keith Johnson's book *Acoustic and Auditory Phonetics*). Linguists and speech pathologists need to understand how certain sounds become confused with one another. We can give better descriptions of some sounds (such as vowels) by describing their acoustic structures rather than by describing the articulatory movements involved. Knowledge of acoustic phonetics is also helpful for understanding how computers synthesize speech and how speech recognition works (topics that are addressed more fully in Peter Ladefoged's book *Vowels and Consonants*). Furthermore, often the only permanent data that we can get of a speech event is an audio recording, as it is often impossible to obtain movies or x-rays showing what the speaker is doing. Accordingly, if we want permanent data that we can study, it will often have to come from analyzing an audio recording.

Speech sounds, like other sounds, can differ from one another in three ways. They can be the same or different in (1) pitch, (2) loudness, and (3) quality. Thus, two vowel sounds may have exactly the same pitch in the sense that they are said on the same note on the musical scale, and they may have the same loudness, yet still may differ in that one might be the vowel in *bad* and the other the vowel in *bud*. On the other hand, they might have the same vowel quality but differ in that one was said on a higher pitch or that one of them was spoken more loudly.

Sound consists of small variations in air pressure that occur very rapidly one after another. These variations are caused by actions of the speaker's vocal organs that are (for the most part) superimposed on the outgoing flow of lung air. Thus, in the case of voiced sounds, the vibrating vocal folds chop up the stream of lung air so that pulses of relatively high pressure alternate with moments of lower pressure. Variations in air pressure in the form of sound waves move through the air somewhat like the ripples on a pond. When they reach the ear of a listener, they cause the eardrum to vibrate. A graph of a sound wave is very similar to a graph of the movements of the eardrum.

The upper part of Figure 1.4 shows the variations in air pressure that occur during a production of the word *father*. The ordinate (the vertical axis) represents air pressure (relative to the normal surrounding air pressure), and the abscissa (the horizontal axis) represents time (relative to an arbitrary starting point). As you can see, this particular word took about 0.6 seconds to say. The lower part of the figure shows part of the first vowel in *father*. The major peaks in air pressure recur about every 0.01 seconds (i.e., every one-hundredth of a second). This is because the vocal folds were vibrating approximately one hundred times a second, producing a pulse of air every hundredth of a second. This part of the diagram shows the air pressure corresponding to four vibrations of the vocal folds. The smaller variations in air pressure that occur within each period of one-hundredth of a second are due to the way air vibrates when the vocal tract has the particular shape required for this vowel.

In the upper part of Figure 1.4, which shows the waveform for the whole word *father*, the details of the variations in air pressure are not visible because the time scale is too compressed. All that can be seen are the near-vertical lines corresponding to the individual pulses of the vocal folds. The sound [f] at the beginning of the word *father* has a low amplitude (it is not very loud, so the pressure fluctuation is not much different from zero) in comparison with the vowel that follows it, and the variations in air pressure are smaller and more nearly random. There are no regular pulses because the vocal folds are not vibrating.

The ear's response to sound is to break it down into different frequency components; in fact, fibers in the auditory nerve are tuned to specific frequencies of

Figure 1.4 The variations in air pressure that occur during Peter Ladefoged's pronunciation of the vowel in *father*.

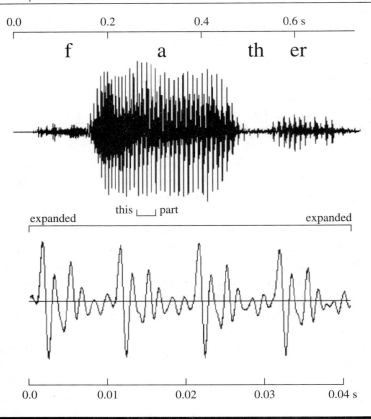

the sound. In order to visualize what the ear hears, we simulate this property of hearing by performing a spectral analysis of the sound, which results in a **sound spectrogram**. The process is illustrated in Figure 1.5 (the web version of this figure is annotated further).

EXAMPLE 1.4

As we saw in Figure 1.4, the waveform of speech shows differences between fricative noises and vowels in both amplitude and periodicity (regular repetition of a waveform pattern). In Figure 1.5, the utterance under consideration is of the sequence [ʃɑ] as in the word "shah." The figure shows a spectral analysis of a small window of time during the "sh" sound (arrow 1 in the figure) and another during the vowel (arrow 2). The windows are shaded grey in the waveform. The spectrum shows the amplitudes of different frequency components in the sound. These amplitudes change over time, so we take spectra from many small windows of time, rotate the axes (arrows 3 and 4), and place them side to side in a three dimensional graph (the spectrogram) that shows time on the horizontal axis, frequency on the vertical axis, and amplitude in a grey scale. The spectra in

Sound Waves 9

Figure 1.5 Where spectrograms come from. Small windows (shaded grey) of the acoustic waveform are spectrally analyzed, and amplitude is coded on a grey scale: darker = higher amplitude. Then the spectral slices are rotated and stacked together with each other in a three dimensional display (the spectogram). The dimensions are time on the horizontal axis, frequency on the vertical axis, and amplitude in the grey scale.

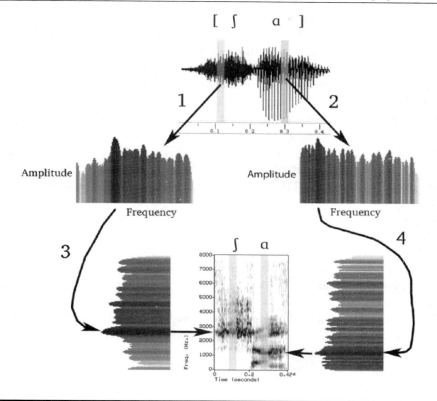

Figure 1.5 are filled with different shades of grey, depending on the height of the amplitude peak to illustrate how grey scale is used to code amplitude in spectrograms. The spectrogram in Figure 1.5 is composed of 213 spectral "slices," with one new spectrum calculated every 2 milliseconds during the utterance.

Spectrograms are a very informative visual display of speech sounds because they mimic the analysis performed by the ear. The information that we see in spectrograms is directly relevant for understanding how listeners perceive speech. Spectrograms also are very informative for deducing articulatory gestures because articulations leave acoustic "signatures" that we can see in spectrograms. For instance, in Figure 1.5, the "sh" noise is noticeably different from the noise we would expect to see in an "s" (to the trained eye). You will see quite a few spectrograms in this book, and especially on the book's website, and will become adept at reading them.

PLACES OF ARTICULATORY GESTURES

The parts of the vocal tract that can be used to form sounds are called *articulators*. The articulators that form the lower surface of the vocal tract are highly mobile. They make the gestures required for speech by moving toward the articulators that form the upper surface. Try saying the word *capital* and note the major movements of your tongue and lips. You will find that the back of the tongue moves up to make contact with the roof of the mouth for the first sound and then, comes down for the following vowel. The lips come together in the formation of *p* and then, come apart again in the vowel. The tongue tip comes up for the *t* and again, for most people, for the final *l*.

The names of the principal parts of the upper surface of the vocal tract are given in Figure 1.6. The upper lip and the upper teeth (notably the frontal incisors) are familiar enough structures. Just behind the upper teeth is a small protuberance that you can feel with the tip of the tongue. This is called the **alveolar ridge**. You can also feel that the front part of the roof of the mouth is formed by a bony structure. This is the **hard palate**. You will probably have to use a fingertip to feel farther back. Most people cannot curl the tongue up far enough to touch the **soft palate**, or **velum**, at the back of the mouth. The soft palate is a muscular flap that can be raised to press against the back wall of the pharynx and shut off the nasal tract, preventing air from going out through the nose. In this case, there is said to be a **velic closure**. This action separates the nasal tract from the oral tract so that the air can go out only through the mouth. At the lower end of the soft palate is a small appendage hanging down that is known as the *uvula*. The part of the vocal tract between the uvula and the larynx is the pharynx. The back wall of the pharynx may be considered one of the articulators on the upper surface of the vocal tract.

Figure 1.6 The principal parts of the upper surface of the vocal tract.

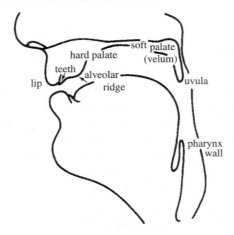

Figure 1.7 The principal parts of the lower surface of the vocal tract.

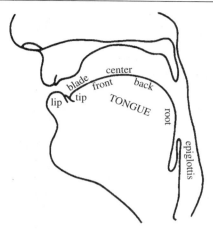

Figure 1.7 shows the lower lip and the specific names for the parts of the tongue that form the lower surface of the vocal tract. The tip and blade of the tongue are the most mobile parts. Behind the blade is what is technically called the *front* of the tongue; it is actually the forward part of the body of the tongue and lies underneath the hard palate when the tongue is at rest. The remainder of the body of the tongue may be divided into the center, which is partly beneath the hard palate and partly beneath the soft palate; the back, which is beneath the soft palate; and the root, which is opposite the back wall of the pharynx. The *epiglottis* is attached to the lower part of the root of the tongue. You may find it helpful to review the names of the articulators using the web version of Homework Exercise A for Chapter 1. It is a fun interactive way to study this information.

Bearing all these terms in mind, say the word *peculiar* and try to give a rough description of the gestures made by the vocal organs during the consonant sounds. You should find that the lips come together for the first sound. Then the back and center of the tongue are raised. But is the contact on the hard palate or on the velum? (For most people, it is centered between the two.) Then note the position in the formation of the *l*. Most people make this sound with the tip of the tongue on the alveolar ridge.

Now compare the words *true* and *tea*. In which word does the tongue movement involve a contact farther forward in the mouth? Most people make contact with the tip or blade of the tongue on the alveolar ridge when saying *tea*, but slightly farther back in *true*. Try to distinguish the differences in other consonant sounds, such as those in *sigh* and *shy* and those at the beginning of *fee* and *thief*.

When considering diagrams such as those we have been discussing, it is important to remember that they show only two dimensions. The vocal tract is a tube, and the positions of the sides of the tongue may be very different from the position of the center. In saying *sigh*, for example, there is a deep hollow in the center of the tongue that is not present when saying *shy*. We cannot represent this difference in a two-dimensional diagram that shows just the midline of the tongue—a so-called *mid-sagittal* view. We will be relying on mid-sagittal diagrams of the vocal organs to a considerable extent in this book. But we should never let this simplified view become the sole basis for our conceptualization of speech sounds.

In order to form consonants, the airstream through the vocal tract must be obstructed in some way. Consonants can be classified according to the place and manner of this obstruction. The primary articulators that can cause an obstruction in most languages are the lips, the tongue tip and blade, and the back of the tongue. Speech gestures using the lips are called **labial** articulations; those using the tip or blade of the tongue are called **coronal** articulations; and those using the back of the tongue are called **dorsal** articulations.

If we do not need to specify the place of articulation in great detail, then the articulators for the consonants of English (and of many other languages) can be described using these terms. The word *topic*, for example, begins with a coronal consonant; in the middle is a labial consonant; and at the end is a dorsal consonant. Check this by feeling that the tip or blade of your tongue is raised for the first (coronal) consonant, your lips close for the second (labial) consonant, and the back of your tongue is raised for the final (dorsal) consonant.

These terms, however, do not specify articulatory gestures in sufficient detail for many phonetic purposes. We need to know more than which articulator is making the gesture, which is what the terms *labial, coronal,* and *dorsal* tell us. We also need to know what part of the upper vocal tract is involved. More specific places of articulation are indicated by the arrows going from one of the lower articulators to one of the upper articulators in Figure 1.8. Because there are so many possibilities in the coronal region, this area is shown in more detail at the right of the figure. The principal terms for the particular types of obstruction required in the description of English are as follows.

1. **Bilabial**

    (Made with the two lips.) Say words such as *pie, buy, my* and note how the lips come together for the first sound in each of these words. Find a comparable set of words with bilabial sounds at the end.

2. **Labiodental**

    (Lower lip and upper front teeth.) Most people, when saying words such as *fie* and *vie*, raise the lower lip until it nearly touches the upper front teeth.

3. **Dental**

    (Tongue tip or blade and upper front teeth.) Say the words *thigh* and *thy*. Some people (most speakers of American English as spoken in the Midwest and on the West Coast) have the tip of the tongue protruding between the upper and lower front teeth; others (most speakers of British English)

Figure 1.8 A sagittal section of the vocal tract, showing the places of articulation that occur in English. The coronal region is shown in more detail at the right.

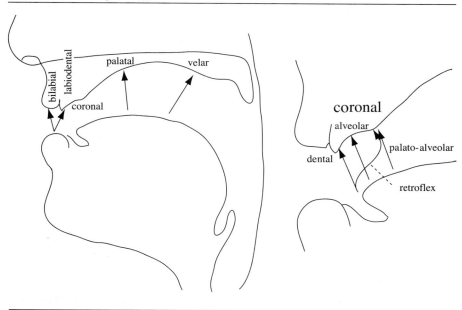

have it close behind the upper front teeth. Both sounds are normal in English, and both may be called *dental*. If a distinction is needed, sounds in which the tongue protrudes between the teeth may be called **interdental**.

4. **Alveolar**

    (Tongue tip or blade and the alveolar ridge.) Again there are two possibilities in English, and you should find out which you use. You may pronounce words such as *tie, die, nigh, sigh, zeal, lie* using the tip of the tongue or the blade of the tongue. You may use the tip of the tongue for some of these words and the blade for others. For example, some people pronounce [s] with the tongue tip tucked behind the lower teeth, producing the constriction at the alveolar ridge with the blade of the tongue; others have the tongue tip up for [s]. Feel how you normally make the alveolar consonants in each of these words, and then try to make them in the other way. A good way to appreciate the difference between dental and alveolar sounds is to say *ten* and *tenth* (or *n* and *nth*). Which *n* is farther back? (Most people make the one in *ten* on the alveolar ridge and the one in *tenth* as a dental sound with the tongue touching the upper front teeth.)

5. **Retroflex**

    (Tongue tip and the back of the alveolar ridge.) Many speakers of English do not use retroflex sounds at all. But some speakers begin words such as *rye*, *row*, *ray* with retroflex sounds. Note the position of the tip of your tongue in these words. Speakers who pronounce *r* at the ends of words may also have retroflex sounds with the tip of the tongue raised in words such as *ire*, *hour*, and *air*.

6. **Post-Alveolar**

    (Tongue blade and the back of the alveolar ridge.) Say words such as *shy*, *she*, and *show*. During the consonants, the tip of your tongue may be down behind the lower front teeth or up near the alveolar ridge, but the blade of the tongue is always close to the back part of the alveolar ridge. Because these sounds are made at the boundary between the alveolar ridge and the hard palate, they can also be called **palato-alveolar**. It is possible to pronounce them with either the tip or blade of the tongue. Try saying *shipshape* with your tongue tip up on one occasion and down on another. Note that the blade of the tongue will always be raised. You may be able to feel the place of articulation more distinctly if you hold the position while taking in a breath through the mouth. The incoming air cools the region where there is greatest narrowing, the blade of the tongue and the back part of the alveolar ridge.

7. **Palatal**

    (Front of the tongue and hard palate.) Say the word *you* very slowly so that you can isolate the consonant at the beginning. If you say this consonant by itself, you should be able to feel that it begins with the front of the tongue raised toward the hard palate. Try to hold the beginning consonant position and breathe in through the mouth. You will probably be able to feel the rush of cold air between the front of the tongue and the hard palate.

8. **Velar**

    (Back of the tongue and soft palate.) The consonants that have the place of articulation farthest back in English are those that occur at the end of words such as *hack*, *hag*, and *hang*. In all these sounds, the back of the tongue is raised so that it touches the velum.

As you can tell from the descriptions of these articulatory gestures, the first two, bilabial and labiodental, can be classified as labial, involving at least the lower lip; the next four—dental, alveolar, retroflex, and palato-alveolar (post-alveolar)—are coronal articulations, with the tip or blade of the tongue raised; and the last, velar, is a dorsal articulation, using the back of the tongue. Palatal sounds are sometimes classified as coronal articulations and sometimes as dorsal articulations, a point to which we shall return.

To get the feeling of different places of articulation, consider the consonant at the beginning of each of the following words: *fee*, *theme*, *see*, *she*. Say these consonants by themselves. Are they voiced or voiceless? Now note that the place of articulation moves back in the mouth in making this series of voiceless consonants, going from labiodental, through dental and alveolar, to palato-alveolar.

THE ORO-NASAL PROCESS

Consider the consonants at the ends of *rang*, *ran*, and *ram*. When you say these consonants by themselves, note that the air is coming out through the nose. In the formation of these sounds in sequence, the point of articulatory closure moves forward, from velar in *rang*, through alveolar in *ran*, to bilabial in *ram*. In each case, the air is prevented from going out through the mouth but is able to go out through the nose because the soft palate, or velum, is lowered.

In most speech, the soft palate is raised so that there is a velic closure. When it is lowered and there is an obstruction in the mouth, we say that there is a nasal consonant. Raising or lowering the velum controls the oro-nasal process, the distinguishing factor between oral and nasal sounds.

MANNERS OF ARTICULATION

At most places of articulation, there are several basic ways in which articulatory gestures can be accomplished. The articulators may close off the oral tract for an instant or a relatively long period; they may narrow the space considerably; or they may simply modify the shape of the tract by approaching each other.

Stop

(Complete closure of the articulators involved so that the airstream cannot escape through the mouth.) There are two possible types of stop.

Oral stop If, in addition to the articulatory closure in the mouth, the soft palate is raised so that the nasal tract is blocked off, then the airstream will be completely obstructed. Pressure in the mouth will build up and an **oral stop** will be formed. When the articulators come apart, the airstream will be released in a small burst of sound. This kind of sound occurs in the consonants in the words *pie*, *buy* (bilabial closure), *tie*, *dye* (alveolar closure), and *kye*, *guy* (velar closure). Figure 1.9 shows the positions of the vocal organs in the bilabial stop in *buy*. These sounds are called **plosives** in the International Phonetic Association's (IPA's) alphabet (see inside the front cover of this book).

Nasal stop If the air is stopped in the oral cavity but the soft palate is down so that air can go out through the nose, the sound produced is a **nasal stop**. Sounds of this kind occur at the beginning of the words *my* (bilabial closure) and *nigh* (alveolar closure), and at the end of the word *sang* (velar closure). Figure 1.10 (on page 16) shows the position of the vocal organs during the bilabial nasal stop in *my*. Apart from the presence of a velic opening, there is no difference between this stop and the one in *buy* shown in Figure 1.9 (on page 16). Although both the nasal sounds and the oral sounds can be classified as stops, the term **stop** by itself is almost always used by phoneticians to indicate an oral stop, and the term **nasal** to indicate a nasal stop. Thus, the consonants at the beginnings of the words *day*

Figure 1.9 The positions of the vocal organs in the bilabial stop in *buy*.

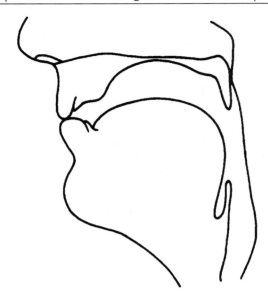

Figure 1.10 The positions of the vocal organs in the bilabial nasal (stop) in *my*.

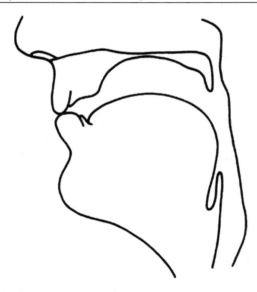

and *neigh* would be called an alveolar stop and an alveolar nasal, respectively. Although the term **stop** may be defined so that it applies only to the prevention of air escaping through the mouth, it is commonly used to imply a complete stoppage of the airflow through both the nose and the mouth.

Figure 1.11 The positions of the vocal organs in the palato-alveolar (post-alveolar) fricative in *shy*.

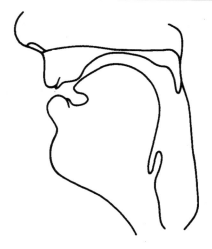

Fricative

(Close approximation of two articulators so that the airstream is partially obstructed and turbulent airflow is produced.) The mechanism involved in making these slightly hissing sounds may be likened to that involved when the wind whistles around a corner. The consonants in *fie*, *vie* (labiodental), *thigh*, *thy* (dental), *sigh*, *zoo* (alveolar), and *shy* (palato-alveolar) are examples of fricative sounds. Figure 1.11 illustrates one pronunciation of the palato-alveolar fricative consonant in *shy*. Note the narrowing of the vocal tract between the blade of the tongue and the back part of the alveolar ridge. The higher-pitched sounds with a more obvious hiss, such as those in *sigh* and *shy*, are sometimes called **sibilants**.

Approximant

(A gesture in which one articulator is close to another, but without the vocal tract being narrowed to such an extent that a turbulent airstream is produced.) In saying the first sound in *yacht*, the front of the tongue is raised toward the palatal area of the roof of the mouth, but it does not come close enough for a fricative sound to be produced. The consonants in the word *we* (approximation between the lips and in the velar region) and, for some people, in the word *raw* (approximation in the alveolar region) are also examples of approximants.

Lateral (Approximant)

(Obstruction of the airstream at a point along the center of the oral tract, with incomplete closure between one or both sides of the tongue and the roof of the mouth.) Say the word *lie* and note how the tongue touches near the center of the alveolar ridge. Prolong the initial consonant and note how, despite the closure formed by the tongue, air flows out freely, over the side of the tongue. Because there is no stoppage of the air, and not even any fricative noises, these sounds are classified as approximants. The consonants in words such as *lie* and *laugh* are alveolar lateral approximants, but they are usually called just *alveolar laterals*, their approximant status being assumed. You may be able to find out which side of the tongue is not in contact with the roof of the mouth by holding the consonant position while you breathe inward. The tongue will feel colder on the side that is not in contact with the roof of the mouth.

Additional Consonantal Gestures

In this preliminary chapter, it is not necessary to discuss all of the manners of articulation used in the various languages of the world—nor, for that matter, in English. But it might be useful to know the terms **trill** (sometimes called **roll**) and **tap** (sometimes called **flap**). Tongue-tip trills occur in some forms of Scottish English in words such as *rye* and *raw*, and as the "rolled *r*" in Spanish. Taps, in which the tongue makes a single tap against the alveolar ridge, occur in the middle of a word such as *pity* in many forms of American English.

The production of some sounds involves more than one of these manners of articulation. Say the word *cheap* and think about how you make the first sound. At the beginning, the tongue comes up to make contact with the back part of the alveolar ridge to form a stop closure. This contact is then slackened so that there is a fricative at the same place of articulation. This kind of combination of a stop immediately followed by a fricative is called an **affricate**, in this case a palato-alveolar (or post-alveolar) affricate. There is a voiceless affricate at the beginning and end of the word *church*. The corresponding voiced affricate occurs at the beginning and end of *judge*. In all these sounds the articulators (tongue tip or blade and alveolar ridge) come together for the stop and then, instead of coming fully apart, separate only slightly so that a fricative is made at approximately the same place of articulation. Try to feel these movements in your own pronunciation of these words.

Words in English that start with a vowel in the spelling (like *eek*, *oak*, *ark*, etc.) are pronounced with a **glottal stop** at the beginning of the vowel. This "glottal catch" sound isn't written in these words and is easy to overlook; but in a sequence of two words in which the first word ends with a vowel and the second starts with a vowel, the glottal stop is sometimes obvious. For example, the phrase *flee east* is different from the word *fleeced* in that the first has a glottal stop at the beginning of *east*.

To summarize, the consonants we have been discussing so far may be described in terms of five factors:

1. state of the vocal folds (voiced or voiceless);
2. place of articulation;

3. central or lateral articulation;
4. soft palate raised to form a velic closure (oral sounds) or lowered (nasal sounds); and
5. manner of articulatory action.

Thus, the consonant at the beginning of the word *sing* is a (1) voiceless, (2) alveolar, (3) central, (4) oral, (5) fricative; and the consonant at the end of *sing* is a (1) voiced, (2) velar, (3) central, (4) nasal, (5) stop.

On most occasions, it is not necessary to state all five points. Unless a specific statement to the contrary is made, consonants are usually presumed to be central, not lateral, and oral rather than nasal. Consequently, points (3) and (4) may often be left out, so the consonant at the beginning of *sing* is simply called a voiceless alveolar fricative. When describing nasals, point (4) has to be specifically mentioned and point (5) can be left out, so the consonant at the end of *sing* is simply called a voiced velar nasal.

THE ACOUSTICS OF CONSONANTS

At this stage, we will not go too deeply into the acoustics of consonants, simply noting a few distinctive points about them from waveforms and spectrograms. The places of articulation are not obvious in any waveform, but the differences in some of the principal manners of articulation—stop, nasal, fricative, and approximant—are usually apparent. Furthermore, as already pointed out, you can also see the differences between voiced and voiceless sounds. Place of articulation is more apparent in spectrograms, though it can still be a surprisingly subtle feature given how important it is for speech communication.

The top part of Figure 1.12 (on page 20) shows the waveform of the phrase *It's very central and the apartment is really nice*, labeled roughly in ordinary spelling. The lower part shows a spectrogram of the same utterance (this utterance is one of several contributed by a Dubliner—listen to it in the "Extras" section of the website for this book). This phrase took about two seconds.

Looking at the labels in the middle of the figure, you can see that fricatives (in *it's* and *nice*) are very different from vowels in both the waveform and in the spectrogram. But notice that the nasal in *and* and the lateral in *really* are much easier to see in the spectrogram than in the waveform.

Try to guess where the "n" of *nice* is in the waveform and then look for it in the spectrogram. Even though you don't know exactly what to look for in the spectrogram, it is probably apparent that something changed in the spectrogram (there is less energy, hence less ink, as if someone took an eraser and made a vertical white stripe), where it would be next to impossible to identify the nasal in the waveform.

Figure 1.12 The waveform and spectrogram of the phrase *It's very central and the apartment's really nice.*

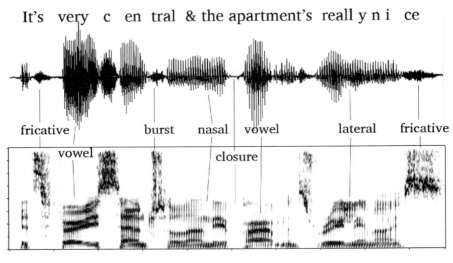

THE ARTICULATION OF VOWEL SOUNDS

In the production of vowel sounds, the articulators do not come very close together, and the passage of the airstream is relatively unobstructed. For this reason, it is much more difficult to feel the position of the tongue during vowel sounds, than in consonants. We can describe vowel sounds roughly in terms of the position of the highest point of the tongue and the position of the lips. (As we will see later, more accurate descriptions can be made in acoustic terms.) Figure 1.13 shows the articulatory position for the vowels in *heed, hid, head, had, father, good, food*. Of course, in saying these words, the tongue and lips are in continuous motion throughout the vowels, as we saw in the x-ray movie in example 1.1 on the book's website. The positions shown in the figure are best considered as the targets of the gestures for the vowels.

As you can see, in all these vowel gestures, the tongue tip is down behind the lower front teeth, and the body of the tongue is domed upward. Check that this is so in your own pronunciation. You will notice that you can prolong the [h] sound and that there is no mouth movement between the [h] and the following vowel; the [h] is like a voiceless version of the vowel that comes after it. In the first four vowels, the highest point of the tongue is in the front of the mouth. Accordingly, these vowels are called **front vowels**. The tongue is fairly close to the roof of the mouth for the vowel in *heed* (you can feel that this is so by breathing inward while holding the target position for this vowel), slightly less close for the vowel in *hid* (for this and most other vowels it is difficult to localize the position by breathing inward; the articulators are too far apart), and

Figure 1.13 The positions of the vocal organs for the vowels in the words 1 *heed*, 2 *hid*, 3 *head*, 4 *had*, 5 *father*, 6 *good*, 7 *food*. The lip positions for vowels 2, 3, and 4 are between those shown for 1 and 5. The lip position for vowel 6 is between those shown for 1 and 7.

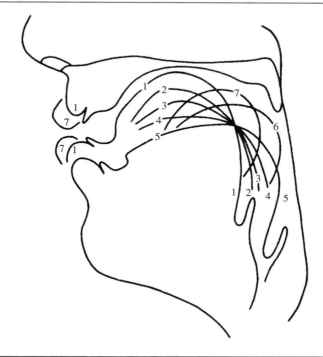

lower still for the vowels in *head* and *had*. If you look in a mirror while saying the vowels in these four words, you will find that the mouth becomes progressively more open while the tongue remains in the front of the mouth. The vowel in *heed* is classified as a *high front vowel*, and the vowel in *had* as a *low front vowel*. The height of the tongue for the vowels in the other words is between these two extremes, and they are therefore called *mid-front vowels*. The vowel in *hid* is a mid-high vowel, and the vowel in *head* is a mid-low vowel.

Now try saying the vowels in *father, good, food*. Figure 1.13 also shows the articulatory targets for these vowels. In all three, the tongue is close to the back surface of the vocal tract. These vowels are classified as **back vowels**. The body of the tongue is highest in the vowel in *food* (which is therefore called a *high back vowel*) and lowest in the first vowel in *father* (which is therefore called a *low back vowel*). The vowel in *good* is a mid-high back vowel. The tongue may be near enough to the roof of the mouth for you to be able to feel the rush of cold air when you breathe inward while holding the position for the vowel in *food*.

Lip gestures vary considerably in different vowels. They are generally closer together in the mid-high and high back vowels (as in *good, food*), though in some forms of American English this is not so. Look at the position of your lips in a mirror while you say just the vowels in *heed, hid, head, had, father, good, food.* You will probably find that in the last two words, there is a movement of the lips in addition to the movement that occurs because of the lowering and raising of the jaw. This movement is called *lip rounding.* It is usually most noticeable in the inward movement of the corners of the lips. Vowels may be described as being **rounded** (as in *who'd*) or **unrounded** (as in *heed*).

In summary, the targets for vowel gestures can be described in terms of three factors: (1) the height of the body of the tongue; (2) the front–back position of the tongue; and (3) the degree of lip rounding. The relative positions of the highest points of the tongue are given in Figure 1.14. Say just the vowels in the words given in the figure caption and check that your tongue moves in the pattern described by the points. It is very difficult to become aware of the position of the tongue in vowels, but you can probably get some impression of tongue height by observing the position of your jaw while saying just the vowels in the four words *heed, hid, head, had.* You should also be able to feel the difference between front and back vowels by contrasting words such as *he* and *who.* Say these words silently and concentrate on the sensations involved. You should feel the tongue going from front to back as you say *he, who.* You can also feel your lips becoming more rounded.

As you can see from Figure 1.14, the specification of vowels in terms of the position of the highest point of the tongue is not entirely satisfactory for a number of reasons. First, the vowels classified as high do not have the same tongue height. The back high vowel (point 7) is nowhere near as high as the front vowel (point 1). Second, the so-called back vowels vary considerably in their degree of "backness." Third, as you can see by looking at Figure 1.13, this kind of specification disregards considerable differences in the shape of the tongue in front vowels and in back vowels. Nor does it take into account the width of the pharynx, which varies considerably and is not entirely dependent on the height of the tongue in different vowels. We will discuss better ways of describing vowels in Chapters 4 and 9.

Figure 1.14 The relative positions of the highest points of the tongue in the vowels in 1 *heed*, 2 *hid*, 3 *head*, 4 *had*, 5 *father*, 6 *good*, 7 *food*.

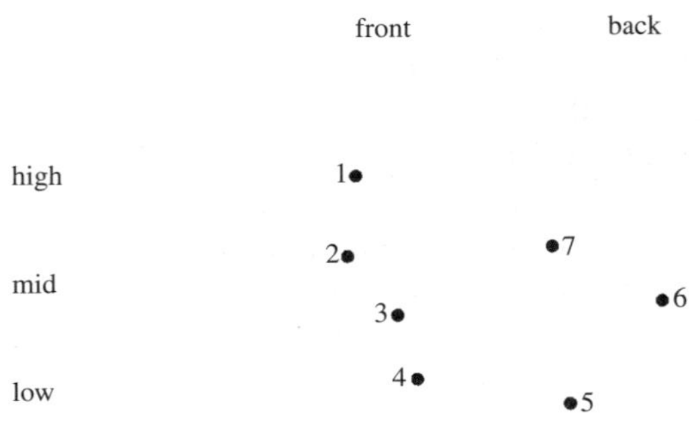

	front	back
high	1●	
mid	2●	●7
	3●	●6
low	4●	
		●5

THE SOUNDS OF VOWELS

Studying the sounds of vowels requires a greater knowledge of acoustics than we can handle at this stage of the book. We can, however, note some comparatively straightforward facts about vowel sounds. Vowels, like all sounds except the pure tone of a tuning fork, have complex structures. We can think of them as containing a number of different pitches simultaneously. There is the pitch at which the vowel is actually spoken, which depends on the pulses being produced by the vibrating vocal folds; and, quite separate from this, there are overtone pitches that depend on the shape of the resonating cavities of the vocal tract. These overtone pitches give the vowel its distinctive quality. Look back at Figure 1.12 to see what these overtone pitches look like in a spectrogram. The second vowel in *apartment* is labeled in that figure, and when you look at it in the spectrogram one key visual feature is that there are three dark bands running horizontally through the vowel. These bands occur at different frequencies for different vowels. We will enlarge on this notion in Chapter 8. Here we will consider briefly how one vowel is distinguished from another by the pitches of the overtones.

Normally, one cannot hear the separate overtones of a vowel as distinguishable pitches. The only sensation of pitch is the note on which the vowel is said, which depends on the rate of vibration of the vocal folds. But there are circumstances in which the overtones of each vowel can be heard. Try saying just the vowels in the words *heed, hid, head, had, hod, hawed, hood, who'd*, making all of them long vowels. Now whisper these vowels. When you whisper, the vocal folds are not vibrating, and there is no regular pitch of the voice. Nevertheless, you can hear that this set of vowels forms a series of sounds on a continuously descending pitch. What you are hearing corresponds to a group of overtones that characterize the vowels. These overtones are highest for the vowel in *heed* and lowest for the vowel in either *hawed, hood*, or *who'd*. Which of the three vowels is the lowest depends on your regional accent. Accents of English differ slightly in the pronunciation of these vowels. In the audio examples that accompany this chapter, you can hear these vowels whispered.

There is another way to produce something similar to this whispered pitch. Try whistling a very high note, and then the lowest note that you can. You will find that for the high note you have to have your tongue in the position for the vowel in *heed*, and for the low note your tongue is in the position for one of the vowels in *hawed, hood, who'd*. From this, it seems as if there is some kind of high pitch associated with the high front vowel in *heed,* and a low pitch associated with one of the back vowels. The lowest whistled note corresponds to the tongue and lip gestures very much like those used for the vowel in *who*. A good way to learn how to make a high back vowel is to whistle your lowest note possible, and then add voicing.

EXAMPLE 1.5

Another way of minimizing the sound of the vocal fold vibrations is to say the vowels in a very low, creaky voice (listen to example 1.4 in the supplemental materials). It is easiest to produce this kind of voice with a vowel such as that in *had* or *hod*. Some people can produce a creaky-voice sound in which the rate of vibration of the vocal folds is so low that you can hear the individual pulsations.

Try saying just the vowels in *had, head, hid, heed* in a creaky voice. You should be able to hear a change in pitch, although, in one sense, the pitch of all of them is just that of the low, creaky voice. When saying the vowels in the order *heed, hid, head, had,* you can hear a sound that steadily increases in pitch by approximately equal steps with each vowel. Now say the vowels in *hod, hood, who'd* in a creaky voice. These three vowels have overtones with a steadily decreasing pitch. Example 1.4 has an audio file of Peter Ladefoged saying the vowels in the words *heed, hid, head, had, hod, hawed, hood, who'd* in his British accent. The first four of these vowels have a quality that clearly goes up in pitch, and the last four have a declining pitch.

In summary, vowel sounds may be said on a variety of notes (voice pitches), but they are distinguished from one another by two characteristic vocal tract pitches associated with their overtones. One of them (actually the higher of the two) goes downward throughout most of the series *heed, hid, head, had, hod, hawed, hood, who'd* and corresponds roughly to the difference between front and back vowels. The other is low for vowels in which the tongue position is high and high for vowels in which the tongue position is low. It corresponds (inversely) to what we called *vowel height* in articulatory terms. These characteristic overtones are called the **formants** of the vowels. The one with the lower pitch (distinguishable in creaky voice) is called the *first formant*, and the higher one (the one heard when whispering) is the *second formant*.

The notion of a formant (actually the second formant) distinguishing vowels has been known for a long time. It was observed by Isaac Newton, who, in about 1665, wrote in his notebook: "The filling of a very deepe flaggon with a constant streame of beere or water sounds ye vowells in this order *w, u, ω, o, a, e, i, y.*" He was about twelve years old at the time. (The symbols used here are the best matches to the letters in Newton's handwriting in his notebook, which is in the British Museum. They probably refer to the vowels in words such as *woo, hoot, foot, coat, cot, bait, bee, ye.*) Fill a deep narrow glass with water (or beer!) and see if you can hear something like the second formant in the vowels in these words as the glass fills up.

SUPRASEGMENTALS

Vowels and consonants can be thought of as the segments of which speech is composed. Together they form the syllables that make up utterances. Superimposed on the syllables are other features known as *suprasegmentals*. These include variations in stress and pitch. Variations in length are also usually considered to be suprasegmental features, although they can affect single segments as well as whole syllables. We will defer detailed descriptions of the articulation and the corresponding acoustics of these aspects of speech till later in this book.

Variations in stress are used in English to distinguish between a noun and a verb, as in *(an) insult* versus *(to) insult*. Say these words yourself, and check which syllable has the greater stress. Then compare similar pairs such as *(a) pervert, (to) pervert* or *(an) overflow, (to) overflow*. Listen to these words in the supplemental materials. You should find that in the nouns, the stress is on the first syllable, but in the verbs, it is on the last. Thus, stress can have a grammatical function in English. It can also be used for contrastive emphasis (as in *I want a **red** pen, not a **black** one*). Stress in English is produced by (1) increased activity of the respiratory muscles, producing greater loudness, as well as by (2) exaggeration of consonant and vowel properties such as vowel height and stop aspiration, and (3) exaggeration of pitch so that low pitches are lower and high pitches are higher.

You can usually find where the stress occurs on a word by trying to tap with your finger in time with each syllable. It is much easier to tap on the stressed syllable. Try saying *abominable* and tapping first on the first syllable, then on the second, then on the third, and so on. If you say the word in your normal way, you will find it easiest to tap on the second syllable. Many people cannot tap on the first syllable without altering their normal pronunciation.

Pitch changes due to variations in laryngeal activity can occur independently of stress changes. They are associated with the rate of vibration of the vocal folds. Earlier in the chapter, we called this the "voice pitch" to distinguish between the characteristic overtones of vowels ("vocal tract pitches") and the rate of vocal fold vibration. Pitch of the voice is what you alter to sing different notes in a song. Because each opening and closing of the vocal folds causes a peak of air pressure in the sound wave, we can estimate the pitch of a sound by observing the rate of occurrence of the peaks in the waveform. To be more exact, we can measure the *frequency* of the sound in this way. **Frequency** is a technical term for an acoustic property of a sound—namely, the number of complete repetitions (cycles) of a pattern of air pressure variation occurring in a second. The unit of frequency measurement is the hertz, usually abbreviated Hz. If the vocal folds make 220 complete opening and closing movements in a second, we say that the frequency of the sound is 220 Hz. The frequency of the vowel [a] shown in Figure 1.4 was 100 Hz, as the vocal fold pulses occurred every 10 ms (one-hundredth of a second).

The **pitch** of a sound is an auditory property that enables a listener to place it on a scale going from low to high, without considering its acoustic properties. In practice, when a speech sound goes up in frequency, it also goes up in pitch. For the most part, at an introductory level of the subject, the pitch of a sound may be equated with its fundamental frequency, and, indeed, some books do not distinguish between the two terms, using *pitch* for both the auditory property and the physical attribute.

The pitch pattern in a sentence is known as the **intonation**. Listen to the intonation (the variations in the pitch of the voice) when someone says the sentence *This is my father.* (You can either say the sentences yourself, or listen to the recordings of it in the supplemental materials.) Try to find out which syllable has the highest pitch and which the lowest. In most people's speech, the highest pitch will occur on the first syllable of *father* and the lowest on the second, the last syllable in the sentence. Now observe the pitch changes in the question *Is this your father?* In this sentence, the first syllable of *father* is usually on a lower pitch than the last syllable. In English, it is even possible to change the meaning of a sentence, such as *That's a cat,* from a statement to a question without altering the order of the words. If you substitute a mainly rising for a mainly falling intonation, you will produce a question spoken with an air of astonishment: *That's a cat?*

All the suprasegmental features are characterized by the fact that they must be described in relation to other items in the same utterance. It is the relative values of pitch, length, or degree of stress of an item that are significant. You can stress one syllable as opposed to another irrespective of whether you are shouting or talking softly. Children can also use the same intonation patterns as adults, although their voices have a higher pitch. The absolute values are never linguistically important. But they do, of course, convey information about the speaker's age, sex, emotional state, and attitude toward the topic under discussion.

RECAP

This chapter introduces several key concepts that provide a foundation for later chapters in the book.

- Vocal tract anatomy. We named the major parts of the vocal tract used in speech production.
- Taxonomy of terms describing consonants centering around five aspects of consonant articulation: (1) place of articulation, (2) manner of articulation, (3) voicing, (4) nasality, and (5) laterality.
- Acoustic properties of consonants in waveforms and in spectrograms including amplitude, periodicity, and frequency.
- Taxonomy of vowel description, with three main parameters: front/back, high/low, and rounding.
- Acoustic properties of vowels with a focus on formant frequencies.
- A brief introduction to suprasegmentals, mainly word stress, sentence stress, and intonation.

The organization of this book is cyclical. Each of the concepts introduced in this chapter will appear twice more in the book—once in connection with English phonetics (Part 2) and again in connection with general phonetics (Part 3).

EXERCISES

(Printable versions of all the exercises are available on the website.)

A. Fill in the names of the vocal organs numbered in Figure 1.15.

1. _____
2. _____
3. _____
4. _____
5. _____
6. _____
7. _____
8. _____
9. _____
10. _____
11. _____
12. _____
13. _____
14. _____

Figure 1.15

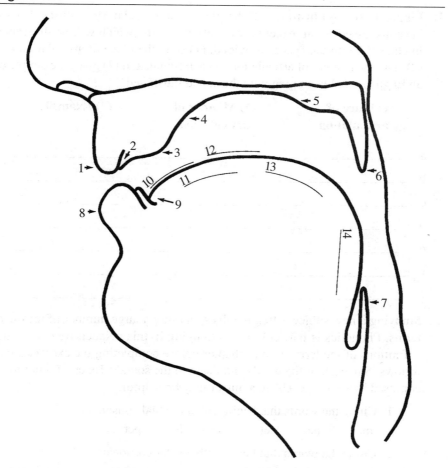

28 CHAPTER 1 Articulation and Acoustics

B. Describe the consonants in the word *skinflint* using the chart below. Fill in all five columns, and put parentheses around the terms that may be left out, as shown for the first consonant.

C.

	1 Voiced or voiceless	2 Place of articulation	3 Central or lateral	4 Oral or nasal	5 Articulatory action
s	voiceless	alveolar	(central)	(oral)	fricative
k					
n					
f					
l					
t					

D. Figure 1.16 a–g illustrates all the places for articulatory gestures that we have discussed so far, except for retroflex sounds (which will be illustrated in chapter 7). In the spaces provided, (1) state the place of articulation and (2) state the manner of articulation of each sound, and (3) give an example of an English word beginning with the sound illustrated.

	(1) Place of articulation	**(2) Manner of articulation**	**(3) Example**
a	_____	_____	_____
b	_____	_____	_____
c	_____	_____	_____
d	_____	_____	_____
e	_____	_____	_____
f	_____	_____	_____
g	_____	_____	_____

E. Studying a new subject often involves learning a large number of technical terms. Phonetics is particularly challenging in this respect. Read over the definitions of the terms in this chapter before completing the exercises that follows. Say each of the words and listen to the sounds. Be careful not to be confused by spellings. Using a mirror may be helpful.

1. Circle the words that begin with a bilabial consonant.
   met   net   set   bet   let   pet

2. Circle the words that begin with a velar consonant.
   knot   got   lot   cot   hot   pot

Figure 1.16 Sounds that illustrate all the places of articulation discussed so far, except for retroflex sounds.

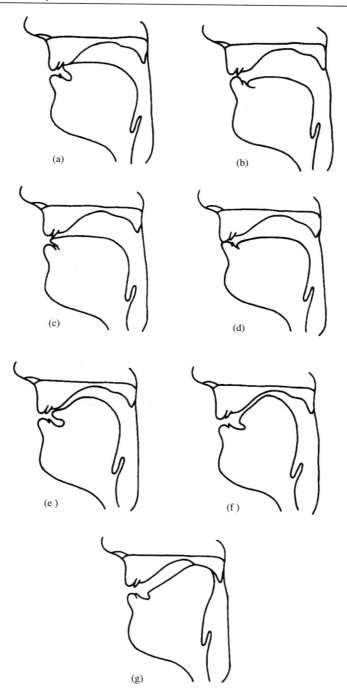

3. Circle the words that begin with a labiodental consonant.
   fat   cat   that   mat   chat   vat
4. Circle the words that begin with an alveolar consonant.
   zip   nip   lip   sip   tip   dip
5. Circle the words that begin with a dental consonant.
   pie   guy   shy   thigh   thy   high
6. Circle the words that begin with a palato-alveolar consonant.
   sigh   shy   tie   thigh   thy   lie
7. Circle the words that end with a fricative.
   race   wreath   bush   bring   breathe   bang
   rave   real   ray   rose   rough
8. Circle the words that end with a nasal.
   rain   rang   dumb   deaf
9. Circle the words that end with a stop.
   pill   lip   lit   graph   crab   dog   hide
   laugh   back
10. Circle the words that begin with a lateral.
    nut   lull   bar   rob   one
11. Circle the words that begin with an approximant.
    we   you   one   run
12. Circle the words that end with an affricate.
    much   back   edge   ooze
13. Circle the words in which the consonant in the middle is voiced.
    tracking   mother   robber   leisure   massive
    stomach   razor
14. Circle the words that contain a high vowel.
    sat   suit   got   meet   mud
15. Circle the words that contain a low vowel.
    weed   wad   load   lad   rude
16. Circle the words that contain a front vowel.
    gate   caught   cat   kit   put
17. Circle the words that contain a back vowel.
    maid   weep   coop   cop   good
18. Circle the words that contain a rounded vowel.
    who   me   us   but   him

F. Define the consonant sounds in the middle of each of the following words as indicated in the example.

	Voiced or voiceless	Place of articulation	Manner of articulation
a**dd**er	*voiced*	*alveolar*	*stop*
fa**th**er			
si**ng**ing			
e**tch**ing			
ro**bb**er			
e**th**er			
plea**s**ure			
ho**pp**er			
se**ll**ing			
su**nn**y			
lo**dg**er			

G. Complete the diagrams in Figure 1.17 to illustrate the target for the gesture of the vocal organs for the first consonants in each of the words given. If the sound is voiced, schematize the vibrating vocal folds by drawing a wavy line at the glottis. If it is voiceless, use a straight line.

H. Figure 1.18 shows the waveform of the phrase *Tom saw ten wasps*. Mark this figure in a way similar to that in Figure 1.12. Using just ordinary spelling, show the center of each sound. Also indicate the manner of articulation.

I. Make your own waveform of a sentence that will illustrate different manners of articulation. You can use the WaveSurfer application that is available at http://www.speech.kth.se/wavesurfer/ or Praat, which is available at http://www.praat.org.

J. Recall the pitch of the first formant (heard best in a creaky voice) and the second formant (heard best when whispering) in the vowels in the words *heed, hid, head, had, hod, hawed, hood, who'd*. Compare their formants to those in the first parts of the vowels in the following words:

	First formant similar to that in the vowel in:	Second formant similar to that in the vowel in:
bite	_____	_____
bait	_____	_____
boat	_____	_____

Figure 1.17

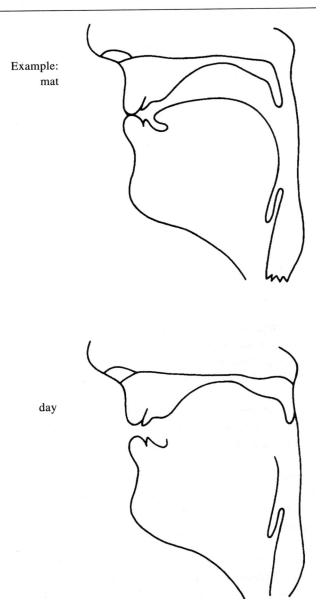

Example: mat

day

Exercises 33

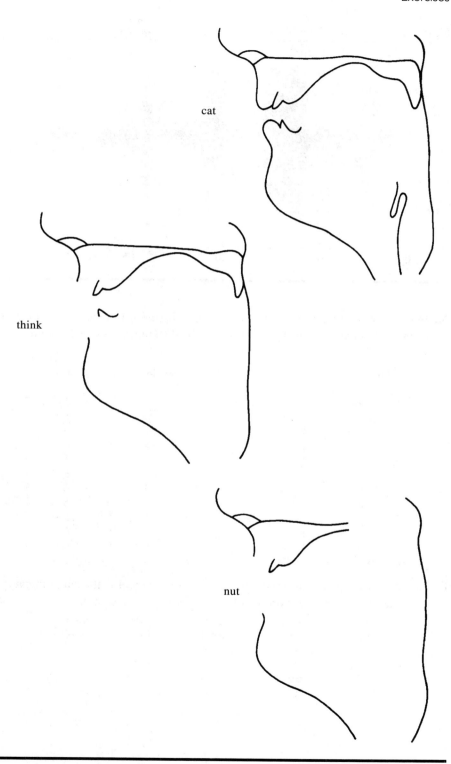

Figure 1.18 The waveform of the phrase *Tom saw ten wasps.*

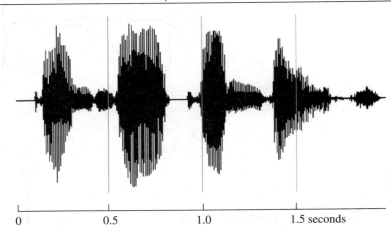

K. In the next chapter, we will start using phonetic transcriptions. The following exercises prepare for this by pointing out the differences between sounds and spelling.

How many distinct sounds are there in each of the following words? Circle the correct number.

		1	2	3	4	5	6	7
1.	laugh	1	2	3	4	5	6	7
2.	begged	1	2	3	4	5	6	7
3.	graphic	1	2	3	4	5	6	7
4.	fish	1	2	3	4	5	6	7
5.	fishes	1	2	3	4	5	6	7
6.	fished	1	2	3	4	5	6	7
7.	batting	1	2	3	4	5	6	7
8.	quick	1	2	3	4	5	6	7
9.	these	1	2	3	4	5	6	7
10.	physics	1	2	3	4	5	6	7
11.	knock	1	2	3	4	5	6	7
12.	axis	1	2	3	4	5	6	7

L. In the following sets of words, the sound of the vowel is the same in every case but one. Circle the word that has a different vowel sound.

1.	pen	said	death	mess	mean
2.	meat	steak	weak	theme	green
3.	sane	paid	eight	lace	mast
4.	ton	toast	both	note	toes
5.	hoot	good	moon	grew	suit
6.	dud	died	mine	eye	guy

2

Phonology and Phonetic Transcription

Many people think that learning phonetics means simply learning to use phonetic transcription. But there is really much more to the subject than learning to use a set of symbols. A phonetician is a person who can describe speech, who understands the mechanisms of speech production and speech perception, and who knows how languages use these mechanisms. Phonetic transcription is no more than a useful tool that phoneticians use in the description of speech. It is, however, a very important tool.

In this chapter, we are concerned with the phonetic transcription of careful speech—the style of speech you use to show someone how to pronounce a word. This is called the **citation style** of speech. Transcriptions of citation style are particularly useful in language documentation and lexicography, and also serve as the basic phonetic observations described in phonology. In Chapter 5, we will discuss phonetic transcription of **connected speech**—the style used in normal conversation. When phoneticians transcribe a citation speech utterance, we are usually concerned with how the sounds convey differences in meaning. For the most part, we describe only the significant articulations rather than the details of the sounds. For example, when saying the English word *tie*, some people pronounce the consonant with the blade of the tongue against the alveolar ridge, others with the tip of the tongue. This kind of difference in articulation does not affect the meaning of the word (in English) and is not usually transcribed. We will begin by considering just this simplest form of transcription, sometimes called a *broad transcription*.

In order to understand what we transcribe and what we don't, it is necessary to understand the basic principles of phonology. **Phonology** is the description of the systems and patterns of sounds that occur in a language. It involves studying a language to determine the **distributions** of sounds in words, that is, we must discover when a phonetic contrast is distinctive, that is, when the sounds in contrast convey a difference in meaning and when a phonetic contrast does not convey a difference in meaning. Children have to do this when they are learning to speak. They may not realize at first that, for example, there is a difference between the consonants at the beginnings of words such as *white* and *right*. They later realize that these words begin with two distinct sounds. Conversely, they may notice that the first sound of *lip* is different from the last sound in *pill*, and may expect to make words by putting the "l" of *lip* at the end of *pill*. In order to develop a native-sounding accent in English, they must implicitly learn how sounds are distributed in the words of their language. Thus, in addition to learning to distinguish all the sounds that can change the meanings of words, and learning to control their vocal organs to produce the sounds, children must learn the usage patterns, the distributions, of sounds.

One of the most important properties of a phonological distribution is the relationship called **distinctiveness**, or **contrast**. When two sounds can be used to differentiate words, they are said to be distinct, or contrastive. The phonetic difference is **phonemic**—as opposed to a simple phonetic difference. [In phonetics and phonology, these three terms are used synonymously—*distinctive*, *contrastive*, *phonemic*.] Notice, for example, that your tongue touches the roof of the mouth at a different location in the "l" of *pill* than it does in the "l" of *lip*. Suppose you said the word *lip* with the "l" from *pill*—we could write this *llip*. These two pronunciations are phonetically different because the tongue has a different position or shape. However, the difference is not contrastive, not phonemic, because it is not used in English to differentiate words—*lip* and *llip* are not (and importantly could not be) different words of English.

This means that if two words (such as *white* and *right* or *cat* and *bat*) differ in only a single sound, the sounds that differ are distinctive in the language. Distinctive sounds get a special status in phonetic transcription because sometimes we want to simplify the transcription, which means that we don't try to record every single phonetic detail, but we would never want to leave out so much information that we end up disregarding contrastive/phonemic differences.

We cannot rely on the spelling to tell us whether two sounds contrast. For example, the words *phone* and *foam* begin with the same sounds, although they have different spellings. To take a more complex example, the words *key* and *car* begin with what we can regard as the same sound, despite the fact that one is spelled with the letter *k* and the other with *c*. But in this case, the two sounds are not exactly the same. The words *key* and *car* begin with slightly different sounds. If you whisper just the first consonants in these two words, you can probably hear the difference, and you may be able to feel that your tongue touches the roof of the mouth in a different place for each word. This example shows that there may be very subtle differences between sounds that do not contrast with each other. The sounds at the beginning of *key* and *car* are slightly different, but it is not a difference that changes the meaning of a word in English. The phonetic difference is not a phonemic difference.

We noted other small changes in sounds that do not affect the meaning in Chapter 1, where we saw that the tongue is farther back in *true* than in *tea*, and the *n* in *tenth* is likely to be dental, whereas the *n* in *ten* is usually alveolar. In some cases, noncontrastive phonetic differences can be larger than these subtle phonetic differences. For example, most Americans (and some younger speakers of British English) have a *t* in the middle of *pity* that is very different from the *t* at the end of the word *pit*. The one in *pity* sounds more like a *d*. Consider also the *l* in *play*. You can say just the first two consonants in this word without any voicing, but still hear the *l* (try doing this). When you say the whole word *play*, the *l* is typically voiceless, and very different from the *l* in *lay*. Say the *l* at the beginning of *lay*, and you'll hear that it is definitely voiced.

We often want to record all—and only—the variations between sounds that cause a difference in meaning—differences that are contrastive. Transcriptions of this kind are called *phonemic transcriptions*. Languages that have been written down only comparatively recently (such as Swahili and most of the other languages of Africa) have a fairly phonemic spelling system. There is very little difference between a written version of a Swahili sentence and a phonemic transcription of that sentence. But because English pronunciation has changed over the centuries while the spelling has remained basically the same, phonemic transcriptions of English are different from written texts.

THE TRANSCRIPTION OF CONSONANTS

A good way to find consonants that are contrastive in a language is to find sets of words that rhyme. Take, for example, all the words that rhyme with *pie* and have only a single consonant at the beginning. A set of words in which each differs from all the others by only one sound is called a *minimal set*. The second column of Table 2.1 lists a set of this kind. There are obviously many other words that rhyme with *pie*, such as *spy*, *try*, *spry*, but these words begin with sequences of two or more of the sounds already in the minimal set. Some of the words in the list begin with two consonant letters (*thigh*, *thy*, *shy*), but they each begin with a single consonant sound. *Shy*, for example, does not contain a sequence of two consonant sounds in the way that *spy* and *try* do. You can record these words and see the sequences in *spy* and *try* for yourself.

Some consonants do not occur in words rhyming with *pie*. If we allow using the names of the letters as words, then we can find another large set of consonants beginning words rhyming with *pea*. A list of such words is shown in the third column of Table 2.1. (Speakers of British English will have to remember that in American English, the name of the last letter of the alphabet belongs in this set rather than in the set of words rhyming with *bed*.)

Even in this set of words, we are still missing some consonant sounds that contrast with others only in the middles or at the ends of words. The letters *ng* often represent a single consonant sound that does not occur at the beginning of a word. You can hear this sound at the end of the word *rang*, where it contrasts with other nasals in words such as *ram* and *ran*, though the vowel sound in *rang* is a little different in most varieties of English. There is also a contrast between the consonants in the middles of *mission* and *vision*, although there are very few pairs of words that are distinguished by this contrast in English. (One such pair for some speakers involves the name of a chain of islands—*Aleutian* versus

CHAPTER 2 Phonology and Phonetic Transcription

TABLE 2.1 Symbols for transcribing English consonants. (Alternative symbols that may be found in other books are given in parentheses.) The last column gives the conventional names for the phonetic symbols in the first column.

p	pie	pea		lowercase *p*
t	tie	tea		lowercase *t*
k	kye	key		lowercase *k*
b	by	bee		lowercase *b*
d	dye	D		lowercase *d*
g	guy			lowercase *g*
m	my	me	ram	lowercase *m*
n	nigh	knee	ran	lowercase *n*
ŋ			rang	eng (or angma)
f	fie	fee		lowercase *f*
v	vie	V		lowercase *v*
θ	thigh			theta
ð	thy	thee		eth
s	sigh	sea	listen	lowercase *s*
z		Z	mizzen	lowercase *z*
ʃ (š)	shy	she	mission	esh (or long *s*)
ʒ (ž)			vision	long *z* (or yogh)
l	lie	lee		lowercase *l*
ɹ	rye			turned *r*
j (y)		ye		lowercase *j*
h	high	he		lowercase *h*

Note also the following:
tʃ (tš)	chi(me)	chea(p)	
dʒ (dž)	ji(ve)	G	

allusion.) Words illustrating these consonants are given in the fourth column of Table 2.1.

Most of the symbols in Table 2.1 are the same letters we use in spelling these words, but there are a few differences. One difference between spelling and phonetic usage occurs with the letter *c*, which is sometimes used to represent a [k] sound, as in *cup* or *bacon*, and sometimes to represent an [s] sound, as in *cellar* or *receive*. Two *c*'s may even represent a sequence of [k] and [s] sounds in the same word, as in *accent* and *access*. A symbol that sometimes differs from the corresponding letter is [g], which is used for the sound in *guy* and *guess*, but never for the sound in *age* or the sound in the name of the letter *g*.

EXAMPLE 2.1

A few other symbols are needed to supplement the regular alphabet. The phonetic symbols we will use are part of the set approved by the International Phonetic Association, a body founded in 1886 by a group of leading phoneticians from France, Germany, Britain, and Denmark. The complete set of IPA symbols is given in the chart on the inside covers of this book. It will be discussed in detail in Chapters 6 through 10. Because we often need to talk about the symbols, the names that have been given to them are shown in the last column of Table 2.1.

The velar nasal at the end of *rang* is written with [ŋ], a letter *n* combined with the tail of the letter [g] descending below the line. Some people call this symbol *eng*; others pronounce it *angma*. The symbol [θ], an upright version of the Greek letter theta, is used for the voiceless dental fricative in words such as *thigh, thin, thimble, ether, breath,* and *mouth*. The symbol [ð], called *eth*, is derived from an Anglo-Saxon letter. It is used for the corresponding voiced sound in words such as *thy, then, them,* and *breathe*. Both these symbols are ascenders (letters that go up from the line of writing rather than descending below it). The spelling system of the English language does not distinguish between [θ] and [ð]. They are both written with the letters *th* in pairs such as *thigh, thy*.

The symbol for the voiceless palato-alveolar (post-alveolar) fricative [ʃ] (long *s*) in *shy, sheep, rash* is both an ascender and a descender. It is like a long, straightened *s* going both above and below the line of writing. The corresponding voiced symbol [ʒ] is like a long *z* descending below the line. This sound occurs in the middle of words such as *vision, measure, leisure* and at the beginning of foreign words such as the French *Jean, gendarme,* and foreign names such as *Zsa Zsa*.

The sound at the beginning of the word *rye* is symbolized by [ɹ], an upside-down letter *r*. It might not matter too much in transcribing English whether we use the *turned r* [ɹ] or the regular [r] to write the first sound of *rye*, but in order to be consistent with the conventions of the IPA we will use [ɹ].

You see, the most common *r* sound in the world's languages is the trilled or rolled [r] that is found in Spanish, Finish, Russian, Arabic, Persian, Thai, and so on. Reflecting its use as a general phonetic alphabet, then, the IPA uses the most common variant of the letter for the most common variant of the sound. This raises the issue that different books on phonetics use different forms of phonetic transcription. In this book, where we are concerned with general phonetics, we use the IPA symbol [j] for the initial sound in *yes, yet, yeast* because the IPA reserves the symbol [y] for another sound, the vowel in the French word *tu*. Another reason for using [j] is that in many languages (German, Dutch, Norwegian, Swedish, and others) this letter is used in words such as *ja*, which are pronounced with a sound that in the English spelling system would be written with the letter *y*. Books that are concerned only with the phonetics of English often use [y] where this one uses [j]. Some books on phonetics also use [š] and [ž] in place of the IPA symbols [ʃ] and [ʒ], respectively. The first and last sounds in both *church* and *judge* are transcribed with the digraph symbols [tʃ] and [dʒ]. These affricate sounds are phonetically a sequence of a stop followed by a fricative (hence the IPA symbols for them are digraphs), yet they function in English as if they are really a single unit, comparable in some ways to other stop consonants. You can see that a word such as *choose* might be said to begin with [tʃ] if you compare your pronunciation of the phrases *white shoes* and *why choose*. In the first phrase, the [t] is at the end of one word and the [ʃ] at the beginning of the next; but in the second phrase, these two sounds occur together at the beginning of the second word. The difference between the two phrases is one of the timing of the articulations involved. The affricate in *why choose* has a more abrupt fricative onset, and the timing of the stop and fricative is more rigid than is the timing of the sequence in *white shoes*. Also, for some speakers, the final [t] of *white* may be said with simultaneous alveolar and glottal stops, while the [t] in the affricate [tʃ] is never said with glottal stop. Other pairs of phrases that demonstrate this point are *heat sheets* versus *he cheats* and *might shop* versus *my chop*. There are no pairs of phrases illustrating the same point for the voiced counterpart [dʒ] found in *jar, gentle, age*, because no English word begins with [ʒ].

Some other books on phonetics transcribe [tʃ] and [dʒ] (as in *church* and *judge*) with single symbols, such as [č] and [ǰ]. These transcriptions highlight the fact that affricates are single units by using a single letter to transcribe them. We will see that some linguistic segments have two phonetic elements (e.g., vowel diphthongs) and it is usually helpful to represent both of the elements in phonetic transcription. When we wish to make perfectly clear that we are writing an affricate and not a consonant cluster, the ligature symbol [͡] is used to tie symbols together. Thus, the affricate in *why choose* can be written [t͡ʃ] to distinguish it from the cluster [tʃ] in *white shoes*. The glottal stop that begins words that are spelled with an initial vowel (recall the example from Chapter 1 of the difference between *flee east* and *fleeced*) is written phonetically with [ʔ], a symbol based on the question mark. So *flee east* is pronounced [fliʔist], while *fleeced* is [flist]. The status of glottal stop as a consonant phoneme in English is questionable because its distribution is limited. Where other consonants may appear in a variety of positions in words (e.g., note the [k] in *cat, scab, back, active, across*, etc.), glottal stop only occurs at the beginnings of words (i.e., word-initially) before vowels in American English. Compare the pronunciation of *east* [ʔist] and *yeast* [jist]. The "vowel initial" word *east* is pronounced with an initial glottal stop. In London Cockney, glottal stop also appears between vowels in words like *butter* and *button* where other dialects have a variant of [t]. In American casual speech, the final [t] in words like *cat* and *bat* can be "glottalized"—replaced by glottal stop, or more usually pronounced with simultaneous glottal stop (e.g., [bæt͡ʔ] and [kæt͡ʔ]).

There is one minor matter still to be considered in the transcription of the consonant contrasts of English. In most forms of both British and American English, *which* does not contrast with *witch*. Accordingly, both *why* and *we* in Table 2.1 are said to begin simply with [w]. But some speakers of English contrast pairs of words such as *which, witch; why, wye; whether, weather*. The first consonants of each of these pairs of words sounds a little like the sequence [hw] and that is a reasonable way to transcribe this voiceless *w*, but naturally the IPA provides a contrastive symbol [ʍ] that can be used to record this constrastive sound.

THE TRANSCRIPTION OF VOWELS

The transcription of the contrastive vowels (the vowel phonemes) in English is more difficult than the transcription of consonants for two reasons. First, accents of English differ more in their use of vowels than in their use of consonants. Second, authorities differ in their views of what constitutes an appropriate description of vowels.

Taking the same approach in looking for contrasting vowels as we did for contrasting consonants, we might try to find a minimal set of words that differ only in the vowel sounds. We could, for example, look for monosyllables that begin with [h] and end with [d] and supplement this minimal set with other lists of monosyllables that contrast only in their vowel sounds. Table 2.2 shows five such sets of words. You should listen to the recordings of these words on the website while reading the following discussion of the vowels.

We will consider one form of British and one form of American English. The major difference between the two is that speakers of American English

TABLE 2.2 Symbols for transcribing contrasting vowels in English. Column 1 applies to many speakers of American English, and Column 2 to most speakers of British English. The last column gives the conventional names for the phonetic symbols in the first column unless otherwise noted.

1	2						
i	i	heed	he	bead	heat	keyed	lowercase *i*
ɪ	ɪ	hid		bid	hit	kid	small capital *I*
eɪ	eɪ	hayed	hay	bayed	hate	Cade	lowercase *e*
ɛ	ɛ	head		bed			epsilon
æ	æ	had		bad	hat	cad	ash
ɑ	ɑ	hard		bard	heart	card	script *a*
ɑ	ɒ	hod		bod	hot	cod	turned script *a*
ɔ	ɔ	hawed	haw	bawd		cawed	open *o*
ʊ	ʊ	hood				could	upsilon
oʊ	əʊ	hoed	hoe	bode		code	lowercase *o*
u	u	who'd	who	booed	hoot	cooed	lowercase *u*
ɝ	ɜ	herd	her	bird	hurt	curd	reversed epsilon
aɪ	aɪ	hide	high	bide	height		lowercase a (+I)
aʊ	aʊ		how	bowed		cowed	(as noted above)
ɔɪ	ɔɪ		(a)hoy	Boyd			(as noted above)
ɪɹ	ɪə		here	beard			(as noted above)
ɛɹ	ɛə		hair	bared		cared	(as noted above)
aɪɹ	aə	hired	hire				(as noted above)

Note also:
| ju | ju | hued | hue | Bude | | cued | (as noted above) |

pronounce [ɹ] sounds after vowels, as well as before them, whereas in most forms of British English, [ɹ] can occur only before a vowel. American English speakers distinguish between words such as *heart* and *hot* not by making a difference in vowel quality (as in Peter Ladefoged's form of British English), but rather by pronouncing *heart* with an [ɹ] and *hot* with the same vowel but without an [ɹ] following it. In *here, hair, hire*, these speakers may use vowels similar to those in *he, head, high* respectively, but in each case with a following [ɹ]. Most speakers of British English distinguish these words by using different **diphthongs**—movements from one vowel to another within a single syllable.

EXAMPLE 2.2

Even within American English, there are variations in the number of contrasting vowels that occur. Many Midwestern speakers and most speakers in the western half of the United States do not distinguish between the vowels in pairs of words such as *odd, awed* and *cot, caught*. Some forms of American English make additional distinctions not shown in Table 2.2. For example, some speakers (mainly from the East Coast) distinguish the auxiliary verb *can* from the noun *can*, the latter being more diphthongal. But we will have to overlook these small differences in this introductory textbook.

There are several possible ways of transcribing the contrasting vowels in Table 2.2. The two principal forms that will be used in this book are shown in the first and second columns. The first column is suitable for many forms of American English and the second for many forms of British English. The two columns have been kept as similar as possible; as you will see in Chapter 4, we have tried to make the transcriptions reasonably similar to those of well-known authorities on the phonetics of English.

As in the case of the consonant symbols, the vowel symbols in Table 2.2 are used in accordance with the principles of the IPA. Those symbols that have the same shapes as ordinary letters of the alphabet represent sounds similar to the sounds these letters have in French or Spanish or Italian. Actually, the IPA usage of the vowel letters conforms with usage in the great majority of the world's languages when they are written with the Roman alphabet, including such diverse languages as Swahili, Turkish, and Navajo. The present spelling of English reflects the way it sounded many centuries ago when it still had vowel letters with values similar to those of the corresponding letters in all these other languages.

One of the principal problems in transcribing English phonetically is that there are more vowel sounds than there are vowel letters in the alphabet. In a transcription of the English word *sea* as [si], the [i] represents a similar (but not identical) sound to that in the Spanish or Italian *si*. But unlike Spanish and Italian, English differentiates between vowels such as those in *seat, sit,* and *heed, hid*. The vowels in *seat, heed* differ from those in *sit, hid* in two ways: They have a slightly different quality and they are longer. Because the vowels in *sit, hid* are somewhat like those in *seat, heed*, they are represented by the symbol [ɪ], a small capital *I*. The difference in length may also be shown by adding the symbol [:], which, as we will see later, can be used when it is necessary to distinguish sounds that differ in length. Adding this symbol to some vowels shows additional phonetic detail, but it isn't necessary in a phonemic transcription because words in English aren't distinguished, for example, by long and short [ɪː] and [ɪ].

The vowels in words such as *hay, bait, they* are transcribed with a sequence of two symbols, [eɪ], indicating that for most speakers of English, these words contain a diphthong. The first element in this diphthong is similar to sounds in Spanish or Italian that use the letter *e*, such as the Spanish word for 'milk,' which is written *leche* and pronounced [letʃe]. The second element in the English words *hay, bait, they* is [ɪ], the symbol used for transcribing the vowel in *hid*.

Two symbols that are not ordinary letters of the alphabet, [ɛ] and [æ], are used for the vowels in *head* and *had*, respectively. The first is based on the Greek letter epsilon and the second on the letters *a* and *e* joined together. They may be referred to by the names *epsilon* and *ash*.

Most Americans use the same vowel sound in the words *heart* and *hot* and can use one form of the letter *a*. They would transcribe these words as [hɑɹt] and [hɑt]. But some East Coast Americans and speakers of British English who do not pronounce [ɹ] sounds after a vowel distinguish between these words by the qualities of the vowels and have to use two different forms of the letter *a*. They would transcribe these words as [hɑt] and [hɒt].

Most speakers of British forms of English, and many American speakers, distinguish between pairs of words such as *cot, caught; not, naught*. The symbol [ɔ], an open letter *o*, may be used in the second of each of these pairs of words and in words such as *bawd, bought, law*. Many Midwestern and Western American speakers do not need to use this symbol in any of these words, as they do not distinguish between the vowels in words such as *cot* and *caught*. They may have different vowels in words in which there is a following [ɹ] sound, such as *horse, hoarse*, but if there is no opposition between *cot, caught* or *not, naught*, there is no need to mark this difference by using the symbol [ɔ]. Doing so would simply be showing extra phonetic detail, straying from the principle of showing just the differences between phonemes.

Another special symbol is used for the vowel in *hood, could, good*. This symbol, [ʊ], may be thought of as a letter *u* with the ends curled out.

The vowel in *hoe, dough, code* is a diphthong. For most American English speakers, the first element is very similar to sounds that are written in Spanish or Italian with the letter *o*. Many speakers of English from the southern parts of Britain use a different sound for the first element of the diphthong in these words, which we will symbolize with [ə], an upside-down letter *e* called *schwa*. We will discuss this sound more fully in a later section. The final element of the diphthong in words such as *hoe* and *code* is somewhat similar to the vowel [ʊ] in *hood*.

An upside-down letter *v*, [ʌ], is used for the vowel in words such as *bud* and *hut*. This symbol is sometimes called *wedge*. The sound is very similar to [ə], the sound we noted at the beginning of some of the diphthongs in British English. This symbol is usually called by its German name *schwa*. Another symbol, [ɜ], a reversed form of the Greek letter epsilon, is used for the sound in *pert, bird, curt* as pronounced by most speakers of British English and those speakers of American English who do not have an [ɹ] in these words. In most forms of American English, the *r* in these words is fully combined with the vowel, and the symbol [ɚ] is used. The little hook [˞] indicates the *r*-coloring of the vowel. A somewhat whimsical name for [ɚ] is *schwar*.

The next three words in Table 2.2 contain diphthongs composed of elements that have been discussed already. The vowel in *hide* [haɪd] begins with a sound between that of the vowel in *cat* [kæt] and that in *hard* [hɑd] or [hɑrd], and moves toward the vowel [ɪ] as in *hid* [hɪd]. The symbol [a] is used for the first part of this diphthong. The vowel in *how* [aʊ] begins with a similar sound but moves toward [ʊ] as in *hood*. The vowel in *boy* [bɔɪ] is a combination of the sound [ɔ] as in *bawd* and [ɪ] as in *hid*.

Most Americans pronounce the remaining words in Table 2.2 with one of the other vowels followed by [ɹ], while most British English speakers have additional diphthongs in these words. In each case, the end of the diphthong is [ə], the same symbol we used for the beginning of the diphthong in *hoe* for most British English speakers. We will discuss this symbol further in the next paragraph. Some (usually old-fashioned) British English speakers also use a diphthong in words like *poor, cure* that can be transcribed as [ʊə]. Some people have a diphthong [aə] in words such as *fire, hire* [faə, haə]. Others pronounce these words as two syllables (like *higher, liar*), transcribing them as [faɪə, haɪə].

The words in Table 2.2 are all monosyllables except for *ahoy*. Consequently, none of them contains both stressed and unstressed vowels. By far, the most common unstressed vowel is [ə], *schwa*. It occurs at the ends of words such as *sofa, soda* [ˈsoʊfə, ˈsoʊdə], in the middles of words such as *emphasis, demonstrate* [ˈɛmfəsɪs, ˈdɛəmənstreɪt], and at the beginnings of words such as *around, arise* [əˈraʊnd, əˈraɪz]. (In all these words, the symbol [ˈ] is a stress mark that has been placed before the syllable carrying the main stress. It is almost always a good idea to mark stress in words of more than one syllable.) One common recommendation in transcribing English is to reserve [ə] for use in unstressed syllables only, but many speakers of American English produce words such as *bud* and *hut* with [ə] rather than with [ʌ]. For these speakers, the stressed and unstressed vowels in words such as *above* and *among* differ more in duration than in vowel quality—[əˈbəːv] and [əˈməːŋ].

In British English, [ə] is usually the sole component of the *-er* part of words such as *brother, brotherhood, simpler* [ˈbrʌðə, ˈbrʌðəhʊd, ˈsɪmplə]. In forms of American English with *r*-colored vowels, these words are usually [ˈbrʌðɚ, ˈbrʌðɚhʊd, ˈsɪmplɚ]. Both [ə] and [ɚ] are very common vowels, [ə] occurring very frequently in unstressed monosyllables such as the grammatical function words *the, a, to, and, but*. In connected speech, these words are usually [ðə, ə, tə, ənd, bət].

Some of the other vowels also occur in unstressed syllables, but because of differences in accents of English, it is a little more difficult to say which vowel occurs in which word. For example, nearly all speakers of English differentiate between the last vowels in *Sophie, sofa* or *pity, patter*. But some accents have the vowel [i] as in *heed* at the end of *Sophie* and *pity*. Others have [ɪ] as in *hid*. Similarly, most accents make the vowel in the second syllable of *taxis* different from that in *Texas*. Some have [i] and some have [ɪ] in *taxis*. Nearly everybody pronounces *Texas* as [ˈtɛksəs]. (Note that in English, the letter *x* often represents the sounds [ks].) Compare your pronunciation of these words with the recordings on the website and decide which unstressed vowels you use.

This is an appropriate moment to start doing some transcription exercises. There are a large number of them at the end of this chapter. To ensure that you have grasped the basic principles, you should try Exercises A through D.

CONSONANT AND VOWEL CHARTS

So far, we have been using the consonant and vowel symbols mainly as ways of representing the contrasts that occur among words in English. But they can also be thought of in a completely different way. We may regard them as shorthand descriptions of the articulations involved. Thus, [p] is an abbreviation for *voiceless bilabial stop,* and [l] is equivalent to *voiced alveolar lateral approximant*. The consonant symbols can then be arranged in the form of a chart as in Figure 2.1. The places of articulation are shown across the top of the chart, starting from the most forward articulation (bilabial) and going toward those sounds made in the back of the mouth (velar) and in the throat (glottal). The manners of articulation are shown on the vertical axis of the chart. By convention, the voiced–voiceless distinction is shown by putting the voiceless symbols to the left of the voiced symbols. The symbol [w] is shown in two places in the consonant chart in Figure 2.1 (on page 46). This is because it is articulated with both a narrowing of the lip aperture, which makes it bilabial, and a raising of the back of the tongue toward the soft palate, which makes it velar. The affricate symbols [tʃ] and [dʒ] are not listed separately in the table even though they are contrastive sounds in English. Note that if we were to include them in the table, we would have the problem of deciding whether to put them in the palato-alveolar column (the place of the fricative element) or in the alveolar column (the place of the stop element). The international phonetic alphabet avoids the inaccuracy that is inevitable when the stop element and fricative element of the affricate have different place of articulation by listing only stop and fricative symbols in the consonant chart.

The symbols we have been using for the contrasting vowels may also be regarded as shorthand descriptions for different vowel qualities. There are problems in this respect in that we have been using these symbols somewhat loosely, allowing them to have different values for different accents. But the general values can be indicated by a vowel chart as shown in Figure 2.2 (on page 46). The symbols have been placed within a quadrilateral, which shows the range of

Figure 2.1 A phonetic chart of the English consonants we have dealt with so far. Whenever there are two symbols within a single cell, the one on the left represents a voiceless sound. All other symbols represent voiced sounds. Note also the consonant [h], which is not on this chart, and the affricates [tʃ, dʒ], which are sequences of symbols on the chart.

Place of articulation

Manner of articulation	bilabial	labio-dental	dental	alveolar	palato-alveolar	palatal	velar	glottal
nasal (stop)	m			n			ŋ	
stop	p b			t d			k g	ʔ
fricative		f v	θ ð	s z	ʃ ʒ			h
(central) approximant	(w)			ɹ		j	w	
lateral (approximant)				l				

Figure 2.2 A vowel chart showing the relative vowel qualities represented by some of the symbols used in transcribing English. The symbols [e, a, o] occur as the first elements of diphthongs.

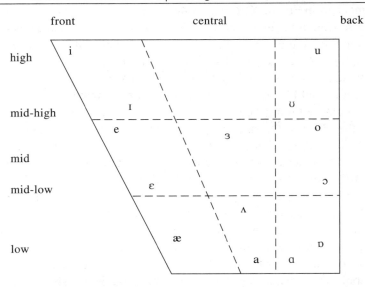

possible vowel qualities. Thus, [i] is used for a high front vowel, [u] for a high back one, [ɪ] for a mid-high front vowel, [e] for a raised mid-front vowel, [ɛ] for a mid-low, and so on.

The simple vowel chart in Figure 2.2 shows only two of the dimensions of vowel quality. If they are taken to be descriptions of what the tongue is doing, these dimensions are not represented very accurately (as we will see in later chapters). Furthermore, Figure 2.2 does not show anything about the variations in the degree of lip rounding in the different vowels, nor does it indicate anything about vowel length. It does not show, for example, that in most circumstances, [i] and [u] are longer than [ɪ] and [ʊ].

The consonant and vowel charts enable us to understand the remark made in Chapter 1, when we said that the sounds of English involve about twenty-five different gestures of the tongue and lips. The consonant chart has twenty-three different symbols, but only eleven basic gestures of the tongue and lips are needed to make these different sounds. The sounds [p, b, m] are all made with the same lip gesture, and [t, d, n] and [k, g, ŋ] with the same tongue gestures. (There are slight differences in timing when these gestures are used for making the different sounds, but we will neglect them here.) Four more gestures are required for the sounds in the fricative row, three more for the (central) approximants, and another one for the lateral approximant, making eleven in all. The vowel chart has fourteen symbols, each of which may be considered to require a separate gesture. But, as we have seen, accents of English vary in the number of vowels that they distinguish, which is why we said that English requires *about* twenty-five different gestures of the tongue and lips.

All these sounds will also require gestures of the other three main components of the speech mechanism—the airstream process, the phonation process, and the oro-nasal process. The airstream process involves pushing air out of the lungs for all the sounds of English. The phonation process is responsible for the gestures of the vocal folds that distinguish voiced and voiceless sounds, and the oro-nasal process will be active in raising and lowering the velum so as to distinguish nasal and oral sounds.

PHONOLOGY

At the beginning of this chapter, we discussed another reason why it is only approximately true that in our transcriptions of English, the symbols have the values shown in Figures 2.1 and 2.2. In the style of transcription we have been using so far, we have focused on sounds that are distinctive, or phonemic, in English. From this point on, we will use slash lines / / to mark off symbols when we are explicitly using them to represent a phonemic transcription.

As we have noted, it is also possible to include more phonetic information than this in a phonetic transcription. For example, the final / t / sound in words such as *hut* and *cat* may be released with a puff of air [hʌtʰ] or may be pronounced without a noisy release of the stop [hʌt̚]. This is the exact opposite of a contrastive phonetic distribution—in the case of the released and unreleased

[tʰ] and [t̚] we say that they are in **free variation**. It is important to note that this pattern of variation is a property of English that may not be shared by other languages. For example, final / t / in Cantonese is almost always unreleased, while released stops are the norm in Tsou.

A much more interesting type of phonetic distribution occurs when phonetic patterns seem to be conditioned by particular **environments**. For example, we mentioned above that the / l / of *lip* is different from the / l / of *pill*. When / l / occurs at the beginning of a syllable the body of the tongue is held low in the mouth, but when / l / occurs at the end of a syllable the body of the tongue is raised in the mouth. In this case, the / l / is described as velarized and written with the diacritic mark for velarization [ɫ]. The distribution of these two / l / sounds is called a **complementary distribution**—the plain [l] occurs in one environment (beginning of the syllable), and the velarized [ɫ] occurs in another environment (end of the syllable). A similar non-overlapping, or complementary, set of environments is evident in the phonetic realization of the "p" sounds in the words *peak* and *speak*. In *peak* the / p / is released with a puff of air, an aspiration noise, while the / p / in *speak* is much less noisy. This difference is written with the same small superscript [h] that we used above to indicate the aspirated release of / t / in [kætʰ], so we write *peak* as [pʰik] and *speak* as [spik]. The complementary variants [pʰ] and [p] are called **allophones** of / p / because native speakers think of them both as "p" sounds (and probably don't notice the phonetic difference that we are pointing out here).

The three types of phonetic distributions are illustrated in Figure 2.3. In the first two types of distributions (contrast and free variation), the sounds occur in overlapping distributions—for example, the rhyming words of Table 2.1 and the minimal sets of Figure 2.2, and the identical environments in which free variants occur—while in complementary distribution the sounds never appear in the same environment—syllable initial versus syllable final position, or after an / s / or not after an / s /. The different types of phonetic distributions have important ramifications for the practice of phonetic transcription, but before we turn to these issues we would like to make one point: All of the phonetic variations that we are discussing here occur in citation speech and are not simply the result of sloppy speech or failing to "hit the target" when speaking quickly. The noncontrastive phonetic variations that we observe in free variation and complementary distribution are a part of what the native speaker knows about how to say the words of the language. That means that if you want to sound like a native speaker of a language, you have to master the phonology of the language; you not only have to learn how to say the sounds of the language, but you also have to learn the distributions of the sounds. It also means that if we are to have an accurate phonetic description of a language, we must not only describe the sounds but also the phonetic distributions of the sounds.

When you look closely at the phonetics of a language, the number of complementary distributions is remarkable and remarkably complex. In fact, a whole subdiscipline of linguistics (phonology) is dedicated to describing patterns of

Figure 2.3 Phonetic variation comes in three basic types: contrastive (also called phonemic or distinctive distribution), free variation, or complementary distribution. As the figure indicates, the difference between contrastive distribution and free variation is that phonetic variation results in different words in phonemic variation while phonetic variation does not result in a different word in free variation.

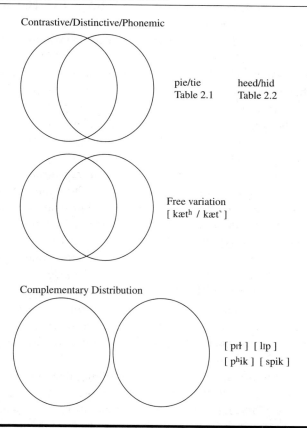

complementary distributions. Chapters 3 and 4 focus on several of the sound patterns of English, but it doesn't hurt to give a few more examples here, so you will get a flavor of why we need to think carefully about different types of phonetic transcription.

The symbols / l / and / r / normally stand for voiced approximants. But in words such as *ply* / plaɪ / and *try* / traɪ /, the influence of the preceding stops makes them voiceless. Vowel sounds also vary. The / i / in *heed* / hid / is usually very different from the / i / in *heel* / hil /, and much longer than the / i / in *heat*.

Many of the variations we have been discussing can be described in terms of simple statements about the phonetic distributions because the sound patterns are found in all words that have the relevant phonetic environments. In most forms of American English, for example, / t / becomes voiced not only in *catty*, but on all occasions when it occurs immediately after a vowel and before an unstressed vowel (e.g., in *pity, matter, utter, divinity*, etc.). In English of nearly all kinds, we also find that whenever / t / occurs before a dental fricative, it is pronounced as a dental stop. We can show that this is a different kind of / t / by adding a small mark [̪] under it, making it [t̪]. (As this symbol is not representing a phonemic contrast, it is placed between [ ].) The same is true of / d /, as in *width* [wɪd̪ð]; / n /, as in *tenth* [tɛn̪θ]; and / l /, as in *wealth* [wɛl̪θ]. In all these cases, the mark [̪] may be added under the symbol to indicate that it represents a dental articulation.

Small marks that can be added to a symbol to modify its value are known as **diacritics**. They provide a useful way of increasing the phonetic precision of a transcription. Another diacritic, [̥], a small circle beneath a symbol, can be used to indicate that the symbol represents a voiceless sound. Earlier we noted that the /l/ in *play* is voiceless. Accordingly, we can transcribe this word as [pl̥eɪ]. Similarly, *ply* and *try* can be written [pl̥aɪ] and [tr̥aɪ].

In addition to transcribing variants that occur in free variation or in complementary distribution, there is another way we can show more phonetic detail. We can use more specialized phonetic symbols. For example, we noted that the vowel / i / is longer than the vowel / ɪ /, as in *sheep* versus *ship*. This difference in length is always there as long as the two vowels are in the same phonetic context (between the same sounds and with the same degree of stress, etc.). We could transcribe this difference in length by adding a length mark to the longer of the two sounds. The IPA provides the symbol [ː] to show that the preceding symbol represents a longer sound. Accordingly, we could transcribe the two sounds as / iː / and / ɪ /. We would still be representing a phonemic contrast in this particular accent of English, but doing so with greater phonetic precision.

Students sometimes make the mistake of thinking that allophonic transcription is written with diacritics while phonemic contrasts are written with simple phonetic symbols. Consider, though, the pronunciation of the word *letter*. For most speakers of American English, there is no [t] sound in this word. Instead, the medial consonant sounds like a very short [d]. It is different enough from [d] (compare *seedy* and *see Dee*) that the IPA has a unique symbol for the **tap** allophone of / t / and / d /. The alveolar tap sound in *letter* is written with the symbol [ɾ], a letter derived from the letter *r*. Note, therefore, that transcription of allophones may use simple phonetic symbols as well as symbols with diacritic marks.

The term **broad transcription** is often used to designate a transcription that uses the simplest possible set of symbols. Conversely, a **narrow transcription** is one that shows more phonetic detail, either by using more specific symbols or by representing some allophonic differences. A broad transcription of *please* and *trip* would be / pliz / and / trɪp /. A narrow (but still phonemic) transcription could be / pliːz / and / trɪp /. This transcription would be phonemic as long as we always used / iː / for this contrastive vowel sound. In this way, we would be distinguishing contrastive sounds without showing any allophonic variation. A narrow allophonic transcription would be [pl̥iːz] and [tɹ̥ɪp], in which [l̥] and [ɹ̥] are allophones of / l / and / r /.

Every transcription should be considered as having two aspects, one of which is often not explicit. There is the phonetic text itself and, at least implicitly, there is a set of conventions for interpreting the text. These conventions are usually of two kinds. First, there are the conventions that ascribe general phonetic values to the symbols. It was these conventions we had in mind when we said earlier that a symbol could be regarded as an approximate specification of the articulations involved. If we want to remind readers of the implicit statements accompanying a transcription, we can make them explicit. We could, for instance, say that, other things being equal, / i / is longer than / ɪ /, perhaps stating at the beginning of the transcription / i / = / iː /. We could also make explicit the phonological analysis that guides the choice of particular symbols in the transcription, a topic we will return to in Chapter 4.

When writing down an unknown language or when transcribing the speech of a child or a patient not seen previously, one does not know which phonetic differences are contrastive and which are not. In these circumstances, the symbols indicate only the phonetic value of the sounds without a phonological analysis to determine the patterns of contrast and complementary distributions. This kind of transcription is called an **impressionistic transcription**.

We hope this brief survey of different kinds of transcription makes plain that there is no such thing as *the* IPA transcription of a particular utterance. Sometimes, one wants to make a detailed phonetic transcription; at other times, it is more convenient to make a phonemic transcription. Sometimes, one wants to point out a particular phonetic feature such as vowel length; at other times, the vowels are not of concern and details of the consonants are more important. IPA transcriptions take many forms.

RECAP

This chapter introduces the letters of the **International Phonetic Alphabet** that are used to phonetically transcribe the contrastive/phonemic sounds of English. The vowel sounds of American English are contrasted with the vowels of British English (don't miss the audio examples of these vowel sounds on the website). These IPA symbols are arranged in **consonant** and **vowel charts** that highlight the phonetic properties that the symbols stand for. The chapter also considers the types of **distributions** in which sounds occur (contrastive, complementary, or free variation) and how these patterns relate to phonemic, broad, and narrow phonetic transcription. We emphasize that there is no one correct IPA transcription—that what one conveys by transcription depends to an extent on the focus of your attention.

52 CHAPTER 2 Phonology and Phonetic Transcription

EXERCISES

(Printable or interactive versions of the exercises are available on the website.)

A. Find the errors in the transcriptions of the consonant sounds in the following words. In each word, there is one error, indicating an impossible pronunciation of that word for a native speaker of English of any variety. Make a correct transcription in the space provided after the word.

1. strength [stɹɛŋθ] should be [   ]
2. crime [cɹaɪm] [   ]
3. wishing [wɪʃɪŋ] [   ]
4. wives [waɪvs] [   ]
5. these [θiz] [   ]
6. hijacking [haɪjækɪŋ] [   ]
7. chipping [tʃɪppɪŋ] [   ]
8. yelling [ˈyɛlɪŋ] [   ]
9. sixteen [ˈsɪxtin] [   ]
10. thesis [ˈðisɪs] [   ]

B. Now try another ten words in which the errors are all in the vowels. Again, there is only one possible error, but because of differences in varieties of English, there are sometimes alternative possible corrections.

11. man-made [ˈmanmeɪd] should be [   ]
12. football [ˈfʊtbol] [   ]
13. tea chest [ˈtitʃest] [   ]
14. tomcat [ˈtomkæt] [   ]
15. tiptoe [ˈtɪptoʊ] [   ]
16. avoid [æˈvɔɪd] [   ]
17. remain [ɹəˈman] [   ]
18. bedroom [ˈbɛdɹɔm] [   ]
19. umbrella [umˈbɹɛlə] [   ]
20. manage [ˈmænædʒ] [   ]

C. Make a correct transcription of the following words. There is still only one error per word, but it may be among the vowels, the consonants, or the stress marks.

21. magnify [ˈmægnɪfaɪ] should be [   ]
22. traffic [ˈtɹæfɪc] [   ]
23. simplistic [ˈsɪmplɪstɪk] [   ]
24. irrigate [ˈɪɹɪgeɪt] [   ]
25. improvement [ɪmˈpɹʊvmənt] [   ]

26. demonstrate	[ˈdəmɑnstɹeɪt]	[	]
27. human being	[humən ˈbiɪŋ]	[	]
28. appreciate	[əˈpɹeʃieɪt]	[	]
29. joyful	[ˈdʒɔyfʊl]	[	]
30. wondrous	[ˈwondɹəs]	[	]

D. Transcribe the following words or phrases as they are pronounced by either the British or the American speaker on the website (follow the "audio clips" link for this exercise). Be careful to put in stress marks at the proper places. Use a phonemic transcription and note which speaker you are transcribing.

31. languages
32. impossibility
33. boisterous
34. youngster
35. another
36. diabolical
37. nearly over
38. red riding hood
39. inexcusable
40. chocolate pudding

E. What kind of distribution is found for the sounds in these words (free variation, complementary distribution, or contrastive)?

1. "l" sounds in: play, lean, feel _____
2. The first sounds in: pie, tie, sigh _____
3. The last sounds in: pat˺, matʰ, seat˺ _____
4. The "t" sounds in: bat, tub, steep, butter _____
5. The "n" sound in: ten, tenth _____
6. The medial sounds in: awesome, autumn, awning _____

F. Pirahã, a language spoken by about 300 hunter-gatherers in the Amazonian rain forest, has only three vowels (**i, a, o**) and eight consonants (**p, t, k, ʔ, b, g, s, h**). (The glottal stop, **ʔ**, does not have any lip or tongue action.) How many different gestures of the tongue and lips do the speakers of this language have to make? Note which are vocalic (vowel) gestures and which are consonantal gestures.

G. Hawaiian, now undergoing a revival although spoken natively by only a few hundred people, has the following vowels and consonants: **i, e, a, o, u, p, k, ʔ, m, n, w, l, h**. How many different gestures of the tongue and lips do the speakers of this language have to make? Note which are vocalic gestures and which are consonantal gestures.

54 CHAPTER 2 *Phonology and Phonetic Transcription*

H. Transcribe the following phrases as they are pronounced by either the British English or the American English speaker on the website. Say whether the British or American English speaker is being transcribed.

1. We can see three real trees.
2. He still lives in the big city.
3. The waiter gave the lady stale cakes.
4. They sell ten red pens for a penny.
5. His pal packed his bag with jackets.
6. Father calmly parked the car in the yard.
7. The doll at the top costs lots.
8. He was always calling for more laws.
9. Don't stroll slowly on a lonely road.
10. The good-looking cook pulled sugar.
11. Sue threw the soup into the pool.
12. He loved a dull, muddy-colored rug.
13. The girl with curls has furs and pearls.
14. I like miles of bright lights.
15. He howled out loud as the cow drowned.
16. The boy was annoyed by boiled oysters.

I. Transcribe the following phrases as they are pronounced by either the British English or the American English speaker on the website. Make both (*a*) a broad transcription and (*b*) a narrower transcription. Say whether the British or American English speaker is being transcribed.

Please come home.

(a)

(b)

He is going by train.

(a)

(b)

The tenth American.

(a)

(b)

His knowledge of the truth.

(a)

(b)

I prefer sugar and cream.

(a)

(b)

Sarah took pity on the young children.

(a)

(b)

J. Read the following passages in phonetic transcription. The first, which represents a form of British English of the kind spoken by Peter Ladefoged, is a broad transcription. The second, which represents an American pronunciation typical of a Midwestern or Western speaker, is slightly narrower, showing a few allophones. By this time, you should be able to read transcriptions of different forms of English, although you may have difficulty pronouncing each word exactly as it is represented. Nevertheless, read each passage several times and try to pronounce it as indicated. Take care to put the stresses on the correct syllables, and say the unstressed syllables with the vowels as shown. Now listen to these passages on the website, and comment on any problems with the transcriptions.

British English

ɪt ɪz ˈpɒsəbl tə tɹænˈskɹaɪb fəˈnetɪklɪ

ˈeni ˈʌtɹəns, ɪn ˈeni ˈlæŋgwɪdʒ,

ɪn ˈsevɹəl ˈdɪfɹənt ˈweɪz

ˈɔl əv ðəm ˈjuzɪŋ ði ˈælfəbət ənd kənˈvenʃnz

əv ði ˈaɪ ˈpi ˈeɪ.

ðə ˈseɪm ˈθɪŋ ɪz ˈpɒsəbl

wɪð ˈməʊst ˈʌðə ɪntəˈnæʃənl fəˈnetɪk ˈælfəbəts.

ə tɹænˈskɹɪpʃn wɪtʃ ɪz ˈmeɪd baɪ ˈjuzɪŋ ˈletəz əv ðə ˈsɪmplɪst ˈpɒsəbl ˈʃeɪps,

ənd ɪn ðə ˈsɪmplɪst ˈpɒsəbl ˈnʌmbə,

ɪz ˈkɔld ə ˈsɪmpl fəʊˈnimɪk tɹænˈskɹɪpʃn.

American English

ɪf ðə ˈnʌmbɚ əv ˈdɪfɹənt ˈlɛɾɚz ɪz ˈmɔɹ ðen̩ ðə ˈmɪnəməm

əz dəˈfaɪnd əˈbʌv

ðə tɹænˈskɹɪpʃn wɪl ˈnɑt bi ə fəˈnimɪk,

bɚr ən æləˈfɑnɪk wʌn.

ˈsʌm əv ðə ˈfoʊnimz, ˈðæɹ ɪz tə ˈseɪ,

wɪl bi ɹɛpɹəˈzɛntəd baɪ ˈmɔɹ ðən ˈwʌn ˈdɪfɹənt ˈsɪmbl̩.
ɪn ˈʌðɚ ˈwɝdz ˈsʌm ˈæləfoʊnz əv ˈsʌm ˈfoʊnimz
wɪl bi ˈsɪŋɡld̩ ˈaʊt fɚ ɹɛpɹəzɛnˈteɪʃn̩ ɪn̩ ðə tɹænˈskɹɪpʃn̩,
ˈhɛns ðə ˈtɝm ˈæləˈfɑnɪk.

(Both the above passages are adapted from David Abercrombie, *English Phonetic Texts* [Salem, N.H.: Faber & Faber, 1964].)

PERFORMANCE EXERCISES

It is extremely important to develop practical phonetic skills as you learn the theoretical concepts. One way to do this is to learn to pronounce nonsense words. You should also transcribe nonsense words that are dictated to you. By using nonsense words, you are forced to listen to the sounds that are being spoken. Audio examples of all the following words are on the website.

A. Learn to say simple nonsense words. A good way is to start with a single vowel, and then add consonants and vowels one by one at the beginning. In this way, you are always reading toward familiar material, rather than having new difficulties ahead of you. Make up sets of words such as:

ɑ
zɑ
rˈzɑ
trˈzɑ
ˈœtrˈzɑ
ˈmœtrˈzɑ
ʌˈmœtrˈzɑ
tʌˈmœtrˈzɑ

B. Read the following words and listen to them as they appear on the website. Ask a partner to click on the words in a different order. Enter the order in which the words are played.

piˈsuz
piˈsus
piˈzus
piˈzuz
piˈzuʒ

C. Repeat Exercise B with the following sets of words.

| tɑˈθɛð | ˈkipik | ˈlæmæm | ˈmʌlʌl |
| tɑˈθɛθ | ˈkɪpik | ˈlæmæn | ˈmʌrʌl |

tɑˈðɛθ	ˈkipɪk	ˈlænæm	ˈmʌwʌl
tɑˈðɛð	ˈkɪpɪk	ˈlænæn	ˈnʌlʌl
tɑˈfɛð	ˈkɪpɪt	ˈlænæŋ	ˈnʌɾʌl

D. There is a set of nonsense words on the website numbered D 1–5. Play them one at a time and try to transcribe them.

1. _____
2. _____
3. _____
4. _____
5. _____

E. After you have done Exercise D, look at the following nonsense words, which are the answers to Exercise D. Now make up a set of similar words, and say these to a partner. Your words can differ from the sample set in as many sounds as you like. But we suggest that you should not make them much longer at first. You will also find it helpful to write down your words and practice saying them for some time by yourself so that you can pronounce them fluently when you say them to your partner.

ˈskɑnzil

ˈbɹaɪɡbluzd

ˈdʒɪŋsmœŋ

flɔɪʃˈθɹaɪðz

pjutˈpeɪtʃ

When you have finished saying each word several times and your partner has written the words down, compare notes. Try to decide whether any discrepancies were due to errors in saying the words or in hearing them. If possible, the speaker should try to illustrate discrepancies by pronouncing the word in both ways, saying, for example, "I said [ˈskɑnzil] but you wrote [ˈskɑnsil]."

There is no one best way of doing ear-training work of this kind. It is helpful to look carefully at a person pronouncing an unknown word, then try to say the word yourself immediately afterward, getting as much of it right as possible but not worrying if you miss some things on first hearing. Then write down all that you can, leaving blanks to be filled in when you hear the word again. It seems important to get at least the number of syllables and the placement of the stress correct on first hearing so that you have a framework in which to fit later observations. Repeat this kind of production and perception exercise as often as you can. You should do a few minutes' work of this kind every day, so that you spend at least an hour a week doing practical exercises.

PART II
ENGLISH PHONETICS

3

The Consonants of English

 We begin this chapter by reviewing some of the gestures involved in producing the consonants of English. In the materials for this chapter on the website, there are two movies. The first shows the pronunciation of consonants that have different places of articulation. The stops [p, t, k] are illustrated in the nonsense utterances [həpa, həta, həka]. These stops are said to be bilabial, alveolar, and velar. But it is not just the different places on the roof of the mouth that distinguish these sounds. They are equally characterized by the movements of the lips and different parts of the tongue. Look at the movie and note the rapid movements of the lips for the first consonant, of the tip of the tongue for the second, and of the back of the tongue for the third.

The second movie shows different manners of articulation, illustrating the consonants [d, n, s] in the nonsense words [hədɛ, hənɛ, həsɛ]. Look at the movie, and then go through it slowly. In [hədɛ], note how, at the left of the picture, the soft palate rises to form a velic closure in the first few frames, even before the tip of the tongue moves up to form a closure on the alveolar ridge. Conversely, in [hənɛ], note that the soft palate moves up before the tongue moves, but this time only slightly. The soft palate does not make a complete closure and thus allows air to escape through the nose after the tongue tip has made a closure on the alveolar ridge for [n]. The third nonsense word in this movie, [həsɛ], has tongue and soft palate gestures very similar to those in [hədɛ]. The small differences in tongue shape are hard to see in this film, even when you step through it one frame at a time. But if you superimpose tracings of the articulators at the [d] and [s] midpoints, you will find that in the [s], the center of the tongue is slightly hollowed; the location of the constriction in [d] is slightly behind that for [s]. Also, during the [s], the teeth are closer together and slightly more forward than during the [d]. Much of the sound of [s] is produced by a jet of air striking the edges of the teeth. The rapidly moving airstream is formed by the narrow gap between the tongue and the alveolar ridge. These requirements of the [s] sound may explain why this speaker has slightly different tongue and jaw positions for [d] and [s].

STOP CONSONANTS

Consider the difference between the words in the first column in Table 3.1 and the corresponding words in the second column. This opposition may be said to be between the set of voiceless stop consonants and the set of voiced stop consonants. But the difference is really not just one of voicing during the consonant closure, as you can see by saying these words yourself. Most people have very little voicing going on while the lips are closed during either *pie* or *buy*. Both stop consonants are essentially voiceless. But in *pie*, after the release of the lip closure, there is a moment of **aspiration**, a period of voicelessness after the stop articulation and before the start of the voicing for the vowel. If you put your hand in front of your lips while saying *pie*, you can feel the burst of air that comes out during the period of voicelessness after the release of the stop. In the spectrograms linked to example 3.2, this puff of air is noticeable at the start of *pie* and *tie* and *kye*.

In a narrow transcription, aspiration may be indicated by a small raised *h*, [ʰ]. Accordingly, these words may be transcribed as [pʰaɪ, tʰaɪ, kʰaɪ]. You may not be able to feel the burst of air in *tie* and *kye* because these stop closures are made well inside the mouth cavity. But listen carefully and notice that you can hear the period of voicelessness after the release of the stop closure in each of the words. It is this interval that indicates that the stop is aspirated. The major difference between the words in the first two columns is not that one has voiceless stops and the other voiced stops. It is that the first column has (voiceless) aspirated stops and the second column has (perhaps voiced) unaspirated stops. The amount of voicing in each of the stops [b, d, g] depends on the context in which it occurs. When it is in the middle of a word or phrase in which a voiced sound occurs on either side (as in column 3 in Table 3.1), voicing usually occurs throughout the stop closure. However, most speakers of English have no voicing during the closure of so-called voiced stops in sentence initial position, or when they occur after a voiceless sound as in *that boy*.

One of the main objects of this book is to teach you to become a phonetician by learning to listen very carefully. You should be able to hear these differences, but

TABLE 3.1 Words illustrating allophones of English stop consonants.

1	2	3	4	5	6
pie	buy	a buy	spy	nap	nab
tie	dye	a dye	sty	mat	mad
kye	guy	a sky	sky	knack	nag

Figure 3.1 The waveforms of the words *tie* and *die*.

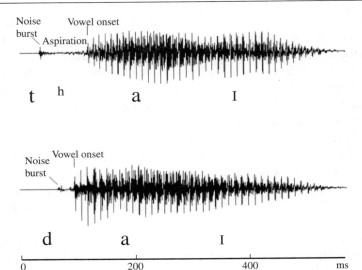

you can also see them in acoustic waveforms. Figure 3.1 is a record of the words *tie* and *die*. It is quite easy to see the different segments in the sound wave. In the first word, *tie*, there is a spike indicating the burst of noise that occurs when the stop closure is released, followed by a period of very small semi-random variations during the aspiration, and then a regular, repeating wave as the vocal folds begin to vibrate for the vowel. In *die*, the noise burst is smaller, and there is very little gap between the burst and the start of the wave for the vowel. As you can see, the major difference between *tie* and *die* is the increase in time between the release of the stop and the start of the vowel. We will discuss this distinction further in Chapter 6.

EXAMPLE 3.2 Now consider the words in the fourth column of Table 3.1. Are the sounds of the stop consonants more like those in the first column or those in the second? As in many cases, English spelling is misleading, and the sounds are in fact more like those in the second column. There is no opposition in English between words beginning with / sp / and / sb /, or / st / and / sd /, or / sk / and / sg /. English spelling has words beginning with *sp*, *st*, *sc*, or *sk*, and none that begin with *sb*, *sd*, or *sg*, but the stops that occur after / s / are really somewhere between initial / p / and / b /, / t / and / d /, / k / and / g /, and usually more like the so-called voiced stops / b, d, g / in that they are completely unaspirated. Figure 3.2 shows the acoustic waveform in *sty*. You can see the small variations in the waveform corresponding to the fricative / s /, followed by a straight line during the period in which there is no sound because there is a complete stop for the / t /. This is followed by a sound wave very similar to that of the / d / in Figure 3.1.

Figure 3.2 The waveform of the word *sty*.

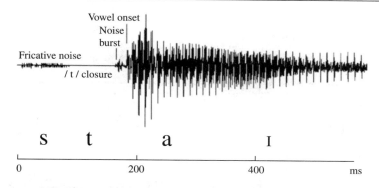

If you have access to a computer that can record sounds and let you see the waveforms of words, you can verify this for yourself. We recommend three different free programs for acoustic phonetics (you can find them with an Internet search): WaveSurfer for the great visualization of spectra and spectrograms, and for each plain text output of analyses; Praat for great user support and a large base of user scripts; Audacity for good recording interface and simple editing. Record words such as *spy, sty, sky, spill, still, skill*, each said as a separate word. Now find the beginning and end of each / s /, and cut this part out. When you play the edited recordings to others and ask them to write down the words they hear, they will almost certainly write *buy, die, guy, bill, dill, gill*.

What about the differences between the words in the fifth and sixth columns? The consonants at the end of *nap, mat, knack* are certainly voiceless. But if you listen carefully to the sounds at the end of the words *nab, mad, nag*, you may find that the so-called voiced consonants / b, d, g / have very little voicing and might also be called voiceless. Try saying these words separately. You can, of course, say each of them with the final consonant released with a noise burst and a short vowel-like sound afterward. But it would be more normal to say each of them without releasing the final consonants, or at least without anything like a vowel. You could even say *cab* and not open your lips for a considerable period of time if it were the last word of an utterance. In such circumstances, it is quite clear that the final consonants are not fully voiced throughout the closure.

There is, however, a clear distinction between the words in the fifth and sixth columns. Say these words in pairs—*nap, nab; mat, mad; knack, nag*—and try to decide which has the longer vowel. In these pairs, and in all similar pairs—such as *cap, cab; cat, cad; back, bag*—the vowel is much shorter before the voiceless consonants / p, t, k / than it is before the voiced consonants / b, d, g /. In addition to hearing the difference, when you look at the spectrograms for example 3.2, you can see the length difference. The major difference between such pairs of words is in the vowel length, not in the voicing of the final consonants.

Figure 3.3 The waveforms of the words *mat* and *mad*.

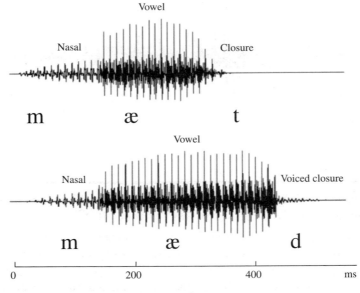

You can hear that both speakers on the website also distinguish these words by vowel length. In these recordings, each of the speakers said the words *nap, nab*; *mat, mad*; *knack, nag* in the same phonetic context, *I'll say again*. By saying each word in a separate sentence, it's easier to give each of them the same stress and intonation, and thus avoid the influence of these factors on the length of a word.

This length difference is very evident in Figure 3.3, which shows the waveforms of the words *mat* and *mad*. In this case, the vowel in *mad* is almost twice as long as the vowel in *mat*. You can see small voicing vibrations during the / d / in *mad*, but there is nothing noteworthy at the end of *mat* except the slightly irregular voicing at the time of the closure. We will return to this point later in this section.

Try comparing the length differences in short sentences such as *Take a cap now* and *Take a cab now*. If you say these sentences with a regular rhythm, you will find that the length of time between *Take* and *now* is about the same in both. This is because the whole word *cap* is only slightly shorter than the whole word *cab*. The vowel is much shorter in *cap* than in *cab*. But the consonant / p / makes up for this by being slightly longer than the consonant / b /. It is a general rule of English (and of most other languages) that syllable final voiceless consonants are longer than the corresponding voiced consonants after the same vowel.

The phrases *Take a cap now* and *Take a cab now* also illustrate a further point about English stop consonants at the end of a word (or, in fact, at the end of a stressed syllable). Say each of these phrases without a pause before *now*. Do your lips open before the [n] of *now* begins, or do they open during the [n]? If they open before the [n], there will be a short burst of aspiration or a short vowel-like sound between the two words. Releasing the stops produces a somewhat unnatural pronunciation. Generally, final stops are unreleased when the next word begins with a nasal. The same is true if the next word begins with a stop. The final [t] in *cat* is nearly always unexploded in phrases like *the cat pushed*. In a narrow transcription, we can symbolize the fact that a consonant is unreleased by adding a small raised mark [˺], which stands for "no audible release." We could therefore transcribe the phrase as [ð ə ˈkʰæt˺ pʰʊʃt].

The same phenomenon occurs even within a word such as *apt* [æp˺t] or *act* [æk˺t]. Furthermore, across a word boundary, the two consonants involved can even be identical, as in the phrase *white teeth*. To convince yourself that there are two examples of / t / in this phrase, try contrasting it with *why teeth*. Not only is the vowel in *white* much shorter than the vowel in *why* (because the vowel in *white* is in a syllable with a voiceless consonant at the end), but also the stop closure in *white teeth* is much longer than the stop in the phrase with only one / t /. In *white teeth*, there really are two examples of / t / involved, the first of which is unreleased.

Other languages do not have this pattern. For example, it is a mark of speakers with an Italian accent (at least as caricatured in films and on television) that they release all their final stop consonants, producing an extra vowel at the end, as they normally would in their own language. Authors trying to indicate an Italian speaking English will write the sentence *It's a big day* as *It's a bigga day*. They are presumably trying to indicate the difference between the normal [ɪts ə ˈbɪg˺ ˈdeɪ] and the foreign accent [ɪts ə ˈbɪgə ˈdeɪ].

It is interesting that words such as *rap*, *rat*, *rack* are all distinguishable, even when the final consonants are unreleased. The difference in the sounds must therefore be in the way that the vowels end—after all, the rest is silence. The consonants before and after a vowel always affect it, so there is a slight but noticeable difference in its quality. Compare your pronunciation of words such as *pip*, *tit*, and *kick*. Your tongue tip is up throughout the word *tit*, whereas in *pip* and *kick* it stays behind the lower front teeth. In *kick*, it is the back of the tongue that is raised throughout the word, and in *pip*, the lip gestures affect the entire vowel. The same is true for words with voiced consonants such as *bib*, *did*, and *gig*. The consonant gestures are superimposed on the vowel in such a way that their effect is audible throughout much of the syllable.

The sounds [p, t, k] are not the only voiceless stops that occur in English. Many people also pronounce a glottal stop in some words. A glottal stop is the sound (or, to be more exact, the lack of sound) that occurs when the vocal folds are held tightly together. As we have seen, the symbol for a glottal stop is [ʔ], resembling a question mark without the dot.

When you lift something heavy you will probably produce a glottal stop to trap the air in your lungs and stabilize your abdomen and chest, and then release the stop with a grunt. Glottal stops also occur whenever one coughs. You should be able to get the sensation of the vocal folds being pressed together by making small coughing noises. Next, take a deep breath and hold it with your mouth open. Listen to the small plosive sound that occurs when you let the breath go. Now, while breathing out through your mouth, try to check and then release the breath by making and releasing a short glottal stop. Then, do the same while making a voiced sound such as the vowel [ɑ]. Practice producing glottal stops between vowels, saying [ɑʔɑ] or [iʔi] so that you get to know what they feel like.

One of the most common occurrences of a glottal stop is in the utterance meaning *no,* often spelled *uh-uh.* If someone asks you a question, you can reply *no* by saying [ˈʔʌʔʌ] (usually with a nasalized vowel, which we will symbolize later). Note that there is a contrast between the utterance meaning *no* and that meaning *yes* that is dependent on the presence of the glottal stop. If you had meant to say *yes,* you might well have said [ˈʌhʌ]. We can tell that it is the glottal stop that is important in conveying the meaning by the fact that one could be understood equally well by using a syllabic consonant (shown by putting the mark [ˌ] under the consonant) instead of a vowel, and saying [ˈm̩hm̩] for *yes* and [ˈʔm̩ʔm̩] for *no.* As long as there is a glottal stop between the two syllables, the utterance will mean *no,* irrespective of what vowel or nasal is used.

Glottal stops frequently occur as variants of / t /. Probably most Americans and many British speakers have a glottal stop followed by a syllabic nasal in words such as *beaten, kitten, fatten* [ˈbiʔn̩, ˈkɪʔn̩, ˈfæʔn̩]. London Cockney and many forms of Estuary English also have a glottal stop between vowels such as in *butter, kitty, fatter* [ˈbʌʔə, ˈkɪʔi, ˈfæʔə]. Many speakers in both Britain and America have a glottal stop just before final voiceless stops in words such as *rap, rat,* and *rack.* Usually, the articulatory gesture for the other stop is still audible, so these words could be transcribed [ɹæʔ͡p, ɹæʔ͡t, ɹæʔ͡k]. When Peter Ladefoged recorded the word *mat* for Figure 3.3, he pronounced it as [mæʔ͡t], with the glottal stop and the closure for [t] occurring almost simultaneously.

EXAMPLE 3.5

Practice producing words with and without a glottal stop. After you have some awareness of what a glottal stop feels like, try saying the words *rap, rat,* and *rack* in several different ways. Begin by saying them with a glottal stop and a final release [ɹæʔ͡pʰ, ɹæʔ͡tʰ, ɹæʔ͡kʰ]. Next, say them without a glottal stop and with the final stops unexploded [ɹæp̚, ɹæt̚, ɹæk̚]. Then, say them with a glottal stop and a final unexploded consonant [ɹæʔ͡p̚, ɹæʔ͡t̚, ɹæʔ͡k̚]. Finally, say them with a glottal stop and no other final consonant [ɹæʔ, ɹæʔ, ɹæʔ].

EXAMPLE 3.6

When a voiced stop and a nasal occur in the same word, as in *hidden,* the stop is not released in the usual way. Both the [d] and the [n] are alveolar consonants. The tongue comes up and contacts the alveolar ridge for [d] and stays there for the nasal, which becomes syllabic [ˈhɪdn̩]. Consequently, as shown in Figure 3.4, the air pressure built up behind the stop closure is released through the nose by the lowering of the soft palate (the velum) for the nasal consonant. This phenomenon, known as **nasal plosion**, is normally used in pronouncing words such as *sadden, sudden, leaden* [ˈsædn̩, ˈsʌdn̩, ˈlɛdn̩]. It is considered a mark of a foreign accent to add a vowel [ˈsædən, ˈsʌdən, ˈlɛdən]. Nasal plosion also occurs in the pronunciation of words with [t] followed by [n], as in *kitten* [ˈkɪtn̩], for those people who do not have a glottal stop instead of the [t], but the majority of speakers of English pronounce this word with a glottal stop [ˈkɪʔn̩].

Figure 3.4   Nasal plosion.

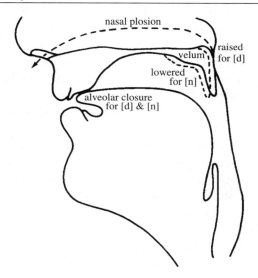

It is worth spending some time thinking exactly how you and others pronounce words such as *kitten* and *button*, in that it enables you to practice making detailed phonetic observations. There are a number of different possibilities. Most British and American English speakers make a glottal stop at the end of the vowel, before making an alveolar closure. Then, while still maintaining the glottal stop, they lower the velum and raise the tongue for the alveolar closure. But which comes first? If they lower the velum before making the alveolar closure, there is only [ʔn] and no [t]. If they make the alveolar closure first, we could say that there is [ʔtn], but there would not be any nasal plosion, as there would be no pressure built up behind the [t] closure. Nasal plosion occurs only if there is no glottal stop, or if the glottal stop is released after the alveolar closure has been made and before the velum is lowered.

These are fairly difficult sequences to determine, but there are some simple things you can do to help you find out what articulations you use. First of all, find a drinking straw and something to drink. Put one end of the straw between your lips and hold the other end just (and only just) below the surface of the liquid. Now say [ɑpɑ], and note how bubbles form during [p]. This is because pressure is built up behind your closed lips. Now push the straw slightly farther into your mouth and say [ɑtɑ]. It will not sound quite right because the straw gets in the way of your tongue when it makes the alveolar closure. You may have to try different positions of the straw. Go on until you can see bubbles coming out, and convince yourself that pressure builds up behind the [t]. Now try saying *button*. Of course there will be bubbles during the [b], but are there any at the end of the word, or do you have a glottal stop and no [t] behind which pressure builds up?

EXAMPLE 3.7

When two sounds have the same place of articulation, they are said to be **homorganic**. Thus, the consonants [d] and [n], which are both articulated on the alveolar ridge, are homorganic. For nasal plosion to occur within a word, there must be a stop followed by a homorganic nasal. Only in these circumstances can there be pressure first built up in the mouth during the stop, and then released through the nose by lowering the soft palate. Many forms of English do not have any words with a bilabial stop [p] or [b] followed by the homorganic nasal [m] at the end of the word. Nor in most forms of English are there any words in which the velar stops [k] or [g] are normally followed by the velar nasal [ŋ]. Consequently, both bilabial and velar nasal plosion are less common than alveolar nasal plosion in English. But when talking in a rapid conversational style, many people pronounce the word *open* as [ˈoʊpm̩], particularly if the next word begins with [m], as in *open my door, please*. Quite frequently, when counting, people will pronounce *seven* as [ˈsɛbm̩], and *something, captain, bacon* are sometimes pronounced [ˈsʌmpm̩ ˈkæpm̩ ˈbeɪkm̩]. You should try to pronounce all these words in these ways yourself.

A phenomenon similar to nasal plosion may take place when an alveolar stop [t] or [d] occurs before a homorganic lateral [l], as in *little, ladle* [ˈlɪtl̩, ˈleɪdl̩]. The air pressure built up during the stop can be released by lowering the sides of the tongue; this effect is called **lateral plosion**. Say the word *middle* and note the action of the tongue. Many people (particularly British speakers) maintain the tongue contact on the alveolar ridge through both the stop and the lateral, releasing it only at the end of the word. Others (most Americans) pronounce a very short vowel in the second syllable. For those who have lateral plosion, no vowel sound occurs in the second syllables of *little, ladle*. The final consonants in all these words are syllabic. There may also be lateral plosion in words such as *Atlantic*, in which the [t] may be resyllabified so that it is at the beginning of

Figure 3.5 Stop consonant releases.

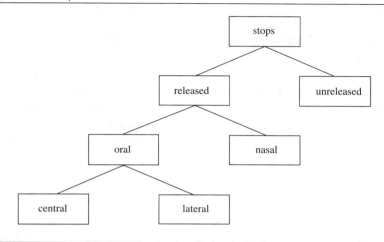

the stressed (second) syllable. We should also note that most Americans, irrespective of whether they have lateral plosion, do not have a voiceless stop in *little*. There is a general rule in American English that whenever / t / occurs after a stressed vowel and before an unstressed syllable other than [n̩], it is changed into a voiced sound. For those Americans who have lateral plosion, this will be the stop [d].

EXAMPLE 3.8   This brings us to another important point about coronal stops and nasals. For many speakers, including most Americans, the consonant between the vowels in words such as *city, better, writer* is not really a stop but a quick tap in which the tongue tip is thrown against the alveolar ridge. This sound is written in the IPA with the symbol [ɾ] so that *city* can be transcribed as [ˈsɪɾi]. Many Americans also make this kind of tap when / d / occurs after a stressed vowel and before an unstressed vowel. As a result, they do not distinguish between pairs of words such as *latter* and *ladder*. But some maintain a distinction by having a shorter vowel in words such as *latter* that have a voiceless consonant in their underlying form. Vowel duration is usually just a redundant cue to the voicing of the intervocalic consonant, and the consonant voicing is the main cue. However, in words with a tapped / t / or / d / the consonant voicing cue has been neutralized, leaving the redundant cue (vowel length) to carry the contrast on its own. Some dialects of North American English, particularly from central Canada, also distinguish between word pairs like *writer* and *rider*, which are both said with a tap [ɾ] with an additional vowel quality difference that is redundant with the vowel length difference found in other dialects. So, where a Midwesterner in the United States would say [ɹaɪɾɚ] and [ɹaːɪɾɚ], with a length difference in the diphthong, in Canadian vowel "raising" we hear [ɹəɪɾɚ] and [ɹaːɪɾɚ] with a short "schwa."

We can summarize the discussion of stop consonants by thinking of the possibilities there are in the form of a branching diagram, as shown in Figure 3.5. The first question to consider is whether the gesture for the stop is released (exploded) or not. If it is released, then is it oral plosion, or is the release due to the lowering of the velum, with air escaping through the nose, making it nasal plosion? If it is oral plosion, then is the closure in the mouth entirely removed, or is the articulation in the midline retained and one or both sides of the tongue lowered so that air escapes laterally? You should be able to produce words illustrating all these possibilities. For coronal stops, there is an additional point not shown in Figure 3.5; namely, is the [t] or [d] sound produced as a tap [ɾ]?

FRICATIVES

The fricatives of English vary less than the stop consonants, yet the major allophonic variations that do occur are in many ways similar to those of the stops. Earlier we saw that when a vowel occurs before one of the voiceless stops / p, t, k /, it is shorter than it would be before one of the voiced stops / b, d, g /. The same kind of difference in vowel length occurs before voiceless and voiced fricatives. The vowel is shorter in the first word of each of these pairs: *strife, strive* [stɹaɪf, stɹaɪv]; *teeth, teethe* [tiθ, tið]; *rice, rise* [raɪs, raɪz]; *mission, vision* ['mɪʃn̩, 'vɪʒn̩].

Stops and fricatives are the only English consonants that can be either voiced or voiceless. Consequently, our observation that vowels are shorter before voiceless stops than before voiced stops should be revised. The correct observation is that vowels are shorter before all voiceless consonants than before all voiced consonants, whether fricatives or stops.

We also saw that a voiceless stop at the end of a syllable (as in *hit*) is longer than the corresponding voiced stop (as in *hid*). Similarly, the voiceless fricatives are longer than their voiced counterparts in each of the pairs *safe, save* [seɪf, seɪv], *lace, laze* [leɪs, leɪz], and all the other pairs of words we have been discussing in this section. Again, because fricatives behave like stops, a linguistically significant generalization would have been missed if we had regarded each class of consonants completely separately.

Fricatives are also like stops in another way. Consider the degree of voicing that occurs in the fricative at the end of the word *ooze*, pronounced by itself. In most pronunciations, the voicing that occurs during the final [z] does not last throughout the articulation but changes in the last part to a voiceless sound like [s]. In general, voiced fricatives at the end of a word, as in *prove, smooth, choose, rouge* [pɹuv, smuð, tʃuz, ɹuʒ], are voiced throughout their articulation only when they are followed by another voiced sound. In a phrase such as *prove it,* the [v] is fully voiced because it is followed by a vowel. But in *prove two times two is four* or *try to improve*, where the [v] is followed by a voiceless sound [t] or by a pause at the end of the phrase, it is not fully voiced.

Briefly stated, then, fricatives are like stops in three ways. First, stops and fricatives influence vowel length in similar ways—vowels before voiceless stops or fricatives are shorter than before voiced stops or fricatives. Second, final voiceless stops and fricatives are longer than final voiced stops and fricatives. Third, the final stops and fricatives classified as voiced are not actually voiced throughout the articulation unless the adjacent sounds are also voiced. In addition, both these types of articulation involve an obstruction of the airstream. Because they have an articulatory feature in common and because they act together in phonological patterns, we refer to fricatives and stops together as a natural class of sounds called **obstruents**.

However, fricatives do differ from stops in that they sometimes involve actions of the lips that are not immediately obvious. Try saying *fin, thin, sin, shin* [fɪn, θɪn, sɪn, ʃɪn]. There is clearly a lip action in the first word as it involves the labiodental sound [f]. But do your lips move in any of the other three words? Most people find that their lips move slightly in any word containing / s / (*sin, kiss*) and quite considerably in any word containing / ʃ / (*shin, quiche*), but that there is no lip action in words containing / θ / (*thin, teeth*). There is also lip movement in the voiced sounds corresponding to / s / and / ʃ /, namely / z / as in *zeal, zest* and / ʒ / in *leisure, treasure*, but none in / ð /, as in *that, teethe.*

The primary articulatory gesture in these fricatives is the close approximation of two articulators so that friction can be heard. The lip rounding is a lesser articulation in that the two articulators (the lower lip and the upper lip) approach one another but not sufficiently to cause friction. A lesser degree of closure by two articulators not involved in the primary articulation is called a *secondary articulation*. This particular one, in which the action of the lips is added to another articulation, is called *labialization*. The English fricatives / ʃ, ʒ / are strongly labialized, and the fricatives / s, z / are slightly labialized.

AFFRICATES

This is a convenient place to review the status of affricates in English. An affricate is a sequence of a stop followed by a fricative that functions as if it were a single sound. Some stop, fricative sequences, for example the dental affricate [tθ] as in *eighth* or the alveolar affricate [ts] as in *cats*, are simply consonant clusters comparable to those at the beginning of *spy* and *sky*. But, as we noted in the discussion of symbols for transcribing English, it is sometimes appropriate to regard the sequences [tʃ] and [dʒ] as different from other sequences of consonants. They are the only stop, fricative sequences in English that can occur at both the beginning and the end of words. In fact, even the other stop, fricative sequences that can occur at the end of words will usually do so only as the result of the formation of a plural or some other suffix, as in *eighth*. From the point of view of a phonologist considering the sound pattern of English, the post-alveolar affricates are plainly single units, but [ts] as in *cats* is simply a sequence of two consonants. One way to convince yourself that the affricates [tʃ] and [dʒ] are phonetic sequences of stop followed by fricative is to record yourself saying *itch* and *badge*, and then play them backwards (e.g., use the WaveSurfer "reverse" function to do this). The fricative stop sequence is usually pretty easy to hear in the backwards versions.

NASALS

The nasal consonants of English vary even less than the fricatives. Nasals, together with [ɹ, l], can be syllabic when they occur at the end of words. As we have seen, the mark [ˌ] under a consonant indicates that it is syllabic. (Vowels, of course, are always syllabic and therefore need no special mark.) In a narrow transcription, we may transcribe the words *sadden* and *table* as [ˈsædn̩, ˈteɪbl̩]. In most pronunciations, *prism* and *prison* can be transcribed [ˈpɹɪzm̩, ˈpɹɪzn̩], as these words do not usually have a vowel between the last two consonants. Syllabic consonants can also occur in phrases such as *Jack and Kate* [ˈdʒæk n̩ ˈkeɪt].

The nasal [ŋ] differs from the other nasals in a number of ways. No English word can begin with [ŋ]. This sound can occur only within or at the end of a word, and even in these circumstances it does not behave like the other nasals. It can be preceded only by the vowels / ɪ, ɛ, æ, ʌ / and / ɑ / (American English) or / ɒ / (British English), and it cannot be syllabic (except in slightly unusual pronunciations, such as *bacon* [ˈbeɪkn̩], and phrases such as *Jack and Kate* mentioned earlier).

One way to consider the different status of [ŋ] is that in the history of English, it was derived from a sequence of the phonemes / n / and / g /. Looking at it this way, *sing* was at an earlier time in history / sɪng /, and *sink* was / sɪnk /. There was then a sound change in which / n / became the new phoneme / ŋ / in those words where it occurred before / g / and / k /, turning / sɪng / into / sɪŋg / and / sɪnk / into / sɪŋk /. Another change resulted in the deletion of / g / (but not of / k /) whenever it occurred after / ŋ / at the end of either a word (as in *sing*) or a stem followed by a suffix such as *-er* or *-ing*. In this way, the / g / would be dropped in *singer*, which contains a suffix *-er*, but is retained in *finger*, in which the *-er* is not a suffix. The second change has been undone by some New Yorkers who make *singer* rhyme with *finger*.

APPROXIMANTS

The voiced approximants are / w, ɹ, j, l / as in *whack, rack, yak,* and *lack*. The first three of these sounds are central approximants, and the last is a lateral approximant. The articulation of each of them varies slightly depending on the articulation of the following vowel. You can feel that the tongue is in a different position in the first sounds of *we* and *water*. The same is true for *reap* and *raw*, *lee* and *law*, and *ye* and *yaw*. Try to feel where your tongue is in each of these words.

These consonants also share the possibility of occurring in consonant clusters with stop consonants. The approximants / ɹ, w, l / combine with stops in words such as *pray*, *bray*, *tray*, *dray*, *Cray*, *gray*, *twin*, *dwell*, *quell*, *Gwen*, *play*, *blade*, *clay*, and *glaze*. The approximants are largely voiceless when they follow one of the voiceless stops / p, t, k / as in *play*, *twice*, and *clay*. This voicelessness is a manifestation of the aspiration that occurs after voiceless stops, which we discussed at the beginning of this chapter. At that time, we introduced a small raised *h* symbol, [ʰ], which can be used to show that the first part of the vowel is voiceless. When there is no immediately following vowel, we can use the diacritic [̥] to indicate a voiceless sound. We can transcribe the words *play*, *twice*, *clay*, in which there are approximants after initial voiceless plosives, as [pl̥eɪ, tw̥aɪs, kl̥eɪ]. The approximant / j / as in *you* [ju] can occur in similar consonant clusters, as in *pew*, *cue* [pj̥u, kj̥u], and, for speakers of British English, *tune* [tj̥un]. We will discuss the sequence [ju] again when we consider vowels in more detail.

In most forms of British English, there is a considerable difference in the articulation of / l / before a vowel or between vowels, as in *leaf* or *feeling*, as compared with / l / before a consonant or at the end of a word, as in *field* or *feel*. In most forms of American English, there is less distinction between these two kinds of / l /. Note the articulation of / l / in your own pronunciation. Try to feel where the tongue is during the / l / in *leaf*. You will probably find that the tip is touching the alveolar ridge, and one or both sides are near the upper side teeth, but not quite touching. Now compare this articulation with the / l / in *feel*. Try playing *leaf* backwards to see if it sounds like *feel*. Does *feel* backwards sound like *leaf*? Most (but not all) speakers make / l / with the tongue tip touching the alveolar ridge. But in both British and American English, the center of the tongue is pulled down and the back is arched upward as in a back vowel. If there is contact on the alveolar ridge, it is the primary articulation. The arching upward of the back of the tongue forms a secondary articulation, which we will call **velarization**. In most forms of American English, all examples of / l / are comparatively velarized, except perhaps, those that are syllable initial and between high front vowels, as in *freely*. In British English, / l / is usually not velarized when it is before a vowel, as in *lamb* or *swelling*, but it is velarized when word final or before a consonant, as in *ball or filled*. Also, compare the velarized / l / in *Don't kill dogs* with the one in *Don't kill it*. Most people don't have a velarized / l / in *kill it,* despite the fact that it is seemingly at the end of a word. This is because the *it* in *kill it* acts like a suffix (technically a *clitic*), just like the suffix *-ing* in *killing*. (Note: The differences between the two types of / l / are more noticeable in British English.)

One symbol for velarization, that was introduced briefly in Chapter 2, is the mark [˜] through the middle of the symbol. Accordingly, a narrow transcrip-

EXAMPLE 3.11

tion of *feel* would be [fit]. For many speakers, the whole body of the tongue is drawn up and back in the mouth so that the tip of the tongue no longer makes contact with the alveolar ridge. Strictly speaking, therefore, this sound is not an alveolar consonant, but more like some kind of back vowel. This variant is called a "vocalized / l /."

Finally, we must consider the status of / h /. Earlier we suggested that the English / h / is the voiceless counterpart of the surrounding sounds. At the beginning of a sentence, / h / is like a voiceless vowel, but / h / can also occur between vowels in words or phrases like *behind the head*. As you move from one vowel through / h / to another, the articulatory movement is continuous, and the / h / is signaled by a weakening of the voicing, which may not even result in a completely voiceless sound.

In many accents of English, / h / can occur only before stressed vowels or before the approximant / j /, as in *hue* [hju]. Some speakers of English also sound / h / before / w / so that they contrast *which* [hwɪtʃ] and *witch* [wɪtʃ]. The symbol [ʍ] (an inverted *w*) is a better transcription for this contrastive, phonemic voiceless approximant. The contrast between / w / and / ʍ / is disappearing in most forms of English. In those dialects in which it occurs, [ʍ] is more likely to be found only in the less common words such as *whether* rather than in frequently used words such as *what*.

OVERLAPPING GESTURES

All the sounds we have been considering involve movements of the articulators. They are often described in terms of the articulatory positions that characterize these movements. But, rather than thinking in terms of static positions, we should really consider each sound as a movement. This makes it easier to understand the overlapping of consonant and vowel gestures in words such as *bib, did, gig*, mentioned earlier in this chapter. As we noted, in the first word, *bib*, the tongue tip is behind the lower front teeth throughout the word. In the second word, *did*, the tip of the tongue goes up for the first / d / and remains close to the alveolar ridge during the vowel so that it is ready for the second / d /. In the third word, *gig*, the back of the tongue is raised for the first / g / and remains near the soft palate during the vowel. In all these cases, the gestures for the vowels and consonants overlap.

The same kind of thing happens with respect to gestures of the lips. Lip rounding is an essential part of / w /. Because there is a tendency for gestures to overlap with those for adjacent sounds, stops are slightly rounded when they occur in clusters in which / w / is the second element, as in *twice, dwindle, quick* [tw̥aɪs, ˈdwɪndl̩, kw̥ɪk]. This kind of gestural overlapping, in which a second gesture starts during the first gesture, is sometimes called *anticipatory coarticulation*. The gesture for the approximant is anticipated during the gesture for the stop. In many people's speech, / ɹ / also has some degree of lip rounding. Try saying words such as *reed* and *heed*. Do you get some movement of the lips in the first word but not in the second? Use a mirror to see whether you get anticipatory lip rounding for the stops [t, d] so that they are slightly rounded in words such as *tree* and *dream*, as opposed to *tee* and *deem*.

We can often think of the gestures for different articulations as movements toward certain targets. A target is something that one aims at but does not necessarily hit, perhaps because one is drawn off by having to aim at a second target. Ideally, the description of an utterance might consist of the specification of a string of target gestures that must be made one after another. The data in Figure 3.6 are traces of the vocal tract during [b], [d], and [ɡ] in a variety of vowel contexts in French; similar observations have been made for English as well. The patterns of stability and variation are interesting. For instance, the traces for [b] show that the lips, jaw, and soft palate have about the same position no matter what the vowel context is, while the tongue position and larynx height varies quite a bit. If you look at the tongue traces closely, you can see tongue positions during [b] for the French vowels [i], [u], [ɑ], and the *umlaut u*, which is transcribed [y] in the IPA. In the traces for [d], we see again that some parts of the vocal tract take the same position in all of the vowel contexts (the tongue tip, soft palate, and jaw are the least variable). Interestingly, tongue body variation is much smaller in [d], which requires a tongue tip or blade gesture, than it is in [b], while in [d] the lip position is more variable. We also see a good deal of variation in the lip positions for [ɡ], as well as a good deal of variation in the front/back location of the tongue—unlike [b] and [d], the place of articulation of [ɡ] varies a good deal as a function of the neighboring vowel. The increased coarticulation of [ɡ] with surrounding vowels, as compared with [d], suggests that the specifications of the consonant and vowel gestures are competing with each other for control of the tongue body. The vowel [u] wants the tongue body to go quite far back in the mouth, as you can see it does in the [b] traces, while the [ɡ] wants the tongue body to be located a bit farther toward the front than this. Similarly, the vowel [i] wants the tongue body to be further front than is required or specified for [ɡ]. What we see in the figure is that the exact location of the [ɡ] stop closure is more variable than are the locations of the stop closures in [b] or [d]. This is probably because [ɡ] requires significant tongue body movement, just as do vowels.

Coarticulation between sounds will always result in the positions of some parts of the vocal tract being influenced quite a lot, whereas others will not be so much affected by neighboring targets. The extent to which anticipatory coarticulation occurs depends on the extent to which the position of that part of the vocal tract is specified in the two gestures. The degree of coarticulation also depends on the interval between them. For example, a considerable amount of lip rounding occurs during [k] when the next sound is rounded, as in *coo* [ku]. Slightly less lip rounding occurs if the [k] and the [u] are separated by another sound, as in *clue* [klu], and even less occurs if there is also a word boundary between the two sounds, as in the phrase *sack Lou* [sæklu]. Nevertheless, some rounding may occur, and sometimes anticipatory coarticulations can be observed over even longer sequences. In the phrase *tackle Lou* [tækl̩lu], the lip rounding for the [u] may start in the [k], which is separated from it by two segments and a word boundary.

There is no simple relationship between the description of a language in terms of phonetic distributions and the description of utterances in terms of gestural targets. Sometimes the different members of a phonetic distribution arise because of overlapping gestures. The difference between the [k] in *key* and the [k] in *caw* may be simply due to their overlapping with different vowels. Similarly, we do not necessarily have to specify separate targets for the alveolar [n] in *ten* and the dental [n̪] in *tenth*. Both may be the result of aiming at the same target, but in *tenth,* the realization of the phoneme / n / is influenced by the dental target required for the following sound. However, some phonetic variation is actually the result of aiming at different targets. For many American English speakers, the initial [ɹ] in *reed* is made with a tongue gesture that is very different from that for the final [ɹ] in *deer*. In most forms of British English, the [l] in *leaf* and the [l] in *feel* differ in ways that cannot be ascribed to coarticulation. To drive home the point that coarticulation isn't the only source of phonetic variation, consider the realization of the / t / in *button* spoken carefully [bʌtʰən] and quickly [bʌʔn̩], in which one word is realized with two completely different gestures for the medial consonant, [tʰ] and [ʔ]. Sometimes, phonetic variation is the result of overlapping gestures, producing what have been called *intrinsic allophones;* sometimes, they involve different gestures, which may be called *extrinsic allophones.*

To summarize, gestural targets are units that can be used in descriptions of how a speaker produces utterances. Virtually all the gestures for neighboring sounds overlap. Differences in the timing of one gesture with respect to another account for a wide range of the phenomena that we observe in speech. The next section provides a number of additional examples.

ENGLISH CONSONANT ALLOPHONES

A good way of summarizing (and slightly extending) all that we have said about English consonants so far is to list a number of phonetic distributions that describe the consonant allophones of English. The first of these deals with consonant length.

(1) Consonants are longer when at the end of a phrase.

You can see this pattern by comparing the duration of / s / in "*what will you miss*" to the duration of / s / in "*I'll miss it all.*" Use WaveSurfer or Praat to make recordings and spectrograms of words in phrases such as this (where the word is at the end of one phrase and in the middle of the other). You can check the duration to see if consonants really are longer at the ends of phrases.

Most patterns of phonetic variation apply to only selected groups of consonants.

(2) Voiceless stops (i.e., / p, t, k /) are aspirated when they are syllable initial, as in words such as *pip, test, kick* [pʰɪp, tʰɛst, kʰɪk].

(3) Obstruents—stops and fricatives—classified as voiced (i.e., / b, d, g, v, ð, z, ʒ /) are voiced through only a small part of the articulation when they occur at the end of an utterance or before a voiceless sound. Listen to the / v / when you say *try to improve*, and the / d / when you say *add two*.

(4) So-called voiced stops and affricates / b, d, g, dʒ / are voiceless when syllable initial, except when immediately preceded by a voiced sound (as in *a day* as compared with *this day*). Listen to the *sday* part of your own recording of *this day*. Does it sound like *stay*?

(5) Voiceless stops / p, t, k / are unaspirated after / s / in words such as *spew, stew, skew*.

(6) Voiceless obstruents / p, t, k, tʃ, f, θ, s, ʃ / are longer than the corresponding voiced obstruents / b, d, g, dʒ, v, ð, z, ʒ / when at the end of a syllable.

Words exemplifying this rule are *cap* as opposed to *cab* and *back* as opposed to *bag*. Try contrasting these words in sentences, and you may be able to hear the differences more clearly.

(7) The approximants /w, ɹ, j, l / are at least partially voiceless when they occur after initial / p, t, k /, as in *play, twin, cue* [pl̥eɪ, tw̥ɪn, kj̥u].

This is due to the overlapping of the gesture required for aspiration with the voicing gesture required for the approximants. (Note that the observation is that they are *at least partially voiceless*, but the transcription marks the approximants as being completely voiceless. Conflicts between statements and transcriptions of this kind will be discussed further below.)

(8) The gestures for consecutive stops overlap so that stops are unexploded when they occur before another stop in words such as *apt* [æp̚t] and *rubbed* [rʌb̚d].

(9) In many accents of English, syllable final / p, t, k / are accompanied by an overlapping glottal stop gesture, as in pronunciations of *tip, pit, kick* as [tɪʔ͡p, pɪʔ͡t, kɪʔ͡k]. (This is another case where transcription cannot fully describe what is going on.)

This is not found in all varieties of English. Some people do not have any glottal stops in these circumstances, and others have glottal stops completely replacing some or all of the voiceless stops. In any case, even for those who simply add a glottal stop, the statement is not completely accurate. Many people will have a glottal stop at the end of *cat* in phrases such as *that's a cat* or *the cat sat on the mat*, but they will not have this allophone of / t / in *the cat eats fish*.

(10) In many accents of English, / t / is replaced by a glottal stop when it occurs before an alveolar nasal in the same word, as in *beaten* [ˈbiʔn̩].

(11) Nasals are syllabic at the end of a word when immediately after an obstruent, as in *leaden, chasm* [ˈlɛdn̩, ˈkæzm̩].

Note that we cannot say that nasals become syllabic whenever they occur at the end of a word and after a consonant. The nasals in *kiln* and *film* are not syllabic in most accents of English. We can, however, state a rule describing the syllabicity of / l / by saying simply:

(12) The lateral / l / is syllabic at the end of a word when immediately after a consonant.

This statement summarizes the fact that / l / is syllabic not only after stops and fricatives (as in *paddle, whistle* [ˈpædl̩, ˈwɪsl̩]), but also after nasals (as in *kennel, channel* [ˈkɛnl̩, ˈtʃænl̩]). The only problem with this rule is what happens after / ɹ /. It is correct for words such as *barrel* [ˈbærl̩] but does not work in most forms of American English in words such as *snarl* [snɑɹl] when / ɹ / has to be considered as part of the vowel.

When it is not part of the vowel, / ɹ / is like / l / in most forms of American English in that it, too, can be syllabic when it occurs at the end of a word and after a consonant, as in *saber, razor, hammer, tailor* [ˈseɪbɹ̩, ˈɹeɪzɹ̩, ˈhæmɹ̩, ˈteɪlɹ̩]. If we introduce a new term, **liquid**, which is used simply as a cover term for the consonants / l, ɹ /, we may rephrase the observation in (12) and say:

(12a) The liquids / l, ɹ / are syllabic at the end of a word when immediately after a consonant.

The next statement also applies more to American English than to British English. It accounts for the / t / in *fatty, data* [ˈfæɾi, ˈdeɪɾə]. But note that these are not the only contexts in which these changes occur. This is not simply a change that affects / t / after a stressed vowel and before an unstressed one, in that / t / between two unstressed vowels (as in *divinity*) is also affected. However, not all cases of / t / between vowels change in this way. The / t / in *attack* (i.e., before a stressed syllable) is voiceless, and / t / after another consonant (e.g., in *hasty* and *captive*) is also voiceless. Note also that most American English speakers have a very similar articulatory gesture in words containing / d / and / n / in similar circumstances, such as *daddy* and *many*. The first of these two words could well be transcribed [ˈdæɾi]. The second has the same sound, except that it is nasalized, so it could be transcribed [ˈmɛɾ̃i] in a narrow transcription. Nasalization is shown by the diacritic [˜] over a symbol. The following statement accounts for all these facts:

(13) Alveolar stops become voiced taps when they occur between two vowels, the second of which is unstressed.

Many speakers of American English show a similar pattern in a sequence of an alveolar nasal followed by a stop. In words such as *painter* and *splinter*, the / t / is lost and a nasal tap occurs. This has resulted in *winter* and *winner* and *panting* and *panning* being pronounced in the same way. For these speakers, we can restate (13), making it:

(13a) Alveolar stops and alveolar nasal plus stop sequences become voiced taps when they occur between two vowels, the second of which is unstressed.

There is a great deal of variation among speakers with respect to this. Some make taps in familiar words such as *auntie*, but not in less common words such as *Dante*. Some make them only in fast speech. What is the pattern in your own speech?

(14) Where we would expect to have an alveolar consonant, we find it to be dental when the next segment is a dental consonants, as in *eighth, tenth, wealth* [eɪt̪θ, tɛn̪θ, wɛl̪θ]. Note that this statement applies to all alveolar consonants, not just stops, and often applies across word boundaries, as in *at this* [æt̪ ðɪs]. This phenomenon, in English, may be from gestural overlap so that the place of articulation for the first consonant is changed.

In a more rapid style of speech, some of these dental consonants tend to be omitted altogether. Say these words first slowly and then more rapidly, and see what you do yourself. It is difficult to make precise statements about when consonants get deleted, because this depends so much on the style of speech being used. Alveolar stops often appear to get dropped in phrases such as *fact finding*. Most people say *most people* as ['moʊs 'pipl] with no audible [t], and they produce phrases such as *send papers* with no audible [d]. We could state this as follows:

(15) Alveolar stops are reduced or omitted when between two consonants.

This raises an interesting point of phonetic theory. Note that we said "alveolar stops often *appear* to get dropped," and there may be "no *audible* [d]." However, the tongue tip gesture for the alveolar stop in *most people* may be present but just not audible because it is completely overlapped by the labial stop that follows. More commonly, it is partially omitted; that is to say, the tongue tip moves up for the alveolar stop but does not make a complete closure. When we think in terms of phonetic symbols, we can write ['moʊs 'pipl̩] or ['moʊst 'pipl̩]. This makes it a question of whether the [t] is there or not. But that is not really the issue. Part of the tongue tip gesture may have been made, a fact that we have no way of symbolizing.

Check how you say phrases such as *best game* and *grand master*. Say these and similar phrases with and without the alveolar stop. You may find it difficult to formulate a statement that takes into account all the contexts where alveolar stops may not appear in your speech.

We must state not only where consonants get dropped, but also where they get added. Words such as *something* and *youngster* often get pronounced as ['sʌmpθɪŋ] and ['jʌŋkstɚ]. In a similar way, many people do not distinguish between *prince* and *prints,* or *tense* and *tents*. All these words may be pronounced with a short voiceless stop between the nasal and the voiceless fricative. But the stop is not really an added gesture. It is simply the result of changing the timing of the nasal gesture with respect to the oral gesture. By rushing the raising of the velum for the nasal, a moment of complete closure—a stop—occurs. The apparent insertion of a stop into the middle of a word in this way is one type of **epenthesis**. One way to state the observation is to say:

(16) A homorganic voiceless stop may occur after a nasal before a voiceless fricative followed by an unstressed vowel in the same word.

Note that it is necessary to mention that the following vowel must be unstressed. Speakers who have an epenthetic stop in the noun *concert* do not usually have one in verbal derivatives such as *concerted,* or in words such as *concern.* Nothing need be said about the vowel before the nasal. Epenthesis may—like the [t]-to-[ɾ] change described in (13)—occur between unstressed vowels. It is possible to hear an inserted [t] in both *agency* and *grievances.*

Pattern (16) raises a theoretical point similar to that discussed in connection with (15), where we were concerned with whether a segment had been deleted. Now we are concerned with whether a segment has been added. In each case, it is better to treat these as misleading questions and to think about the gestures involved rather than worry about the symbols that might or might not represent separate segments. It may be convenient to transcribe *something* as [ˈsʌmpθiŋ], but transcription is only a tool and should not be thought of as necessarily portraying the units used in the production of speech.

EXAMPLE 3.12

Observation (17) accounts for the shortening effects that occur when two identical consonants come next to one another, as in *big game* and *top post.* It is usually not accurate to say that one of these consonants is dropped. There are two consonantal gestures, but they overlap considerably. Even in casual speech, most people would distinguish between *stray tissue, straight issue,* and *straight tissue.* (Try saying these in sentences such as *That's a stray tissue* and see for yourself.) But there clearly is a shortening effect that we can state as follows:

(17) A consonant is shortened when it is before an identical consonant.

We can describe the overlapping gestures that result in more advanced articulations of / k / in *cap, kept, kit, key* [kʰæp, kʰɛpt, kʰɪt, kʰi] and of / g / in *gap, get, give, geese* [gæp, gɛt, gɪv, gis]. You should be able to feel the fronted position of your tongue contact in the latter words of these series. We can say:

(18) Velar stops are more front before front vowels.

Finally, we need to note the difference in the quality of / l / in *life* [laɪf] and *file* [faɪɫ], or *clap* [klæp] and *talc* [tæɫk], or *feeling* [filɪŋ] and *feel* [fiɫ].

(19) The lateral / l / is velarized when after a vowel or before a consonant at the end of a word.

Note that there are clearly distinct gestures required for / l / in the different circumstances. These are not differences that can be ascribed to overlapping gestures.

DIACRITICS

In this and the previous chapter, we have seen how the transcription of English can be made more detailed by the use of diacritics, small marks added to a symbol to narrow its meaning. The six diacritics we have introduced so far are shown in Table 3.2. You should learn the use of these diacritics before you attempt any further detailed transcription exercises. Note that the nasalization diacritic is a small wavy line above a symbol (the "tilde" symbol), and the

TABLE 3.2 Some diacritics that modify the value of a symbol.

̥	Voiceless	w̥	l̥	kw̥ɪk, pl̥eɪs	*quick, place*
ʰ	Aspirated	tʰ	kʰ	tʰæp, kʰɪs	*tap, kiss*
̪	Dental	t̪	d̪	æt̪ðə, həl̪θ	*at the, health*
ˠ	Velarized	ɫ		pʰɪɫ	*pill*
̩	Syllabic	n̩	l̩	ˈmɪʔn̩	*mitten*
̃	Nasalized	æ̃		mæ̃n	*man*

velarization diacritic is a tilde through the middle of a symbol. You can also mark velarization with a small superscript version of the Greek letter *gamma* (the "baby gamma"). Nasalization is more common among vowels, which will be discussed in the next chapter.

RECAP

This chapter goes into considerable detail on the consonants of English. And the main observations of the chapter are summarized in the section on consonant allophones. Perhaps the most important point to emerge from the many details covered in this chapter is that consonant sounds are not emitted from the mouth of the speaker like letters typed on a computer screen. (1) The information we use to identify speech sounds is spread over several adjacent sounds. For example, the most reliable difference between the / d / and / t / in *mad* versus *mat* is the duration of the vowel before the stop consonants. (2) Speech sounds in sequence influence each other. For example, the [n] in *button* is "pronounced" without a tongue movement—the tongue stays in place from the preceding [t] and the pronunciation involves adding voicing and nose opening to this existing tongue gesture. We notice also in Figure 3.6 the extensive degree of vocal tract variation that results from particular vowel and consonant combinations. These observations lead us to conclude that underlying the descriptive convenience of using letters in a phonetic alphabet, and describing the distributions of sounds as contrastive versus complementary, is a more fundamental reality. Ultimately, we have a more explanatory view of language sound patterns, and particularly the phonetic details of these patterns by focusing on the gestures that are used to produce speech.

EXERCISES

(Printable versions of all the exercises are available on the website.)

A. The sequence of the following annotated diagrams illustrates the actions that take place during the consonants at the end of the word *bench*. Fill in the blanks.

Before the vowel ends the soft palate
_____ so that air _____
_____.

At the end of the vowel, the blade of the tongue is raised to make contact with _____, preventing air from _____
_____.

The lips remain _____.
The vocal folds continue _____.

Then the _____ is raised and the _____ of the tongue is raised,
while the _____ of the tongue remains in the same place.
The lips become more _____.
The vocal folds _____.

The _____ remains _____ throughout the end of the word.
After a short period the _____
_____ moves downward, but the _____ remains close enough to the alveolar ridge to _____
_____.
The _____ are _____.
The vocal folds _____.

B. Annotate the diagram so as to describe the actions required for the consonants in the middle of the word *implant*. Make sure that your annotations mention the action of the lips, the different parts of the tongue, the soft palate, and the vocal folds in each diagram. Try to make clear which of the vocal organs moves first in going from one consonant to another. The pronunciation illustrated is that of a normal conversational utterance; note the position of the tongue during the bilabial nasal.

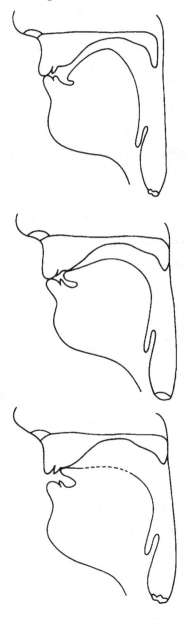

C. Draw and annotate diagrams similar to those in the previous exercises, but this time illustrate the actions that occur in pronouncing the consonants in the middle of the phrase *thick snow*. Make sure you show clearly the sequence of events, noting what the lips, tongue, soft palate, and vocal folds do at each moment. Before you begin, say the phrase to yourself several times at a normal speed. Note especially whether the back of your tongue lowers before or after the tip of the tongue forms the articulation for subsequent consonants.

D. As a transcription exercise, give a number of examples for each observation (2 through 19) given in this chapter. Give a narrow transcription of some additional words that illustrate the pattern. Your examples should not include any words that have been transcribed in this book so far. Remember to mark the stress on words of more than one syllable.

Statement (2)	three examples (one for each voiceless stop)
	_____ _____ _____
Statement (3)	seven examples (one for each voiced obstruent)
	_____ _____ _____
	_____ _____ _____
	_____
Statement (4)	eight examples (two for each voiced stop or affricate)
	_____ _____ _____
	_____ _____ _____
	_____ _____
Statement (5)	three examples (one for each voiceless stop)
	_____ _____ _____
Statement (6)	four contrasting pairs (one for each place of articulation)
	_____ _____
	_____ _____
	_____ _____
	_____ _____
Statement (7)	four examples (one for each approximant)
	_____ _____
	_____ _____
Statement (8)	six examples (one for each voiced and voiceless stop)
	_____ _____ _____
	_____ _____ _____

Statement (9)   three examples (not necessarily from your own speech)
                _____   _____   _____

Statement (10) three examples (use three different vowels)
                _____   _____   _____

Statement (11) three examples (use at least two different nasals)
                _____   _____   _____

Statement (12a) six examples (three each with / l / and / r /)
                _____   _____   _____
                _____   _____   _____

Statement (13a) six examples (two each with / t, d, n /, one being after an unstressed vowel)
                _____   _____   _____
                _____   _____   _____

Statement (14) three examples (one each for / t, d, n /)
                _____   _____   _____

Statement (15) three examples (any kind)
                _____   _____   _____

Statement (16) two examples (use two different nasals)
                _____   _____

Statement (17) three examples (any kind)
                _____   _____   _____

Statement (18) four examples (use four different vowels)
                _____   _____
                _____   _____

Statement (19) two contrasting pairs (try to make them reversible words)
                _____   _____
                _____   _____

E. As a more challenging exercise, try to list two exceptions to some of these statements.

Statement ( )   _____

Statement ( )   _____

F. Write a statement that describes the phonetic distribution of / h /.

_____

_____

_____

_____

G. Transcribe both the British and the American speaker saying these statements.

British English speaker

Once there was a young rat named Arthur,
who could never make up his mind.
Whenever his friends asked him
    if he would like to go out with them,
he would only answer, "I don't know."
He wouldn't say "yes" or "no" either.
He would always shirk making a choice.

American English speaker

Once there was a young rat named Arthur,
who could never make up his mind.
Whenever his friends asked him
    if he would like to go out with them,
he would only answer, "I don't know."
He wouldn't say "yes" or "no" either.
He would always shirk making a choice.

PERFORMANCE EXERCISES

A. Learn to produce some non-English sounds. First, in order to recall the sensation of adding and subtracting voicing while maintaining a constant articulation, repeat the exercise saying [sssszzzssszzz]. Now try a similar exercise, saying [mmm m̥m̥m̥mmmm m̥m̥m̥]. Make sure that your lips remain together all the time. During [m̥], you should be producing exactly the same action as when breathing out through the nose. Now say [m̥] between vowels, producing sequences such as [ɑm̥ɑ, im̥i], and so on. Try not to have any gap between the consonant and the vowels.

B. Repeat this exercise with [n, ŋ, l, ɹ, w, j], learning to produce [ɑn̥ɑ, ɑŋ̥ɑ, ɑl̥ɑ, ɑɹ̥ɑ, ɑw̥ɑ, ɑj̥ɑ] and similar sequences with other vowels.

C. Make sure that you can differentiate between the English words *whether*, *weather*; *which*, *witch*, even if you do not normally do so.

Say:

[ʍɛðə(ɹ)]	*whether*
[wɛðə(ɹ)]	*weather*
[ʍɪtʃ]	*which*
[wɪtʃ]	*witch*

D. Learn to produce the following Burmese words. (You may for the moment neglect the tones, indicated by accents above the vowels. The voiceless diacritic is placed on top of [ŋ̊] because the descender of the letter clashes with it [ŋ̥].)

Voiced nasals	**Voiceless nasals**
mâ 'lift up'	m̥â 'from'
nă 'pain'	n̥ă 'nose'
ŋa 'fish'	ŋ̊a 'borrow'

E. Working with a partner, produce and transcribe several sets of nonsense words. You should use slightly more complicated sets than previously. Make up your own sets on the basis of the illustrative set given below, including glottal stops, nasal and lateral plosion, and some combinations of English sounds that could not occur in English. Remember to mark the stress.

'kl̪ɑntʃʊps'kweɪdʒ

'ʒiʒm̩'spobm̩

'tsɪʔɪ'bɛʔɪdl̩

mbu'tr̪ɪgŋ

'tw̪aɪbrɛʔɪp

F. To increase your memory span in perceiving sounds, include some simpler but longer words in your production–perception exercises. A set of possible words is given below. Words such as the last two, which have eight syllables each, may be too difficult for you at the moment. But try to push your hearing ability to its limit. When you are listening to your partner dictating words, remember to try to (1) look at the articulatory movements; (2) repeat to yourself as much as you can immediately afterward; and (3) write down as much as you can, including the stress, as soon as possible.

'kiputu'pikitu

'bɛgɪ'gɪdɛ'dɛdɪ

tr̪i'tʃɪʔitʃu'drudʒi

'rilɛ'tolɛ'mɑnu'dʊli

'faɪθiði'vɔɪðuvu'θifi

4

English Vowels

TRANSCRIPTION AND PHONETIC DICTIONARIES

The vowels of English can be transcribed in many different ways, partly because accents of English differ greatly in the vowels they use and partly because there is no one right way of transcribing even a single accent of English. The set of symbols used depends on the reason for making the transcription. If one is aiming to reduce English to the smallest possible set of symbols, then *sheep* and *ship*, *Luke* and *look*, and all the other pairs of vowels that differ in length could be transcribed using one symbol per pair plus a length mark [ː], as [ʃiːp, ʃip], [luːk, luk], and so on. In this way, one could reduce the number of vowel symbols considerably, but at the expense of making the reader remember that the vowel pairs that differed by the use of the length mark also differed in quality. A different approach would be to emphasize all the differences between English vowels. This would require noting that both length and quality differences occur, making [ʃiːp, ʃɪp] the preferable transcription. Using this kind of transcription would hide the fact that vowel quality and vowel length are linked, and there is no need to mark both. In this book, we have chosen to use the transcription that most phonetics instructors prefer and write [ʃip, ʃɪp], leaving the reader to infer the difference in length.

Using this simple style of transcription, which was introduced in Chapter 2, carries a small penalty. There are some widely accepted reference books that specify pronunciations in both British and American English, none of which use exactly this style. One is an updated version of the dictionary produced by the English phonetician Daniel Jones, whose acute observations of English dominated British phonetics in the first half of the twentieth century. The current edition, *English Pronouncing Dictionary*, 18th edition (Cambridge: Cambridge University Press, 2011), is familiarly known as "EPD 18." It still bears Daniel Jones's name but has been completely revised by the new editors, Peter Roach, Jane Setter, and John Esling. It now shows both British and American pronunciations. A CD accompanies one version so that you can hear both the British and American pronunciations.

Another authoritative work is the *Longman Pronunciation Dictionary*, 3rd edition (Harlow, U. K.: Pearson, 2008), by John Wells. This dictionary, known as "LPD 3," also gives the British and American pronunciations, and has an accompanying CD. Professor Wells until recently held the chair in phonetics at University College, London, that Daniel Jones previously held. He is clearly the leading authority on contemporary English pronunciation in all its forms—British, American, and other variants of the worldwide language. Both these dictionaries, EPD 18 and LPD 3, use transcriptions in which the length differences in vowels are marked, not just the quality differences as in this book. They write [ʃiːp, ʃɪp] where we have [ʃip, ʃɪp]. A third dictionary, *Oxford Dictionary of Pronunciation for Current English* (Oxford: Oxford University Press, 2003) by Clive Upton, William Kretzschmar, and Rafal Konopka, is slightly different from the other two dictionaries in that it gives a wider range of both British and American pronunciations. To show more detail, it also uses a larger set of symbols and a more allophonic transcription than either of the other two dictionaries.

Everyone seriously interested in English pronunciation should be using one of these dictionaries. Each of them shows the pronunciations typically used by national newscasters—what we may regard as "Standard American Newscaster English" and "Standard BBC English" (often shortened to just "American English" and "British English" in this book). Of course, in neither country is there really a standard accent. Some newscasters in both countries have notable local accents. The dictionaries give what would be accepted as reasonable pronunciations for communicating in the two countries. They allow one to compare British and American pronunciations in great detail, noting, for example, that most British speakers pronounce *Caribbean* as [kæɹɪˈbiən], with the stress on the third syllable, whereas Americans typically say [kəˈɹɪbiən], with the stress on the second syllable.

Ordinary American college dictionaries also provide pronunciations, but the symbols they use are not in accordance with the principles of the IPA and are of little use for comparative phonetic purposes. American dictionary makers sometimes say that they deliberately do not use IPA symbols because their dictionaries are used by speakers with different regional accents, and they want readers to be able to learn how to pronounce an unfamiliar word correctly in their own accent. But, as we have been observing, IPA symbols are often used to represent broad regions of sounds, and there is no reason why dictionary makers should not assign them values in terms of key words, just as they do for their ad hoc symbols.

Two of the three dictionaries we have been discussing, LPD 3 and EPD 18, use virtually the same set of symbols, differing only in the way they transcribe the vowel in American English *bird:* LPD 3 has [ɝ], whereas EPD 18 has [ɜr]. *Oxford Dictionary of Pronunciation for Current English* uses a slightly different set of symbols, but they are readily interpretable within the IPA tradition. This book keeps to the style of transcription used in Wells's LPD 3 except for the omission of the length mark and a few simple typographical changes. We use [ɛ] in words such as *head, bed* instead of [e]. In later chapters, we will be comparing vowels in other languages such as French and German, and we will need to use both [e] and [ɛ]. We also use [ɹ] instead of [r] as the IPA does, reserving [r] for the cross-linguistically more common tongue tip trill.

VOWEL QUALITY

In the discussion so far, we have deliberately avoided making precise remarks about the quality of the different vowels. This is because, as we said in Chapter 1, the traditional articulatory descriptions of vowels are not very satisfactory. Try asking people who know as much about phonetics as you do to describe where the tongue is at the beginning of the vowel in *boy*, and you will get a variety of responses. Can you describe where your own tongue is in a set of vowels?

Figure 4.1 (on page 92) shows a set of MRI images taken from the midpoints of vowels in British English (kindly made available by Prof. John Coleman, head of the Oxford Phonetics Lab). In these images IPA vowel symbols are placed on the tongue, and the vocal tract airway is shaded dark. (Prof. Coleman recommends the IPA symbol [a] to transcribe the vowel in *pat* for this speaker.) The speaker is facing to the left, but unfortunately the MRI receiver did not capture the lips. As we saw with the x-ray tongue traces in Figure 1.13, the vowel height difference among front vowels is pretty clearly visible. The vocal tract airway between the front of the tongue and the hard palate is very small (not much black space) in [i] while the airway is quite expanded in [a]. It is possible also to see that the tongue is retracted in the mouth in the back vowels [u] and [ʊ]. So what is unsatisfactory about articulatory descriptions of vowels? Part of the problem for English has to do with vowels that we don't show in Figure 4.1—[eɪ] and [oʊ] generally have higher tongue positions than [ɪ] and [ʊ]. This is unexpected given the description of these vowels. Another source of trouble with the articulatory description of vowels has to do with the low vowels in Figure 4.1. The articulatory differences between [a], [ɒ], and [ɑ] are quite subtle, but the auditory differences are substantial. This comparison isn't entirely fair because we don't get to see the lips, which probably distinguish [ɒ] and [ɑ]. Nonetheless, the magnitude of the articulatory differences doesn't seem to match the auditory and linguistic contrasts that are evident among the vowels.

To compound the difficulties, because the tongue doesn't touch the midline of the roof of the mouth in vowels, it is difficult to feel the tongue position of a vowel in one's own speech. This makes it difficult to have an intuition about what another person might be doing to produce the vowel, and thus leads to confusion in phonetic vowel transcription. Very often, people can only repeat what the books have told them—they cannot determine for themselves where their tongues are. It is quite easy for a book to build up a set of terms that are not really descriptive but are in fact fairly undefined labels.

We started introducing an auditory basis for vowel transcription in Chapters 1 and 2 and will continue with this procedure here. But it is important for you to remember that though the terms we are using ostensibly refer to tongue position, it is more accurate to think of them as labels that describe how vowels sound in relation to one another. They are not absolute descriptions of the position of the body of the tongue.

Figure 4.1 MRI images of tongue positions in the vowels of British English. (© John Coleman. Used with permission. All rights reserved.)
NB: It fails to get the authorization for the MRI images. Here are some sketches.

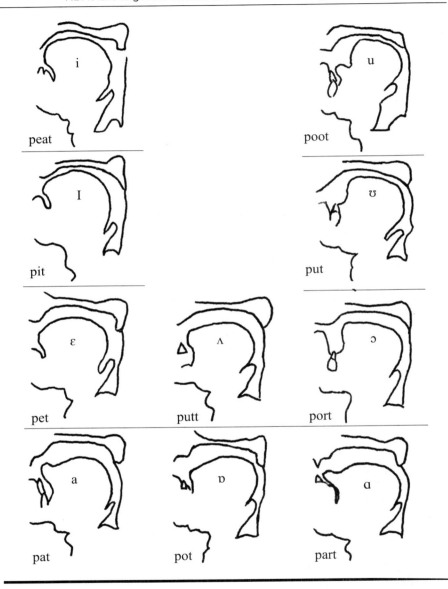

Part of the problem in describing vowels is that there are no distinct boundaries between one type of vowel and another. When talking about consonants, the categories are much more distinct. A sound may be a stop or a fricative, or a sequence of the two. But it cannot be halfway between a stop and a fricative. Vowels are different. It is perfectly possible to make a vowel that is halfway between a high vowel and a mid vowel. In theory (as opposed to what a particular individual can do in practice), it is possible to make a vowel at any specified distance between any two other vowels. In order to appreciate the fact that vowel sounds form a continuum, try gliding from one vowel to another. Say [æ] as in *had* and then try to move gradually to [i] as in *he*. Do not say just [æ–i], but try to spend as long as possible on the sounds between them. When you do this, you should pass through sounds that are something like [ɛ] as in *head* and [eɪ] as in *hay*. If you have not achieved this effect already, try saying [æ–ɛ–eɪ–i] again, slurring slowly from one vowel to another.

Now do the same in the reverse direction, going slowly and smoothly from [i] as in *he* to [æ] as in *had*. Take as long as possible over the in-between sounds. You should learn to stop at any point in this continuum so that you can make, for example, a vowel like [ɛ] as in *head*, but slightly closer to [æ] as in *had*. Next, try going from [æ] as in *had* slowly toward [ɑ] as in *father*. When you say [æ–ɑ], you may not pass through any other vowel of your own speech. But there is a continuum of possible vowel sounds between these two vowels. You may be able to hear sounds between [æ] and [ɑ] that are more like those used by people with other accents in *had* and *father*. Some forms of Scottish English, for example, do not distinguish between the vowels in these words (or between *cam* and *calm*). Speakers with these accents pronounce both *had* and *father* with a vowel about halfway between the usual Midwestern American pronunciation of these two vowels. Some speakers of American English in the Boston area pronounce words such as *car* and *park* with a vowel between the more usual American vowels in *cam* and *calm*. They do, however, also distinguish the latter two words.

Last, in order to appreciate the notion of a continuum of vowel sounds, glide from [ɑ] as in *father* to [u] as in *who*. In this case, it is difficult to be specific as to the vowels that you will go through on the way, because English accents differ considerably in this respect. But you should be able to hear that the movement from one of these sounds to the other covers a range of vowel qualities that have not been discussed so far in this section.

THE AUDITORY VOWEL SPACE

When you move from one vowel to another, you are changing the auditory quality of the vowel. You are, of course, doing this by moving your tongue and your lips, but, as we have noted, it is very difficult to say exactly how your tongue is moving. Consequently, because phoneticians cannot be very precise about the positions of the vocal organs in the vowels unless we use x-ray or MRI to monitor the tongue, we often simply use labels for the auditory qualities of the different vowels. The vowel [i] as in *heed* is called *high front*, meaning, roughly, that the tongue is high and in the front of the mouth but, more precisely, that it has the auditory quality we will call *high*, and the auditory quality *front*. Similarly, the vowel [æ] as in *had* has a low tongue position and, more important, an auditory quality that may be called *low front*. The vowel [ɛ] as in *head* sounds somewhere between [i] and

Figure 4.2 The vowel space.

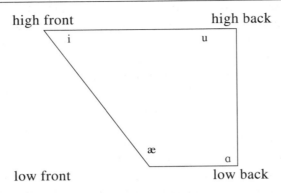

[æ], but a little nearer to [æ], so we call it *mid-low front*. (Say the series [i, ɛ, æ] and check for yourself that this is true.) The vowel [ɑ] as in *father* has a tongue position that is low and back in the mouth and auditory qualities that we will call *low back*. Last, the vowel [u] in *who* is a high, fairly back vowel. The four vowels [i, æ, ɑ, u], therefore, give us something like the four corners of a space showing the auditory qualities of vowels, which may be drawn as in Figure 4.2.

None of the vowels has been put in an extreme corner of the space in Figure 4.2. It is possible to make a vowel that sounds more back than the vowel [u] that most people use in *who*. You should be able to find this fully back vowel for yourself. Start by making a long [u], then round and protrude your lips a bit more. Now, try to move your tongue back in your mouth while still keeping it raised toward the soft palate. The result should be a fully back [u]. Another way of making this sound is to whistle the lowest note that you can and then, while retaining the same tongue and lip position, voice this sound. Again, the result will be an [u] sound that is farther back than the vowel in *who*. Try saying [i] as in *heed*, [u] as in *who*, and then this new sound, which we may symbolize with an added underline [u̱]. If you say the series [i, u, u̱], you should be able to hear that [u] is intermediate between [i] and [u̱], but—for most speakers—much nearer [u̱].

Similarly, it is possible to make vowels with a more extreme quality than the usual English vowels [i, æ, ɑ]. If, for example, while saying [æ] as in *had*, you lower your tongue or open your jaw slightly farther, you will produce a vowel that sounds relatively farther from [i] as in *heed*. It will probably also sound a little more like [ɑ] as in *father*.

Given a notion of an auditory vowel space of this kind, we can plot the relative quality of the different vowels. Remember that the labels *high/low* and *front/back* should not be taken as descriptions of tongue positions. They are simply indicators of the way one vowel *sounds* relative to another. The labels describe the relative auditory qualities, not the articulations.

Students of phonetics often ask why we use terms like *high*, *low*, *back*, and *front* if we are simply labeling auditory qualities and not describing tongue positions. The answer is that it is largely a matter of tradition. For many years, phoneticians thought they were describing tongue positions when they used these terms to specify vowel quality. But there is only a rough correspondence between the traditional descriptions in terms of tongue positions and the actual auditory qualities of vowels. If you could take x-ray pictures showing the position of your tongue while you were saying the vowels [i, æ, ɑ, u], you would find that the relative positions were not as indicated in Figure 4.2. But, as we will see in Chapter 8, if you use acoustic phonetic techniques to establish the auditory qualities, you will find that these vowels do have the relationships indicated in this figure.

Indeed, linguists have used terms such as *acute* and *grave* instead of *front* and *back* in the description of vowels. But, for a variety of reasons, these terms did not become widely used. It seems preferable to stick with the old terms *high*, *low*, *front*, and *back*, even though they are being used to describe auditory qualities rather than tongue positions.

AMERICAN AND BRITISH VOWELS

Most of the vowels of a form of Standard American Newscaster English typical of many Midwestern speakers are shown in the upper part of Figure 4.3 (on page 96). A comparable diagram of the vowels of British English as spoken by BBC newscasters is shown in the lower part of Figure 4.3. In both diagrams, the solid points represent the vowels that we are treating as monophthongs, and the lines represent the movements involved in the diphthongs. The symbols labeling the diphthongs are placed near their origins. There is a good scientific basis for placing the vowels as shown here. The positions of both monophthongs and diphthongs are not just the result of auditory impressions. The data are taken from the acoustic analyses of a number of authorities, a point we will return to in Chapter 8 when we discuss acoustic phonetics. Meanwhile, when you listen to the speakers of American English and British English linked on the website, you should be able to hear that the relative vowel qualities are as indicated. Other varieties of English will differ in some respects, but you should find that in most accents, the majority of the relationships are the same. We will note the cases in which there are substantial differences as we discuss the individual vowels.

EXAMPLE 4.1

Listen first of all to your pronunciation of the vowels [i, ɪ, ɛ, æ] as in *heed, hid, head, had*. (Use the website example 4.1 in connection with this section and listen to the speakers there, and compare their speech with your own. If you are not a native speaker of English, you can listen to recordings of these words on the website. Do these vowels sound as if they differ by a series of equal steps? Make each vowel about the same length (although in actual words they differ considerably), saying just [i, ɪ, ɛ, æ]. Now say them in pairs, first [i, ɪ], then [ɪ, ɛ], then [ɛ, æ]. In many forms of English, [i] sounds about the same distance

Figure 4.3 The relative auditory qualities of some of the vowels of Standard American Newscaster English and British (BBC newscaster) English.

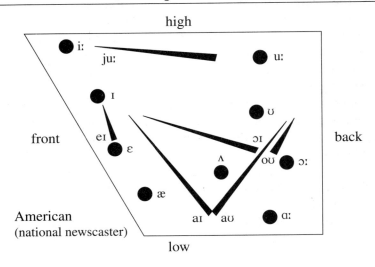

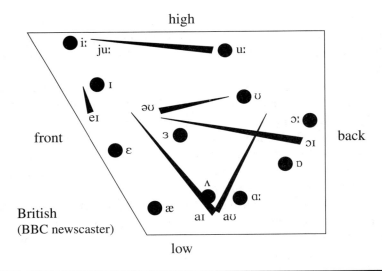

from [ɪ] as [ɪ] is from [ɛ], and as [ɛ] is from [æ]. Some Eastern American speakers make a distinct diphthong in *heed* so that their [i] is really a glide starting from almost the same vowel as that in *hid*. Other forms of English, for example as spoken in the Midlands and the North of England, make a lower and more back vowel in *had*, making it sound a little more like the [ɑ] in *father*. This may result in the distance between [ɛ] and [æ] being greater than that between [ɛ] and [ɪ]. But speakers who have a lower [æ] may also have a slightly lower [ɛ], thus keeping the distances between the four vowels [i, ɪ, ɛ, æ] approximately the same.

The remaining front vowel in English is [eɪ] as in *hay*. We will discuss this vowel after we have discussed some of the back vowels. The back vowels vary considerably in different forms of English, but no form of English has them evenly spaced like the front vowels. Say for yourself [ɑ, ɔ, ʊ, u] as in *father, author, good, food*. As before, make each vowel about the same length, and say just [ɑ, ɔ, ʊ, u]. (If, like many Californians, you do not distinguish between the vowels in *father* and *author*, just say the three vowels [ɑ, ʊ, u].) Consider pairs of vowels as you did the front vowels. Estimate the distances between each of these vowels, and compare them with those shown in Figure 4.3.

We noted that many Californian and other speakers in the western United States do not distinguish [ɑ] and [ɔ] as in *cot* and *caught*. They usually have a vowel intermediate in quality between the two points shown on the chart but closer to [ɑ]. On the other hand, most speakers of British English have an additional vowel in this area. They distinguish between the vowels [ɑ, ɒ, ɔ] as in *balm, bomb, bought*. This results in a different number of vowel qualities, as shown in the lower diagram in Figure 4.3. The additional vowel [ɒ] is more back and slightly more rounded than [ɑ].

The vowels [ʊ, u] as in *good, food* also vary considerably. Many speakers have a very unrounded vowel in *good* and a rounded but central vowel in *food*. Look in a mirror and observe your own lip positions in these two vowels.

British speakers have a mid-low central vowel [ʌ] as in *bud* while in American English the vowel in bud is [ə]. The lower [ʌ] in British English is thus more distinct from the central vowel [ɜ] in *bird*. The vowel in American English *bird* is not shown in the upper part of Figure 4.3 because it is distinguished from the vowel in *bud* by having *r*-coloring, which we will discuss later.

DIPHTHONGS

We will now consider the diphthongs shown in Figure 4.3. Each of these sounds involves a change in quality within the one vowel. As a matter of convenience, they can be described as movements from one vowel quality to another. In English, the first part of the diphthong is usually more prominent than the last. In fact, the last part is often so brief and transitory that it is difficult to determine its exact quality. Furthermore, the diphthongs often do not begin and end with any of the sounds that occur in simple vowels.

For maximum clarity, the difference in the prominence of the two vowel qualities of a diphthong can be indicated by writing the "nonsyllabic" diacritic symbol under the less prominent portion, as in [aɪ̯]. This makes explicit the distinction between a two-syllable vowel sequence (*gnaw it* [nɑɪt]) and a single-syllable vowel sequence (*night* [nɑɪ̯t]). It is also common among phoneticians to use another method to mark diphthongs: with the nonsyllabic element printed as a superscript letter (e.g., [aⁱ]).

You can see from Figure 4.3 that the diphthongs [aɪ, aʊ], as in *high, how,* start from more or less the same low central vowel position, midway between [æ] and [ɑ] and, in BBC English, closer to [ʌ] than to any of the other vowels. (The *Oxford Dictionary of Pronunciation for Current English* transcribes the American [aɪ] as [ʌɪ] in British English.) Say the word *eye* very slowly and try to isolate the first part of it. Compare this sound with the vowels [æ, ʌ, ɑ] as in *bad, bud, father*. Now make a long [ɑ] as in *father*, and then say the word *eye* as if it began with this sound. The result should be something like some forms of New York or London Cockney English pronunciations of *eye*. Try some other pronunciations, starting, for example, with the vowel [æ] as in *bad*. In this case, the result is a somewhat affected pronunciation.

The diphthong [aɪ], as in *high, buy,* moves toward a high front vowel, but in most forms of English, it does not go much beyond a mid-front vowel. Say a word such as *buy*, making it end with the vowel [ɛ] as in *bed* (as if you were saying [baɛ]). A diphthong of this kind probably has a smaller change in quality than occurs in your normal pronunciation (unless you are one of the speakers from Texas or elsewhere in the South and Southwest who make such words as *buy, die* into long monophthongs—[baː, daː]). Then say *buy*, deliberately making it end with the vowel [ɪ] as in *bid*. This vowel is usually slightly higher than the ending of this diphthong for many speakers of English. Finally, say *buy* with the vowel [i] as in *heed* at the end. This is a much larger change in quality than normally occurs in this word. But some speakers of Scottish English and Canadian English have a diphthong of this kind in words such as *sight*, which is different from the diphthong that they have in *side*.

The diphthong [aʊ] in *how* usually starts with a quality very similar to that at the beginning of *high*. Try to say *owl* as if it started with [æ] as in *had*, and note the difference from your usual pronunciation. Some speakers of the type of English spoken around London and the Thames estuary (often called Estuary English) have a complicated movement in this diphthong, making a sequence of qualities like those of [ɛ] as in *bed*, [ʌ] as in *bud*, and [u] as in *food*. Say [ɛ–ʌ–u] in quick succession. Now say the phrase *how now brown cow* using a diphthong of this type.

The diphthong [eɪ], as in *hay*, varies considerably in different forms of English. Some American English speakers have a diphthong starting with a vowel very much like [ɛ] in *head* (as shown in the upper part of Figure 4.3). Most BBC English speakers and many Midwestern Americans have a smaller diphthong, starting closer to [ɪ] as in *hid*. Estuary English, as described above, has a larger diphthong so that words such as *mate, take* sound somewhat like *might, tyke*. Conversely, others (including many Scots) have a higher vowel, a monophthong that can be written [e]. Check your own pronunciation of *hay* and try to decide how it should be represented on a chart as in Figure 4.3.

The diphthong [oʊ], as in *hoe*, may be regarded as the back counterpart of [eɪ]. For many speakers of American English, it is principally a movement in the high-low dimension, but in most forms of British English, the movement is more in the front-back dimension, as you can see in Figure 4.3. Some British English speakers make this vowel start near [ɛ] and end a little higher than [ʊ]. Say each part of this diphthong and compare it with other vowels.

The remaining diphthong moving in the upward direction is [ɔɪ], as in *boy*. Again, this diphthong does not end in a very high vowel. It often ends with a vowel similar to that in *bed*. We might well have transcribed *boy* as [bɔɛ] if we had not been trying to keep the style of transcription used in this book as similar as possible to other widely used transcriptions.

The last diphthong, [ju], as in *cue*, differs from all the other diphthongs in that the more prominent part occurs at the end. Because it is the only vowel of this kind, many books on English phonetics do not even consider it a diphthong; they treat it as a sequence of a consonant followed by a vowel. We have considered it to be a diphthong because of the way it patterns in English. Historically, it is a vowel, just like the other vowels we have been considering. Furthermore, if it is not a vowel, then we have to say that there is a whole series of consonant clusters in English that can occur before only one vowel. The sounds at the beginning of *pew*, *beauty*, *cue*, *spew*, *skew* and (for most speakers of British English) *tune*, *due*, *sue*, *Zeus*, *new*, *lieu*, *stew* occur only before / u /. (Note that in British English, *do* and *due* are pronounced differently, the one being [du] and the other [dju].) There are no English words beginning with / pje / or / kjæ /, or any combination of stop plus [j] before any other vowel. In stating the distributional properties of English sounds, it seems much simpler to recognize / ju / as a diphthong and thus reduce the complexity of the statements one has to make about the English consonant clusters.

RHOTIC VOWELS

The only common stressed vowel of American English not shown in Figure 4.3 is [ɚ] as in *sir*, *herd*, *fur*. This vowel does not fit on the chart because it cannot be described simply in terms of the features high-low, front-back, and rounded-unrounded. The vowel [ɚ] can be said to be ***r*-colored**. It involves an additional feature called **rhotacization**. Just like high-low and front-back, the feature rhotacization describes an auditory property, the *r*-coloring, of a vowel. When we describe the height of a vowel, we are saying something about how it sounds rather than something about the tongue gesture necessary to produce it. Similarly, when we describe a sound as a *rhotacized vowel*, we are saying something about how it sounds. In most forms of American English, there are both stressed and unstressed rhotacized vowels. For younger speakers there is very little difference in vowel quality as a function of stress—so the two vowels of *further* are practically identical [fɚðɚ]. For speakers who do have different rhotic qualities in stressed and unstressed syllables, the transcription for the phrase *my sister's bird* would be [maɪ ˈsɪstɚs ˈbɝd].

Rhotacized vowels are often called *retroflex vowels*, but there are at least two distinct ways in which the *r*-coloring can be produced (see Figure 4.4).

Figure 4.4 Magnetic resonance imaging (MRI) scans of two American English speakers producing [ɚ]. (© Xinhui Zhou, Carol Espy-Wilson, Mark Tiede, Suzanne Boyce. Used with permission. All rights reserved.)

NB: It fails to get the authorization for the MRI images. Here are the sketches.

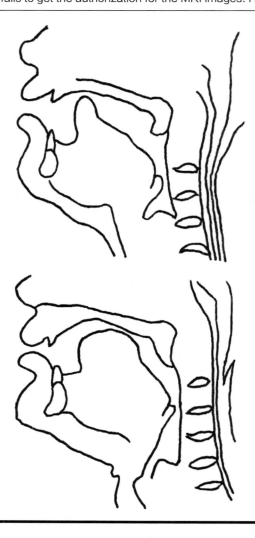

Some speakers have the tip of the tongue raised, as in a retroflex consonant. The speaker shown in the top panel of Figure 4.4 has this type of tongue configuration in [ɚ]. Others (such as the speaker in the bottom panel) keep the tip down and produce a high bunched tongue position. These two gestures produce a very similar auditory effect. X-ray studies of speech have shown that in both these ways of producing a rhotacized quality, there is usually a constriction in the pharynx caused by retraction of the part of the tongue near the epiglottis.

The most noticeable difference among accents of English is in whether they have *r*-colored vowels. In many forms of American English, rhotacization occurs when vowels are followed by [ɹ], as in *beard, bared, bard, board, poor, tire, hour*. Accents that permit some form of [ɹ] after a vowel are said to be **rhotic**. The rhotacization of the vowel is often not so evident at the beginning of the vowel, and something of the quality of the individual vowel remains. But in *sir, herd, fur* the whole vowel is rhotacized (which is why [ɚ] is preferable to [ər]). Insofar as the quality of this vowel can be described in terms of the features high-low and front-back, it appears to be a mid-central vowel such as [ə] with added rhotacization.

Rhotic accents are the norm in most parts of North America. They were prevalent throughout Britain in Shakespeare's time, and still occur in the West Country, Scotland, and other regions distant from London. Shortly after it became fashionable in the Southeast of England to drop the post-vocalic / ɹ /, this habit spread to areas of the United States in New England and parts of the South. These regions are now non-rhotic to various degrees. Try to find a speaker of English with an accent that is the opposite of yours—rhotic or non-rhotic, as the case may be. Listen to their vowels in words such as *mirror, fairer, surer, poorer, purer* and compare them with your own.

Standard BBC English is not rhotic and has diphthongs (not shown in Figure 4.3) going from a vowel near the outside of the vowel space toward the central vowel [ə]. In words such as *here* and *there*, these are transcribed [ɪə] and [ɛə]. Some speakers have a long [ɛ] instead of [ɛə] particularly before [ɹ] as in *fairy* and *bearing*. Some people have a centering diphthong [ʊə] in words such as *poor*, but this is probably being replaced by [ɔ] in most non-rhotic accents of British English. We also noticed in Chapter 2 that some speakers have a centering diphthong (though we did not call it that at the time) in *hire, fire*, which are [haə, faə].

LEXICAL SETS

One of the challenges facing the student of English phonetics is that the accents of English differ from each other quite substantially. Each accent contrasts a certain number of vowels. The first difference between two accents may be in the number of vowels they contrast. Californian English, for example, differs from many Midwestern accents of English in having lost the contrast between [ɑ] and [ɔ], as in *cot* versus *caught*, so there is one fewer vowel in the Californian system. Similarly, most British English accents have systemic differences from most American English accents in that they have additional vowels, distinguishing *cart, cot, court* by vowels that we can represent by / ɑ, ɒ, ɔ /. Another way in which accents can differ is in the vowels that occur in certain words. Both BBC English and American Newscaster English have vowels that can be symbolized by / æ / and / ɑ /, as in *fat* and *father*, but BBC English has / ɑ / in *glass* and *last*, while American English has / æ /. An even more pointed comparison of this kind of difference occurs between some Standard Northern accents of British English and BBC English. Both these accents have the same number of vowel contrasts (the same vowel systems), but they use /æ/ and /ɑ/ in different words, Standard Northern having /æ/ in *castle*, *glass*, and much the same words as those for which this vowel is used in American English. This kind of difference between accents is known as a difference in *distribution* (of vowel qualities) as opposed to a difference in *system* (the number of distinct vowels). Finally, some differences between accents have to do with the particular phonetic vowel qualities that they use. Two accents can have exactly the same number of vowel distinctions and the same vowel distributions, but the vowels can differ in phonetic quality. Thus, Texans and Midwestern Americans have similar vowel systems and distributions, but use different ways of distinguishing the vowels in words such as *pie* and the word for 'father,' *pa*. Texans are likely to have a long monophthong in each of these words, making them best symbolized as [paː] and [pɑː], whereas Midwestern Americans are more likely to say [paɪ] and [pɑ]. Or, to take a British English example, an old-fashioned Cockney English and a modern Estuary English accent may have the same vowel distinctions (the same systems) and use them in the same words (the same distributions), but use different vowel qualities. Cockney will have vowels best represented as [ʌɪ] and [ɑɪ] in *mate* and *might*; Estuary English pronounces these words more like [meɪt] and [mʌɪt].

To help keep the comparison of many English accents organized, the phonetician J. C. Wells devised a system of **lexical sets** as a way of naming English vowels. Table 4.1 illustrates Wells's lexical sets. The vowels are ordered from KIT to CURE from vowel types that show the (roughly) least amount of variation across accents to vowels that are most different from accent to accent. This means that in Wells's estimation KIT and DRESS tend to have the same quality [ɪ] and [ɛ] in most accents, while rhotic vowels show the greatest range of variation. The key words are also chosen to highlight vowel differences by embedding them in familiar and unmistakably different words—sort of the opposite of the idea behind the minimal sets we used in Chapter 2. There is one lexical key word for each subset of words that tend to pattern together across accents. For example, Wells (1982) defined the BATH lexical set as "those words whose citation form contains the stressed vowel /æ/ in General American, but /ɑː/ in RP [the "received pronunciation of British English]" (p. 133).

The lexical set system provides information (obviously schematic in nature) about the three important parameters of accent variation in English vowels: (1) the number of **phonological vowel categories** in an accent is indicated by the number of distinct vowel symbols in each column, (2) the **phonetic vowel qualities** in an accent is given by the IPA symbols in each column, and (3) the **distribution of vowels** in the lexicon is given by overlapping and intersecting word sets. On this last point about distributions, consider the TRAP, PALM, and BATH vowels in American and British English. The table shows that there are two sets of words in American English that are pronounced with [æ] (the TRAP

| TABLE 4.1 | Lexical sets illustrating the vowel qualities, and distributions for four accents of English. |

	American	British	Australian	Irish
KIT	ɪ	ɪ	ɪ	ɪ
DRESS	ɛ	ɛ	e	ɛ
TRAP	æ	æ	æ	æ
LOT	ɑ	ɒ	ɔ	ɔ
STRUT	ə	ʌ	ɐ	ʊ
FOOT	ʊ	ʊ	ʊ	ʊ
BATH	æ	ɑː	ɐː	æː
CLOTH	ɔ	ɒ	ɔ	
NURSE	ɚ	ɜː	ɜː	ʊɹ
FLEECE	i	iː	iː	iʲə
FACE	eɪ	eɪ	æɪ	eː
PALM	ɑ	ɑː	ɐː	
THOUGHT	ɔ	ɔː	oː	aː
GOAT	oᵘ	əʊ	əʉ	ʌɔ
GOOSE	u	uː	ʉː	uʲə
PRICE	aɪ	aɪ	ɑə	əɪ
CHOICE	ɔɪ	ɔɪ	oɪ	aɪ
MOUTH	aʊ	aʊ	æɔ	ɛʊ
NEAR	ɪɹ	ɪə	ɪə	iːɹ
SQUARE	ɛɹ	ɛə	eː	ɛːɹ
START	ɑɹ	ɑː	ɐː	æːɹ
NORTH	ɔɹ	ɔː	oː	aːɹ
FORCE	oɹ	ɔː	oː	ɒːɹ
CURE	ʊɹ	ʊə		uʲəɹ

words, and the BATH words) while only one of these sets (the TRAP set) is pronounced with [æ] in British English.

The difference between the vowel qualities in an accent and their lexical distribution is also highlighted by comparing Australian and Irish English. Both accents have an [eː] vowel, but in Australian the vowel is used in the SQUARE set of words, while in Irish English [eː] is used in the FACE set. Compare Australian *hair* [heː] with Irish *hay* [heː]. Comparisons such as this emphasize that accent differences involve lexical vowel distributions as well as phonetic vowel qualities.

Try to compare your own accent of English with another accent and say which of the vowel differences are best described as differences in the system of vowels, which are differences of distribution, and which involve just differences in vowel quality. Often all three of these factors—systemic differences, distributional differences, and vowel quality differences—distinguish one accent from another. Nevertheless, considering the three factors provides a useful way of looking at differences between accents.

UNSTRESSED SYLLABLES

In all forms of English, the symbol [ə] may be used to specify a range of mid-central vowel qualities. As we saw in Chapter 2, this vowel occurs in grammatical function words such as *to, the, at* [tə, ðə, ət]. It also occurs at the end of the words *sofa, China* [ˈsoʊfə, ˈtʃaɪnə], and for most British speakers, *better, farmer* [ˈbɛtə, ˈfɑmə]. In American English, the vowel at the end of words with the *–er* spelling is usually [ɚ], a very similar quality, but with added *r*-coloring. As the vowel chart in Figure 4.3 represents a kind of auditory space, vowels near the outside of the chart are more distinct from one another than vowels in the middle, and differences in vowel quality become progressively reduced among vowels nearer the center. The symbol [ə] is often produced when vowels have a central, **reduced vowel** quality.

We will be considering the nature of stress in English in the next chapter, but we can note here that vowels in unstressed syllables do not necessarily have a completely reduced quality. All the English vowels can occur in unstressed syllables in their full, unreduced forms. Many of them can occur in three forms, as shown in Table 4.2. In this table, the vowel to be considered is in the first column. The words in the second column illustrate the full forms of the vowels. The third column gives an example of the same unreduced vowel in an unstressed syllable. The fourth column illustrates a reduced variant of the vowel. For many people, the reduced vowels in this last column are all very similar. Some accents have slightly different qualities in some of these words, but all are still within the range of a mid-central vowel that can be symbolized by [ə]. Others have [ɪ] in some of these words, such as *recitation*, or a high-central vowel, which may be symbolized by [ɨ]—a symbol that is sometimes called "barred i." Yet others, particularly speakers of various forms of American English, do not reduce the vowels in the fourth column appreciably, keeping them with much the same vowel quality as in the third column. The transcription of vowels with one symbol or another sometimes disguises the fact that the vowel in question might have an intermediate quality, neither that of the unstressed vowel nor that of a vowel fully reduced to [ə]. Say all the words in Table 4.2 yourself and find out which vowels you have.

EXAMPLE 4.2 Some reduced vowels are in correspondence with unreduced vowels in related words, as illustrated by some of the pairs in the second and fourth columns in Table 4.2. It is important, however, to recognize that these lexical correspondences are the result of diachronic processes of sound change rather than the result of a synchronic process of phonetic reduction. Many, if not most, reduced vowels in English words are not in correspondence with a full vowel in a semantically related word. For example, the [ə] in *along* [əlɔŋ] does not correspond with any full vowel (hypothetically consider *alongize* [ˈeɪləŋˌaɪz]). *Along* has come to be pronounced with an initial schwa through some path of historical development, but now [ə] is the vowel target that speakers intend to reach. This [ə] is reduced in the sense that it is near the center of the auditory vowel space,

TABLE 4.2	Examples of vowels in stressed and unstressed syllables and in reduced syllables. The boldface type shows the vowel under consideration.		
Vowels	Stressed Syllable	Unstressed Syllable	Reduced Syllable
i	appr**e**ciate	cr**e**ation	depr**e**cate
ɪ	impl**i**cit	simpl**i**stic	impl**i**cation
ɔ	c**au**se	c**au**sality	
ʊ	h**oo**dwink	neighborh**oo**d	
ʌ	confr**o**nt	**u**mbrella	confr**o**ntation
ɚ, ɜ	conf**i**rm	v**e**rbose	conf**i**rmation
aɪ	rec**i**te	c**i**tation	rec**i**tation
ɔɪ	expl**oi**t	expl**oi**tation	
ju	comp**u**te	comp**u**tation	circ**u**lar

but it is not a phonetically reduced version of an underlying full vowel. The idea (probably correct) that reduced vowels in English may have their historic origin in full vowels is suggested by correspondences like [aɪ]/[ə] in *recite/recitation*, but the presence of reduced vowels without corresponding full vowels indicates that the emergence of reduced vowels in English is a completed historical process.

Most British and some American English speakers have a vowel more like [ɪ] in suffixes such as *–ed, –(e)s* at the ends of words with alveolar consonants such as *hunted, houses* ['hʌntɪd, 'haʊzɪz]. For these speakers, both vowels in *pitted* ['pɪtɪd] have much the same quality. A reduced vowel more like [ʊ] may occur in the suffix *–ful* as in *dreadful* ['dɹɛdfʊl], but for many people this is just a syllabic [l̩], ['dɹɛdfl̩].

TENSE AND LAX VOWELS

The vowels of English can be divided into what may be called **tense** and **lax** sets. These terms are really just labels used to designate two groups of vowels that behave differently in English words. There are phonetic differences between the two groups, but they are not simply a matter of muscular tenseness versus laxness. To some extent, the differences between the two sets are due to developments in the history of the English language that are still represented in the spelling. The tense vowels occur in the words with a final, so-called silent *e* in the spelling, for example, *mate, mete, kite, cute*. The lax vowels occur in the corresponding words without a silent *e*: *mat, met, kit, cut*. In addition, the vowel in *good*, which, for reasons connected with the history of English, has no silent *e* partner, is also a member of the lax set. This spelling-based distinction is, however, only a rough indication of the difference between the two sets. It is better exemplified by the data in Table 4.3.

TABLE 4.3 The distribution of tense and lax vowels in stressed syllables in American English.

Tense Vowels	Lax Vowels	Most Closed Syllables	Open Syllables	Syllables Closed By [r]	Syllables Closed By [ŋ]	Syllables Closed By [ʃ]
i		beat	bee	beer		(leash)
	ɪ	bit			sing	wish
eɪ		bait	bay			
	ɛ	bet		bare	length	fresh
oʊ		boat	low	(boar)		
	ʊ	good				push
u		boot	boo	tour		
	ə/ʌ	but		burr	hung	crush
aɪ		bite	buy	fire		
	ɔɪ	void	boy	(coir)		
ju		cute	cue	pure		

EXAMPLE 4.3

The difference between the two sets can be discussed in terms of the different kinds of syllables in which they can occur. Table 4.3 shows some of the restrictions for one form of American English. The first column of words illustrates a set of **closed syllables**—those that have a consonant at the end. All of the vowels can occur in these circumstances. The next column shows that in **open syllables**—those without a consonant at the end—only a restricted set of vowels can occur.

None of the vowels [ɪ, ɛ, æ, ʊ, ʌ] as in *bid, bed, bad, good, bud* can appear in stressed open syllables. This is the set of vowels that may be called *lax vowels*, as opposed to the tense vowels in the other words. To characterize the differences between tense and lax vowels, we can consider some of them in pairs, each pair consisting of a tense vowel and the lax vowel that is nearest to it in quality. Three pairs of this kind are [i, ɪ] as in *beat, bit*; [eɪ, ɛ] as in *bait, bet*; and [u, ʊ] as in *boot, foot*. In each of these pairs, the lax vowel is shorter, lower, and slightly more centralized than the corresponding tense vowel. There are no vowels that are very similar in quality to the remaining two lax vowels in most forms of American English, [æ] as in *hat, cam* and [ʌ] as in *hut, come*. But both of these low lax vowels are shorter than the low tense vowel [ɑ] as in *spa*. Speakers of most forms of British English have an additional lax vowel. They have the tense vowel [ɑ] as in *calm, car, card* in both open and closed syllables, and they also have a lax vowel [ɒ] as in *cod, common, con* [kɒd, kɒmən, kɒn], which occurs only in closed syllables.

The fifth column in Table 4.3 shows the vowels that can occur in syllables closed by /ɹ/ in American English. In a syllable closed by /ɹ/, there is no contrast in quality between a tense vowel and the lax vowel nearest to it. Consequently, as often happens in contexts in which there is no opposition between two sounds, the actual sound produced is somewhere between the two. (We have already observed another example of this tendency. We saw that after / s / at the beginning of a word, there is no contrast between / p / and / b /, or / t / and / d /, or / k / and / g /. Consequently, the stops that occur in words such as *spy, sty, sky* are between the corresponding voiced and voiceless stops; they are unaspirated, but they are never voiced.)

The words *boar* and *coir* are in parentheses in this column because for many people, [oʊ] and [ɔɪ] do not occur before / ɹ /. The word *coir* [kɔɪɹ], perhaps the only word in English pronounced with [ɔɪ], is not in many people's vocabularies, and many people make no difference between *bore* and *boar*. But some speakers do contrast [ɔ] and [oʊ] in these two words, or in other pairs such as *horse* and *hoarse*.

The next column shows the vowels that occur before [ŋ]. In these circumstances, again, there is no possible contrast between tense and lax vowels. But, generally speaking, it is the lax vowels that occur. However, many younger Americans pronounce *sing* with a vowel closer to that in *scene* rather than that in *sin*. And in some accents, *length* is regularly pronounced with virtually the same vowel as that in *bait* rather than that in *bet*; in others, it is pronounced with the vowel in *bit*. The pronunciation of *long* varies. It is [lɑŋ] or [lɔŋ] in most forms of American English and [lɒŋ] in most forms of British English. Several other changes are true of vowels before all nasals in many forms of American English. For example, [æ] may be considerably raised in *ban, lamb* as compared with *bad, lab*. In many accents, *pin, pen* and *gym, gem* are not distinguished.

The last column shows that there are similar restrictions in the vowels that can occur before [ʃ]. By far, the majority of words ending in / ʃ / have lax vowels for most speakers, although some accents (e.g., that used in parts of Appalachia) have [i] in *fish* (making it like *fiche*) and [u] in *push* and *bush*. In Peter Ladefoged's speech, the only words containing the tense vowel / i / before / ʃ / are *leash, fiche, quiche*. Some speakers have tense vowels in a few new or unusual words such as *creche, gauche*, which may be [kreɪʃ, goʊʃ]. The pronunciation of *wash* varies in much the same way as that of *long*. Both [wɑʃ] and [wɔʃ] occur in American English.

ENGLISH VOWEL ALLOPHONES

As we did in the previous chapter in discussing consonant allophones, we can conclude this chapter by listing some observations about vowels in English. The first concerns vowel length.

(1) Other things being equal, a given vowel is longest in an open syllable, next longest in a syllable closed by a voiced consonant, and shortest in a syllable closed by a voiceless consonant.

If you compare words such as *sea, seed, seat* or *sigh, side, site*, you will hear that the vowel is longest in the first word in each set, next longest in the second, and shortest in the last. You can see an example of this in Figure 3.3, which showed the waveforms of the words *mat* and *mad*. Because some vowels (particularly the tense vowels) are inherently longer than others (the lax vowels), we have to restrict statement (1) to a vowel of a given quality. Although it is in a syllable closed by a voiced consonant, the lax vowel in *bid* is often shorter than the tense vowel in *beat*, which is a syllable closed by a voiceless consonant. We also have to note "other things being equal" because, as we will see in the next statement, there are other things that affect vowel length.

Even when we are considering the same vowel in syllables with the same consonants, there may be a difference in vowel length. Stressed syllables are longer than the corresponding unstressed syllables. Compare words such as *below* and *billow*. You will find that the vowel [oʊ] in the stressed syllable in the first word is longer than the same vowel in the second word, where it occurs in an unstressed syllable. We therefore have the following formal statement:

(2) Other things being equal, vowels are longer in stressed syllables.

We still have to hedge this statement with the phrase "other things being equal," as there are other causes of variation in vowel length. Another kind of length variation is exemplified by sets of words such as *speed, speedy, speedily*. Here, the vowel in the stressed syllable gets progressively shorter as extra syllables are added to the same word. The reasons for this phenomenon will be dealt with in the next chapter. Here, we will simply state:

(3) Other things being equal, vowels are longest in monosyllabic words, next longest in words with two syllables, and shortest in words with more than two syllables.

We should also add a statement about unstressed vowels, which may become voiceless in words such as *potato, catastrophe*. For some people, this happens only if the following syllable begins with a voiceless stop, but for many, it also happens in a normal conversational style in words such as *permission, tomato, compare*. In terms of the gestures involved, this is simply a case of the voiceless gesture for the glottis associated with the initial voiceless stops overlapping with the voicing gesture normally associated with the vowels. The observation is thus:

(4) A reduced vowel may be voiceless after a voiceless stop (and before a voiceless stop).

The parenthesized phrase can be omitted for many people.

(5) Vowels are nasalized in syllables closed by a nasal consonant.

The degree of nasalization in a vowel varies extensively. Many people will have the velum lowered throughout a syllable beginning and ending with a nasal, such as *man*, making the vowel fully nasalized.

Finally, we must note the variants produced when vowels occur in syllables closed by / l /. Compare your pronunciation of / i / in *heed* and *heel*, of / eɪ / in *paid* and *pail*, and [æ] in *pad* and *pal*. In each case, you should be able to hear a noticeably different vowel quality before the velarized [ɫ]. All the front vowels become considerably retracted in these circumstances. It is almost as if they became diphthongs with an unrounded form of [ʊ] as the last element. In a narrow transcription, we could transcribe this element so that *peel, pail, pal* would be [pʰiʊɫ, pʰeʊɫ, pʰæʊɫ]. Note that we omitted the usual second element of the diphthong [eɪ] in order to show that in these circumstances the vowel moved from a mid-front to a mid-central (rather than to a high front) quality.

Back vowels, as in *haul, pull, pool*, are usually less affected by the final [ɫ] because they already have a tongue position similar to that of [ɫ]. But there is often a great difference in quality in the vowels in *hoe* and *hole*. As we have seen, many speakers of British English have a fairly front vowel as the first element in the diphthong [əʊ]. This vowel becomes considerably retracted before / ɫ / at the end of the syllable. You can observe the change by comparing words such as *holy*, where there is no syllable final [ɫ], and *wholly*, where the first syllable is closed by [ɫ].

The change of vowel quality before [ɫ] is yet another example of overlapping gestures. The exact form of the statement for specifying vowel allophones before [ɫ] will vary from speaker to speaker. But, so that we can include a statement in our set summarizing some of the main allophones of vowels in English, we may say:

(**6**) Vowels are retracted before syllable final [ɫ].

Some speakers also have vowel retraction before / r / as in *hear, there*, which might be [hiəɹ, ðeəɹ]. Note again how / l, ɹ / act in similar ways, as we found in the preceding chapter when discussing consonants.

Again, it is important to understand that these observations only cover some of the major aspects of the pronunciation of English. They do not state everything that is generally true about the phonology of English vowels, nor are they formulated with complete accuracy. There are problems, for example, in saying exactly what is meant by *word* or *syllable*, and it is possible to find both exceptions to these statements and additional generalizations that can be made.

RECAP

This chapter emphasized that vowel sounds are best described as sounds—in terms of their auditory properties. We suggested that a focus on properties of their articulation, such as the highest point of the tongue, does not lead to classifications that are reliable for linguistic description. We redefined the terms "high," "low," "front," and "back" to refer to positions within an auditory vowel space, and encouraged you to practice hearing auditory similarities and differences among the vowels—vowel quality. We discussed the monophthongs and diphthongs of American and British English, the particular effects of / ɹ / on vowels, the reduced vowel quality found in unstressed vowels, and the tense/lax distinction in the English vowel system. We also mentioned the use of lexical sets as a way of exploring vowel differences among the many English accents, and ended with a short discussion of phonological variation in vowels. We suggested that the distribution of vowel qualities in English is such that one could consider that there are different phonetic inventories in different environments—a vowel system in closed syllables, and a separate system in open syllables, and yet another system of contrasts in syllables closed by / ɹ / or / l /.

EXERCISES

(Printable versions of all the exercises are available on the website.)

A. Put your own vowels in this chart, using the lexical sets in Table 4.1. Which of the words in Table 2.2 best fit the words in Table 4.1? Listen to each vowel carefully and try to judge how it sounds relative to the other vowels. You will probably find it best to say each vowel as the middle vowel of a three-member series, with the vowels in the words above and below forming the first and last vowels in the series. In the case of the diphthongs, you should do this with both the beginning and the ending points.

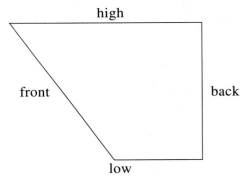

B. Try to find a speaker with an accent different from your own (or perhaps someone who speaks English as a second language) and repeat Exercise A using this blank chart.

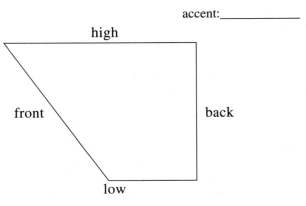

C. List words illustrating the occurrence of vowels in monosyllables closed by / p /. Do not include names or words of recent foreign origin. You will find that some vowels cannot occur in these circumstances.

i

ɪ

eɪ

ɛ

æ

ɑ

ɔ

oʊ

ʊ

u

ʌ

aɪ

aʊ

ɔɪ

D. Considering only the vowels that *cannot* occur in monosyllables closed by / p / as in Exercise C, give words, if possible, illustrating their occurrence in syllables closed by the following consonants.

b	l
m	s
f	z
t	k
n	g

E. Which vowel occurs before the smallest number of consonants? Also, which class of consonants occurs after the largest number of vowels? (Define the class in terms of the place of articulation at which these consonants are made.)

_____

_____

_____

_____

_____

112 CHAPTER 4 English Vowels

F. Look at Table 4.2. Find additional examples illustrating the relationship between the words in the second and fourth columns. Transcribe each pair of words as shown for the vowel / i /.

Vowel	Stressed Syllable	Reduced Syllable
i	secrete [sə'kɹit]	secretive ['sikɹətɪv]
ɪ		
eɪ		
ɛ		
æ		
ɑ or ɒ		
oʊ		
aɪ		

G. Make up and transcribe a sentence containing at least eight different vowels.

_____

_____

_____

H. Give a number of examples for each of statements (1) through (6) by making a transcription of some additional words that fit the rules. Your examples should not include any words that have been transcribed in this book so far. Remember to mark the stress on words of more than one syllable.

  (1) three examples (one for each syllable type)

  _____ _____ _____

  (2) two pairs of examples (each showing words differing principally in stress)

  _____ _____

  _____ _____

  (3) two sets of examples (each containing a one-syllable, a two-syllable, and a three-syllable word, with the first stressed syllable remaining constant)

  _____ _____ _____

  _____ _____ _____

  (4) four examples

  _____ _____

  _____ _____

(5) four examples (use different vowels and different nasals)

_____   _____

_____   _____

(6) two sets of examples, each containing a contrasting pair of words

_____   _____

_____   _____

I. Transcribe the following sentences as recorded by the British and American speakers (the audio files are linked at the book website).

(1) I've called several times, but never found you there.
(2) Someone, somewhere, wants a letter from you.
(3) We were away a year ago.
(4) We all heard a yellow lion roar.
(5) What did you say before that?
(6) Never kill a snake with your bare hands.
(7) It's easy to tell the depth of a well.
(8) I enjoy the simple life.

As instructors vary in the kinds of transcription exercises they wish to assign, additional exercises will not be given at the end of this and subsequent chapters. Instead, more exercises may be found on the book's website in the materials for Chapter 11, and in the "extras" section of the website.

PERFORMANCE EXERCISES

A. Learn to produce only the first part of the vowel [eɪ] as in *hay*. Try saying this sound in place of your normal diphthong in words such as *they came late*. Similarly, learn to produce a mid-high back vowel [o], and say it in words that you have been transcribing with the diphthong [oʊ] such as *Don't go home*. You can hear example utterances such as this at the books website, in the Chapter 4 materials for the "performance exercises."

B. Incorporate [e] and [o] in nonsense words for production and perception exercises. These words might also now include the voiceless sounds [m̥, n̥, ŋ̊, w̥, j̊]. Remember to practice saying the words by yourself so that you can say them fluently. As we mentioned in the performance exercises for Chapter 3, it is often very helpful to work with a partner. Start with easy words such as:

ma'ŋa

'n̥eme

'ŋ̊ale

'moʔi

'l̥ele

Then go on to more difficult words like:

heˈm̥an̥e

ˈŋambm̥bel̥

ˈspoʔetn̥ʔɔɪ

ˈw̥oθʃoˈr̥esfi

ˈtlep̥ridʒiˈkuʒ

C. Again, working with a partner, write the numbers 1 through 5 somewhere on a vowel chart as, for example, shown here.

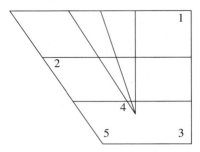

Now say vowels corresponding to these numbered positions in nonsense monosyllables. For example, say something like [dub]. Your partner should try to plot these vowels on a blank chart. When you have pronounced five words, compare notes and then discuss the reasons for any discrepancies between the two charts. Then reverse roles and repeat the exercise.

D. Repeat Exercise C with as many different partners as you can. It is difficult to make perceptual judgments of the differences among vowels, but you should be able to find a rough consensus.

E. In addition to nonsense words of the kind given in Exercise B, continue practicing with words to increase your auditory memory span. Say each word only two or three times. Remember that you should be spending at least one hour a week on production and perception exercises.

θeˈmifeˈðim̥e

ˈsɑrɑpoˈsɑpofiˈpos

moˈpretepleteˈki

n̥ɑˈkotoˈtɑkpoto

lɑˈkimitiˈnoneʔe

5

English Words and Sentences

WORDS IN CONNECTED SPEECH

In previous chapters, we considered lists of words that illustrated the contrasts between consonants and the contrasts between vowels. This is a good way of starting to look at the gestures that make up the words of English (or, indeed, of any language, as we will see later). But speech is not really composed of a series of distinct gestures, and, anyway, we don't usually speak using isolated words. As we saw in Chapter 1, when looking at the short movie clip of *on top of his deck*, all the actions run together, making it very hard to see separate gestures. It's useful to look at short, specially constructed phrases to be able to see the main aspects of individual vowels and consonants, as we did using x-ray clips in Chapters 2 and 3. But now we must look at how pronunciations of individual words compare with what happens in more normal, connected speech.

The form of a word that occurs when you say it by itself is called the **citation form**. At least one syllable is fully stressed and there is no reduction of the vowel quality. But in connected speech, many changes may take place. Consider, for example, the spectrogram in Figure 5.1. This is our first spectrogram of speech, so you shouldn't expect to get much out of it at first, but even with only a little explanation of how to "read" a spectrogram, you should be able to tell that the word *opposite* was said in two different ways in this utterance. The speaker was being interviewed, and the topic of life choices came up. He was talking about choosing between a life of crime or a life in a religious discipline, and he said, "*or* I was going to go in the opposite direction, and I went in the opposite direction." Before reading on, listen to this utterance at the website. Can you hear any differences in the word *opposite* between the first time he says it and the second? They both seem to be perfectly acceptable (American) pronunciations of the word, but the spectrogram shows some differences. The second *opposite* is phonetically **reduced**. There are arrows under the portions of the spectrogram that correspond to vowel sounds. The first *opposite* has three arrows corresponding to the three vowels that we expect in the citation form of the word, while in the second production we can only identify two vowel segments.

Figure 5.1 A spectrogram of the utterance "the opposite direction, and I went in the opposite direction."

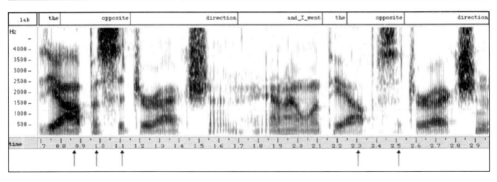

In reading spectrograms, the first and most basic observation to make is that there are three basic types of sounds. A stop appears as a white gap (silence) followed by a very thin vertical stripe (the release burst). You can see this pattern in the [p] of both productions of *opposite* in Figure 5.1. Fricatives appear as dark patches near the top of the spectrogram. The [s] of *opposite* is visible in both productions, as is the [ʃ] of *direction* [ˈdɹɛkʃn̩]. The third basic type of sound includes vowels, approximants, and nasals and has anywhere from two to five roughly parallel horizontal bands, generally with one band below a thousand Hertz (Hz on the vertical scale), one between one thousand and two thousand Hz, and another between two thousand and three thousand Hz. You can see that the unstressed vowels of the first *opposite* are quite short in duration—less than 0.05 seconds on the horizontal scale—and one of the two has completely vanished in the second *opposite* so that it is now pronounced [ˈapsɪt]. There are other indications of reduced pronunciation in the second production of this word—all of the segments are shorter, the first vowel has no steady-state portion (see how the second highest dark band goes down in frequency throughout the vowel, where in the first production there was a plateau), and the [s] is lighter at the top of the spectrogram.

When words are said in connected speech, they may be pronounced with varying degrees of emphasis, and this results in varying degrees of deviation from the citation form (which can be taken as the most emphatic, phonetically **full** form of the word). In Chapters 3 and 4, we discussed consonant and vowel allophones that help us describe the patterns of pronunciation found in citation forms. The range of phonetic variability found in connected speech is a good deal greater and more subtle than the variability found in citation forms, and this makes it difficult to describe the sound patterns of conversational speech as alternations among phonetic symbols; quantitative measurement of duration, amplitude, and frequency is often a more insightful ways to proceed. Nevertheless, some useful observations about phonetic reduction in conversational speech can be based on careful phonetic transcription.

The key difference between citation speech and connected speech is the variable degree of emphasis placed on words in connected speech. This "degree of emphasis" is probably related to the amount of information that a word conveys in a particular utterance in conversation. For example, repetitions such as the second *opposite* in Figure 5.1 are almost always reduced compared to the first mention of the word—but here we will focus on the phonetics of reduction, not its semantics. The citation speech/conversational speech difference is particularly noticeable for one class of words. Closed-class words such as determiners (*a*, *an*, *the*), conjunctions (*and*, *or*), and prepositions (*of*, *in*, *with*)—the grammatical words—are very rarely emphasized in connected speech, and thus their normal pronunciation in connected speech is quite different from their citation speech forms.

As with other words, closed-class words show a **strong form**, which occurs when the word is emphasized, as in sentences such as *He wanted pie **and** ice cream, not pie **or** ice cream*. There is also a **weak form**, which occurs when the word is in an unstressed position. Table 5.1 lists strong and weak forms of a number of common English words.

Several of the words in Table 5.1 have more than one weak form. Sometimes, as in the case of *and*, there are no clear rules as to when one as opposed to another of these forms is likely to occur. After a word ending with an alveolar consonant, most speakers of English have a tendency to drop the vowel and say [n̩] or [nd] in phrases such as *cat and dog* or *his and hers*. But this is far from invariable.

For some words, however, there are rules that are nearly always applicable. The alternation between *a* [ə] before a consonant and *an* [ən] before a vowel

EXAMPLE 5.2

TABLE 5.1 Strong and weak forms of some common English words. Over five times as many could easily have been listed.

Word	Strong form	Weak form	Example of a Weak Form
a	eɪ	ə	a cup [ə ˈkʌp]
and	ænd	ənd, n̩d, ən, n̩	you and me [ˈju ən ˈmi]
as	æz	əz	as good as [əz ˈɡʊd əz]
at	æt	ət	at home [ət ˈhoʊm]
can	kæn	kən, kn̩	I can go [aɪ kn̩ ˈɡoʊ]
has	hæz	həz, əz, z, s	He's left [hɪz ˈlɛft]
he	hi	i, hɪ, ɨ	Will he go? [wɪl i ˈɡoʊ]
must	mʌst	məst, məs, m̩s	I must sell [aɪ m̩s ˈsɛl]
she	ʃi	ʃɨ	Did she go? [ˈdɪd ʃɨ ˈɡoʊ]
that	ðæt	ðət	He said that it did [hi ˈsɛd ðət ɪt ˈdɪd]
to	tu	tʊ, tə	to Mexico [t ə ˈmɛksɪkoʊ]
would	wʊd	wəd, əd, d	It would do [ˈɪ t əd ˈdu]

is even recognized in the spelling. Similar alternations occur with the words *the* and *to*, which are [ðə, tə] before consonants and are often [ði, tu] or [ðɨ, tʊ] before vowels. Listen to your own pronunciation of these words in the sentence *The* [ðə] *man and the* [ðɨ] *old woman went to* [tə] *Britain and to* [tʊ] *America.* The two examples of *the* will often be pronounced differently. It should be noted, however, that there is a growing tendency for younger American English speakers to use the form [ðə] in all circumstances, even before a vowel. If a glottal stop is inserted before words beginning with a vowel (another growing tendency in American English), then the form [ðə] is even more likely to be used.

Some of the words in Table 5.1 are confusing in that the same spelling represents two words with different meanings (two homonyms). Thus, the spelling *that* represents a demonstrative pronoun in a phrase such as "that boy and the man," but it represents a subordinate conjunction in *he said that women were better*. The conjunction is much more likely to have a weak form. The demonstrative *that* is always pronounced [ðæt]. Similarly, when *has* is an auxiliary verb, it may be [z], as in *she's gone*, but it is [həz] or [əz] when it indicates possession, as in *she has nice eyes*.

At this point, we should note a weakness in the above discussion and in Table 5.1. We have been using phonetic transcription to note changes that occur. But although transcription is a wonderful tool for phoneticians to use (please go on practicing it), it is not a perfect one. All transcriptions use a limited set of symbols, giving the impression that a sound is one thing or another. The word *has*, for example, has been transcribed as [hæz] or [əz] or [z], but there are really lots of intermediate gestures. The word *to* has more possibilities than [tu, tʊ, tə]. Similarly, in the previous chapter, we discussed the first syllable in words such as *potato*, noting that the vowel can be there or not. But it's really not as absolute as that. There may be anything from just the [pʰ], through a single glottal pulse of a vowel, to (rather unusually) a full vowel [oʊ]. Speech is a continuum of gestures that may be produced fully or in a reduced form, or may be virtually not present at all.

These considerations also apply to another way in which words can be affected when they occur in connected speech. As you already know, sounds are often affected by adjacent sounds—for example, the [n] in *tenth* is articulated on the teeth (or nearer to them) because of the following dental fricative [θ]. Similar effects commonly occur across word boundaries, so that in phrases such as *in the* and *on the*, the [n] is realized as a dental [n̪] because of the following [ð]. But it isn't a simple choice of the nasal being either dental or alveolar. Using phonetic transcription, we have only those two possibilities. Transcription puts things in one category or another, but in fact there is a continuum of possibilities between the two possible transcriptions.

Finally, in this discussion of the limitations of transcription, think how you say phrases such as *fact finding*. Do you pronounce the [t] at the end of *fact*? Most people don't say [ˈfækfaɪndɪŋ] with no [t] gesture, nor do they say [ˈfæktfaɪndɪŋ] with a complete [t] gesture. Instead, there is probably a small [t] gesture in which the tip of the tongue moves up slightly. A similar partial gesture probably occurs in phrases like *apt motto* and *wrapped parcel*. You cannot say that there is or is not a [t].

When one sound is changed into another because of the influence of a neighboring sound, there is said to be a process of **assimilation**. There is an assimilation of [n] to [n̪] because of the [ð] in the phrase *in the*. The assimilation may be complete if the nasal becomes absolutely dental, or partial if it is somewhere between dental and alveolar, a form we cannot symbolize in transcription. Anticipatory coarticulation is by far the most common cause of assimilations in English. In this process, the gesture for one sound is affected by anticipating the gesture for the next sound. But there are also perseverative assimilations in which the gesture for one sound perseveres into the gesture for the next sound. The pronunciation of the phrase *it is* [ɪt ɪz] as *it's* [ɪts] is a result of the perseveration of the voicelessness of [t].

There is, of course, nothing slovenly or lazy about using weak forms and assimilations. Only people with artificial notions about what constitutes so-called good speech could use adjectives such as these to label the kind of speech we have been describing. Rather than being labeled lazy, it could be described as being more efficient, in that it conveys the same meaning with less effort. Weak forms and assimilations are common in the speech of every sort of speaker in both Britain and America. Foreigners who make insufficient use of them sound stilted.

STRESS

Stress is most easily identified in citation forms. In conversational speech, words can be unemphasized, and when this happens, some of the properties of stressed syllables may not be realized. In citation forms, a stressed syllable is usually produced by pushing more air out of the lungs in one syllable relative to others. A stressed syllable thus has greater respiratory energy than neighboring unstressed syllables. It may also have an increase in laryngeal activity. Stress can always be defined in terms of something a speaker does in one part of an utterance relative to another.

It is difficult to define stress from a listener's point of view. A stressed syllable is often, but not always, louder than an unstressed syllable. In declarative utterances it is usually, but not always, on a higher pitch. The most reliable thing for a listener to detect is that a stressed syllable frequently has a longer vowel than it would have if it were unstressed. But this does not mean that all long vowels are necessarily stressed. The second and third vowels in *radio*, for example, are comparatively long, but they do not have the extra push of air from the lungs that occurs on the first vowel. Conversely, the vowels in the first syllables of *cupcake* and *hit man* are comparatively short, but they have extra respiratory energy and so are felt to be stressed.

Stress can always be correlated with something a speaker does rather than with some particular acoustic attribute of the sounds. Consequently, you will find that the best way to decide whether a syllable is stressed is to try to tap out the beat as a word is said. This is because it is always easier to produce one increase in muscular activity—a tap—in time with an existing increase in activity. When as listeners we perceive the stresses that other people are making, we are probably putting together all the cues available in a particular utterance in order to deduce the motor activity (principally the respiratory gestures) we would use to produce those same stresses. It seems as if listeners sometimes perceive an utterance by reference to their own motor activities. When we listen to speech, we may be considering, in some way, what we would have to do in order to make similar sounds. We will return to this point when we discuss phonetic theories in a later chapter.

Stress has several different functions in English. In the first place, it can be used in sentences to give special emphasis to a word or to contrast one word with another. As we have seen, even a word such as *and* can be given a contrastive stress. The contrast can be implicit rather than explicit. For example, if someone else says, or if you even thought that someone else might possibly say (using stress marks within regular orthography):

'John or 'Mary should 'go.

You might, without any prior context actually spoken, say:

'I think 'John 'and 'Mary should 'go.

Another major function of stress in English is to indicate the syntactic category of a word. There are many noun–verb oppositions, such as *an 'insult, to in'sult*; *an 'overflow, to over'flow*; *an 'increase, to in'crease*. In these three pairs of words, the noun has the stress on the first syllable and the verb has it on the last. The placement of the stress indicates the syntactic category of the word. (Of course, there are nouns with second-syllable stress—like *gui'tar, pi'ano*, and *trom'bone*—and verbs with first-syllable stress—like *to 'tremble, to 'flutter*, and *to 'simper*—so stress placement is not determined by syntactic category but is simply a cue in certain noun–verb pairs as to the identity of the word.)

Similar oppositions occur in cases where two-word phrases form compounds, such as a *'walkout, to 'walk 'out*; a *'put-on, to 'put 'on*; a *'pushover, to 'push 'over*. In these cases, there is a stress only on the first element of the compound for the nouns but on both elements for the verbs. Stress also has a syntactic function in distinguishing between a compound noun, such as a *'hot dog* (a form of food), and an adjective followed by a noun, as in the phrase a *'hot 'dog* (an overheated animal). Compound nouns have a single stress on the first element, and the adjective-plus-noun phrases have stresses on both elements.

Many other variations in stress can be associated with the grammatical structure of the words. Table 5.2 exemplifies the kinds of alternations that can occur. All the words in the first column have the main stress on the first syllable. When the noun-forming suffix *–y* occurs, the stress in these words shifts to the second syllable. But as you can see in the third column, the adjectival suffix *–ic* moves the stress to the syllable immediately preceding it, which in these words is the

TABLE 5.2	English word stress alternations.

ˈ _ _ _	_ ˈ _ _ _	_ _ _ ˈ _
diplomat	diplomacy	diplomatic
monotone	monotony	monotonic

third syllable. If you make a sufficiently complex set of rules, it is possible to predict the location of the stress in the majority of English words. There are very few examples of lexical items such as *differ* and *defer* that have the same syntactic function (they are both verbs) but different stress patterns. *Billow* and *below* are another pair of words illustrating that differences in stress are not always differences between nouns and verbs.

DEGREES OF STRESS

In some longer words, it may seem as if there is more than one stressed syllable. For example, say the word *multiplication* and try to tap on the stressed syllables. You will find that you can tap on the first and the fourth syllables—ˈmultipliˈcation. The fourth syllable seems to have a higher degree of stress. The same is true of other long words such as ˈmagnifiˈcation and ˈpsycholinˈguistics. But this apparently higher degree of stress on the later syllable occurs only when the word is said in isolation or at the end of a phrase. Try saying a sentence such as *The ˈpsycholinˈguistics ˈcourse was ˈfun*. If you tap on each stressed syllable, you will find that there is no difference between the first and fourth syllables of *psycholinguistics*. If you have a higher degree of stress on the fourth syllable in *psycholinguistics*, this word will be given a special emphasis, as though you were contrasting some other psychology course with a psycholinguistics course. The same is true of the word *magnification* in a sentence such as *The deˈgree of ˈmagnifiˈcation deˈpends on the ˈlens*. The word *magnification* will not have a larger stress on the fourth syllable as long as you do not break the sentence into two parts and leave this word at the end of a phrase.

Why does it seem as if there are two degrees of stress in a word when it occurs at the end of a phrase or when it is said alone—which is, of course, at the end of a phrase? The answer is that in these circumstances another factor is present. As we will see in the next section, the last stressed syllable in a phrase often accompanies a special peak in the intonation (the "tonic accent"). In longer words containing two stresses, the apparent difference in the levels of the first and the second stress is really due to the superimposition of an intonation pattern. When these words occur within a sentence in a position where the word does not receive tonic accent, then there are no differences in the stress levels.

A lower level of stress may also seem to occur in some English words. Compare the words in the two columns in Table 5.3. The words in both columns have

TABLE 5.3	Three-syllable words exemplifying the difference between an unreduced vowel in the final syllable (first column) and a reduced vowel in the final syllable (second column).
ˈmultiply	ˈmultiple
ˈregulate	ˈregular
ˈcopulate	ˈcopula
ˈcirculate	ˈcircular
ˈcriticize	ˈcritical
ˈminimize	ˈminimal

the stress on the first syllable. The words in the first column might seem to have a second, weaker, stress on the last syllable as well, but this is not so. The words in the first column differ from those in the second by having a full vowel in the final syllable. This vowel is always longer than the reduced vowel—usually [ə]—in the final syllable of the words in the second column. The result is that there is a difference in the rhythm of the two sets of words. This is due to a difference in the vowels that are present in the final vowel; it is not a difference in stress.

In summary, we can note that the syllables in an utterance vary in their degrees of prominence, but these variations are not all associated with what we want to call stress. A syllable may be especially prominent because it accompanies the final peak in the intonation. We will say that syllables of this kind have a *tonic accent*. Given this, we can note that English syllables are either stressed or unstressed. If they are stressed, they may or may not be the tonic stress syllables that carry the major pitch changes in the phrase. If they are unstressed, they may or may not have a reduced vowel. These relationships are shown in Figure 5.2.

As an aid to understanding the difference between these processes, consider the set of words *explain, explanation,* and *exploit, exploitation*. If each of these words

Figure 5.2 Degrees of prominence of different syllables in a sentence.

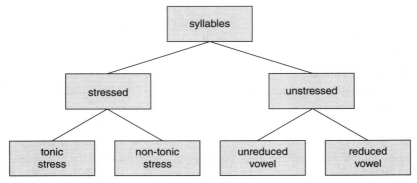

is said in its citation form, as a separate tone group, the set will be pronounced as shown below (using a schematic representation of the intonation peak).

Intonation peak	↑	↑	↑	↑
Stress	ex'plain	'expla'nation	ex'ploit	'exploi'tation
Segments	ɪks'pleɪn	'ɛksplə'neɪʃən	ɪks'plɔɪt	'ɛksplɔɪ'teʃən

Another way of representing some of these same facts is shown in Table 5.4. This table shows just the presence (+) or absence (–) of an intonation peak (a tonic accent), a stress, and a full vowel in each syllable in these four words. Considering first the stress (in the middle row), note that the two-syllable words are marked [+ stress] on the second syllable, and the four-syllable words are marked [+ stress] on both the first and the third syllables.

As you can see by comparing the middle row with the top row, the last [+ stress] syllable in each word has been marked [+ tonic accent]. There is a [+] in the third row if the vowel is not reduced. Note that the difference in rhythm between *explanation* and *exploitation* is that the second syllable of *explanation* has a reduced vowel, but this syllable in *exploitation* has a full vowel. As we saw in the previous chapter, there are a number of vowels that do not occur in reduced syllables. Furthermore, the actual phonetic quality of the vowel in a reduced syllable varies considerably from accent to accent. We have transcribed the first vowel in *explain* as [ɪ] because that is the form Peter Ladefoged used. But other accents (such as Keith Johnson's) have [ɛ].

Some other books do not make the distinctions described here, maintaining instead that there are several levels of stress in English. The greatest degree of stress is called *stress level one*, the next is *level two*, the next *level three*, a lower level still is *level four*, and so on. Note that in this system, a smaller degree of stress has a larger number.

You can easily convert our system into a multilevel stress system by adding the number of [+] marks on a syllable in a table of the sort just used and subtracting this number from four. If there are three [+] marks, it is stress level one; if two, stress level two; if one, stress level three; and if none, stress level four. Try this for yourself with the data in Table 5.4. Writing the stress levels as superscripts after the vowels, you will find that *explanation* and *exploitation* are $e^2xpla^4na^1tio^4n$ (a pattern of 2–4–1–4) and $e^2xploi^3ta^1tio^4n$ (a pattern of 2–3–1–4).

TABLE 5.4 The combination of stress, intonation, and vowel reduction in a number of words.

	Explain	Explanation	Exploit	Exploitation
stress	– +	+ – + –	– +	+ – + –
full vowel	– +	+ – + –	– +	+ + + –

We do not consider it useful to think of stress in terms of a multilevel system, feeling that descriptions of this sort are not in accord with the phonological facts. But as it is so commonly said that there are many levels of stress in English, we thought we should explain how these terms are used. In this book, however, we will continue to regard stress as something that either does or does not occur on a syllable in English, and we will view vowel reduction and intonation as separate processes.

We can sometimes predict whether a vowel will be reduced to [ə] or not. For example, [ɔɪ] never reduces. But other cases seem to be a matter of how recently the word came into common use. Factors of this sort seem to be the reason why there should be reduced vowels at the end of *postman*, *bacon*, and *gentleman*, but not at the end of *mailman*, *moron*, and *superman*.

SENTENCE RHYTHM

The stresses that can occur on words sometimes become modified when the words are part of sentences. The most frequent modification is the dropping of some of the stresses. There is a stress on the first syllable of each of the words *Mary, younger, brother, wanted, fifty, chocolate, peanuts* when these words are said in isolation. But there are normally fewer stresses when they occur in a sentence, for example, *Mary's younger brother wanted fifty chocolate peanuts*. Tap with your finger at each stressed syllable while you say this phrase in a normal conversational style. You will probably find it quite natural to tap on the first syllables marked with a preceding stress mark in *'Mary's younger 'brother wanted 'fifty chocolate 'peanuts*. Thus, the first syllables of *younger, wanted,* and *chocolate* are pronounced without stresses (but with their full vowel qualities).

The same kind of phenomenon can be demonstrated with monosyllabic words. Say the sentence *The big brown bear bit ten white mice*. It sounds unnatural if you put a stress on every word. Most people will say *The 'big brown 'bear bit 'ten white 'mice*. As a general rule, English does not have stresses too close together. Very often, stresses on alternate words are dropped in sentences where they would otherwise come too near one another.

The tendency to avoid having stresses too close together may cause the stress on a polysyllabic word to be on one syllable in one sentence and on another syllable in another. Consider the word *clarinet* in *He had a 'clarinet 'solo* and in *He 'plays the clari'net*. The stress is on the first or the third syllable, depending on the position of the other stresses in the sentence. Similar shifts occur in phrases such as *'Vice-president 'Jones* versus *'Jones, the vice-'president*. Numbers such as *'fourteen, 'fifteen, 'sixteen* are stressed on the first syllable when counting, but sometimes not in phrases such as *She's 'only six'teen*. Read all these phrases with the stresses as indicated and check that it is natural to tap on the stressed syllables. Then try tapping on the indicated syllables while you read the next paragraph.

*'Stresses in 'English 'tend to re'cur at 'regular 'intervals of 'time (') It's 'often 'perfectly 'possible to 'tap on the 'stresses in 'time with a 'metronome. (') The

'rhythm can 'even be 'said to de'termine the 'length of the 'pause between 'phrases. (') An 'extra 'tap can be 'put in the 'silence, (') as 'shown by the 'marks with'in the pa'rentheses. (')

Figure 5.3 shows another example of speech rhythm. This musical notation of the rhythm of the first forty-seven seconds of Barack Obama's victory speech after the Iowa primary election of 2008 shows that he came in "on the beat" after interruptions by a cheering crowd of supporters—even a long interruption of sixteen beats. This and other instances of public speaking are so noticeably rhythmic that some artists have set them to music, dubbing rhythm tracks under the spoken word.

EXAMPLE 5.10

Of course, not all sentences are as regular as those discussed in the preceding paragraphs. Stresses *tend* to recur at regular intervals. It would be quite untrue to say that there is always an equal interval between stresses in English. It is just that English has a number of processes that act together to maintain the rhythm. We have already mentioned two of these processes. First, we saw that some words that might have been stressed are nevertheless often unstressed, thus preventing too many stresses coming together. To give another example, both

Figure 5.3 The first forty-seven seconds of Barack Obama's Iowa victory speech.

wanted and *pretty* can be stressed in *She 'wanted a 'pretty 'parrot*, but they may not be in *My 'aunt wanted 'ten pretty 'parrots*. Second, we saw that some words have variable stress; compare *the 'unknown 'man* with the *'man is un'known*.

We can also consider some of the facts mentioned in the previous chapter as part of this same tendency to reduce the variation in the interval between stresses. We saw that the vowel in *speed* is longer than the first vowel in speedy, and this in turn is longer than the first vowel in *speedily*. This can be interpreted as a tendency to minimize the variation in the length of words containing only a single stress, so that adjacent stresses remain much the same distance apart.

Taking all these facts together, along with others that will not be dealt with here, it is as if there were a conspiracy in English to maintain a regular rhythm. However, this conspiracy is not strong enough to completely override the irregularities caused by variations in the number and type of unstressed syllables. In a sentence such as *The 'red 'bird flew 'speedily 'home*, the interval between the first and second stresses will be far shorter than that between the third and fourth. Stresses tend to recur at regular intervals. But the sound pattern of English does not make it an overriding necessity to adjust the lengths of syllables so as to enforce complete regularity. The interval between stresses is affected by the number of syllables within the stress group, by the number and type of vowels and consonants within each syllable, and by other factors such as the variations in emphasis that are given to each word.

INTONATION

Listen to the pitch of the voice while someone says a sentence. You will find that it is changing continuously. The difference between speaking and singing is that in singing, you hold a given note for a noticeable length of time and then jump to the pitch of the next note. But when one is speaking, there are no steady-state pitches. Throughout every syllable in a normal conversational utterance, the pitch is going up or down. (Try talking with steady-state pitches and notice how odd it sounds.)

The intonation of a sentence is its pattern of pitch changes. The part of a sentence over which a particular pattern extends is called an **intonational phrase**. A short sentence forming a single intonational phrase is shown in sentence (1) below. In this and all the subsequent illustrations of different intonations in this chapter, two curves are shown. The top one always represents the changes in pitch for a British English speaker, and the lower one for an American English speaker. They are not completely smooth curves because they show the actual pitches of the utterances. This sentence and all of the sentences illustrating intonation are available for you to listen to and analyze on the book website. The irregularities reflect how the vocal folds vibrated when producing these sentences. In most cases, there is no pitch scale indicated, as it is usually the relative pitches within a phrase that are important. The time scale varies from utterance to utterance, allowing the graphs to fit the dimensions of the page.

Below the American speaker, there is always a thin line representing a duration of 500 ms (half a second). Phonetic transcription of the intonation contour is marked with starred tones (H*) on prominent pitch accents, and percent tones (L%) marking the tones at the boundary of the phrase. This transcription system is discussed in more detail in the next section.

The sentence spoken is shown below the pitch curve in ordinary spelling, but with IPA stress marks added, and one syllable preceded by an asterisk. Within an intonational phrase, stressed syllables usually have a pitch change; but there is also a single syllable that stands out because it carries the major pitch change. This syllable, which carries the **tonic accent**, will be marked in this section by an asterisk. In sentence (1), the first syllable of *mayor* has the tonic accent, and, as you can see, this word is the last one with a large overall pitch change. There is a pitch peak on the stressed syllable *know*, indicating that this syllable also had an accent, though the tonic accent on *mayor* is more prominent.

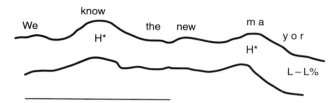

(1) We ˈknow the new *mayor.

The tonic accent usually occurs on the last stressed syllable in a tone group in neutral intonation if you don't intend to put any special focus on any of the words in the utterance. But it may occur earlier, if some word requires emphasis. If we want to emphasize that we know the *new* mayor but not the old one, then we can put the tonic accent on *new*, as in sentence (2). There are no further accents after *new*.

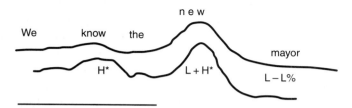

(2) We ˈknow the *new ˈmayor.

Sometimes, there are two or more intonational phrases within an utterance. When this happens, the first one ends in a small rise, which we may call a *continuation rise*. It indicates that there is more to come and the speaker has not yet completed the utterance. The break between two intonational phrases may be marked, as in sentence (3), by a single vertical stroke. The British English speaker in (3) signals that there is more to come by having a fall on *in*, the last word in the phrase, followed by a marked continuation rise. The American speaker does this by prolonging the word *in* (which starts at the peak of the pitch contour) and making a very large fall followed by a more slight continuation rise. In this way of showing there is more to come (which occurs quite frequently), it is not that there is much of a continuation rise, it's more that there is no sentence final fall. Note also that the British speaker put a high accent on *when*, while the American speaker didn't.

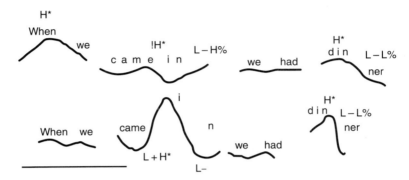

(3) ˈWhen we came ˈin, | we had *ˈdinner.

In (3), the two intonational phrases can be associated with the two syntactic clauses within the sentence, but the clause structure does not always determine the intonation. An intonational phrase is a unit of information rather than a syntactically defined unit. Because it is the information that matters, it is difficult to tell not only where the intonation breaks occur but also where the tonic accent will fall. As one linguist put it, "Intonation is predictable (if you are a mind reader)." You have to know what is in the speaker's mind before you can say exactly what will be accented. The intonation is also considerably affected by the speaker's style. When speaking slowly in a formal style, a speaker may choose to break a sentence up. Obamian oratory will produce a large number of intonational phrases, but in a rapid conversational style, there is likely to be only one per sentence.

Although one cannot entirely predict which syllable will be the tonic syllable in an intonational phrase, some general statements can be made. New information is more likely to receive a tonic accent than material that has already been mentioned. The topic of a sentence is less likely to receive the tonic accent than the comment that is made on that topic. Thus, if you were telling someone a number of facts about lions, you might say the sentence shown in (4). The topic of the discussion is lions, and the comment on that topic is that a lion is a mammal. The two speakers in (4) differ slightly in that the American English speaker puts accents on both *lion* and *mammal* and uses the more prominent L+H* accent. Nevertheless, even for this speaker, the tonic accent is the last accent of the intonational phrase; for both speakers, this is on the last word, *mammal*, making it clear that this is the comment, the new information that is being given about an already known topic.

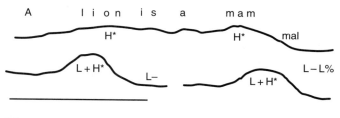

(4) A 'lion is a *mammal.

In a discussion of mammals, and considering all the animals that fit into that category, the comment—the new information—is that a lion fits into the category, as illustrated in sentence (5). Here, for both speakers, the tonic accent is on *lion*.

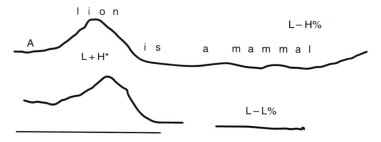

(5) A *lion is a 'mammal.

Various pitch changes are possible within the tonic accent. In sentences (1) through (5), the intonation may be simply described as having a falling contour, except for the continuation rise in the middle of (3). Another possibility is that the tonic syllable is marked by a low target followed by a rise. This kind of pitch change, which we will refer to as a *rising contour*, is typical in questions requiring *yes* or *no* answers, as exemplified in (6). For the British speaker (the upper pitch curve), the first part of the sentence is on a fairly level pitch, with most of the rise on the last word. The American speaker asks the question without a rising contour. He does have a rising pitch for much of the last two-thirds of the sentence starting from the low accent on *mail* to the high accent on *money*, and then a final fall.

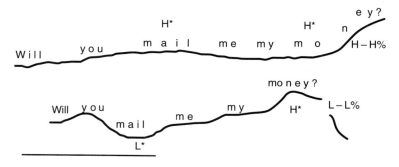

(6) Will you 'mail me my *money?

As with falling contours, the syllable that has the prominent rising contour is not necessarily the last stressed syllable in an intonational phrase. If the question in (6) is really about whether the money will be mailed or whether it has to be picked up, then emphasis will be on an earlier word, and the pitch will start going up at that point, as illustrated in (7). For the British speaker, there is a major rise on *mail*, and then, after a comparatively level piece, a further rise on *money*. The American speaker, who says this sentence considerably faster, has a rise starting on mail and a fall on the first syllable of *money*, followed by a small rise on the last syllable in the sentence.

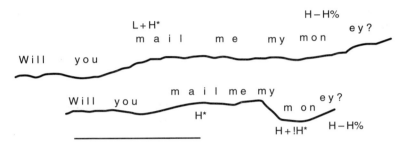

(7) Will you *mail me my 'money?

Now consider what you do in questions that cannot be answered by *yes* or *no*, such as that in (8). Of course, there are many possible ways of saying this sentence, but probably the most neutral is with a falling contour starting on the final stressed syllable. Apparently, the British English speaker has instead put an accent very early in the question—on *when*—and then a lower, less prominent accent on *mail*. [This example illustrates that intonation transcription requires listening as well as looking at pitch traces—be sure to go to the website and see if you can hear why we put an accent on *mail* in the British speaker's rendition of (8).] Questions that begin with *wh*-question words—*where, when, who, why, what*—are usually pronounced with a falling intonation, though as the pitch traces illustrate the words can be put to many different tunes even when the tunes share a feature like the falling final contour.

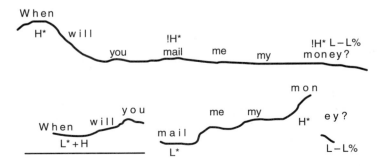

(8) 'When will you 'mail me my *money?

As we saw in (3), a small rising intonation occurs in the middle of sentences, typically at the end of an intonational phrase. Another example is given in (9). Again, there is a difference between the British and the American English speaker. The British English speaker has a fall followed by a rise in the word *winning*. The American English speaker has a sharp rise followed by a large fall that levels off at the end.

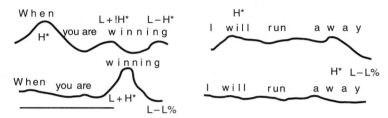

(9) 'When you are *winning, | I will run a*way.

A list of items can also have rising intonation on each item in the list, as in sentence (10). The first three names in this list have much higher pitches on their second syllables. The fourth name, the last, falls—as is usual—at the end of a sentence.

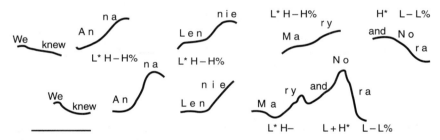

(10) We knew 'Anna, 'Lenny, 'Mary, and *Nora.

Note that *yes/no* questions can often be reworded so that they fit into this rising pattern, signaling that there is more to come. The British speaker has a rise on *mail* and *money*, followed by a regular sentence ending with a fall on *or not*. The American English speaker has a rise starting on *money* and continuing through *or not*, which again drops rapidly into a creaky voice at the end.

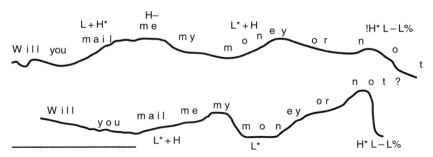

(11) Will you 'mail me my 'money or *not?

It is useful to distinguish between two kinds of rising intonation. In one, which typically occurs in *yes/no* questions, there is a large upward movement of pitch. In the other, the continuation rise that usually occurs in the middle of sentences, there is a smaller upward movement. These two intonations are often used contrastively. Thus, a low rising intonation on an utterance means that there is something more to come. There is a slightly rising intonation in the utterances in (12) and (13). These are the kinds of utterances one makes when listening to someone telling a story. They are equivalent to *I hear you; please continue*. In the center of this illustration are two vertical lines, indicating the normal voice ranges of the two speakers. The British English speaker (the upper pair of graphs) uses about half his pitch range in these words. The American English speaker (the lower pair of graphs) uses a slightly wider range.

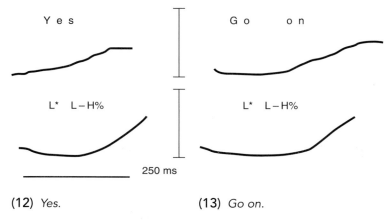

(12) Yes. (13) Go on.

If there is a larger rise in pitch, as in sentences (14) and (15), there is a change in meaning to something more like *Did you say "Yes"?* or *Did you say "Go on"?* The British English speaker uses more than 75 percent of his full range, and the American English speaker uses an even greater range. It should be noted, however, that people are not entirely consistent in the way they use this difference in intonation.

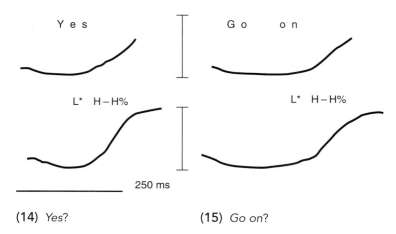

(14) Yes? (15) Go on?

Both rising and falling intonations can occur within the same tonic accent. If someone tells you something that surprises you, you might have a distinct fall–rise on the tonic syllable followed by a further rise on the remainder of the intonational phrase. Both speakers in (16) follow this pattern.

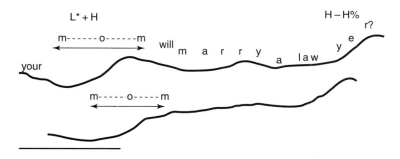

(16) *Your *mom will marry a 'lawyer?*

One can also use distinct intonation patterns when answering, addressing, or calling someone. The answer to a question such as *Who is that over there?* is shown in (17). The British English speaker has a falling intonation over the lower half of his pitch range. The American English speaker has a rise and then, a fall to nearly the bottom of his range. When addressing someone, perhaps indicating that it is their turn to speak, as in (18), there is a smaller fall or, in the case of the American English speaker, a pitch change with half the range of the answer to a question. Calling to someone normally involves a fall over a larger interval than that in the response to a question. There is also a stereotypical way of calling to someone not in sight with comparatively steady pitches after the first rise, as in (19).

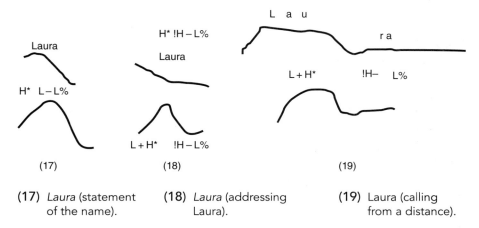

(17) *Laura* (statement of the name).

(18) *Laura* (addressing Laura).

(19) *Laura* (calling from a distance).

We can sum up many differences in intonation by referring to the different ways in which a name can be said, particularly if the name is long enough to show the pitch curve reasonably fully. Curves (20) through (24) show different pronunciations of the name *Amelia*. (20) is a simple statement, equivalent to

Her name is Amelia. In (21) the question is equivalent to *Did you say Amelia?* The form with the continuation rise in (22) might be used when addressing Amelia, indicating that it is her turn to speak. The question expressing surprise in (23) is equivalent to *Was it really Amelia who did that?* The British English speaker does this by an initial fall followed by a high rise. The American English speaker follows the reverse procedure, a sharp rise followed by a deep fall. Last, (24) is the form for a strong reaction, reprimanding Amelia.

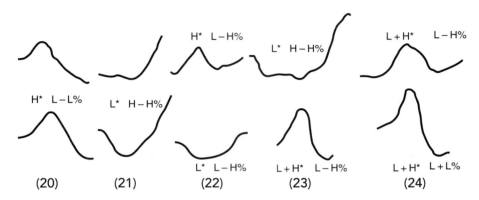

Several considerations emerge from this look at the intonation patterns of a British and an American speaker. Many of them apply to other accents of English, and to other languages. One of the most important points is that intonation cannot be as neatly specified as other aspects of speech. In the first four chapters of this book, English has been described mainly by considering phonemic contrasts. We have noted that there are twenty-two consonants in most forms of English and a specific number of vowels in each accent. Each of the contrasting vowels and consonants has certain phonetic properties. Contrasts in intonation are often more difficult to pin down. Usually, in an intonational phrase, the last stressed syllable that conveys new information is the tonic syllable. It has a falling pitch, unless it is part of a sentence in which there is another intonational phrase to follow, in which case there may be a continuation rise (or, at least, a lack of a final fall) in the pitch. Questions that can be answered by *yes* or *no* usually have a rising intonation, one that is larger than the continuation rise. Questions beginning with a question word —*where, when, what, why, how*—usually have a falling pitch. But intonation is highly colored by individual variation. It is much more affected by nuances of meaning than are the vowels and consonants that make up words in the discussion. In a sense, intonation is how the words of an utterance are put to music. The music adds information to the utterance, but it is highly contextual and individual in nature.

TARGET TONES

The examples of intonation have used some high (H) and low (L) tone marks to transcribe the intonation patterns. In this section we will discuss this system of transcription. It is common to think of intonation in terms of tunes that apply over whole sentences or phrases, and sometimes we give names to these basic tunes (such as "statement intonation", "question intonation", "calling contour", "list intonation", and so on). There are a number of other ways in which intonation can be phonetically described. Instead of considering the shape of the pitch curve over a whole phrase, we could describe the intonation in terms of a sequence of high (H) and low (L) target pitches. When people talk, they aim to make either a high or a low pitch on a stressed syllable and to move upward or downward as they go into or come away from this target. One system for representing pitch changes of this kind is known as **ToBI**, standing for *tone and break indices*. In this system, target tones H* and L* (called *H star* and *L star*) are typically written on a line (called a *tier*) above the segmental symbols that represent stressed syllables. The star (*) indicates the alignment of the target tone with the stressed syllable. A high tone, H*, can be preceded by a closely attached low pitch, written L+H*, so that the listener hears a sharply rising pitch onto a stressed syllable. Similarly, L* can be followed by a closely attached high pitch, L*+H, so that the listener hears a scoop upward in pitch after the low pitch at the beginning of the stressed syllable. Sometimes, a stressed syllable can be high but nevertheless can contain a small step-down of the pitch. This, known as *high plus downstepped high*, is written H+!H*, with the exclamation mark indicating the small downstep in pitch. In special circumstances, to be discussed at the end of this section, a downstepped high syllable, !H*, can itself be a pitch accent. There are therefore six possibilities, shown in Table 5.5, that can be regarded as the possible pitch accents that occur in English.

The last pitch accent in a phrase is called the *nuclear pitch accent*. The ToBI system notes that the pitch pattern after the nuclear pitch accent is meaningful. The post-nuclear pitch pattern (at least in simple phrases) is described with two

TABLE 5.5 The ToBI system for characterizing English intonations. Each intonational phrase (tone group) must have one item from each of the last three columns, and may also have additional pitch accents marked on other stressed syllables, as shown in the first column. The parenthesized accent, (!H*), will be explained at the end of this section.

Optional Pre-nuclear Pitch Accents on Stressed Syllables	Nuclear Pitch Accent	Phrase Accent	Boundary Tone
H*	H*		
L*	L*		
L + H*	L + H*	L–	H%
L* + H	L* + H		
H + !H*	H + !H*	H–	L%
(!H*)	(!H*)		

components. The first is called the *phrase accent* and is written H– (H minus) or L– (L minus). The second is called the boundary tone, which is marked H% or L%. The four combinations of phrase accent and boundary tone define four ways to close a tune—fall (L–L%), rise (H–H%), plateau (H–L%), and low rise (L–H%).

In this framework, all English intonations consist of a sequence of tones formed as shown in Table 5.5. As you can see exemplified by the first column, there may or may not be a number of pitch accents on stressed syllables before the nuclear pitch accent. The second column shows the nuclear pitch accents, one of which must always be present in a phrase. The part of the intonational phrase after the nuclear pitch accent must be high or low, and there must be a high or low boundary tone.

The ToBI system also allows us to transcribe the strength of the boundary between words by means of a number called a *break index*. If there is no break, as, for example, in *you're* (which is usually identical with *your*), the break index can be marked as 0. This is a useful way of showing that a phrase such as *to Mexico* is usually pronounced as if it were a single word—there is no added break in *to Mexico* as compared with that in *tomorrow*. Intervals between words are more usually classified as having break index 1 (although there is usually no acoustic pause that can be called a break between words). Higher levels of break indices show, roughly speaking, greater pauses. A break index of 3 is usual between clauses that form intermediate intonational phrases, and a break index of 4 occurs between larger intonational phrases such as whole sentences.

The American speaker's intonation curves in examples (20) through (24) were ToBI transcribed as follows (without indicating the break indices, which would always be a 4 at the end of each of these utterances):

(20) A'melia.	TONE TIER	[H* L–L%]
Simple statement in response to	SEGMENTAL TIER	[ə m i ː l iː ə]
What is her name?		
(21) A'melia?	TONE TIER	[L* H–H%]
A question, equivalent to	SEGMENTAL TIER	[ə m i ː l iː ə]
Did you say Amelia?		
(22) A'melia—	TONE TIER	[L* L–H%]
Addressing Amelia, indicating	SEGMENTAL TIER	[ə m i ː l iː ə]
that it is her turn to speak.		
(23) A'melia!?	TONE TIER	[L+H* L–H%]
A question indicating surprise.	SEGMENTAL TIER	[ə m i ː l iː ə]
(24) A'melia!!	TONE TIER	[L+H* L–L%]
A strong reaction, reprimanding	SEGMENTAL TIER	[ə m i ː l iː ə]
Amelia.		

The ToBI transcription for (20), [H* L– L%], is typical of a simple statement with only one stressed syllable receiving a pitch accent, and it ends with a falling pitch pattern. Similarly, the transcription for (21), [L* H– H%], is a typical tune for a question that can be answered by *yes* or *no*, which ends with a fairly large pitch rise. At the end of the next phrase, (22), there is a smaller rise of the kind that occurs in an unfinished utterance, or in a list of words such as those exemplified in (10), ... *Anna, Lenny, Mary, and* .... The way in which ToBI separates the large pitch rise in (21)—the question rise—from the smaller rise in (22)—the continuation rise—is by making the phrase tone L–, so that (22) has the tune [L* L– H%] instead of [L* H– H%], as in (21). The low phrase tone prevents the final high boundary from being so high. The stressed syllables of the final two tunes begin with an L, ensuring that the H* indicates a sharp rise from a low pitch. Thus, in (23), we have [L + H* L– H%], with a low phrase tone and a small pitch rise at the end, much as in (22). This tune can also be used to signal uncertainty. Finally, (24), [L + H* L– L%], is like (23) in that it begins with a strong rise, but it ends with a low boundary tone.

The simple statements, questions, and other intonations that we discussed earlier can be transcribed in a similar way.

(**1**) Simple statement.   *We know the new mayor.*
TONE TIER   [H*   H*   L–L%   ]
SEGMENTAL TIER   [wiː   noʊ   ðə   nu   ˈmɛr   ]

(**6**) Simple *yes/no* question.   *Will you mail me my money?*
TONE TIER   [H*   H*   H–H%]
SEGMENTAL TIER   [wɪl   juː   meɪl   miː   maɪ   mʌni   ]

(**9**) Two clauses.   *When you are winning,   I will run away.*
BREAK INDEX   [1   1   1   4   1   1   4]
TONE TIER   [H*   L=! H* L–H%   H* L–L%   ]
SEGMENTAL TIER [wən   juː   aː   ˈwɪnɪŋ   aɪ   wɪl   ɹʌn   əˈweɪ   ]

The break indices are shown in (9) above. At the end of the first intonational phrase, there is a continuation rise represented by [L– H%], and a break index of 4. All the words are closely joined together, so in each case the break index is 1.

Finally, we must consider how to transcribe another fact about English intonation (which also applies to many other languages). The pitch in most sentences has a tendency to drift down. Earlier, when discussing stress, we considered the sentence *Mary's younger 'brother wanted 'fifty chocolate 'peanuts*, with stresses on alternate words, *Mary's, brother, fifty, peanuts*. If you say this sentence with these stresses, you will find that there is an H* pitch accent on each of the stressed syllables, but each of these high pitches is usually a little lower than the preceding high pitch. This phenomenon is known as **downdrift**. We can represent this in the transcription by marking the H* pitch accents as being downstepped, a notion that was mentioned earlier in connection with a fall from a high pitch within a syllable. In Table 5.5 and example sentence (8), we used an exclamation mark, "!". We can indicate that each of the H* tones is a little lower than the preceding one by transcribing them as **downstepped** highs, !H*, in the tone tier for this sentence:

[H*   !H*   !H*   !H* L– L%]

(25) *Mary's younger brother wanted fifty chocolate peanuts.*

Note that successive H* pitch accents do not have to be downstepped. If we had wanted to put a very slight emphasis on *brother*, indicating that it was Mary's younger brother, not her younger sister, who had this peculiar desire, then we could have made the downstepping begin at "fifty" and said:

[H*   H*   !H*   !H* L– L%]

(26) *Mary's younger brother wanted fifty chocolate peanuts.*

The ToBI system is a way of characterizing English intonation in terms of a limited set of symbols—a set of six possible pitch accents including a downstep mark, two possible phrase accents, two possible boundary tones, and four possible break indices, going from 1 (close connection) to 4 (a boundary between intonation phrases). It was designed specifically for English intonations, but, with a few modifications, it may be appropriate for other languages as well.

RECAP

This chapter highlights phonetic phenomena in English that occur when you put words together in utterances. In connected speech, words may reduce so that their pronunciations are weaker than they are when you cite them from a list of words. Vowels become more like schwa, consonant constrictions are not as stop-like, or may delete entirely. One factor that is related to this weakening is stress. We note that some syllables in multisyllabic words are stressed while others are not. The vowels and consonants that are most prone to weakening in connected speech are those in unstressed syllables. Interestingly, there are two kinds of stress—one we call "tonic stress" and the other is usually called "word stress." Tonic stress is produced when an intonational accent is placed on a word (as it is usually done in isolated word reading). So to predict which syllables will undergo the most reduction in connected speech we must know both the locations of word stresses (which can be looked up in the dictionary) and the locations of intonational accents (which vary from utterance to utterance, as we show in the intonation section of the chapter). The ToBI system for transcribing intonation contours is also introduced in this chapter and many examples are given. One important point, that bears repeating, is that accurate intonation transcription requires careful listening as well as inspection of pitch traces. We also placed words over our pitch traces, showing roughly where the word boundaries are, this information is also vital.

EXERCISES

(Printable versions of all the exercises are available at the book website.)

A. List the strong and weak forms of ten words not mentioned in this chapter. For each word, transcribe a short utterance illustrating the weak form (as in Table 5.1).

Word	Strong Form	Weak Form	Example of Weak Form
____	____	____	____
____	____	____	____
____	____	____	____
____	____	____	____
____	____	____	____
____	____	____	____
____	____	____	____
____	____	____	____
____	____	____	____
____	____	____	____

B. Give two new examples of each of the following kinds of assimilations, one of the examples involving a change within a word, the other involving a change across word boundaries. In each case, show the words in orthography and in a narrow phonetic transcription, as in the examples. (Even if you yourself do not say assimilations of the kind illustrated, make up plausible examples.)

A change from an alveolar consonant to a bilabial consonant.

input	[ɪmpʊt]	*Saint Paul's*	[sm̩' pɔlz]
____	____	____	____

A change from an alveolar consonant to a dental consonant.

tenth	[tɛn̪θ]	*In this*	[ɪn̪ ðɪs]
____	____	____	____

A change from an alveolar consonant to a velar consonant.

synchronous	['sɪŋkrənəs]	*within groups*	[wɪðɪŋ grups]
____	____	____	____

A change from a voiceless consonant to a voiced consonant.

catty	['kædi]	*sit up*	[sɪ'd ʌp]
Or	['kæɾi]		[sɪ'ɾ ʌp]
____	____	____	____

140 CHAPTER 5 English Words and Sentences

C. Give five more examples of assimilation. Choose examples as different as possible from any that have been given before.

_____	[_____]
_____	[_____]
_____	[_____]
_____	[_____]
_____	[_____]

D. Make up pairs of phrases or sentences that show how each of the following words can have two different stress patterns.

Example: *continental*

It's a ˈcontinental ˈbreakfast.

She's ˈvery contiˈnental.

afternoon

artificial

diplomatic

absentminded

New York

E. Fill in plus and minus signs so as to indicate which syllables in the table below have tonic accents, which have stress, and which have full vowels. You may find it useful to refer back to Table 5.4.

computation   compute   inclination   incline (verb)

tonic accent

stress

full vowel

F. About a hundred years ago, the following words had stress as shown. Some of them still do for some people. But many of them (in Peter Ladefoged's speech, all of them) are stressed differently nowadays. Transcribe these words and show the stress on each of them in your own speech. Then state a general rule describing this tendency for the position of the stress to change to a particular syllable.

an'chovy _____

ab'domen _____

'applicable _____

'controversy _____

'nomenclature _____

tra'chea _____

eti'quette _____

re'plica _____

va'gary _____

blas'phemous _____

a'cumen _____

Rule: _____

_____

G. List three more sets of words showing the stress alternations of the kind shown in Table 5.2.

'photograph	*pho'tography*	*photo'graphic*
_____	_____	_____
_____	_____	_____
_____	_____	_____

H. Indicate the stress and intonation patterns that might occur in the situations described for the following utterances. Draw curves indicative of the pitch rather than using ToBI symbols.

(1) *Can you pass me that book?* (said politely to a friend)

(2) *Where were you last night?* (angry father to daughter)

(3) *Must it be printed?* (polite question)

(4) *Who is the one in the corner?* (excitedly to a friend)

PERFORMANCE EXERCISES

A. Pronounce the following phrases exactly as they have been transcribed, with all the assimilations and elisions. (Each of these transcriptions is a record of an utterance actually heard in normal conversations between educated speakers.)

"What are you doing?"	[ˈwɒdʒəˈduɪn]
"I can inquire."	[ˈaɪkŋ ŋ ˈkwaɪə]
"Did you eat yet?"	[ˈdʒiʔjɛʔ]
"I don't believe him."	[aɪˈdoʊmbəˈlivɪm]
"We ought to have come."	[wiˈɔtfˈkʌm]

B. Working with a partner, try to transcribe the intonation of a few sentences. You may find it difficult to repeat a sentence over and over again with the same intonation. If you do, try to work from a recording. In any case, write down the sentence and the intonation you intend to produce. Practice saying it before you say it to your partner.

C. Take turns saying nonsense words such as those shown below, transcribing them and comparing transcriptions.

ʃkeɪʒdʒˈminʒe

ʔɑŋkliθuntθ

sfeˈeʔəmˌɑ

grɔɪpstˈbraɪgz

D. Also make up lists of words for improving your memory span. These words are more difficult if the stress is varied and if the sounds are mainly of the same class (stops, front vowels, voiceless fricatives, etc).

tipeˈkiketiˈpe

θɔrˈsaɪθaʊˈfɔɪʃaʊθaʊ

ˈmonɑɲuˈɲonɔmɑ

woʔɔɪlaʊrɑˈrɔlojɔ

bəbdɪgˈbɛdgɪbɛdˈbɛdəd

PART III
GENERAL PHONETICS

6
Airstream Mechanisms and Phonation Types

In this part of the book, we will start considering the total range of human phonetic capabilities, not just those used in normal English speech. We will look at the sounds of the world's languages, as in this way we can find stable, repeatable examples of almost all the different speech sounds that people can make. To do this, we will have to enlarge the sets of terms we have been using to describe English. In the first place, all English sounds are initiated by the action of lung air going outward; other languages may use additional ways of producing an airstream. Second, all English sounds can be categorized as voiced or voiceless; in some languages, additional states of the glottis are used. This chapter will survey the general phonetic categories needed to describe the airstream mechanisms and phonation types that occur in other languages. Subsequent chapters will survey other ways in which languages differ. These foreign sounds should be studied even by those who are concerned only with the phonetics of English, both because they shed light on general human phonetic capabilities and also because they are important for a precise description of the shades of sounds present in normal English utterances. In addition, practitioners of clinical speech training find that the study of general phonetics is essential because disordered speech contains many non-English forms—the speech pathologist needs the whole IPA, not just the portion used to describe English.

AIRSTREAM MECHANISMS

Air coming out of the lungs is the source of power in nearly all speech sounds. When lung air is pushed out, we say that there is a **pulmonic airstream mechanism**. The lungs are spongelike tissues within a cavity formed by the rib cage and the diaphragm (a dome-shaped muscle indicated by the curved line at the bottom of Figure 1.3). When the diaphragm contracts, it enlarges the lung cavity so that air flows into the lungs. The lung cavity can also be enlarged by raising the rib cage, a normal way of taking a deep breath in. Air can be pushed out of the lungs by pulling the rib cage down, or by pushing the diaphragm upward by contracting the abdominal muscles.

In the description of most sounds, we take it for granted that the pulmonic airstream mechanism is the source of power. But in the case of obstruent consonants (stops and fricatives), other airstream mechanisms may be involved. Stops that use only an egressive, or outward-moving, pulmonic airstream are called **plosives**. Obstruents made with other airstream mechanisms will be specified by other terms.

In some languages, speech sounds are produced by moving different bodies of air. If you make a glottal stop, so that the air in the lungs is contained below the glottis, then the air in the vocal tract itself will form a body of air that can be moved. An upward movement of the closed glottis will move this air out of the mouth. A downward movement of the closed glottis will cause air to be sucked into the mouth. When either of these actions occurs, there is said to be a **glottalic airstream mechanism**.

An egressive glottalic airstream mechanism occurs in about 18% of the languages of the world. Hausa, the principal language of northern Nigeria, uses this mechanism in the formation of a velar stop that contrasts with the voiceless and voiced velar stops [k, g]. The movements of the vocal organs are shown in Figure 6.1. These are estimated, not drawn on the basis of x-rays.

In Hausa, the velar closure and the glottal closure are formed at about the same time. Then, when the vocal folds are tightly together, the larynx is pulled upward, about 1 cm. In this way it acts like a piston, compressing the air in the pharynx. The compressed air is released by lowering the back of the tongue while the glottal stop is maintained, producing a sound with a quality different from that in an English [k]. Very shortly after the release of the velar closure, the glottal stop is released and the voicing for the following vowel begins.

Figure 6.1 The sequence of events that occurs in a glottalic egressive velar stop [k'].

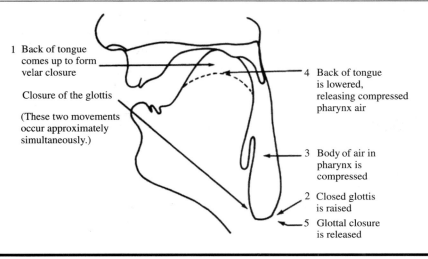

EXAMPLE 6.1

Stops made with a glottalic egressive airstream mechanism are called **ejectives**. The diacritic indicating an ejective is an apostrophe ['] placed after a symbol. The Hausa sound we have just described is a velar ejective, symbolized [k'], as in the Hausa word for 'increase' [k'aːrà], which, as you can hear at the website, contrasts with [kaːràː] 'put near.' (The symbol [ː] indicates that the vowels are long. The accents over the vowels indicate the pitch, a low tone. (We will discuss tones in Chapter 10.) The website also illustrates the contrasts between the Hausa words [kʷ'aːràː] 'pour' and [kʷ'aːràː] 'shea nut.' It is possible to use an ejective mechanism to produce fricatives as well as stops, as Hausa does in the words [saːràː] 'cut' and [s'aːràː] 'arrange,' which are also on the website. Of course, a fricative made in this way can continue only for a short length of time, as there is a comparatively small amount of air that can be moved by raising the closed glottis.

EXAMPLE 6.2

Ejectives of different kinds occur in a wide variety of languages, including Native American languages, African languages, and languages spoken in the Caucasus. Table 6.1 gives examples of ejectives and contrasting sounds made with a pulmonic airstream mechanism in Lakhota, a Native American language. The sounds of Lakhota differ from those of English in many ways, in addition to having contrastive ejectives. Later in this book, we will discuss the unfamiliar symbols in this table.

You can probably hear the difference between the Lakhota syllables [t̯u] and [t̯'u] in the audio files that accompany Table 6.1, and these differences are also apparent in the acoustic waveforms and spectrograms of the syllables shown in Figure 6.2. Both of these syllables begin with a short burst of noise—the **release burst** of the stop. In the case of the pulmonic egressive stop [t̯], the vowel starts about 30 milliseconds later, while in the glottalic egressive stop [t̯'], there is a gap of over 120 milliseconds and then a second stop release burst (the second burst is marked by the double-headed arrow that points at the release burst in the waveform at the top of the figure and in the time-aligned spectrogram at the bottom of the figure). This second stop release is the release of the glottal closure. This is a clear acoustic cue telling us that the stop release burst in [t̯'u] was produced by a glottalic egressive airstream mechanism.

TABLE 6.1	Contrasts involving ejective stops in Lakhota. An ejective mechanism is shown by a following apostrophe.			
Ejective		p'o	t̯'uʃə	k'u
		'foggy'	'at all costs'	'to give'
Voiceless Unaspirated		payõ t̯a	t̯uwa	kah
		'mallard'	'who'	'that'
Voiceless + Velar Fricative		pˣa	t̯ˣawa	kˣant̯a
		'bitter'	'own'	'plum'

Figure 6.2 Acoustic waveforms and spectrograms of the Lakhota dental voiceless unaspirated and ejective stops.

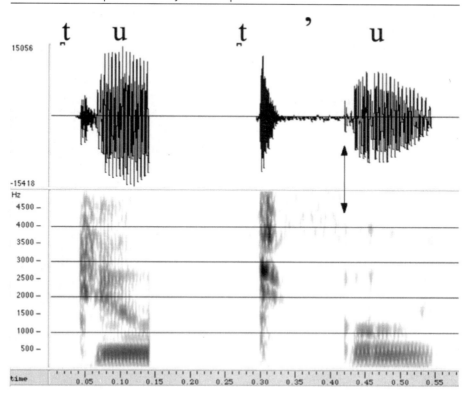

Some people make ejectives at the ends of words in English, particularly in sentence final position. You might notice this in words such as *bike* with a glottal stop accompanying the final [k]. If the velar stop is released while the glottal stop is still being held, a weak ejective may be heard. See if you can superimpose a glottal stop on a final [k] and produce an ejective. Now try to make a slightly more forceful ejective stop. By now, you should be fully able to make a glottal stop in a sequence such as [aʔa], so the next step is to learn to raise and lower the glottis. If you hold your breath and make [k] sounds while you keep holding your breath, you are probably making ejective stops. The glottis remains closed because you are holding your breath, and it moves up and down in the throat to produce the [k]. Feel your larynx and see if it moves up in the throat. Another way to learn to recognize what it feels like to raise the glottis is by singing a very low note and then moving to the position for singing the highest note that you possibly can. Doing this silently makes it easier to concentrate on feeling the muscular sensations involved. Putting your fingers on your throat above the larynx is also a help in feeling the movements.

Repeat (silently) this sequence—low note, very high note—until you have thoroughly experienced the sensation of raising your glottis. Now try to make this movement with a closed glottis. There will, of course, be no sounds produced by these movements alone.

Practice superimposing larynx movement on a velar stop. Say the sequence [ɑk]. Then say this sequence again, very slowly, holding your tongue in the position for the [k] closure at the end for a second or so. Now say it again, and while maintaining the [k] closure, do three things: (1) make a glottal stop; (2) if you can, raise your larynx; and (3) release the [k] closure while maintaining the glottal stop. Don't worry about step (2) too much. The important thing to concentrate on is having a glottal stop and a velar closure going on at the same time, and then releasing the velar closure *before* releasing the glottal stop. The release of the velar closure will produce only a very small noise, but it will be an ejective [k'].

Next, try to produce a vowel after the ejective. This time start from the sequence [ɑkɑ]. Say this sequence slowly, with a long [k] closure. Then, during this closure, make a glottal stop and raise the larynx. Then release the [k] closure while still maintaining the glottal stop. Finally, release the glottal stop and follow it with a vowel. You should have produced something like [ɑk'ʔɑ]. When this sequence becomes more fluent, so that there is very little pause between the release of the velar closure and the release of the glottal stop, it will be simply an ejective followed by a vowel: [ɑk'ɑ]. There is, of course, still a glottal stop after the release of the velar stop and before the vowel, but unless it is exceptionally long, we may consider it to be implied by the symbol for the ejective.

Another way of learning to produce an ejective is to start from the usual American (and common British) pronunciation of *button* as [ˈbʌʔn̩]. Try starting to say *button* but finishing with another vowel [ʌ] instead of the nasal [n]. If you make sure you do include the glottal stop form of / t /, the result will probably be [ˈbʌʔtʌ]. If you say this slowly, you should be able to convert it, first into [ˈbʌʔt'ʔʌ], then into [ˈbʌt'ʌ], and finally, altering the stress, into [bʌˈt'ʌ].

Eventually, you should be able to produce sequences such as [p'ɑ, t'ɑ, k'ɑ] and perhaps [tʃ'ɑ, s'ɑ] as well. Practice producing ejectives before, after, and between a wide variety of vowels. You should also try to say the Lakhota words in Table 6.1. But if you find ejectives difficult to produce, don't worry. As you might gather from this discussion, many people aren't able to say ejectives right away. Just keep on practicing.

It is also possible to use a downward movement of the larynx to suck air inward. Stops made with an ingressive glottalic airstream mechanism are called **implosives**. In the production of implosives, the downward-moving larynx is not usually completely closed. The air in the lungs is still being pushed out, and some of it passes between the vocal folds, keeping them in motion so that the sound is voiced. Figure 6.3 shows the movements in a voiced bilabial implosive of a kind that occurs in Sindhi (an Indo-Aryan language spoken in India and Pakistan). Implosives sometimes occur as allophones in English, particularly in emphatic articulations of bilabial stops, as in *absolutely **billions and billions***.

Figure 6.3 Estimated sequence of events in a Sindhi bilabial implosive [6].

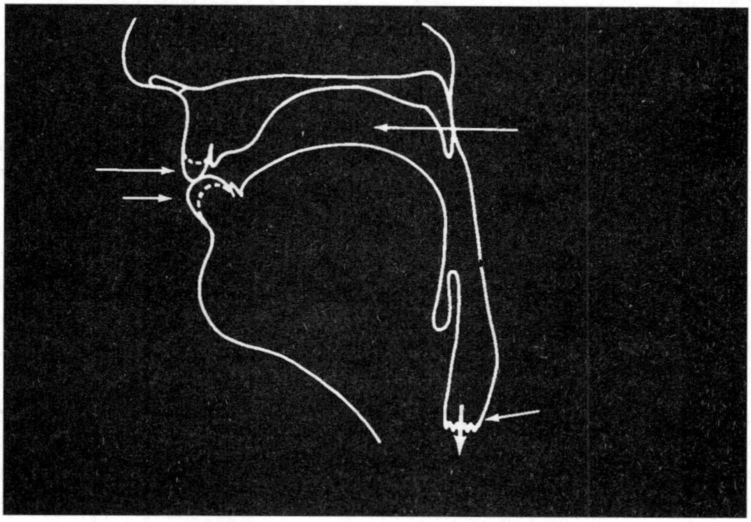

In all the implosives we have measured, the articulatory closure—in this case, the lips coming together—occurs first. The downward movement of the glottis, which occurs next, is like that of a piston that would cause a reduction in the pressure of the air in the oral tract. But it is a leaky piston in that the air in the lungs continues to flow through the glottis. As a result, the pressure of the air in the oral tract is often not affected very much. (In a plosive [b] there is, of course, an increase in the pressure of the air in the vocal tract.) When the articulatory closure is released, there may be implosive action with air sucked into the mouth, but in less emphatic implosives there may not be actual ingressive airflow. Instead, the peculiar quality of the sound arises from the complex changes in the shape of the vocal tract and in the vibratory pattern of the vocal folds.

In many languages, such as Sindhi and several African and Native American languages, implosives contrast with plosives. However, in some languages (e.g., Vietnamese), implosives are simply variants (allophones) of voiced plosives and are not in contrast with those sounds. The top line of Table 6.2 (on page 150) illustrates implosives in Sindhi. The symbols for implosives have a small hook on the top of the regular symbol. For the moment, we will consider only the first and second rows in Table 6.2, which illustrate ingressive glottalic stops (implosives) in the first row, contrasting with regular pulmonic plosives in the second row. Sindhi has unfamiliar places of articulation illustrated in the third and fourth columns, which we will consider in Chapter 7. The lower rows in the table illustrate phonation types that we will consider later in this chapter.

Acoustic waveforms and spectrograms of two of the words in Table 6.2 are shown in Figure 6.4 (on page 150). There are several differences in these displays

EXAMPLE 6.3

CHAPTER 6 Airstream Mechanisms and Phonation Types

TABLE 6.2 Contrasts involving implosives and plosives with different phonation types in Sindhi.

ɓani 'field'		ɗinu 'festival'	ʄatu 'illiterate'	ɠanu 'handle'
banu 'forest'	daru 'door'	ɗoːru 'you run'	ʄatu 'illiterate' [variant]	gunu 'quality'
panu 'leaf'	taru 'bottom'	ʈanu 'ton'	catu 'to destroy'	kanu 'ear'
pʰanu 'snake hood'	tʰaru (district name)	ʈʰaɟu 'thug, cheat'	cʰatu 'crown'	kʰanu 'you lift'
bɦaːnu 'manure'	dɦaru 'trunk'	ɖɦaɟu 'bull'	ɟɦatu 'a grab'	gɦanɪ 'excess'

relating to the differences between the vowels and intervocalic consonants that we will return to later in this book. For now, we would like to focus on the initial consonants [ɖ] and [ɗ]. Both of these start with a short period of low amplitude voicing, which in the spectrogram appears as a gray bar at the bottom of the spectrogram. This is called the voice bar and is an acoustic property of all (phonetically) voiced stops. So, both [ɖ] and [ɗ] are voiced. Interestingly, the

Figure 6.4 Acoustic waveforms and spectrograms of the Sindhi retroflex voiced and implosive stops.

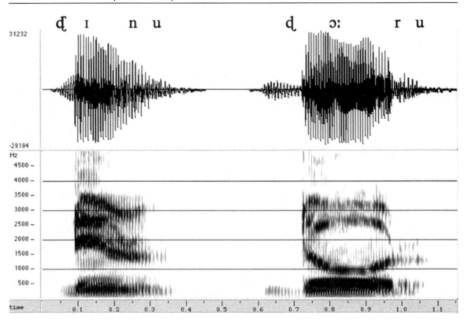

pulmonic voiced stop [d] has a longer voice bar than the glottalic ingressive stop [ɗ]. This characteristic is present for the other Lakhota pairs in Table 6.2, but has not been reported as a phonetic characteristic of the pulmonic/implosive contrast in other languages. There is one other difference between [d] and [ɗ] that is consistently present for contrasts between implosives and plosives. You will notice that in the implosive [ɗ], the voice bar grows louder over time, while in the pulmonic stop [d], the amplitude of the voice bar decreases over time. This difference is almost always seen when we compare regular pulmonic stops and implosives—and might be a good cue to look for as you practice making the distinction.

We do not know any foolproof way of teaching people to make implosives. Some people can learn to make them just by imitating their instructor; others can't. (Peter Ladefoged, incidentally, was one of the latter group. He did not learn to make implosives until nearly the end of a year studying phonetics. Keith Johnson learned to make implosives by imitating his instructor's funny pronunciation of "Alabama" and then realized that he also used the implosive [ʄ] in imitating the noise of liquid pouring from a bottle [ʄə ʄə ʄə ʄə].) The best suggestion we can make is to start from a fully voiced plosive. Say [ɑbɑ], making sure that the voicing continues throughout the closure. Now say this sequence slowly, making the closure last as long as you can while maintaining strong vocal fold vibrations. Release the closure (open the lips) *before* the voicing stops. If you put your fingers on your throat above the larynx while doing this, you will probably be able to feel the larynx moving down during the closure.

There are straightforward mechanical reasons why the larynx moves down in these circumstances. To maintain voicing throughout a [b], air must continue to flow through the glottis. But it cannot continue to flow for very long, because while the articulatory position of [b] is being held, the pressure of the air in the mouth is continually increasing as more air flows through the glottis. To keep the vocal folds vibrating, the air in the lungs must be at an appreciably higher pressure than the air in the vocal tract so that there is a pressure drop across the glottis. One of the ways of maintaining the pressure drop across the glottis is to lower the larynx and thus increase the space available in the vocal tract. Consequently, when saying a long [b], there is a natural tendency to lower the larynx. If you try to make a long, fully voiced [b] very forcibly but open the lips before the voicing stops, you may end up producing an implosive [ɓ]. You can check your progress in learning to produce implosives by using a straw in a drink. Hold a straw immersed in a liquid between your lips while you say [ɑɓɑ]. You should see the liquid move upward in the straw during the [ɓ].

Historically, languages seem to develop implosives from plosives that have become more and more voiced. In many languages, as we mentioned earlier, voiced implosives are simply allophones of voiced plosives. Often, as in Vietnamese, these languages have voiced plosives that have to be fully voiced to keep them distinct from two other sets of plosives that we will discuss in the next section. In languages such as Sindhi, for which we have good evidence of the earlier stages of the language, we can clearly see that the present implosives grew out of older voiced plosives in this way; the present contrasting voiced plosives are due to later influences of neighboring languages.

One other airstream mechanism is used in a few languages. This is the mechanism that is used in producing **clicks**, such as the interjection expressing disapproval that novelists write *tuttut* or *tsktsk*. Another type of click is commonly used to show approval or to signal horses to go faster. Still another click in common use is the gentle, pursed-lips type of kiss that one might drop on one's grandmother's cheek. Clicks occur in words (in addition to interjections or nonlinguistic gestures) in several African languages. Zulu, for example, has a number of clicks, including one that is very similar to our expression of disapproval.

The easiest click to start studying is the gentle-kiss-with-pursed-lips type. In a language that uses bilabial clicks of this sort, the gesture is not quite the same as that used by most people making a friendly kiss. The linguistic gesture does not involve puckering the lips. They are simply compressed in a grimmer manner. Make a "kiss" of this type. Say this sound while holding a finger lightly along the lips. You might be able to feel that air rushes into the mouth when your lips come apart. Note that while you are making this sound, you can continue to breathe through your nose. This is because the back of the tongue is touching the velum, so that the air in the mouth used in making this sound is separated from the airstream flowing in and out of the nose.

Now say the click expressing disapproval (with the blade of the tongue touching the teeth and alveolar ridge), the one that authors sometimes write *tuttut* or *tsktsk* when they wish to indicate a click sound; they do not, of course, mean [tʌt tʌt] or [tɪsk tɪsk]. Say a single click of this kind and try to feel how your tongue moves. The positions of the vocal organs in the corresponding Zulu sound are shown in Figure 6.5. At the beginning of this sound, there are both dental and velar closures. As a result, the body of air shown in the dark shaded area in Figure 6.5 is totally enclosed. When the back and central parts of the tongue move down, this air becomes rarefied. A click is produced when this partial vacuum is released by lowering the tip of the tongue. The IPA symbol for a dental click is [|], a single vertical stroke extending both above and below the line of writing.

Movement of the body of air in the mouth is called a **velaric airstream mechanism**. Clicks are stops made with an ingressive velaric airstream mechanism (as shown in Figure 6.5). It is also possible to use this mechanism to cause the airstream to flow outward by raising the tongue and squeezing the contained body of air, but this latter possibility is not actually used in any known language.

The sound described in Figure 6.5 is a dental click. If the partial vacuum is released by lowering the side of the tongue, a lateral click—the sound sometimes used for encouraging horses—is produced. The phonetic symbol is [‖], a pair of vertical strokes, again going both above and below the line of writing. Clicks can also be made with the tip (*not* the blade) of the tongue touching the posterior part of the alveolar ridge. The phonetic symbol for a click of this kind is [!], an exclamation point (this time resting on the line of writing). These three

Figure 6.5 The sequence of events in a dental click. Initially, both the tip and the back of the tongue are raised, enclosing the small pocket of air indicated by the dark shading. When the center of the tongue moves down, the larger, lightly shaded cavity is formed. Then the tip moves down to the position shown by the dashed line, and, a little later, the back of the tongue comes down to the position shown by the dashed line.

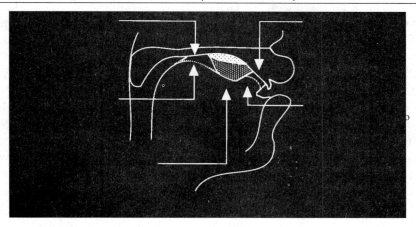

possibilities all occur in Zulu and in the neighboring language Xhosa. Some of the aboriginal South African languages, such as Nama and !Xóõ, have an even wider variety of click articulations. !Xóõ, spoken in Botswana, is one of the few languages that have bilabial clicks—a sort of thin, straight-lips kiss sound, for which the symbol is [ʘ].

In the production of click sounds, there is a velar closure, and the body of air involved is in front of this closure (i.e., in the front of the mouth). Consequently, it is possible to produce a velar sound with a glottalic or pulmonic airstream mechanism while a click is being made. You can demonstrate this for yourself by humming on the velar nasal [ŋ] continuously while producing clicks. This is probably the easiest way to start to learn how to produce clicks. We may symbolize the co-occurrence of a nasal and a click by writing a tie bar [͡] over the two symbols. Thus, a dental click and a velar nasal would be written [ŋ͡|], and the hummed sequence is [ŋ͡|ŋ͡|ŋ͡|ŋ͡|ŋ͡|ŋ͡|ŋ͡|]. In transcribing click languages, the tie bar is usually left off, and simultaneity is assumed.

Even if the soft palate is raised so that air cannot flow through the nose, the pulmonic airstream mechanism can still be used to keep the vocal folds vibrating for a short time during a click. When the back of the tongue is raised for a click and there is also a velic closure, the articulators are in the position for [g]. A voiced dental click of this kind is therefore a combination of [g] and [|] and may be symbolized [g|] (omitting the tie bar).

At this point we should note that, strictly speaking, the transcription of clicks always requires a symbol for both the click itself and for the activity associated with the velar closure. We transcribed the voiced click with a [ɡ] plus the click symbol, and the nasalized click with [ŋ] plus the click symbol. We should also transcribe the voiceless click with [k] plus the click symbol. It is perhaps not necessary for a beginning student in phonetics to be able to produce all sorts of different clicks in regular words. But you should be able to produce at least a simple click followed by a vowel. Try saying [kǀ] followed by [ɑ]. Make a vowel as soon after the click as possible, so that it sounds like a single syllable [kǀɑ] (using the convention that regards the [k] and the click as simultaneous, as if there were a tie bar).

As a more challenging exercise, learn to produce clicks between vowels. Start by repeating [kǀɑ] a number of times, so that you are saying [kǀɑkǀɑkǀɑ]. Now say dental, post-alveolar, and lateral clicks in sequences such as [ɑkǀɑ, ɑk!ɑ, ɑkǁɑ]. Make sure there are no pauses between the vowels and the clicks. Now try to keep the voicing going throughout the sequences, so that you produce [ɑɡǀɑ, ɑɡ!ɑ, ɑɡǁɑ]. Last, produce nasalized clicks, perhaps with nasalized vowels on either side [ɑŋǀɑ, ɑŋ!ɑ, ɑŋǁɑ] (again with the nasal being simultaneous with the click). Repeat with other vowels.

EXAMPLE 6.4

The spelling system regularly used in books and newspapers in Zulu and Xhosa employs the letters *c*, *q*, *x* for the dental, post-alveolar, and lateral clicks for which we have been using the symbols [ǀ, !, ǁ], respectively. The name of the language Xhosa should therefore be pronounced with a lateral click at the beginning. The *h* following the orthographic *X* indicates a short burst of aspiration following the click. Try saying the name of the language with an aspirated lateral click at the beginning. Table 6.3 shows a set of contrasting clicks in Xhosa. Nearly all the words in this table are infinitive forms of words, which is why they begin with the prefix [ukú].

TABLE 6.3 Contrasts involving clicks in Xhosa. The rows differ in phonation types, as discussed later in this chapter.

	Dental	Post-alveolar	Alveolar Lateral
Voiceless unaspirated velar plosive	ukúkǀola 'to grind fine'	ukú!oɓa 'to break stones'	úkǁolo 'peace'
Voiceless aspirated velar plosive	úkukǀʰóla 'to pick up'	ukúk!ola 'perfume'	ukúkǁʰoɓa 'to arm oneself'
Murmured velar plosive	úkuɡǀôɓa 'to be joyful'	ukúɡ!oba 'to scoop'	ukúɡǁoba 'to stir up mud'
Voiced velar nasal	ukúŋǀoma 'to admire'	ukúŋ!ola 'to climb up'	ukúŋǁiɓa 'to put on clothes'
Murmured velar nasal	ukúŋǀola 'to be dirty'	ukúŋ!ala 'to go straight'	ukúŋǁoŋǁa 'to lie on back, knees up'

The website also illustrates clicks in Zulu, a language closely related to Xhosa, and in Nama and !Xóõ, two Khoisan languages spoken in Namibia and Botswana. You can find examples of these languages by going to the index of languages, the index of sounds, or the map index, all of which are accessible in the "Extras" section of the website.

Table 6.4 summarizes the principal airstream mechanisms. Note that pulmonic sounds can be voiced or voiceless. Glottalic egressive sounds—ejectives—are always voiceless. Glottalic ingressive sounds—implosives—are nearly always voiced by being combined with a pulmonic egressive airstream, but voiceless glottalic ingressive sounds (voiceless implosives) have been reported in a few languages, such as the Owerri dialect of Igbo, spoken in Nigeria. (Igbo examples are among the extra material on the website, accessible through the index of languages.) Velaric ingressive sounds (clicks) may be combined with pulmonic egressive sounds so that the resulting combination can be voiced or voiceless. These combinations can also be oral or nasal.

TABLE 6.4	The principal airstream processes.				
Airstream	Direction	Brief Description	Specific Name for Stop Consonant	Examples	Vocal Folds
Pulmonic	egressive	lung air pushed out under the control of the respiratory muscles	plosive	p t k b d g	voiceless or voiced
Glottalic	egressive	pharynx air compressed by the upward movement of the closed glottis	ejective	p' t' k'	voiceless
Glottalic	ingressive	downward movement of the vibrating glottis; pulmonic egressive airstream may also be involved	implosive	ɓ ɗ ʄ	usually voiced by the pulmonic airstream
Velaric	ingressive	mouth air rarefied by the backward and downward movement of the tongue	click	ǀ ǃ ǁ ʘ	combine with the pulmonic airstream for voiced or voiceless velar nasals

STATES OF THE GLOTTIS

So far, we have been considering sounds to be either voiceless, with the vocal folds apart, or voiced, with the folds nearly together so that they will vibrate when air passes between them. But in fact, the **glottis** (which is defined as the space between the vocal folds) can assume a number of other states. Some of these glottal states are important in the description of other languages, and in the description of pathological voices.

Photographs of four states of the glottis are shown in Figure 6.6. These photographs were taken by placing a small mirror at the back of the mouth so that it was possible to look straight down the pharynx toward the larynx. The top of the picture is toward the front of the neck, the lower part toward the back. The vocal folds are the white bands running vertically in each picture. Their position can be adjusted by the movements of the **arytenoid cartilages**,

Figure 6.6 Four states of the glottis. (Photographs by John Ohala and Ralph Vanderslice.)

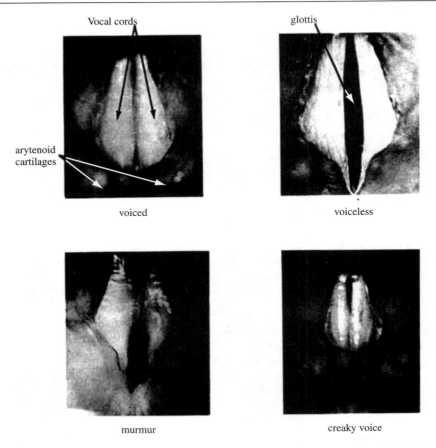

which are underneath the small protuberances visible in the lower part of the pictures.

In a voiced sound, the vocal folds are close together and vibrating, as in the first photograph. In a voiceless sound, as in the second photograph, they are pulled apart. This position will produce a completely voiceless sound if there is little or no airflow through the glottis, as in the case of a voiceless fricative or an unaspirated stop. But if there is considerable airflow, as in an *h*-like sound, the vocal folds will be set vibrating while remaining apart. In this way, they produce what is called **breathy voice**, or **murmur**. The second photograph is labeled "voiceless" because this is the usual position in voiceless fricatives. But in an intervocalic [h] as in *ahead*, the vocal folds are in a very similar position. In these circumstances, they will produce breathy voice, vibrating loosely, so they appear to be simply flapping in the airstream. The third photograph shows another kind of breathy voice. In this sound, the vocal folds are apart between the arytenoid cartilages in the lower (posterior) part of the photograph. They can still vibrate, but at the same time, a great deal of air passes out through the glottis.

Murmured sounds occur in English in the pronunciation of / h / in between vowels as in *ahead* and *behind*. In most of the speakers of English we have been able to observe, the / h / in these words is made with the vocal folds slightly apart along their entire length, but still continuing to vibrate as if they were waving in the breeze. The term "voiced *h*" is sometimes used for this sound, but the vocal fold vibration is different from the usual, or modal, mode of voicing. The term "murmured *h*" is preferable. The symbol for this sound is [ɦ].

Learn to distinguish between the murmured sound [ɦ] as in *aha* and the voiceless sound [h] as at the beginning of an English word such as *heart*. The murmured sound is like a sigh produced while breathing heavily. Take a deep breath and see how long you can make first [ɦ] and then [h]. In the voiceless sound [h], the air from the lungs escapes very rapidly so that this sound cannot be prolonged to any great extent. But you can make the murmured sound [ɦ] last much longer, as the flow of air from the lungs is slowed down by the vibrating vocal folds. Note that [ɦ] can be said on a range of different pitches.

Now say [ɦ] before a vowel. When you say [ɦɑ], you will probably find that the breathiness extends into the vowel. But try to make only the first part of the syllable breathy and produce regular voicing at the end. Finally, try to produce the sequence [ɦɑ] after a stop consonant. Murmured stops of this kind occur in Hindi and in many other languages spoken in India. These sounds will be discussed more fully in the next section. But we can note here that in murmured stops, the murmur occurs only during the release of the stop. There must be a comparatively high rate of flow of air out of the lungs to produce murmur, and this cannot happen during the stop closure.

It is fairly easy to produce the required flow rate for murmur during a vowel. Some languages contrast plain and murmured vowels. Table 6.5 (on page 158) shows a set of words in Gujarati, another language spoken in India. You can hear these words at the Course in Phonetics website. Murmured sounds are indicated by

EXAMPLE 6.8

TABLE 6.5	Murmured vowels in Gujarati.				
	Breathy			**Plain**	
ba̤r	'outside'	bʱar	'burden'	bar	'twelve'
mḛl	'palace'			mɛl	'dirt'

placing two dots below the symbol. In Gujarati, the contrast between murmured or breathy voiced sounds and regular, modal voice can occur in both consonants and vowels. In the first row, you can hear a three-way contrast between a murmured vowel, a murmured release of a stop, and a word that has only modal voice.

In **creaky voice**, which is the fourth state of the glottis illustrated in Figure 6.6, the arytenoid cartilages are tightly together so that the vocal folds can vibrate only at the anterior end (the small opening at the top of the photograph). Note that the vocal folds appear to be much shorter in this photograph. This is partly because the posterior portion at the bottom of the photograph is not visible when the arytenoid cartilages are pulled together. But it is also the case that in creaky voice, the folds are not stretched from front to back as they are on higher pitches. It is not possible to make accurate measurements of the lengths of the vibrating folds in these photographs, as the glottis is at varying distances from the camera, but this probably accounts for only a small proportion of the variation in length apparent in the photographs. Creaky voice is a very low-pitched sound that occurs at the ends of falling intonations for some speakers of English. Other speakers (generally younger speakers in the United States) produce a creaky phonation most of the time in a voice quality that has been noticed in the popular press as vocal "fry." You can probably learn to produce creaky voice, if you don't already use it, by singing the lowest note that you can, and then trying to go even lower. Creaky-voiced sounds may also be called **laryngealized**.

EXAMPLE 6.1

In some languages, laryngealization is used to distinguish one sound from another. Hausa and many other Chadic languages of northern Nigeria distinguish between two palatal approximants. One has regular voicing, rather like the English sound at the beginning of *yacht*, and the other has creaky voice. The IPA diacritic to indicate creaky voice is [˷] placed under the symbol. Hausa orthography uses an apostrophe (') before the symbol for the corresponding voiced sound, thus contrasting *y* and *'y*. The Hausa letters *y* and *'y* correspond to IPA [j] and [j̰]. Try differentiating between the laryngealized and nonlaryngealized sounds in the Hausa words [jaː] *ya* ('he') and [j̰aː] *'ya* ('daughter'), which are included at the website with the other Hausa words discussed earlier in this chapter.

A slightly more common use of laryngealization is to distinguish one stop from another. Hausa and many other West African languages have voiced stops [b, d] contrasting with laryngealized stops [b̰, d̰], which are sometimes implosives. In these sounds, the creaky voice is most evident not during the stop closure itself but during the first part of the following vowel. Similar sounds occur in some Native American languages. You can find examples on the website in the "Extras" section.

VOICE ONSET TIME

We saw earlier that the terms *voiced* and *voiceless* refer to the state of the glottis during a given articulation. We also saw that the terms *aspirated* and *unaspirated* refer to the presence or absence of a period of voicelessness during and after the release of an articulation. The interval between the release of a consonant closure and the start of the voicing is called the **voice onset time** (usually abbreviated VOT). The easiest way to visualize VOT is by reference to the waveform of a sound. This is the technique used in Chapter 3 to discuss the differences between *tie* and *die*. The VOT is measured in milliseconds (ms) from the spike indicating the release of the stop closure to the start of the oscillating pattern indicating the vibrations of the vocal folds in the vowel. If the voicing begins during the stop closure (i.e., before the release), the VOT has a negative value.

The top part of Figure 6.7 (on page 160) shows the waveforms of the first parts of three of the Sindhi words in Table 6.2: [daru] ('door'), [taru] ('bottom'), and [tʰaru] (name of a district). The dashed line indicates the moment of release of the stop closure. A time scale centered on that moment is at the bottom of the figure. In the waveform for [da], at the top of the figure, there is voicing throughout the closure, the release, and the vowel. This is a fully voiced stop that has a negative VOT of −130 ms.

EXAMPLE 6.3

In the next waveform, [ta], there are no voicing vibrations during the closure (before the dashed line). This is, therefore, a voiceless stop. The voicing starts very shortly after the closure, the VOT being less than 20 ms, making this an unaspirated stop. To produce this stop, the vocal folds are apart during the whole of the closure period but close together at the moment of release of the closure, so that voicing starts as soon as there is sufficient airflow through the glottis. In the middle of the closure, the vocal folds might be in a position similar to that shown in the top right photograph in Figure 6.6.

The third waveform, [tʰa], shows an aspirated stop with a VOT of about 50 ms. In producing this sound, the vocal folds are apart during the stop closure and the glottis is still open at the moment of the release of the stop closure.

There is a continuum of possible voice onset times. Some languages, such as Sindhi, have fully voiced stops with a large negative VOT. Others, such as English, have little or no voicing during the closure unless the stop is preceded by a sound in which the vocal folds are already vibrating, in which case the vibration may continue through the closure. Similarly, languages vary in the VOT they use for aspirated stops. In the Sindhi [tʰa] Figure 6.7, it is only 50 ms. In Navajo, as shown in the last row in Figure 6.7, aspirated stops have a VOT of about 150 ms. When producing a strongly aspirated stop such as this, the maximum opening of

Figure 6.7 Waveforms showing stops with different degrees of voicing and aspiration.

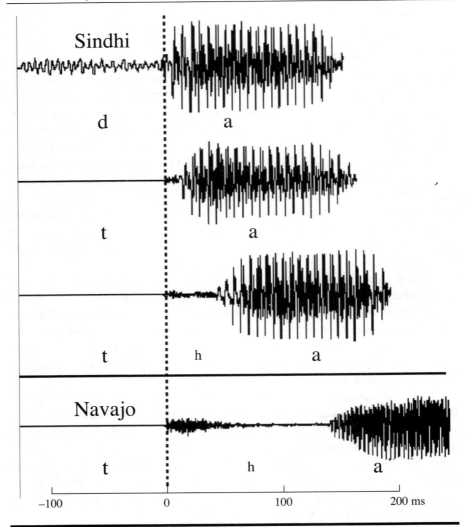

the vocal folds will be much larger than that shown in the top right photograph in Figure 6.6. The maximum opening will occur at about the moment of release of the stop closure. In general, the degree of aspiration (the amount of lag in the voice onset time) will depend on the degree of glottal aperture during the closure. The greater the opening of the vocal folds during a stop, the longer the amount of the following aspiration.

Different languages make use of different points along the VOT continuum in forming oppositions among stop consonants. This point is illustrated in Figure 6.8, in which some of the possibilities that occur in different languages are shown

Figure 6.8 Differences in voice onset time in different languages on a scale going from most voiced (largest negative VOT) to most aspirated (largest positive VOT).

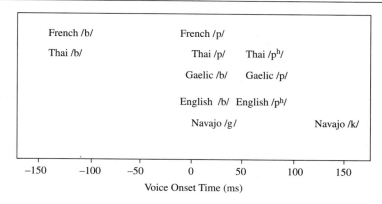

with reference to a scale going from most aspirated (largest positive VOT) at the left to most voiced (largest negative VOT) at the right. The Navajo aspirated stops, shown in the first row, have a very large VOT that is quite exceptional. Navajo does not have a bilabial stop series, but for all the other languages, the positions shown on the scale correspond to bilabial stops. As is indicated, in the second row, a normal value for the VOT of English stressed initial / p / would be between 50 and 60 ms. English initial / b / may have a VOT of about 10 ms, but it may be less and even slightly negative. After an initial / s /, English / p / will have a VOT much like English initial / b /.

Other languages make the contrast between phonemes such as / p, t, k / and / b, d, g / in initial position with very different VOTs. Navajo contrasts initial / k / with a / g / that is far from voiced; it has a VOT of over 40 ms. As this sound is completely voiceless, it might be better to say that the contrast in Navajo is between / kʰ / and / k /, rather than between / k / and / g /. However, both ways of transcribing Navajo are perfectly valid. As we saw in Chapter 2, you can make a broad transcription that shows the phonemic contrasts in a language using the simplest possible symbols, or you can make a narrow transcription that shows the phonetic detail. As long as the broad transcription is accompanied by a statement that specifies how it should be interpreted, it is equally accurate. The choice of symbol depends in part on the reason for making the transcription. In broad transcriptions of English, it is sufficient just to use / b, p /. But if one wants to show more phonetic detail, one can specify that the phoneme / b / is a completely voiceless [b̥] in, for instance, *that boy* [ðæʔtb̥ɔɪ]. Similarly, one might want to show phonetic details such as the aspirated / p / that occurs in *pie* [pʰaɪ] or the unaspirated / p / in *spy* [spaɪ].

The top row in Figure 6.8 shows how the sounds of French line up with those of English and Navajo. The voiced stops in French (and Spanish, Italian, and

TABLE 6.6 Stops in Thai.

Voiced	bâ:	d̪à:
	'crazy'	'curse'
Voiceless Unaspirated	pâ:	t̪a:
	'aunt'	'eye'
Voiceless Aspirated	pʰâ:	t̪ʰâ:
	'cloth'	'landing place'

many other languages) are nearly always fully voiced. Voiceless stops in these languages are unaspirated, making French / p / similar to English initial / b /.

EXAMPLE 6.9

French / p / is even more like Gaelic / b /, which is virtually never voiced, even between vowels. The Gaelic opposition between / b / and / p / is, in a narrow phonetic transcription, / p / versus / pʰ /. In the Gaelic spoken in the Outer Hebrides of Scotland, the VOT of / pʰ / is around 65 ms, not nearly as long as that in Navajo, but longer than that in English.

Some languages contrast three different voice onset times. Thai has voiced, voiceless unaspirated, and aspirated stops, as shown in Figure 6.8. Words illustrating these contrasts in Thai are given in Table 6.6. As in the case of French, the voiced stops are fully voiced, with the duration of the voicing depending on the length of the stop closure.

EXAMPLE 6.10

Many languages spoken in India, such as Hindi and Sindhi, have not only the three possibilities that occur in Thai, but murmured stops as well. After the release of the closure, there is a period of breathy voice or murmur before the regular voicing starts. Some illustrative Hindi words are given in Table 6.7.

TABLE 6.7 Stops in Hindi.

	Voiceless Unaspirated	Voiceless Aspirated	Voiced	Breathy Voiced
Bilabial	pal	pʰal	bal	bʱal
	'take care of'	'knife blade'	'hair'	'forehead'
Dental	t̪al	t̪ʰal	d̪al	d̪ʱal
	'beat'	'plate'	'lentil'	'knife'
Retroflex	ʈal	ʈʰal	ɖal	ɖʱal
	'postpone'	'wood shop'	'branch'	'shield'
Post-alveolar Affricate	tʃʌl	tʃʰʌl	dʒʌl	dʒʱʌl
	'walk'	'deceit'	'water'	'glimmer'
Velar	kan	kʰan	gan	gʱan
	'ear'	'mine'	'song'	'bundle'

The breathy voice release of these stops is indicated by [ʱ], a raised, hooked letter *h*. The Sindhi words in the last row of Table 6.2 also illustrate breathy voiced stops. As shown in the tables, in addition to the breathy voiced stops, both Sindhi and Hindi also contrast stops with three different voice onset times.

Figure 6.9 shows the waveforms of the Hindi dental stops in the second row of Table 6.7. There is voicing during the stop closure of [d̪] (in the top line), but not during the stops in the second and third lines. The second line has a voiceless unaspirated [t̪] with a VOT of about 20 ms. The third line has an aspirated [t̪ʰ] with a VOT of almost 100 ms. In the fourth line, the [d̪ʱ] has voicing during the closure followed by a waveform that has some of the appearance of voicing—a wavy line—but also has noise superimposed on it. This is breathy voicing. It is difficult to say how long this breathy voiced aspiration lasts, as it shades into the regular voicing for the vowel. During this breathy voicing, the vocal folds are drawn into loose vibrations and do not come fully together.

Figure 6.9 Waveforms showing the VOT of the stops in Hindi.

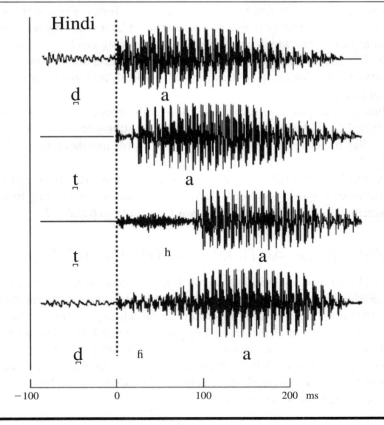

The difference between voiceless unaspirated, aspirated, and murmured stops (the last three rows in Figure 6.9) is largely a matter of the size and timing of the opening of the vocal folds. In voiceless unaspirated stops, the maximum opening of the glottis (which is not very great) occurs during the stop closure. In (voiceless) aspirated stops, the glottal opening is larger and occurs later, near the moment of release of the stop closure. In murmured stops, the glottal opening is similar in size to that in voiceless unaspirated stops, but it occurs later, during the release of the closure. Because there is a rapid flow of air through the vocal folds at this time, the vocal folds vibrate while remaining slightly apart, thus producing breathy voice.

Learn to produce a series of sounds with different voice onset times. Start by producing fully voiced stops [b, d, g]. For instance, to make a fully voiced [b], try first to keep both the lips and the nose closed while you produce voicing—an unreleased the [b]. You should be making a short murmur. See how long you can make the voicing continue during the unreleased stop. You will find that you can make it last longer during [b] than during [d] or [g], because there is a fairly large space above the glottis in [b]. Air from the lungs can flow through the glottis for a longer period of time before the pressure above the glottis begins to approach that of the air in the lungs. The vocal folds can be kept vibrating throughout this period. But in [g], there is only a small space above the glottis into which air can flow, so the voicing can be maintained only briefly. Languages often fail to have fully voiced velar stops. Note that Thai does not have a voiced stop contrasting with a voiceless unaspirated stop at this place of articulation.

When you can produce fully voiced stops satisfactorily, try saying voiceless unaspirated [p, t, k]. You may find it easiest to start with words such as *spy*, *sty*, *sky*. Say these words very slowly. Now say words like them, but without the initial [s].

You will have less difficulty making aspirated stops because they occur in most forms of English—in words such as *pie* [pʰaɪ] and *tie* [tʰaɪ]. But do try pronouncing all of the Thai and Hindi words in Tables 6.6 and 6.7.

SUMMARY OF ACTIONS OF THE GLOTTIS

The vocal folds are involved in many different kinds of actions. They are used in the production of implosives and ejectives, and in forming different phonation types. These two types of activities often are not clearly separable. The implosives of some forms of Hausa are as likely to be marked by creaky voice as by a downward movement of the glottis, and Zulu has weak ejectives that could well be considered simply as glottal stops superimposed on plosives. Consequently, it is convenient to summarize all these activities in a single table. Table 6.8 shows the principal actions of the glottis.

TABLE 6.8	The principal actions of the glottis.	
Glottal stop	Vocal folds together	ʔ
Ejective	Vocal folds together and moving upward	p', t', k', s'
Implosives	Closed vocal folds moving downward	ɓ, ɗ, ʄ
	Usually nearly closed vocal folds moving downward with regular vibrations or creaky voice	ɓ, ɗ, ʄ
Creaky voice	Vocal folds held tightly together posteriorly, but vibrating (usually at a low rate) anteriorly	b̰, d̰, a̰, ḛ
(Modal) voice	Regular vibrations of the vocal folds	b, d (in, e.g., French), a, e
Breathy voice (murmur)	Vocal folds vibrating without coming fully together.	a̤, e̤
	Often during a stop release	ɓʱ, dʱ
Voiceless	Vocal folds apart	p, t, k, s m̥, n̥, ŋ̥
Aspirated	Vocal folds apart during the release of an articulation	pʰ, tʰ, kʰ, sʰ

RECAP

The main aim of this chapter was to expand your phonetic vocabulary (both in terms of what you know about phonetics abstractly and in terms of which of the sounds of the world's languages you can make) by focusing on the different airstream mechanisms and phonations types that are used in languages around the world. We discussed (1) the velaric ingressive airstream mechanism (clicks—[k͡ǃ], [ŋ͡ǀ], etc.), (2) the glottalic egressive mechanism (ejectives—[k'], [s'], etc.), and (3) the glottalic ingressive mechanism (implosives—[ɓ], [ɗ], etc.). We also discussed different phonation types: (1) creaky voice, which is also called laryngealization, and (2) breathy voice, which is also called murmur. The term given to non-creaky and non-breathy phonation is *modal* voice. The chapter ended with a discussion of voice onset time (VOT) and showed how this one phonetic dimension for separating "voiced" and "voiceless" stop consonants is deployed in different ways in different languages.

166 CHAPTER 6 Airstream Mechanisms and Phonation Types

EXERCISES

(Printable versions of all the exercises are available on the website.)

A. Label the diagram to show the sequence of events involved in producing a voiced alveolar implosive.

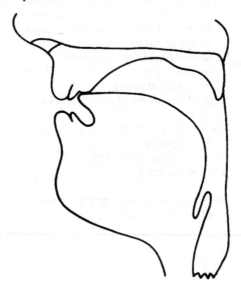

B. Complete the diagram to show the gestures of the vocal organs required for producing [ŋ̊]. Add labels so that the sequence of events is clear.

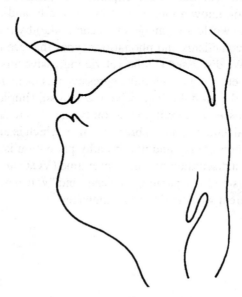

C. Measure (to the nearest 10 ms) the VOT in the waveforms of the stops in *a pie, a buy, a spy.*

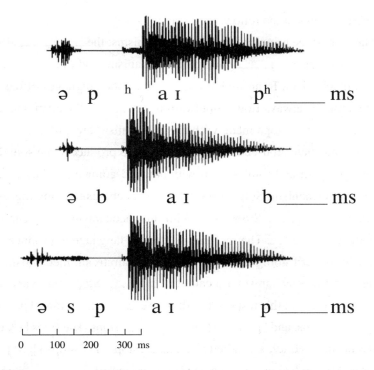

D. Put a narrow transcription above the waveform of the phrase *He started to tidy it*. The phrase has been split during the closure of the [t] in *to*. The location of the [d] in *tidy* is also shown. Measure (to the nearest 10 ms) the VOT in the waveforms of the stops.

First stop in *started* ___ ms.   First stop in *tidy* ___ ms.
Second stop in *started* ___ ms.   Second stop in *tidy* ___ ms.
Stop in *to* ___ ms.

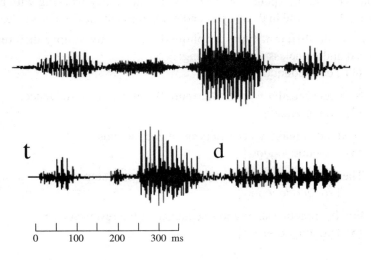

E. Fill in the blanks in the following passage.

There are three principal airstream mechanisms: the _____ airstream mechanism, the _____ airstream mechanism, and the _____ airstream mechanism. In normal utterances in all the languages of the world, the airstream is always flowing outward if _____ the airstream mechanism is involved. Stops made with this mechanism are called _____. The only mechanism used in some languages to produce some sounds with inward-going air and some sounds with outward-going air is the _____ airstream mechanism. Stops made with this mechanism acting ingressively are called _____. Stops made with this mechanism acting egressively are called _____. The mechanism used in language to produce sounds only with inward-going air is the _____ airstream mechanism. Stops made with this mechanism are called _____. Stops may vary in their voice onset time. In this respect, [b, d, g] are _____ stops, [p, t, k] are _____ stops, and [pʰ, tʰ, kʰ] are _____ stops. The stops [bʱ, dʱ, gʱ], which occur in Hindi, are called _____ stops. The stops [ɓ, ɗ], which occur in African languages, such as Hausa, are called _____ stops.

PERFORMANCE EXERCISES

A large number of non-English sounds were discussed in this chapter. About the same number of additional sounds will be considered in the following chapter. Beginning with the exercises that follow, you should spend more time doing practical phonetic work. Try to double the time you spend doing work of this kind. If possible, you should spend about twenty minutes a day working with a partner reviewing the material in the chapter and going through the exercises given below.

A. Review the different types of phonation. Start by simply differentiating voiced and voiceless sounds, saying:

(1) [aaaḁḁḁaaaḁḁḁḁ]

Now add breathy voiced (murmured) sounds to the sequence.

(2) [aaaa̤a̤a̤a̤a̤]

Next, add creaky voiced (laryngealized) sounds.

(3) [a̰a̰a̰aaaa̰a̰a̰a̰a̰]

Then, make the sequence begin with a glottal stop.

(4) [ʔa̰a̰a̰aaaa̰a̰a̰a̰a̰]

Finally, practice saying this sequence in the reverse order.

(5) [a̰a̰a̰a̰a̰aaaa̰a̰a̰ʔ]

B. Try to go in one smooth movement through all these states of the glottis, saying, fairly quickly:

(1) [ʔa̤ɑɑ̰]

and the reverse sequence:

(2) [ɑ̰ɑɑ̤ʔ]

C. Repeat Exercises A and B slowly, quickly, reversed, and so on, with other articulations. For example:

(1) [ʔ m̤ m m̰ m̥]
(2) [ʔ n̤ n n̰ n̥]
(3) [ʔ ŋ̤ ŋ ŋ̰ ŋ̥]
(4) [ʔ l̤ l l̰ l̥]
(5) [ʔ i̤ i ḭ i̥]

D. Try to superimpose breathy voice (murmur) onto intervocalic consonants, saying:

[am̤a, an̤a, al̤a]

Do not worry if the breathy voice is also evident on the adjacent vowels.

E. Now try adding breathy voice to stops. The release of the closure should be followed by a period of murmur extending into the vowel.

[abʱa, adʱa, agʱa]

F. Similarly, add creaky voice (laryngealization) to intervocalic consonants, saying:

[am̰a, an̰a, al̰a]

G. Then produce stops with creaky voice (laryngealization).

[ab̰a, ad̰a, ag̰a]

Again, do not worry if the creaky voice is most evident in the adjacent vowels.

H. Say [aba], making sure that you have a fully voiced intervocalic stop. Now repeat this sequence a number of times, each time increasing the length of the consonant closure. Try to make the consonant closure as long as you can while maintaining the voicing.

I. Repeat Exercise H with the sequences [ada] and [aga].

J. Produce long, fully voiced stops before vowels: [ba, da, ga]. Make sure that there is a velic closure and that you are *not* saying [mba, nda, ŋga], but are correctly saying a long, fully voiced, oral stop.

K. Produce voiceless, unaspirated stops before vowels: [pa, ta, ka]. You may find it helpful to imagine that there is a preceding [s] as in *spar, star, scar*.

L. Say a series of stops with more aspiration than usual: [pʰa, tʰa, kʰa]. Make sure there is a really long period of voicelessness after the release of the closure and before the start of the vowel.

M. Practice saying sequences of voiced, voiceless unaspirated, and aspirated plosives: [ba, pa, pʰa], [da, ta, tʰa], and [ga, ka, kʰa].

N. Try to produce as many intermediate stages as you can in each of these series. You should be able to produce each series with
(1) a long, fully voiced stop.
(2) a slightly shorter, partially voiced stop.
(3) a completely voiceless unaspirated stop.
(4) a slightly aspirated stop.
(5) a strongly aspirated stop.

O. Practice these exercises until you are certain you can reliably produce a distinction between at least (1) voiced, (2) voiceless unaspirated, and (3) aspirated stops at each place of articulation.

P. Extend this series by beginning with a laryngealized stop and ending with a murmured stop. Say:

(1) b̰a	(2) d̰a	(3) g̰a
ba	da	ga
pa	ta	ka
pʰa	tʰa	kʰa
bʱa	dʱa	gʱa

Q. Incorporate all these sounds into simple series of nonsense words. If you are making up your own series to say to someone else, do not make them too difficult. Try saying something like the following.

(1) ˈtemas	(2) ˈbɛkal	(3) ˈgoden
ˈdemas	ˈbʱɛgal	ˈgʱoten
ˈtʰemas	ˈpʰɛkʰal	ˈkoten
ˈd̰emas	ˈb̰egal	ˈkhod̰en
ˈdʱemas	ˈpɛbʱal	ˈgodʱen

R. Review the description of ejectives. When making an ejective, you should be able to *feel* that you (1) make an articulatory closure (e.g., bring your lips together); (2) make a glottal stop (feel that you are holding your breath by closing your glottis); (3) raise the larynx (place your fingers on your throat to feel this movement); (4) release the articulatory closure (open your lips); and (5) release the glottal closure (let go of your breath).

S. If you cannot produce the sequences [p'a, t'a, k'a], reread the section on ejectives to find some useful hints that might help you.

T. Review the description of voiced implosives. Starting from a fully voiced stop, try to feel the downward movement of your larynx. Try to say [ɓa, ɗa, ɠa].

U. Review the description of clicks. Try to say a voiceless version of each click between vowels [ak|a, ak!a, ak‖a], then a voiced version [ag|a, ag!a, ag‖a], and finally a nasalized version [aŋ|a, aŋ!a, aŋ‖a].

V. Incorporate all these sounds into simple series of nonsense words such as:

'dedɑk	'tip'uk	'k'ok|o
'pet'ɑk	'baʄod	'ɓek‖a
'ɓedɑg	'ɗukɑp'	'kak|o
'k'ebɑp	't'eduʄ	't'ik|i

7

Consonantal Gestures

The movements of the lips and tongue in English are only a small subset of those that can be used for making consonants. Scores of other sounds can be made, as we will see by considering different languages. An appropriate way to describe consonantal gestures in the languages of the world is in terms of two of their aspects: the targets of the gestural movements, commonly called the places of articulation, and the way in which the target is approached, often thought of as the manner of articulation. We will use these traditional terms, but always remembering that speech sounds involve gestural movements, not static positions of the vocal organs.

Consonants that occur in other languages are well worth studying even by those concerned mainly with the phonetics of English. Many of the sounds that occur in other languages also occur in regional, accented, or disordered varieties of English. As we noted at the beginning of the previous chapter, the best way to study unfamiliar sounds is by observing them in languages in which they are a regular, easily observable part of the sound system.

ARTICULATORY TARGETS

Many of the possible places of articulation that are used in the languages of the world were defined in Chapter 1. Figure 7.1, which is similar to Figure 1.5, shows three additional places that will be discussed below. The terms for all the places of articulation are not just names for particular locations on the roof of the mouth. They should be thought of as names for the numbered arrows. Each term specifies where the arrow starts (the articulator on the lower surface that makes this particular gesture) and where it ends (the part of the vocal tract that is the target of the gesture).

A large number of non-English sounds are to be found in other languages. Many of them involve using gestures in which the target, or the place of articulation, is different from any found in English. For others it is the type of gesture, what is traditionally called the manner of articulation, that is different. We will illustrate the different targets by considering how each place of articulation is used in English and in other languages for making stops, nasals, and fricatives. The numbers in the following paragraphs refer to the numbered arrows in Figure 7.1.

Figure 7.1 Places of articulation.

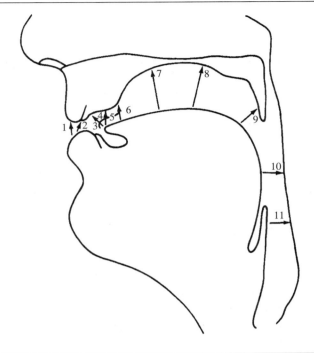

(1) The **bilabial** gesture is common in English, which has bilabial stops and nasals [p, b, m]. But bilabial fricatives in English are simply allophones of the labiodental sounds [f, v]. In some languages (e.g., Ewe of West Africa), bilabial fricatives contrast with labiodental fricatives. The symbols for the voiceless and voiced bilabial fricatives are [ɸ, β]. These sounds are pronounced by bringing the two lips nearly together, so that there is only a slit between them. In Ewe, the name of the language itself is [èβè], whereas the word for *two* is [èvè]. Try to pronounce these contrasting words yourself. Ewe also contrasts voiceless bilabial and labiodental fricatives. Contrasts involving all these sounds are shown in Table 7.1.

EXAMPLE 7.1

We should also note here some other labial sounds not shown in Figure 7.1. A few Austronesian languages spoken in Vanuatu have **linguo-labials**, in which the tongue touches the upper lip. V'enen Taut has nasals, stops, and fricatives made in this way. The diacritic for indicating a linguo-labial articulation is [̼], a shape like a seagull, placed under the coronal symbol. The V'enen Taut for "breadfruit" is [t̼atei], and for "stone" is [nað̼at]. These and other V'enen Taut sounds are on the website.

EXAMPLE 7.2

(2) Many languages are like English in having the **labiodental** fricatives [f, v]. But probably no language has labiodental stops or nasals except as allophones of the corresponding bilabial sounds. In English, a labiodental nasal, [ɱ], may

TABLE 7.1 Contrasting bilabial and labiodental fricatives in Ewe.

Voiceless bilabial fricative	éɸá 'he polished'	éɸlè 'he bought'
Voiceless labiodental fricative	éfá 'he was cold'	éflé 'he spit off'
Voiced bilabial fricative	èβè 'Ewe' (the language)	éβló 'mushroom'
Voiced labiodental fricative	èvè 'two'	évló 'he is evil'

occur when / m / occurs before / f /, as in *emphasis* or *symphony*. Say these words in a normal conversational style and see if your lower lip ever contacts your upper lip during the nasal.

Some languages have affricates in which the bilabial stop is released into a labiodental fricative. Practice these sounds by learning to say the German words *Pfanne* ['pfanə] 'bowl' and *Pflug* [pfluk] 'plough.'

(3) Most speakers of both British and American English have **dental** fricatives [θ, ð] but no dental stops, nasals, or laterals except allophonically before [θ, ð], as in *eighth, tenth, wealth* [eɪt̪θ, tən̪θ, wəl̪θ]. Many speakers of French, Italian, and other languages typically have dental stops, nasals, and laterals. In these languages, [t̪, d̪, n̪] are not just coarticulated allophones that occur only before [θ, ð], as in English. However, there is a great deal of individual variation in the pronunciation of these consonants in all these languages. According to a careful palatographic study, around one-third of Californian English speakers have dental stops, and many French speakers have alveolar rather than dental consonants—well over half of them in the case of the lateral /l/. Say words such as *tip, dip, nip, lip* and try to feel where your tongue touches the roof of your mouth.

Some languages, such as Malayalam, a Dravidian language spoken in southern India, contrast dental and alveolar consonants. Examples of contrasting Malayalam nasals are shown in Table 7.2. The table also includes other consonantal gestures that are used in Malayalam but not in most forms of English. We will discuss these in subsequent paragraphs.

(4) **Alveolar** stops, nasals, and fricatives all occur in English and in many other languages. They need no further comment here.

(5) **Retroflex** stops, nasals, and fricatives do not occur in most forms of English. The outstanding exception is the English spoken in India. Retroflex sounds are made by curling the tip of the tongue up and back so that the underside touches or approaches the back part of the alveolar ridge. The symbols used by IPA for retroflex sounds include [ʈ, ɖ, ɳ]. Remember that, just as *dental* is a gesture that can be defined as an articulator (the tip of the tongue) and a target (the upper teeth), so also *retroflex* describes a gesture involving the underside of the tip

EXAMPLE 7.3

TABLE 7.2	Contrasts involving bilabial, dental, alveolar, retroflex, palatal, and velar places of articulation in Malayalam, illustrating the necessity for six points of articulation. As we saw in Chapter 3, dental articulations are indicated by a subscript [̪].	
Bilabial	**Dental**	**Alveolar**
kʌmmi	pʌn̪n̪i	kʌnni
'shortage'	'pig'	'first'
Retroflex	**Palatal**	**Velar**
kʌɳɳi	kʌɲɲi	kuŋŋi
'link in chain'	'boiled rice and water'	'crushed'

of the tongue and a target, the back of the alveolar ridge. Students sometimes imagine that the term *retroflex* describes a manner of articulation, but in fact it is a place of articulation like dental and alveolar. At each of these places of articulation, it is possible to produce stops, nasals, fricatives, and sounds made with other manners of articulation. As we saw in Tables 6.2 and 6.7, the languages Sindhi and Hindi contrast several types of retroflex stops. Malayalam (Table 7.2) contrasts three coronal gestures—dental, alveolar, and retroflex. In addition, Malayalam has bilabial, palatal, and velar sounds, so that it contrasts nasals with six basic types of gesture, six places of articulation, all of which are exemplified in Table 7.2.

Because a retroflex gesture is made with the undersurface of the tip of the tongue touching or near the back of the alveolar ridge, the blade (the upper surface of the tip) of the tongue is usually a considerable distance from the roof of the mouth. As a result, the tongue is somewhat hollowed, as shown in the diagram of a retroflex fricative [ʂ] in Figure 7.2. Try making this sound yourself. Start with [s], in which the tip of the tongue is raised toward the front part of the alveolar ridge. Now, while maintaining the fricative noise, slowly slide the tip of the tongue back, curling it up as you move it backward. You will be producing a consonant [ʂ], which sounds something like [ʃ], although the articulatory position is different. (See (6) below for discussion of the articulatory position of [ʃ].)

When you have learned to say [ʂ], try adding voice so that you produce [ʐ]. Alternate the voiced and voiceless sounds [sssʐʐʐʂʂʂʐʐʐ]. Next, still with the tip of the tongue curled up and back in this position, make the stops [ʈa, ɖa]. Notice how the stops affect the quality of the following vowel, giving it a sort of *r*-coloring at the beginning. Now produce the corresponding nasal [ɳ]. Learn to say all these sounds before and after different vowels. Finally, try to say the Malayalam words in Table 7.2. You may notice as you imitate these sounds that your tongue tip moves during the retroflex stops, sliding forward from post-alveolar toward a more alveolar place of articulation during the retroflex stop, so that the preceding vowel has more *r*-coloring than the following vowel.

Figure 7.2 The articulation of the retroflex fricative [ʂ]. The dashed lines indicate the position of the sides of the tongue.

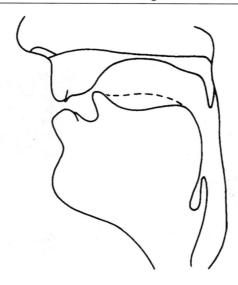

This occurs in Malayalam too. Figure 7.3 (on the next page) shows a spectrogram of the Malayalam word [kʌɳɳi] "link in chain," in which we have traced with a white line the third vowel "formant"—the third highest acoustic resonance of the vocal tract. The third formant is known to go down in frequency for retroflex sounds. Notice in Figure 7.3 that the third formant drops to a low value at the offset of the vowel [ʌ] preceding [ɳɳ] and then at the end of [ɳɳ] picks up at a somewhat higher value at the start of the following vowel [i]. This acoustic dynamic is a reflection of the articulatory dynamics of the tongue tip sliding forward along the roof of the mouth during [ɳɳ].

Retroflex stops and nasals occur in many of the major languages of India, and retroflex fricatives are not at all uncommon. They vary somewhat in the degree to which the tip of the tongue is curled backward. In Hindi and other languages of northern India, retroflex sounds often have the tip of the tongue only slightly behind the most prominent part of the alveolar ridge, much as indicated in Figure 7.2. In Malayalam and other languages spoken in the southern India, the tip is curled farther back, so that the underside of the tip of the tongue touches the roof of the mouth.

(6) The **palato-alveolar** gestures for [ʃ, ʒ] differ from retroflex gestures in the part of the tongue involved. The IPA chart uses the term "post-alveolar" for these sounds. We prefer the somewhat more specific term palato-alveolar. A palato-alveolar gesture is one in which the target on the upper surface of the mouth is about the same as for a retroflex sound—at the margin between the alveolar ridge and the front of the palate. But unlike retroflexes, in this gesture, the front of

178 CHAPTER 7 Consonantal Gestures

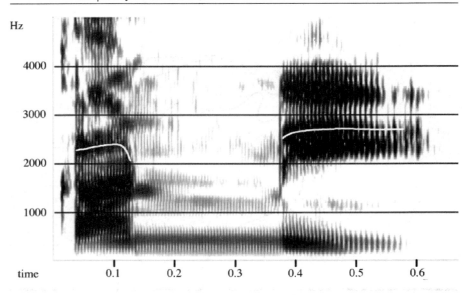

Figure 7.3 A spectrogram of the Malayalam word [kʌɳɳi] *link in chain*. The frequency of the third formant is traced with a white line.

the tongue is slightly domed, as opposed to being hollowed. Compare Figure 1.11, which shows the position of the vocal organs in the palato-alveolar fricative [ʃ] as in *shy*, with the retroflex fricative in Figure 7.2. Note that in both [ʂ] and [ʃ], the maximum constriction of the vocal tract occurs near the back of the alveolar ridge. But these two sounds are said to have different places of articulation, because the terms specify different gestures. The place of articulation designates both the target on the roof of the mouth and the part of the tongue moving toward that target. In retroflex sounds, it is the movement of the underside of the tip of the tongue that forms the gesture, but in palato-alveolar sounds, the active articulator is the tongue blade.

Another way of distinguishing between retroflex and palato-alveolar sounds is to call them all post-alveolar and, in addition, name the part of the tongue involved. Sounds made with the tip of the tongue may be called **apical**, and those made with the blade may be called **laminal**. Thus, the term *retroflex* is exactly equivalent to *apical post-alveolar*, and *palato-alveolar* is equivalent to *laminal post-alveolar*.

EXAMPLE 7.4

There are advantages in introducing the terms *apical* and *laminal* in that they may also apply to other gestures. Dental sounds may be made with the tip of the tongue, or with the blade of the tongue, and so may alveolar sounds. With the use of these extra terms, we can distinguish between the apical dental stops that occur in Hindi (Table 6.7) and the laminal dental stops that occur in French.

In Australian aboriginal languages, the difference between apical and laminal sounds is often very important. If you want to pursue this further, go to the map index under "extras" at the website, and check out the aboriginal languages spoken in Australia.

In English, the only post-alveolar sounds are the palato-alveolar fricatives and affricates [ʃ, ʒ, tʃ, dʒ]. In other languages, such as French and Italian, there are nasals made in either the same or a very similar position. These nasals are often, arbitrarily, considered to be palatal sounds. No language that we know of makes a distinction between a palato-alveolar nasal and a palatal nasal. Some of the palatal sounds in Italian will be discussed later in this chapter.

The IPA chart puts palato-alveolars into the post-alveolar column. A section labeled "other symbols" also mentions **alveolo-palatals** and provides the symbols [ɕ, ʑ]. These symbols are used for voiceless and voiced fricatives in Polish and Chinese. Though similar to [ʃ, ʒ], they have considerable raising of the front of the tongue. They are also made in the post-alveolar region. Tables illustrating contrasting fricatives in Polish and Chinese are at the website. Both these languages are interesting because they have dental or alveolar, post-alveolar (retroflex), and alveolo-palatal fricatives.

EXAMPLE 7.5

We have discussed three kinds of post-alveolar sounds. These are all sounds in which the major constriction lies somewhere between the alveolar ridge and the dome of the palate. As we mentioned, we prefer to use the terms *palato-alveolar*, *alveolo-palatal*, and *retroflex* because they convey more information than the more generic term *post-alveolar*. For instance, a palato-alveolar sound is basically alveolar (in tongue-body shape) with a post-alveolar constriction location, while an alveolo-palatal is basically a palatal sound (with a tongue-body shape more like the vowel [i]) but also with a post-alveolar constriction location. It should be noted though that these sounds are produced with a good deal of individual variation, as small differences in the shape of the roof of the mouth can have a big impact on the acoustic output. So, ultimately what is important from a speaker's point of view is to produce a noise that is accepted as the intended sound, and for some speakers this means that their alveolo-palatal may look quite a lot like another person's palato-alveolar. This highlights the importance of the ear training and production training exercises in each chapter of this book. (Note: There are some disagreements among authorities as to the best descriptions of these sounds.)

(7) **Palatal** sounds can be defined as being made with the front of the tongue approaching or touching the hard palate, and for many speakers, with the tip of the tongue down behind the lower front teeth. There is no clear-cut distinction between these sounds and palato-alveolar sounds. The only true palatal in English is / j /, which is usually an approximant but may be allophonically a voiceless fricative in words such as *hue*. The symbol for a voiceless palatal fricative is [ç], so this word may be transcribed phonemically as /hju/ and phonetically as [çu]. Voiceless palatal fricatives occur in German in words such as *ich* [ɪç], meaning 'I,' and *nicht* [nɪçt], 'not.'

Say [ç] as in *hue* and then try to prolong this sound. Add voice so that you make a fricative something like the [j] as in *you*, but with the front of the tongue nearer the hard palate. The symbol [ʝ], a curly-tailed *j*, is used for a voiced palatal fricative. Say [çççjjjçççjjj], making sure that the tip of the tongue is down behind the lower front teeth. Now change the fricative [ç] into a stop by raising the front of the tongue still more, while keeping the tip of the tongue down. The symbols for voiceless and voiced palatal stops are [c, ɟ]. Say sequences such as [aca] and [aɟa], making sure that the front of your tongue touches the hard palate but that the tip of the tongue is down. Then try making similar sequences with a palatal nasal (for which the symbol is [ɲ], reminding one of [n] and [j] combined).

EXAMPLE 7.11

Palatal nasals occur in several languages, including French, Spanish, Italian, and many non–Indo-European languages. Try saying French words such as *agneau* [aɲo] 'lamb' and Spanish words such as *Señor* [seɲor] 'Mr.' Examples of Italian palatal nasals (and laterals) are at the website. Palatal stops are slightly less common than palatal nasals. They occur, for example, in Hungarian (you can search for them in the language index at the website), and they are part of the set of Sindhi stops discussed in the previous chapter and exemplified in Table 6.2 and at the website. Because of the shape of the roof of the mouth, the contact between the front of the tongue and the hard palate often extends over a fairly large area. As a result, the formation and release of a palatal stop is often not as rapid as in the case of other stops, and they tend to become affricates.

EXAMPLE 6.3

(8) **Velar** stops and nasals [k, g, ŋ] occur in English. But unlike other languages such as German, we no longer have velar fricatives. They are not, however, hard to make. Starting from a syllable such as [ak], build up pressure behind the velar closure, and then lower the tongue slightly. The result will be a voiceless velar fricative, which we write as [x]. The symbol for the corresponding voiced sound is [ɣ]. As with other fricatives, learn to say [xxxɣɣɣxxx]. Then produce sequences such as [axa, exe, oɣo, əɣə].

EXAMPLE 6.2

Examples of words in other languages containing velar fricatives are Lakhota, as shown in Table 6.1; German *Achtung* [ʔaxtʊŋ] 'warning'; *Bach* [bax] 'Bach' (proper name); and Spanish *jamás* [xaˈmas] 'never' *ojo* [ˈoxo] 'eye' *pago* [ˈpaɣo] 'I pay' and *diga* [ˈdiɣa] 'speak.' The Spanish [ɣ] is often not very fricative, and may be more accurately transcribed using the symbol for a voiced velar approximant, which is [ɰ]. The part of the tongue involved in making velar sounds, the back of the tongue, is called the **dorsum**; these sounds are referred to as *dorsal sounds.*

EXAMPLE 7.6

(9) **Uvular** sounds are made by raising the back of the tongue toward the uvula. In a broader grouping of sounds, they, like velar sounds, can be called dorsal. They do not occur at all in most forms of English. But in French, a voiced uvular fricative—[ʁ]—is the common form of *r* in words such as *rouge* [ʁuʒ] 'red' and *rose* [ʁoz] 'rose,' more like an approximant. The voiceless uvular fricative, [χ], also occurs in French as an allophone of / ʁ / after voiceless stops,

TABLE 7.3	Contrasts involving stops in Quechua.		
	Palato-alveolar	**Velar**	**Uvular**
	tʃaka	kujuj	qaʎu
	'bridge'	'to move'	'tongue'
	tʃʰaka	kʰujuj	qʰaʎu
	'large ant'	'to whistle'	'shawl'
	tʃ'aka	k'ujuj	q'aʎu
	'hoarse'	'to twist'	'tomato sauce'

as in *lettre* [lətχ] 'letter.' French differs from English in that it often has perseverative assimilations in which, for example, the voicelessness of one sound continues on through the following sound.

Uvular stops, written [q, ɢ], and nasals, written [ɴ], occur as idiosyncratic pronunciations in English and as part of the regular sound systems of Eskimo, Aleut, and other Native American languages. Table 7.3 illustrates contrasts between uvular and velar stops and palato-alveolar affricates in Quechua, a Native American language widely spoken in Bolivia, Chile, and Peru. Note that Quechua has voiceless unaspirated plosives, aspirated plosives, and ejectives.

One way of learning to produce uvular sounds is to start from a voiceless velar fricative [x]. While making this sound, slide your tongue slightly farther back in your mouth so that it is close to the uvula. The result will be the voiceless uvular fricative [χ]. Learn to make this sound before and after vowels, in sequences such as [aχa, oχo, uχu]. You will find it easier to use back vowels at first; then go on to sequences such as [eχe, iχi]. Next, add voice to this sound, saying [χχχʁʁʁχχχʁʁʁ]. Practice saying [ʁ] before and after vowels. Try saying the French words cited in the first paragraph of this section, (9).

Once you have mastered the pronunciation of uvular fricatives, try changing them into uvular stops. Say [aχa], then make a stop at the same place of articulation, saying [aqa]. Now produce a voiced uvular stop [aɢa] and a uvular nasal [aɴa]. Practice all these sounds before and after different vowels.

(10)(11) The gestures for **pharyngeal** and **epiglottal** sounds involve pulling the root of the tongue or the epiglottis back toward the back wall of the pharynx. Many people cannot make a stop gesture at this position. Furthermore, it would be literally impossible to make a pharyngeal or epiglottal nasal. Closure that deep in the vocal tract would prevent the airstream from coming through the nose. But pharyngeal fricatives, shown by the symbols [ħ, ʕ], can be made, and they do in fact occur in Semitic languages such as Arabic and Hebrew. The Arabic word for 'bath' is [ħammaam], for 'uncle' [ʕamm]. The articulation varies considerably in the Semitic languages, some speakers using epiglottal and others pharyngeal gestures. These sounds also vary considerably with regard to the degree of constriction. For many speakers, there is little or no actual friction, so that approximants rather than fricatives are produced. The voiced fricative made in this region usually has a great deal of laryngealization (creaky voice), perhaps because the necessary constriction in the pharynx also causes a constriction in the larynx. Neither Hebrew, Arabic, nor any of the other Semitic languages distinguish between pharyngeal and epiglottal fricatives; but some of the languages of the Caucasus contrast these two possibilities. The website has a recording of Agul, which contrasts voiceless pharyngeal [ħ] and epiglottal [ʜ] fricatives.

Non-native speakers of Agul find it difficult to distinguish pharyngeal and epiglottal sounds, but it is worth practicing the contrast as you listen to the Agul examples. If you try to constrict your pharynx as much as possible, you will probably be doing so by retracting the epiglottis. Try to produce the voiceless sound [ħ]. Now, if you can, produce this sound before a vowel. Next, try to make the voiced sound [ʕ], not worrying if it turns out to have creaky voice. Produce these sounds in the Arabic words cited above.

Before finishing this section on gestures at different places of articulation, we must note that some sounds involve the simultaneous use of two gestures. The English approximant [w] has both an approximation of the lips (making it a bilabial sound) and of the back of the tongue and the soft palate (making it a velar sound). Sounds that involve these two gestures are called **labial velars**, or, in some more old-fashioned books, **labiovelars**.

Yoruba, Ewe, Tiv, and many other languages spoken in West Africa have labial velar stops. Some of the languages spoken in this area also have labial velar nasals. As in the case of nasal and voiced clicks, we can symbolize two co-occurring articulations with a tie bar joining two symbols. The Yoruba for 'arm' is [ak͡pá] and for 'adult' is [àg͡bà]. In these words, the two closures occur almost simultaneously. Of course you can say the sequence [akpa] and naturally get some overlap of the two stop consonant gestures, but one of the best ways of learning to say the two consonant gestures simultaneously is to start by making a bilabial click (a kissing sound, but with the lips being simply compressed and not puckered) between vowels. Say [a] 'kiss' [a] at first slowly, and then as fast as you can. Then weaken the suction component of the kiss, so that you are making little more than a labial velar articulation between vowels. The result should be a labial velar stop much as in the Yoruba word [ak͡pá], 'arm.' (More information about Yoruba labial velars can be found at the website by using the language index.)

This is a convenient place to review all the places of articulation we have discussed so far. Table 7.4 is a consonant chart showing the symbols for all the nasals, stops, and fricatives that have been mentioned, except for the epiglottal consonants. Check that you know the values of all these symbols. Remember that you can hear Peter Ladefoged's pronunciation of them at the website by clicking on the IPA chart.

TABLE 7.4	Symbols for nasals, stops, and fricatives. As in all consonant charts, when there are two symbols within a single cell, the one on the left indicates a voiceless sound.										
		bilabial	labiodental	dental	alveolar	retroflex	palato-alveolar	palatal	velar	uvular	pharyngeal	labial velar
nasal		m	ɱ	n̪	n	ɳ		ɲ	ŋ	ɴ		ŋ͡m
stop		p b		t̪ d̪	t d	ʈ ɖ		c ɟ	k g	q ɢ		k͡p g͡b
fricative		ɸ β	f v	θ ð	s z	ʂ ʐ	ʃ ʒ	ç ʝ	x ɣ	χ ʁ	ħ ʕ	

TYPES OF ARTICULATORY GESTURES

Stops

We can begin our consideration of the different manners of articulatory gestures that occur in the languages of the world by reviewing what has been said already about stop consonants. Table 7.5 illustrates a number of different types of stops, most of which have been discussed earlier in this book. The first seven possibilities were discussed in Chapter 6. Make sure you understand all these terms and know what all these stops sound like, even if you cannot make them all yourself.

TABLE 7.5	Examples of stop consonants.		
Description	Symbol	Example	
1. voiced	b	banu	(Sindhi 'forest')
2. voiceless unaspirated	p	panu	(Sindhi 'leaf')
3. aspirated	pʰ	pʰanu	(Sindhi 'snake hood')
4. murmured (breathy)	bʱ	bʱaːnu	(Sindhi 'manure')
5. implosive	ɓ	ɓani	(Sindhi 'field')
6. laryngealized (creaky)	b̰	b̰aːtà	(Hausa 'spoil')
7. ejective	k'	k'aːràː	(Hausa 'increase')
8. nasal release	dn	dno	(Russian 'bottom')
9. prenasalized	nd	ndizi	(Swahili 'banana')
10. lateral release	tɬ	tɬàh	(Navajo 'oil, ointment')
11. ejective lateral release	tɬ'	tɬ'éeʔ	(Navajo 'night')
12. affricate	ts	tsaɪt	(German 'time')
13. ejective affricate	ts'	ts'áal	(Navajo 'cradle')

The only comment on the first seven sounds that it is necessary to add here—where they are all listed together—is that no language distinguishes between (5), an implosive [ɓ], and (6), a laryngealized (creaky-voiced) [b̰]. Certain languages have the one sound, and others the other. In a few languages, both sounds occur as allophones or as free variants of the same phoneme. They have not been found in contrast with each other.

Stops with nasal release, the eighth possibility listed in Table 7.5, were discussed in relation to English in Chapter 3. Nasal plosion occurs in English at the ends of words such as *hidden* and *sudden*. In some languages, however, it can occur at the beginning of a word. Try to say the Russian word for 'bottom' which is [dno].

The next possibility listed in Table 7.5 is the prenasalized stop [nd], which is in some senses the reverse of a nasally released stop. In a prenasalized stop, the oral closure—in this case an alveolar gesture—is formed first, while the soft palate is lowered. Then there is a short nasal consonant, after which the soft palate is raised so that there is a stop. This stop is released by removing the oral closure (in this case by lowering the tongue tip) while the soft palate remains raised. Prenasalized stops occur in many African languages. Say the Swahili words *ndege* [ndege] 'bird, airplane,' *ntu* [ntu] 'wax.' (Swahili is a language in which the orthography itself is equivalent to a broad IPA transcription.) When you make these sounds, be careful not to make the initial nasal component into a separate syllable. Make it as short as possible.

Stops with lateral release (see (10) in Table 7.5) were previously discussed in relation to their occurrence in English (e.g., in *little*, *ladle*). In other languages, they can occur initially in a word. Sometimes, as indicated by (11) in Table 7.5, laterally released stops can occur with an ejective airstream mechanism. On these occasions, the stop closure for [t] is formed, the glottalic egressive (ejective) airstream mechanism is set in motion, and then the stop is released laterally by lowering the sides of the tongue. The examples in (10) and (11) in Table 7.5 are from a Native American language, Navajo. (Listen to examples for chapter 11 at the website.)

The only affricates that can occur initially in most forms of English are [tʃ, dʒ]. Some dialects (e.g., London Cockney) have a slightly affricated stop of a kind that might be written [tˢ] in words such as *tea* [tˢəi]. Alveolar affricates also occur in German, as shown in (12) in Table 7.5. In addition, German has a bilabial affricate [pf], as in *Pflug* [pfluk] 'plough.' Affricates can also occur with an ejective airstream mechanism. Example (13) in Table 7.5 is from Navajo, which, in addition to the ejective [ts'], also has the affricate [ts] made with a pulmonic airstream mechanism as in German.

Nasals

We will now consider the other manners of articulation used in the languages of the world. Little more need be said about nasals. Like stops, they can occur voiced or voiceless (e.g., in Burmese, which can be found in the chapter 11 exercises at the website). As voiceless nasals are comparatively rare, they are symbolized simply by adding the voiceless diacritic [̥] under the symbol for the voiced sound. There are no special symbols for voiceless nasals.

Fricatives

There are two ways to produce the rough, turbulent flow that occurs in the airstream during a fricative. It may be just the result of the air passing through a narrow gap, as in the formation of [f]. Or it may be because the airstream is first speeded up by being forced through a narrow gap and then is directed over a sharp edge, such as the teeth, as in the production of [s]. Partly because there are these two possible mechanisms, the total number of different fricatives that have been observed is larger than the number of stops or the number of nasals. Table 7.4 shows ten pairs of fricative symbols, compared with seven pairs of stop symbols and eight nasal symbols.

So far, we have classified fricatives as voiced or voiceless and as made with a number of different articulatory gestures. But we can also subdivide fricatives in accordance with other aspects of the gestures that produce them. Some authorities have divided fricatives into those such as [s], in which the tongue is grooved so that the airstream comes out through a narrow channel, and those such as [θ], in which the tongue is flat and forms a wide slit through which the air flows. Unfortunately, not enough is known about fricatives to be sure how this distinction should be applied in all cases. It is also clearly irrelevant for fricatives made with the lips and the back of the tongue.

A slightly better way of dividing fricatives is to separate them into groups on a purely auditory basis. Say the English voiceless fricatives [f, θ, s, ʃ]. Which two have the loudest high pitches? You should be able to hear that [s, ʃ] differ from [f, θ] in this way. The same kind of difference occurs between the voiced fricatives [z, ʒ] and [v, ð]. The fricatives [s, z, ʃ, ʒ] are called **sibilant** sounds. They have more acoustic energy—that is, greater loudness—at a higher pitch than the other fricatives.

The sound patterns that occur in languages often arise because of auditory properties of sounds. We can divide fricatives into sibilant and nonsibilant sounds only by reference to auditory properties. We need to divide them into these two groups to show how English plurals are formed. Consider words ending in fricatives, such as *cliff, moth, kiss, dish, church, dove, lathe, maze, rouge, judge*. Which of these words add an extra syllable in forming the plural? If you say them over to yourself, you will find that they are all monosyllables in the singular. But those that end with one of the sounds [s, ʃ, z, ʒ]—that is, with a sibilant fricative or an affricate containing a sibilant fricative—become two syllables in the plural. It seems as though English does not favor two sibilant sounds together. It breaks them up by inserting a vowel before adding a sibilant suffix to words ending in sibilants.

Trills, Taps, and Flaps

The most common pronunciation of the sound written with the letter "r" in the languages of the world is the trilled [r]. This is why the IPA uses the common letter [r] for **trill** and the typographically unusual symbol [ɹ] for the phonetically unusual rhotic approximate found in English. Some languages contrast a long and short trilled [r]. You can listen to this contrast in Icelandic at the website— use the language index to find the page. The spectrogram in Figure 7.4 shows an Icelandic minimal pair contrasting these sounds in the words [sauːra] *wound* (gen. pl.) and [sauːra] *sore* (gen. pl.). As the arrows in the spectrogram indicate, in the short [r] there is one contact of the tongue on the roof of the mouth, while in the long [rː] there are three contacts. In both cases, the tongue contacts in the trill are driven by an aerodynamic force in much the same way that vocal fold vibration in voicing is driven by airflow. So, even in the case of a very short trill in which there is only a single contact with the roof of the mouth, the movement is different from that in a tap, or a flap. In a trill, the tip of the tongue is set in motion by the current of air. A **tap** or a **flap** is caused by a single contraction of the muscles so that one articulator is thrown against another. It is often just a very rapid stop gesture.

It is useful to distinguish between taps and flaps. In a tap, the tip of the tongue simply moves up to contact the roof of the mouth in the dental or alveolar region, and then moves back to the floor of the mouth along the same path. In a flap, the tip of the tongue is first curled up and back in a retroflex gesture, and then strikes the roof of the mouth in the post-alveolar region as it returns to its position behind the lower front teeth. The distinction between taps and flaps is thus to some extent bound up with what might be called a distinction in place of articulation. Flaps are typically retroflex articulations, but it is possible to make the articulatory gesture required for a flap at other places of articulation. The tongue can be pulled back and then, as it is flapped forward, made to strike the alveolar ridge or even the teeth, making alveolar or dental flaps. Flaps are distinguished

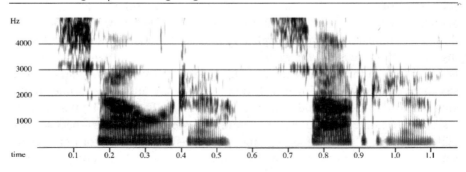

Figure 7.4 A spectrogram of the words [sauːra] *wound* (gen. pl.) and [sauːra] *sore* (gen. pl.) showing long and short trilled [r].

from taps by the direction of the movement—from back to front for flaps, up and down for taps—rather than by the exact point of contact.

Some forms of American English have both taps and flaps. Taps occur as the regular pronunciation of / t, d, n / in words such as *latter, ladder, tanner*. The flap occurs in words that have an *r*-colored vowel in the stressed syllable. In *dirty* and *sorting*, speakers who have the tongue bunched or retracted for the *r*-colored vowel will produce a flap as they move the tongue forward for the non-*r*-colored vowel.

Trills are rare in most forms of English. The stage version of a Scottish accent with trilled / r / is not typical of most Scots. In Scottish English, / r / is more likely to be pronounced as a tap. The American pronunciation of *petal* with a voiced alveolar tap in the middle will sound to a Scotsman from Edinburgh like his regular pronunciation of *pearl*.

The distinction between trills and different kinds of taps and flaps is much more important in other languages. But before this point can be illustrated, we must review the symbols that can be used for different types of *r* sounds. In a broad transcription for English, they can all be transcribed as / r /. But in a narrower transcription, this symbol is restricted to voiced alveolar trills. An alveolar tap may be symbolized by the special symbol [ɾ], and the post-alveolar (retroflex) flap by [ɽ]. The approximant that occurs in most Americans' pronunciation of "r" may be symbolized by [ɹ], an upside-down *r*. If it is important to show that this sound is particularly retroflex, the symbol [ɻ] may be used. Most speakers of American English do not have a retroflex approximant, but for those who do, [ɻ] is an appropriate symbol in a narrow transcription. All these symbols are shown in Table 7.6.

As illustrated in Table 7.6, Spanish distinguishes between a trill and a tap in words such as *perro* [pero] 'dog' and *pero* [peɾo] 'but.' Similar distinctions also occur in some forms of Tamil, a language of southern India. This language, like Hausa (Nigeria), may also distinguish between an alveolar tap and a retroflex flap.

TABLE 7.6	Specific symbols for types of r, and for bilabial trills. Note the use of [*] as a special symbol that can be defined and used when there is no prescribed symbol.		
r	voiced alveolar trill	[pero]	(Spanish 'dog')
ɾ	voiced alveolar tap	[peɾo]	(Spanish 'but')
ɽ	voiced retroflex flap	[báɽà:]	(Hausa 'servant')
ɹ	voiced alveolar approximant	[ɹɛd]	(English 'red')
r̝	voiced alveolar fricative trill	[r̝ɛk]	(Czech 'rivers')
R	voiced uvular trill	[Ruʒ]	(Provençal French 'red')
ʁ	voiced uvular fricative or approximant	[ʁuʒ]	(Parisian French 'red')
ʙ	voiced bilabial trill	[mʙulim]	(Kele 'your face')
*	voiced labiodental flap	[bé*ú]	(Margi 'flying away')

Trills may also have accompanying friction, as in the Czech example in Table 7.6, which uses the IPA diacritic [˒], meaning raised (and thus more fricative).

Learning to make a trill involves placing the tongue, very loosely, in exactly the right position so that it will be set in vibration by a current of air. The easiest position seems to be with the tongue just behind the upper front teeth and very lightly touching the alveolar ridge. If you get the tongue in just the right position and relaxed, you can blow across the top of it, setting it vibrating in a voiceless trill. Many people find it easier to start with a voiceless trill and then add voicing once they can make steady vibrations. The jaw should be fairly closed, leaving a space of 5 mm between the front teeth. Check this by inserting the top of a pencil between your teeth, and then removing it before making the sound. The problem experienced by most people who fail to make trills is that the blade of the tongue is too stiff.

Most people can learn to produce a voiced tap by adopting the typical American English pronunciation of words such as *Betty* (which can be transcribed as [ˈbɛɾi]). You should also be able to produce a retroflex flap. As we have seen, many speakers of American English use this type of articulation in sequences such as *herding* [hɚɽɪŋ], in which the tongue is curled up and back after the *r*-colored vowel, and then strikes the back part of the alveolar ridge as it moves down during the consonant.

EXAMPLE 7.9

When you have mastered all these sounds, try saying them in different contexts. You might also learn to say voiced and voiceless trills, taps, and flaps. Try varying the place of articulation, producing both dental and post-alveolar trills and flaps. Some languages, such as Malayalam and Toda, spoken in southern India, contrast alveolar and dental trills. The word for 'room' in Malayalam is [ara], whereas the word for 'half' is [ara̪]. The Toda rhotics at the website illustrate an even more complex situation in which three kinds of trill are contrasted.

The tongue tip is not the only articulator that can be trilled. Uvular trills occur in some dialects of French, although, as we have noted already, most forms of French have a uvular fricative in words such as 'rose' [ʁoz]. The symbol for a uvular trill is [ʀ]. There is no symbol to distinguish between uvular fricatives and approximants because this phonetic difference is not used to distinguish words in any language. Both sounds are symbolized by [ʁ].

EXAMPLE lg. index

Trills involving the lips occur in a few languages. The IPA symbol for these sounds is a small capital [ʙ] (just as a small capital [ʀ] is used for a uvular trill). In Kele and Titan, two languages spoken in Papua New Guinea, bilabial trills occur in a large number of words. The Titan for 'rat' is [mʙulei]. To pronounce the first part of this word you need to hold the lips loosely together while making [m], and then blow the lips apart. Some people find it easier to trill the lips than the tongue tip. If you are having difficulty making an alveolar trill [r], see if you can get the sensation of making a trill by making a bilabial trill [ʙ]. Kele and Titan bilabial trills are illustrated at the website.

Peter Ladefoged also reported hearing a labiodental flap—in Margi, of northern Nigeria—in which the lower lip is drawn back inside the upper teeth and then allowed to strike against them in passing back to its normal position. There is no IPA symbol for this sound. We included this sound in Table 7.6 to demonstrate how to symbolize a sound for which there is no IPA symbol. In all such cases, it is possible to use an asterisk and define it, as we have done in the table.

Laterals

In Chapter 1, we regarded the term *lateral* as if it specified a manner of articulation in a way comparable to other terms such as *fricative*, or *stop*, or *approximant*. But this is really an oversimplification. The central–lateral opposition can be applied to all these manners of articulation, producing a lateral stop and a lateral fricative as well as a lateral approximant, which is by far the most common form of lateral sound. The only English lateral phoneme is /l/ with, at least in British English, allophones [l] as in *led* [lɛd] and [ɫ] as in *bell* [bɛɫ]. In most forms of American English, initial [l] has more velarization than is typically heard in British English initial [l]. In all forms of English, the air flows freely without audible friction, making this sound a voiced alveolar lateral approximant. It may be compared with the sound [ɹ] in *red* [ɹɛd], which is for many people a voiced alveolar central approximant. Laterals are usually presumed to be voiced approximants, unless a specific statement to the contrary is made.

Try subtracting and adding voice while saying an English [l] as in *led*. You will probably find that the voiceless lateral you produce is a fricative, not an approximant. When the vocal folds are apart, the airstream flows more rapidly, so that it produces a fricative noise in passing between the tongue and the side teeth. The symbol for this sound is [ɬ], so in alternating the voiced and voiceless sounds you will be saying [lllɬɬɬlllɬɬɬ]. It is possible to make a nonfricative voiceless lateral, but you will find that to do this you will have to move the side of the tongue farther away from the teeth. The alternation between a voiced and a voiceless lateral approximant may be symbolized [lllḷḷḷlllḷḷḷ].

It is also possible to make a voiced lateral that is a fricative. Try doing this by starting from an ordinary [l] as in *led*, and then moving the sides of your tongue slightly closer to your teeth. You may find it easier to produce this sound by starting from the voiceless alveolar lateral fricative described in the previous paragraph and then adding voicing, but making sure that you keep the fricative component.

To summarize, there are four lateral sounds under discussion: voiced alveolar lateral approximant, [l]; voiced alveolar lateral fricative, [ɮ]; voiceless alveolar lateral approximant, [l̥]; and voiceless alveolar lateral fricative, [ɬ]. No language uses the difference between the last two sounds contrastively. But some languages make a phonemic distinction between three of the four possibilities. Zulu, for example, has a three-way contrast, as shown in the first row of Table 7.7. As you can see in the second set of Zulu words in Table 7.7, after a nasal, the

190 CHAPTER 7 Consonantal Gestures

TABLE 7.7		Some Zulu laterals (see text for the contrasts in each row).	
1	lálà	ɮálà	ɬânzà
	'sleep'	'play' (imperfect)	'vomit'
2		ínɮàlà	íntɬ'ântɬ'à
		'hunger'	'good luck'
3			ᴋ̲ʟ'iná
			'be naughty'

voiceless fricative may be an ejective. And the final Zulu word in the table illustrates an initial voiceless velar lateral ejective affricate, using the symbol [ʟ] for a velar lateral. Listen to this sound, but don't worry if you can't produce it in your first year of phonetics. Voiceless lateral fricatives can also be exemplified by Welsh words such as [ɬan] 'church' and [ˈkəɬəɬ] 'knife.'

The distinction between a central and a lateral articulation can be applied to other manners of articulation in addition to approximants and fricatives. Trills are always centrally articulated, but flaps can be made with either a central or a lateral articulation. If, when making [ɾ] or [ɽ], you allow the airstream to flow over the sides of the tongue, you will produce a sound that is intermediate in quality between those sounds and [l]. This will be a voiced alveolar or retroflex lateral flap. The symbol for either of these possibilities is [ɺ]. A sound of this kind sometimes occurs in languages such as Japanese that do not distinguish between /r/ and /l/. But some African languages, for example Chaga, spoken in East Africa, make a phonemic distinction among all three of these sounds.

The central–lateral distinction can in some senses be said to apply to stops as well. English stops with lateral plosion, as in *little, ladle*, can, of course, be considered to be sequences of stop plus lateral. But the Navajo sound [tɬ'], in which the ejective airstream mechanism applies to both the stop and the lateral, is appropriately called a lateral ejective. Similarly, we clearly want to distinguish between the central and lateral clicks [ǃ] and [ǁ].

Having seen that the central–lateral distinction can apply to a number of different manners of articulation, we must now consider whether it applies to gestures with different target places of articulation. Here, the limitations are obvious. Generally speaking, laterals are made with the tip, blade, or front of the tongue. They may be either dental (as in Malayalam and Toda), alveolar (as in English), retroflex (also in Malayalam and other Indian languages), or palatal (as in Italian). Velar laterals do occur. We noted a velar lateral in Zulu, but in that language it does not contrast with other laterals in the same context. There are, however, contrastive velar laterals in a few languages spoken in Papua New Guinea such as Mid-Waghi, which you can find at the website. The symbol for palatal laterals is [ʎ]. Try saying Italian words such as *famiglia* [faˈmiʎʎa] 'family' and *figlio* [ˈfiʎʎo] 'son.' In both of these words, the lateral sound is doubled, acting as the final consonant of one syllable and the first consonant of the next. Additional examples of Italian laterals are in the material for this chapter at the website. Note that some forms of Spanish distinguish between [ʎ] and the similar sounding sequence [lj] in words such as *pollo* [ˈpoʎo] 'chicken' and *polio* [ˈpoljo] 'polio.' See if you can make this distinction. There are also retroflex laterals, for which the symbol is [ɭ].

SUMMARY OF MANNERS OF ARTICULATION

Table 7.8 presents a summary of the manners of articulation we have been discussing. Note that the terms *central* and *lateral* have been placed separately, to indicate that they can be used in conjunction with many of the terms in the upper part of the table. This table also lists many of the symbols that have been mentioned in the latter part of this chapter. You should be sure that you can pronounce each of them in a variety of contexts. Again, don't forget that you can find examples of all of them on the IPA chart at the website.

The only consonants we have not considered in detail in this chapter are approximants. Alveolar approximants—both central [ɹ] and lateral [l]—have been discussed. But sounds such as [w, j] as in *wet, yet* have not. Approximants of the latter kind are sometimes called semivowels, or glides. It will be more appropriate to discuss them after we have considered the nature of vowels more fully.

TABLE 7.8 Manners of articulation.

Phonetic Term	Brief Description	Symbols
Nasal (stop)	Soft palate lowered so that air flows out through the nose; complete closure of two articulators	m, n, ŋ, etc.
(Oral) stop	Soft palate raised, forming a velic closure; complete closure of two articulators	p, b, t, etc.
Fricative	Narrowing of two articulators so as to produce a turbulent airstream	f, v, θ, etc.
Approximant	Approximation of two articulators without producing a turbulent airstream	w, j, l, ɹ, etc.
Trill	An articulator set in vibration by the airstream	r, R, ʙ
Tap	Tongue tip hitting the roof of the mouth; a single movement in a trill	ɾ
Flap	One articulator striking another in passing	ɾ, ɺ
Lateral	With a central obstruction, so that air passes out at the side	l, ɫ, ɮ, ɭ, ʎ, ‖
Central	Articulated so that air passes out the center	s, ɹ, w, etc.

But in order to describe vowels, we must first leave the field of articulatory phonetics and consider some of the basic principles of acoustic phonetics.

A summary of the terms required so far for describing consonant gestures is given in the first exercise (see page 193). Note that in order to define a consonant fully, you may need to answer up to eight questions about it: (1) What is the airstream mechanism? (2) What is the direction of the airstream? (3) What is the state of the glottis? (4) What part of the tongue is involved? (5) What is the primary place of articulation? (6) Is it central or lateral? (7) Is it oral or nasal? and (8) What is the manner of articulation? As we will see in Chapter 9, consonants may be even more complicated, so in addition to stating all the characteristics of the primary gesture, it may also be necessary to mention so-called secondary gestures, such as added lip rounding.

RECAP

In a sense, this chapter is one of the two pillars of this book (look at the table of contents and see which chapter might be the other pillar). The topic was the main table of consonants in the International Phonetic Alphabet. We discussed every column and row in that table and presented examples from many languages that exemplify all of the sounds not found in English. Details of the articulatory gestures involved in consonant production were discussed, and perhaps one take-home message from this (apart from the fact that you need to memorize a lot of terms and their definitions) is that a lot of skill is involved in speech production. Almost every language has complicated sounds that speakers of other languages find hard to say. The production exercises of this chapter are designed to help you overcome some of your own linguistic myopia and begin to be prepared to notice and to analyze the sounds you encounter in a new language as a linguist, or in a new client as a speech pathologist.

EXERCISES

(Printable versions of all the exercises are available at the book's website.)
There are fewer exercises at the end of this and subsequent chapters, because by this stage in a course in phonetics it is appropriate for students to think in terms of larger projects. A possible project for students of general linguistics is to find a speaker of another language and give a description of the major phonetic characteristics of that language. Students of English might try to do the same with someone who has an accent of English that is very different from their own. Speech pathologists might describe the speech of a particular child. In each case, students should compile a list of words illustrating the major characteristics of the speech of the person being analyzed. They should then make a recording of this list of words and use it as a basis for their description. A good model to follow is that of the International Phonetic Association, which publishes a series of short (four- to six-page) papers describing the phonetic structures of a language.

Their recommended format for the description is in Sources at the back of the book. Some students will be able to publish papers of this kind.

The table below lists most of the terms required for classifying consonants. Make sure you know the meaning of all these terms. The exercises below refer to the table.

(1) Airstream	(2) Direction	(3) Glottis	(4) Tongue	(5) Place
pulmonic	egressive	voiced	apical	bilabial
glottalic	ingressive	voiceless	laminal	labiodental
velaric		murmured	(neither)	dental
		laryngealized		alveolar
		closed		retroflex
				palato-alveolar
				palatal
				velar
				uvular
				pharyngeal
				labial velar

(6) Centrality	(7) Nasality	(8) Manner
central	oral	stop
lateral	nasal	fricative
		approximant
		trill
		flap
		tap

A. Give a full description of the following sounds, using one term from each of the eight columns in the table above.

[b] _____

[tʰ] _____

[t'] _____

[ɬ] _____

[!] _____

[ʀ] _____

B. List five combinations of terms that are impossible.

_____

_____

_____

_____

_____

C. If we overlook secondary articulations such as rounding, most consonants can be specified by using one term from each of these eight columns. But, in addition to affricates such as [tʃ, dʒ], one of the consonants listed in Chapter 2 cannot be specified in this way. Which consonant is this? How can this deficiency be remedied?

_____

_____

D. Still without considering secondary articulations and affricates, what sounds mentioned in this chapter cannot be specified by taking one term from each of the eight columns?

_____

_____

PERFORMANCE EXERCISES

This chapter, like the last, introduced many non-English sounds. During this part of the course, it is important to do as much practical work as time will allow. But do not try to go too fast. Make sure you have thoroughly mastered the performance exercises at the end of Chapter 6 before going on to do the exercises below. Note that there are no performance exercises at the end of Chapter 8, so you can allow more time for the exercises here and at the end of Chapter 6.

A. Learn to produce voiceless stops before [ɑ] at a number of different places of articulation. Begin by making a clearly interdental stop, [t̪ɑ], with the tongue tip between the teeth. Next, make a very retroflex stop, [ʈɑ], with the tongue tip curled back and up toward the hard palate. Now try to make as many stops as you can with tongue positions between these two extremes. Using the diacritics [̟] and [̠] to mean more forward and more retracted, respectively, a series of this kind could be symbolized [t̪ɑ, t̪ɑ, t̟ɑ, tɑ, t̠ɑ, ʈɑ , ʈɑ]. Try to feel different articulatory positions such as these.

B. Repeat exercise A using a voiced stop:

[d̪ɑ, d̪ɑ, d̟ɑ, dɑ, d̠ɑ, ɖɑ, ɖɑ]

C. Repeat exercise A using a nasal:

[n̪ɑ, n̪ɑ, n̟ɑ, nɑ, n̠ɑ, ɳɑ, ɳɑ]

D. Repeat exercise A using a voiceless sibilant fricative of the [s] type. Note that it is perfectly possible to make a sibilant dental fricative [s̪], but a true interdental sibilant is not possible.

[s̪ɑ, s̪ɑ, sɑ, s̠ɑ, s̠ɑ, s̠ɑ]

E. Repeat exercise A using a voiced sibilant fricative of the [z] type. Say:

[ẓɑ, ẓ, zɑ, z̪ɑ, zɑ̟, z̠ɑ]

F. Make a series of voiceless fricative articulations with the tongue tip down. Start with a palato-alveolar fricative [ʃ] with the blade of the tongue. (Be careful it is not made with the tip of the tongue up, which may be your normal articulation of this sound.) Next, move the point of articulation backward by raising the front of the tongue, so that you produce a palatal fricative [ç]. Then move the articulation farther back, producing first [x] and then [χ]. Finally, pull the tongue root back so that you produce a pharyngeal fricative [ħ]. Try to move in a continuous series, going through all the articulations:

[ʃ, ç, x, χ, ħ]

G. Say these fricatives before vowels:

[ʃɑ, çɑ, xɑ, χɑ, ħɑ]

H. Repeat exercise F with the corresponding voiced sounds, producing the series:

[ʒ, ʝ, ɣ, ʁ, ʕ]

I. Say these fricatives before vowels:

[ʒɑ, ʝɑ, ɣɑ, ʁɑ, ʕɑ]

J. After you are fully aware of the positions of the tongue in all these fricatives, try saying some of the corresponding voiceless stops. There is no significant difference between palato-alveolar and palatal stops, and pharyngeal stops do not occur, so just say:

[cɑ, kɑ, qɑ]

K. Repeat exercise J with the voiced stops:

[ɟɑ, gɑ, ɢɑ]

L. Repeat exercise J with the voiced nasals:

[ɲɑ, ŋɑ, ɴɑ]

M. Consolidate your ability to produce sounds at different places of articulation. Produce a complete series of nasals between vowels:

[ɑmɑ, ɑn̪ɑ, ɑnɑ, ɑɳɑ, ɑɲɑ, ɑŋɑ, ɑɴɑ]

N. Produce a series of voiceless stops between vowels:

[ɑpɑ, ɑt̪ɑ, ɑtɑ, ɑʈɑ, ɑcɑ, ɑkɑ, ɑqɑ]

O. Produce a series of voiced stops between vowels:

[ɑbɑ, ɑd̪ɑ, ɑdɑ, ɑɖɑ, ɑɟɑ, ɑgɑ, ɑɢɑ]

P. Produce a series of voiceless fricatives between vowels:

[ɑɸɑ, ɑfɑ, ɑθɑ, ɑsɑ, ɑṣɑ, ɑʃɑ, ɑçɑ, ɑxɑ, ɑχɑ, ɑħɑ]

Q. Produce a series of voiced fricatives between vowels:

[ɑβɑ, ɑvɑ, ɑðɑ, ɑzɑ, ɑẓɑ, ɑʒɑ, ɑʝɑ, ɑɣɑ, ɑʁɑ, ɑʕɑ]

R. Repeat all these exercises using other vowels.
S. Review the pronunciation of trills, taps, flaps, and similar-sounding approximants. Say:

[ɑrɑ, ɑɾɑ, ɑɽɑ, ɑɹɑ, ɑʀɑ, ɑʁɑ]

T. Some of these sounds are more difficult to pronounce between high vowels. Say:

[iri, iɾi, iɽi, iɹi, iʀi, iʁi]

U. Make sure that you can produce contrasting lateral sounds. Say:

[lɑ, ɮɑ, ɬɑ, ɭɑ, ʎɑ, tɬɑ, tɬ'ɑ, dlɑ]

V. Repeat exercise U with other vowels.
W. Incorporate all these sounds into simple series of nonsense words, such as:

ʁeˈsaʔi	taˈɲoʒe	ˈpʼexonu
ɬupeʐo	ˈbeɾeɬa	doʔeˈɗo
fiɣoˈcɑ	βinoˈɟe	ṣeʃetʼe
koˈɾiɖo	ʀeˈʎɑxɑ	ˈGeɦeɻu
ˈɲeqɸu	ˈɮaɲexo	moˈɓɑle

Remember that you should look at, as well as listen to, anyone saying ear-training words.

8

Acoustic Phonetics

We have looked at a few spectrograms in earlier chapters of this book and on the website. This chapter delves more deeply into the acoustic properties of speech that we can see in spectrograms, aiming to teach you how to "read" spectrograms. Figure 8.1 shows a spectrogram of a woman describing some of her experiences in politics. She says, "First campaign I worked in was for John Kennedy in nineteen-sixty." On the website that accompanies this book, you can listen to this sentence as it was originally recorded and in two filtered versions. In the "high-pass" version of the sentence, the top part of the spectrogram was allowed to pass and everything in the spectrogram below 2500 Hz was erased. Right click to see a spectrogram of the high-pass filtered file and compare it to the spectrogram in Figure 8.1. When you listen to the high-pass filtered version of this sentence, you may notice that it sounds very "tinny." The fricative noises are quite prominent and the intonation is pretty decipherable. In the "low-pass" version, the bottom part of the spectrogram was allowed to pass and all of the sound energy above 1000 Hz was erased. This version of the sentence sounds more "boomy," with prominent vowels and intonation but not much fricative noise. Listening to filtered speech (and looking at spectrograms of filtered speech) can give you an appreciation of the information that is available in speech spectrograms. You can hear that speech has high-frequency components and low-frequency components. In fact, the sounds of language are distinguished largely by the detailed composition of energy in the vertical dimension of the spectrogram (the frequency spectrum). In this chapter, we present the source/filter theory of speech production and discuss many of the acoustic patterns that distinguish the sounds of language.

SOURCE/FILTER THEORY

In the first chapter of this book, we discussed how speech sounds can differ in pitch, in loudness, and in quality. When discussing differences in quality, we noted that the quality of a vowel depends on its overtone structure. Putting this in another way, we can say that a vowel sound contains a number of different pitches simultaneously. There is the pitch at which it is actually spoken, and there are the various overtone pitches that give it its distinctive quality. We distinguish one vowel from another by the differences in these overtones. The overtones are called formants, and the lowest three formants distinguish

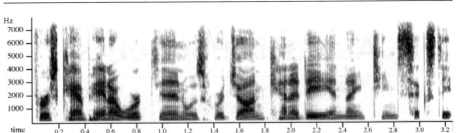

Figure 8.1 Spectrogram of the utterance "First campaign I worked in was for John Kennedy in nineteen-sixty."

vowels from one another. The lowest, formant one, which we can symbolize as F1, can be heard by tapping on your throat. If you open your mouth, make a glottal stop, and flick a finger against your neck just to the side and below the jaw, you will hear a note, just as you would if you tapped on a bottle. If you tilt your head slightly backward so that the skin of the neck is stretched while you tap, you may be able to hear this sound somewhat better. Be careful to maintain a vowel position and not to raise the back of the tongue against the soft palate. If you check a complete set of vowel positions [i, ɪ, e, ɛ, æ, ɑ, ɔ, ʊ, u] with this technique, you should hear the pitch of the first formant going up for the first four vowels and down for the second four vowels.

The second formant, F2, goes down in pitch in the series of vowels [i, ɪ, e, ɛ, æ], as can be heard more easily when these vowels are whispered. The third formant, F3, adds to quality distinctions, but there is no easy way of making it more evident.

How do these formants arise? The answer is that they are echoes in the vocal tract. The air in the vocal tract acts like the air in an organ pipe, or in a bottle. Sound travels from a noise-making source (in voiced sounds, this is the vocal fold vibration) to the lips. Then, at the lips, most of the sound energy radiates away from the lips for a listener to hear, while some of the sound energy reflects back into the vocal tract—it echoes. The addition of the reflected sound energy with the source energy tends to amplify energy at some frequencies and damp energy at others, depending on the length and shape of the vocal tract. The vocal folds are then a **source** of sound energy, and the vocal tract (due to the interaction of the reflected sound waves in it) is a frequency **filter** altering the timbre of the vocal fold sound. In phonetics, the timbre of a vowel is called the **vowel quality**.

This same source/filter mechanism is at work in many musical instruments. In the brass instruments, for example, the noise source is the vibrating lips in the mouthpiece of the instrument, and the filter is provided by the long brass tube. You can verify for yourself that the instrument changes the sound produced by the lips by listening to the lip vibration with the mouthpiece alone (make a circle with your index finger and thumb for a simulated trombone mouthpiece). Similarly, in a marimba, the sound source is produced by striking one of the keys of the instrument, and the filter is provided by the tubes that are mounted underneath each key. One reason the marimba is so much bulkier than a trombone is that it has a separate source/filter system for each note in the scale, in the trombone, there is only one source (lips) and one filter (the tube of the instrument), and both are variable. The human voice is more like the trombone—our vocal fold sound source can be made to vibrate at different pitches and amplitudes, and our vocal tract filter can be made to enhance or damp different frequencies, giving us the many different timbres that we hear as different vowels.

We said above that the filtering action of the vocal tract tends to amplify energy at some frequencies and damp energy at others, depending on the length and shape of the vocal tract. The **length** factor is pretty easy to describe when the shape of the vocal tract is simple. For example, if the vocal tract is shaped like a garden hose—exactly the same diameter from glottis to lips—its resonant frequencies can be defined by a simple formula:

$$F_n = \frac{(2n-1) \times c}{4L}.$$

This formula says that resonant frequency number n (where $n = 1, 2, 3$ for formants F1, F2, and F3) is equal to 1 subtracted from 2 times n, multiplied by the speed of sound c, divided by four times the length of the vocal tract L. For example, Peter Ladefoged's vocal tract was 17.5 cm long, so the $c/4L$ part of the formula for his formant frequencies is $35,000/(4 \times 17.5) = 500$. The constant c is the speed of sound and tells us how quickly a sound wave travels from the lips to the glottis as it bounces around inside the mouth. The first term in the formula $(2n - 1)$ defines a sequence of multipliers for this basic frequency value. So, Peter's first resonant frequency (the F1) was $500 \times 1 = 500$ Hz; the second formant (F2) was $500 \times 3 = 1500$ Hz; and the third formant (F3) was $500 \times 5 = 2500$ Hz.

Different vocal tracts have different resonant frequencies. For example, Keith Johnson's vocal tract is about 16 cm long, so his formants will all be a little higher, with the lowest formant (F1) at $35,000/(4 \times 16) = 547$ Hz, the second formant at $3 \times 547 = 1641$ Hz, and the third formant at $5 \times 547 = 2734$ Hz.

The length of the resonating portion of the vocal tract also differs substantially for different speech sounds. In vowels, the whole vocal tract, from glottis to lips, serves as the acoustic filter for the noise generated by the vibrating vocal folds. In fricatives, the resonating portion of the vocal tract is shorter. For example, in [s], the portion of the vocal tract that serves as the acoustic filter is from the alveolar ridge to the lips. Thus, the lowest formant in [s] (with a vocal tract length of only 2 or 3 cm) will have a much higher frequency than the F1 found in vowels. This explains why the fricative noises were so noticeable in the high-pass filtered version of the utterance in Figure 8.1. The only fricative that does not have higher resonant frequencies than those found in vowels is the glottal fricative [h]. In [h], the whole vocal tract, from glottis to lips, is involved.

In addition to the length of the vocal tract, the frequencies of the resonant overtones, the formants, are determined by the **shape** of the vocal tract. We've been assuming so far with the formula $F_n = (2n - 1) \times c/4L$ that the vocal tract has uniform diameter, as if it were a section of pipe. This is obviously an incorrect assumption for most speech sounds. For example, in nasal consonants, we have numerous side cavities branching off of the main passageway from glottis to nose—the sinus cavities, as well as the mouth cavity. Similarly, in lateral sounds, the shape of the vocal tract is complex. Rather than go into detail for many different speech sounds, we will limit our focus here to vowel sounds. For a more detailed account of vowel acoustics and the acoustics of other speech sounds, see Peter Ladefoged's book *Elements of Acoustic Phonetics* or Keith Johnson's book *Acoustic and Auditory Phonetics*. The acoustics of vowels can be described in two ways: with tube models and with perturbation theory. Both of these descriptions are useful—yet overly simple—descriptions. They are discussed in the next two sections.

TUBE MODELS

The formants that characterize different vowels are the result of the different shapes of the vocal tract. Any body of air, such as that in the vocal tract or that in a bottle, will vibrate in a way that depends on its size and shape. If you blow across the top of an empty bottle, you can produce a low-pitched note. If you partially fill the bottle with water so that the volume of air is smaller, you will be able to produce a note with a higher pitch. Smaller bodies of air are similar to smaller piano strings or smaller organ pipes in that they produce higher pitches. In the case of vowel sounds, the vocal tract has a complex shape so that the different bodies of air produce a number of overtones.

The air in the vocal tract is set in vibration by the action of the vocal folds. Every time the vocal folds open and close, there is a pulse of acoustic energy. These pulses act like sharp taps on the air in the vocal tract, setting the resonating cavities into vibration so that they produce a number of different frequencies, just as if you were tapping on a number of different bottles at the same time. Irrespective of the rate of vibration of the vocal folds, the air in the vocal tract will resonate at these frequencies as long as the position of the vocal organs remains the same. Because of the complex shape of the tract, the air will vibrate in more than one way at once. It's as if the air in the back of the vocal tract might vibrate one way, producing a low-frequency waveform, while the air in front of the tongue, a smaller cavity, might vibrate in another way, producing a higher-frequency waveform. A third mode of vibration of the air in the vocal tract might produce a sound of even higher frequency. What we actually hear in vowels is the sum of these waveforms added together.

The relationship between resonant frequencies and vocal tract shape is actually much more complicated than the air in the back part of the vocal tract vibrating in one way and the air in other parts vibrating in another. Here we will just concentrate on the fact that in most voiced sounds, three formants are produced every time the vocal folds vibrate. Note that the resonance in the vocal tract is independent of the rate of vibration of the vocal folds. The vocal folds may vibrate faster or slower, giving the sound a higher or lower pitch, but the formant frequencies will remain the same as long as there are no changes in the shape of the vocal tract.

There is nothing particularly new about this way of analyzing vowel sounds. The general theory of formants was stated by the great German scientist Hermann Helmholtz about one hundred fifty years ago. Even earlier, in 1829, the English physicist Robert Willis said, "A given vowel is merely the rapid repetition of its peculiar note." We would nowadays say that a vowel is the rapid repetition (corresponding to the vibrations of the vocal folds) of its peculiar two or three notes (corresponding to its formants). We can, in fact, go even further and say that not only vowels but all voiced sounds are distinguishable from one another by their formant frequencies.

The notion that vowels contain several different pitches at the same time is difficult to appreciate. One way of making it clearer is to build up a sentence from the component waves. The speech-synthesis demonstration on the website shows how this can be done. You can listen to the components of the sentence *A bird in the hand is worth two in the bush* in a synthesized version of Peter Ladefoged's voice. The first link in the table on the website enables you to hear just the variations in the first formant, which sounds like a muffled version of the sentence. The vocal fold pulses have been produced at a steady rate so that the "utterance" is on a monotone. What you hear as the changes in pitch are the changes in the overtones of this monotone "voice." These overtone pitch variations convey a great deal of the quality of the voiced sounds. The rhythm of the sentence is apparent because the overtone pitches occur only when the vocal folds would have been vibrating. The amplitude (loudness) of the first formant is turned up only at these times.

The second link in the table does the same for the second formant. This time, the equivalent of a series of monotone vocal fold pulses has been used to excite only the second formant. Again, the variations of these overtone pitches convey much of the vowel quality. The same is not so true of the third formant by itself, which you can hear by playing the third link. This formant adds to the overall quality of the sound, but in this sentence, it does not play a very significant role.

The fourth link plays the sound of the three formants added together. With this, the sentence becomes highly intelligible. A slight improvement in quality occurs by adding some additional, fixed, formants, which you can hear by playing the fifth link. At this point in the synthesis of the sentence, everything is there except the bursts of noise associated with the releases of the stop consonants and the turbulent noises of the fricatives. Play this link again and note that, for example, the final [ʃ] in *bush* is not there.

The sixth link enables you to hear the sounds of the bursts of noise and the turbulence of the fricatives by themselves. When they are added in the correct places, as they are for the seventh link, you can hear the entire sentence in a monotone. The last link adds the fundamental pitch, which varies as the glottal pulses recur at different intervals, so that the sentence is pronounced with a reasonable intonation.

PERTURBATION THEORY

We saw earlier with the formula $F_n = (2n - 1) \times c/4L$ that even a tube with a uniform diameter has simultaneous resonance frequencies—several pitches at the same time. Furthermore, these resonance frequencies change in predictable ways when the tube is squeezed at various locations. This means that we can model the acoustics of vowels in terms of perturbations of the uniform tube. For example, when the lips are rounded, the diameter of the vocal tract is smaller at the lips than at other locations in the vocal tract. With perturbation theory, we know the acoustic effect of constriction at the lips, so we can predict the formant frequency differences between rounded and unrounded vowels.

Here's how perturbation theory works. For each formant, there are locations in the vocal tract where constriction will cause the formant frequency to rise, and locations where constriction will cause the frequency to fall. Figure 8.2 shows these locations for F1, F2, and F3. In this figure, the vocal tract is pictured three times, once for each formant, and is represented as a tube that has the same diameter for its whole length and is closed at the glottis and open at the lips. This is approximately the shape of the vocal tract during the vowel [ə].

The letters "P" and "V" in the F1-F3 tubes indicate the location of pressure maxima (P) and velocity maxima (V) in the resonant waves that are bouncing back and forth between the lips and glottis during a vowel. The fact that three resonant waves can be present in the vocal tract at the same time is difficult to appreciate but true. The perturbation theory says that if there is a constriction at a velocity maximum (V) in a resonant wave, then the frequency of that resonance will decrease, and if there is a constriction at a point of maximum pressure (P), then the frequency of the resonance will increase.

Given these simple rules for how resonant frequency changes when the shape of the resonator changes, consider how to change the F1 frequency in vowels. Constriction near the glottis (as found in low vowels) is closer to a pressure maximum (P) than to a velocity maximum (V), so the F1 frequency will be higher in low vowels than in schwa. Constriction near the lips (as found in high vowels and round vowels) is closer to a velocity maximum, so the F1 frequency will be lower in high vowels than in schwa. The rules apply in the same way to change the frequency of F2 and F3. For example, there are two ways to raise the frequency of F2; one involves a very difficult constriction near the glottis, but

Figure 8.2 Pressure (P) and velocity (V) maxima in the standing waves of the first three vowel formants.

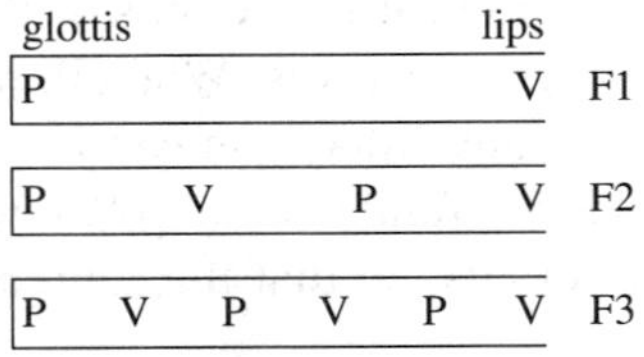

glottis					lips	
P					V	F1
P	V		P		V	F2
P	V	P		V	P V	F3

without tongue root constriction (which is near the first V in the F2 resonance wave). The other involves constriction with the tongue against the roof of the mouth. This is the most common maneuver used to raise the F2 frequency.

ACOUSTIC ANALYSIS

Phoneticians like to describe vowels in terms of numbers. It is possible to analyze sounds so that we can measure the actual frequencies of the formants. We can then represent them graphically, as in Figure 8.3. This figure gives the average of a number of authorities' values of the frequencies of the first three formants in eight American English vowels. Try to see how your own vowels compare with these. Do you have a much larger jump in the frequency of the second formant (which you hear when whispering) between [ɛ] and [æ] as

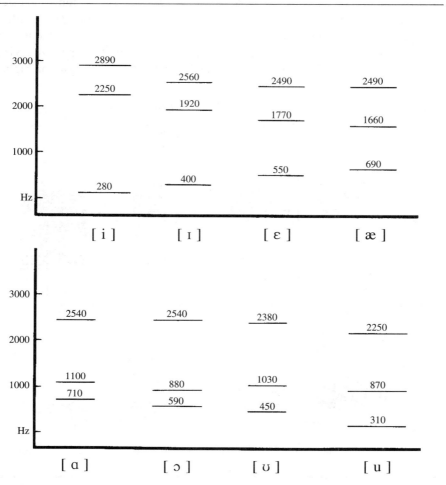

Figure 8.3 The frequencies of the first three formants in eight American English vowels.

204 CHAPTER 8 Acoustic Phonetics

compared with [ɪ] and [ɛ]? Do you distinguish between *hod* and *hawed* in terms of their formant frequencies?

There are computer programs that can analyze sounds and show their components. The display produced is called a **spectrogram**. We have seen spectrograms in prior chapters and described briefly how they are made in connection with Figure 1.5, but there hasn't been much discussion of how to interpret them. Now is the time for a little more detail. In spectrograms, time runs from left to right, the frequency of the components is shown on the vertical scale, and the intensity of each component is shown by the degree of darkness. It is thus a display that shows, roughly speaking, dark bands for concentrations of energy at particular frequencies—showing the source and filter characteristics of speech. There are several free computer programs on the Web that can be used to make spectrograms. One of the best is WaveSurfer from the Centre for Speech Technology (CTT) at KTH in Stockholm, Sweden. Also very widely used is Praat, which is a product of the University of Amsterdam. These programs can be used to open any of the sound files on the book's website so you can produce spectrograms and listen to small snippets of them. If your computer has a built-in microphone, try recording your pronunciation of *heed, hid, head, had* and making spectrograms of them.

EXAMPLE 8.3

Figure 8.4 is a set of spectrograms of an American English speaker saying the words *heed, hid, head, had, hod, hawed, hood, who'd*. Because the higher

Figure 8.4 A spectrogram of the words *heed, hid, head, had, hod, hawed, hood, who'd* as spoken by a male speaker of American English. The locations of the first three formants are shown by arrows.

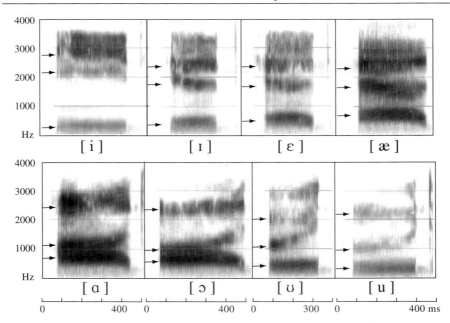

frequencies of the human voice have less energy, the higher frequencies have been given added emphasis. If they had not been boosted by this preemphasis, the higher formants would not have been visible. The time scale along the bottom of the picture shows intervals of 100 ms, so you can see that these words differ in length. The words were actually said one after another, but they have been put in separate frames as there was no point in showing the blank spaces between them. The vertical scale goes up to 4000 Hz, which is sufficient to show the component frequencies of vowels. Because the formants have greater relative intensity, shown by the darkness of the image, they can be seen as dark horizontal bars. The locations of the first three formants in each vowel are indicated by arrows.

There is a great deal of similarity between Figures 8.3 and 8.4. Figure 8.3 is like a schematic spectrogram of the isolated vowels. Figure 8.4 differs in that it represents a particular American English speaker rather than the mean of a number of speakers of American English. It also shows the effects of the consonant at the end of the word (which we will discuss later), and the slightly diphthongal character of some of the vowels. Note, for example, that the vowel [ɪ] starts with a higher second formant, and that the vowel [ʊ] has a large upward movement of the second formant. There is also a small downward movement of the second formant during [æ], indicating diphthongization of this vowel. In addition, there are some extra horizontal bars corresponding to higher formants that are not linguistically significant. The exact position of the higher formants varies a great deal from speaker to speaker. They are not uniquely determined for each speaker, but they certainly are indicative of a person's voice quality.

Figure 8.5 shows spectrograms of Peter Ladefoged's form of British English. It is similar to Figure 8.4, but not exactly the same because of the differences in accent and other individual differences. His vocal tract was longer than that of the American English speaker, so all his formants were slightly lower. Also, his vowels were less diphthongal—they had longer steady states.

Whenever the vocal folds are vibrating, there are regularly spaced vertical lines, close together, on the spectrogram. During a vowel, the vertical lines are visible throughout a large part of the spectrogram. Each vertical line in the vowels is the result of the momentary increase of acoustic energy due to a single movement of the vocal folds. We have seen that it is possible to observe the pulses in a record of the waveform and from this to calculate the pitch. It is equally possible to measure the pitch from observations of the vertical striations on spectrograms. When they are close together, the pitch is higher than when they are farther apart. At the bottom left of Figure 8.5, below the baseline but just above the symbol for [ɒ], there are two small lines, 100 ms apart. Within this tenth of a second, you can see that there are between eight and nine vertical striations in the vowel formants. The vocal folds must have been vibrating at about 85 Hz. This is not the best way of using spectrograms to determine the pitch. As we will see, it is possible to make another kind of spectrographic record that gives a better picture of the variations in pitch.

Figure 8.5 A spectrogram of the words *heed, hid, head, had, hod, hawed, hood, who'd* as spoken in a British accent. The locations of the first three formants are shown by arrows.

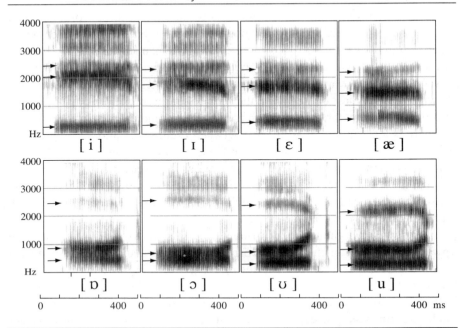

The traditional articulatory descriptions of vowels are related to the formant frequencies. We can see that the first formant frequency (indicated by the lowest of the three arrows in the frame for each vowel) increases as the speaker moves from the high vowel in *heed* to the low vowel in *had*. In these four vowels, the first formant frequency goes up as the vowel height goes down, both for the American English speaker in Figure 8.4 and for Peter Ladefoged in Figure 8.5. In the four vowels in the bottom rows of Figures 8.4 and 8.5, the first formant frequency decreases as the speaker goes from the low vowel in *hod* to the high vowel in *who'd*. Again in these vowels, the first formant frequency is inversely related to vowel height. We can also see that the second formant frequency is much higher for the front vowels in the top row than it is for the back vowels in the bottom row in each figure. But the correlation between the second formant frequency and the degree of backness of a vowel is not as good as that between the first formant frequency and the vowel height. The second formant frequency is considerably affected by the degree of lip rounding as well as by vowel height.

We can see some of the relationships between traditional articulatory descriptions and formants when we plot the formant frequencies given in Figure 8.3 along axes as shown in Figure 8.6. Because the formant frequencies are inversely related to the traditional articulatory parameters, the axes have been placed so that zero frequency would be at the top right corner of the figure rather than at the bottom left corner, as is more usual in graphical representations. In addition, the frequencies

Figure 8.6 A formant chart showing the frequency of the first formant on the ordinate (the vertical axis) plotted against the second formant on the abscissa (the horizontal axis) for eight American English vowels. The scales are marked in Hz, arranged at Bark scale intervals.

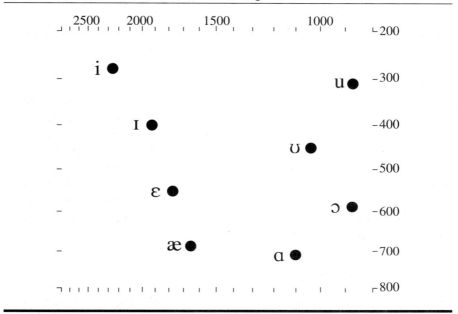

have been arranged in accordance with the Bark scale, in which perceptually equal intervals of pitch are represented as equal distances along the scale. As a further refinement, because the second formant is not as prominent as the first formant (which, on average, has 80 percent of the energy in a vowel), the second formant scale is not as expanded as the first formant scale. (Remember that in Figures 8.4 and 8.5, and in all the spectrograms in this book, the darkness scale does not correspond directly to the acoustic intensity of each sound. The higher frequencies have been given added emphasis to make them more visible.)

On a plot of formant frequencies, [i] and [u] appear at the top left and right of the graph, and [æ] and [ɑ] at the bottom, with all the other vowels in between. Consequently, this arrangement allows us to represent vowels in the way that we have become accustomed to seeing them in traditional articulatory descriptions.

In the preceding paragraphs, we have been careful to refer to the correlation between formant frequencies and the *traditional* articulatory descriptions. This is because, as we noted in Chapter 1, traditional articulatory descriptions are not entirely satisfactory. They are often not in accord with the actual articulatory facts. For well over a hundred years, phoneticians have been describing vowels in terms such as *high* versus *low* and *front* versus *back*. There is no doubt that these terms are appropriate for describing the relationships between different vowel qualities, but to some extent phoneticians have been using these terms as labels to specify acoustic dimensions rather than as descriptions of actual tongue positions. As G. Oscar Russell, one of the pioneers in x-ray studies of vowels, said, "Phoneticians are thinking in terms of acoustic fact, and using physiological fantasy to express the idea."

There is no doubt that the traditional description of vowel "height" is more closely related to the first formant frequency than to the height of the tongue. The so-called front–back dimension has a more complex relationship to the formant frequencies. As we have noted, the second formant is affected by both backness and lip rounding. We can eliminate some of the effects of lip rounding by considering the second formant in relation to the first. The degree of backness is best related to the difference between the first and the second formant frequencies. The closer they are together, the more "back" a vowel sounds.

Formant charts are commonly used to represent vowel qualities. To consolidate acoustic notions about vowels, you should now try to represent the vowels in Figures 8.4 and 8.5 in terms of a formant chart. We have provided arrows that mark what we take to be the formants that characterize these vowels. Measure these frequencies in terms of the scale on the left of each figure. Make a table listing the first and second formant frequencies and plot the vowels. A blank chart is provided as a PDF file on the website.

ACOUSTICS OF CONSONANTS

The acoustic structure of consonants is usually more complicated than that of vowels. In many cases, a consonant can be said to be a particular way of beginning or ending a vowel, and during the consonant articulation itself, there is no distinguishing feature. Thus, there is virtually no difference in the sounds during the actual closures of [b, d, g], and absolutely none during the closures of [p, t, k], for at these moments there is only silence.

Each of the stop sounds conveys its quality by its effect on the adjacent vowel. We have seen that during a vowel such as [ɛ] there will be formants corresponding to the particular shape of the vocal tract. These formants will be present as the lips open in a syllable such as [bɛ]. They will have frequencies corresponding to the particular shape that occurs at the moment that the lips come apart. As the lips come farther apart and the vocal tract shape changes, the formants will move correspondingly. As we saw in the section on perturbation theory and in Figure 8.2, closure of the lips causes a lowering of all the formants. Consequently, the syllable [bɛ] will begin with the formants in a lower position and will be distinguished by their rapid rising to the positions for [ɛ]. Similarly, in the syllable [ɛb], the formants in [ɛ] will descend as the lip closure is formed. Whenever a stop is formed or released, there will be a particular shape of the vocal tract that will be characterized by particular formant frequencies.

When you say *bib* or *bab*, for example, the tongue will be in the position for the vowel even when the lips are closed at the beginning of the word. The formant frequencies at the moment of release will be determined by the shape of the vocal tract as a whole, and hence will vary according to the vowel. The apparent point of

Figure 8.7 Spectrograms of the words *bed*, *dead*, and the nonword [gɛg] spoken by an American English speaker.

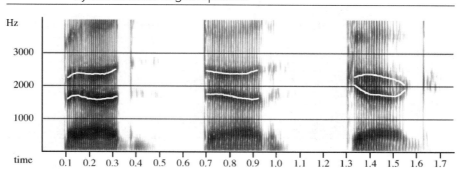

origin of the formant for each place of articulation is called the **locus** of that place of articulation. The point of origin of the formants will depend on the adjacent vowels. This is because the position of that part of the tongue that is not involved in the formation of a consonant closure will be largely that of the adjacent vowel.

Figure 8.7 shows spectrograms of the words *bed*, *dead*, and the nonword [gɛg] spoken by an American English speaker. You can see the faint voicing striations near the baseline for each of the final stops [d, d, g]. Evidence of voicing near the baseline during a consonant closure is called a **voice bar**. Note that this speaker, like many other speakers of English, has no voice bars in the initial "voiced" stops.

In all three words, the first formant rises from a low position. This is simply a mark of a stop closure and does not play a major part in distinguishing one place of articulation from another. What primarily distinguishes these three stops are the onsets and offsets of the second and third formants, which are traced with white lines. At the beginning of the word *bed*, the second and third formants have a lower frequency than they do at the beginning of the word *dead*. The second formant is noticeably rising for the initial [b] from a comparatively low locus. In the word *dead*, the second formant is fairly steady at the beginning and the third formant drops a little. In [gɛg], the second and third formants come close to each other at the margins of the vowel, where the [g] consonants have the most influence over the formant frequencies. It is almost as if the F2 and F3 were going to a common point. This coming together of the second and third formants, sometimes called a **velar pinch**, is very characteristic of velar consonants.

The corresponding voiceless stops [p, t, k] are illustrated in Figure 8.8 in the forms [pʰɛm], [tʰɛn], and [kʰɛŋ], of which only *ten* is an English word. We chose these forms because the vowel [ɛ] is a particularly good environment for showing stop-consonant place-of-articulation differences. As with unaspirated stops, the release of the aspirated stops is marked by a sudden sharp spike corresponding to the onset of a burst of noise. After the release burst, there is a period of aspiration noise marked by absence of energy in F1 and absence of the regular vertical striations of voicing. The aspiration noise separates the burst

Figure 8.8 Spectrograms of the forms [pʰɛm], [tʰɛn] (ten), and [kʰɛŋ].

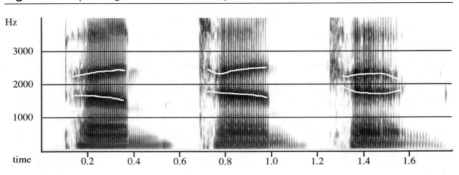

from the voiced portion of the vowel. The burst for [p] has the lowest frequency. For both [t] and [k], the noise extends above the 4000 Hz shown in the spectrogram, as we will see in later figures. The highest frequencies are actually in the [t] burst rather than the [k]. If you whisper a sequence of consonants [t, t, t, k, k, k, p, p, p] in that order, [t, k, p], you can hear that the highest pitch is associated with [t], the next with [k], and the lowest with [p]. You can also hear that [t] is the loudest, [k] next loudest, and [p] the least loud. The intensity of the [p] burst is sometimes so low that there is hardly any evidence of a sharp spike in the spectrogram. Since the formant transitions after voiceless aspirated stops take place during the period of aspiration, they are not as apparent in Figure 8.8 as they are after the voiced stops in Figure 8.7. However, we have traced the centers of F2 and F3 in these spectrograms to help you see that the formants are also present in the aspiration noise. In addition, the transitions into the final nasals from the vowels before them are easily visible. The second and third formants are falling (slightly) before [m]; the second and third formants are almost level before [n]. Most distinctive of all, the second and third formants are coming together for the velar pinch before [ŋ].

The nasal consonants [m, n, ŋ] are also illustrated in Figure 8.8. A clear mark of a nasal (or, as we will see, a lateral) consonant is an abrupt change in the spectrogram at the time of the formation of the articulatory closure. Each of the nasals has a formant structure similar to that of a vowel, except that the bands are fainter and are in particular frequency locations that depend on the characteristic resonances of the nasal cavities. In nasal consonants, there is usually a very low first formant centered at about 250 Hz. The location of the higher formants varies, but generally there is a large region above the first formant with no energy. This speaker has a second, rather faint, nasal formant around 2000 Hz. The difference between each of the nasals is often determinable from the different formant transitions that occur at the end of each vowel. There is a decrease in the second formant of the vowel before [m], and formants two and three are coming together for the velar pinch before the velar nasal at the end of [kʰɛŋ]. But the place cues are sometimes not very clear.

Figure 8.9 A spectrogram of *fie, thigh, sigh, shy*. The frequency scale goes up to 8000 Hz in this figure. The arrows mark the onsets of the second formant transitions. Only the first word is shown in full. The second part of the diphthong has been deleted for the other words.

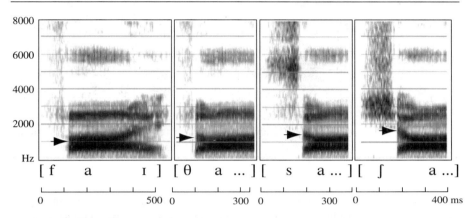

In Figure 8.9, the words *fie, thigh, sigh,* and *shy* illustrate the voiceless fricatives. The frequency scale for these spectrograms has been increased to 8000 Hz, as the highest frequencies in speech occur during fricatives. In [s] sounds, the random noise extends well beyond the upper limits of even this spectrogram. The spectrogram of *fie* shows the diphthong that occurs in each of these words. The first and second formants in this diphthong start close together in the position for a low central vowel. They then move apart so that at the end of the diphthong they are in locations similar to those in [ɪ] in Figure 8.3. As the formant pattern for the diphthong is the same in *fie, thigh, sigh, shy*, only the first part has been shown for the last three words.

All these sounds have random energy distributed over a wide range of frequencies. In [f] and [θ], the pattern is much the same. What distinguishes *fie* and *thigh* is the movement of the second formant into the following vowel, marked by arrows in the figure. There is very little movement in [f], but in [θ], the second formant starts at around 1200 Hz and moves down. Because the differences between these two sounds are so small, they are often confused in noisy settings, and they have fallen together as one sound in some accents of English, such as London Cockney, which does not distinguish between *fin* and *thin*.

The noise in [s] is centered at a high frequency, between 5000 and 6000 Hz in Figure 8.9. In [ʃ], it is lower, extending down to about 2500 Hz. Since both [s] and [ʃ] have a comparatively large acoustic intensity, they produce darker patterns than [f] or [θ]. They are also marked by distinctive formant transitions. The apparent origin (the locus) of the second formant transition increases throughout the four words *fie, thigh, sigh, shy* so that in *shy*, it is in a position comparable to its location in the vowel [i] and falls considerably.

Figure 8.10 A spectrogram of *ever, weather, fizzer, pleasure*.

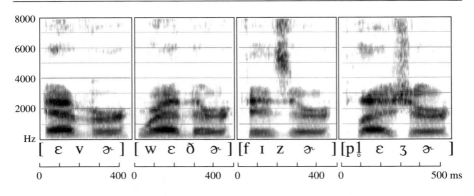

EXAMPLE 8.8

The voiced fricatives corresponding to [f, θ, s, ʃ] do not contrast at the beginnings of words. Accordingly, Figure 8.10 shows [v, ð, z, ʒ] between vowels. These voiced fricatives have patterns similar to their voiceless counterparts, but with the addition of the vertical striations indicative of voicing. The fricative component of [v] in *ever* is even fainter than the [f] in *face* and is really only visible at the start of the following vowel. The vertical striations due to voicing are apparent throughout the articulation. The same is true of [ð] in *whether*. As with their voiceless counterparts, [f, θ], it is the formants in the adjacent vowels that distinguish these words. In this figure, both these fricatives are preceded by [ɛ] and followed by [ɚ]. The second formants are much higher around [ð] than around [v].

The fricative energy in the higher frequencies is very apparent in [z] and [ʒ]. There is a faint voice bar in [z], but in [ʒ], the voicing is hard to see. There are only a few vertical striations due to voicing in the 6000- to 8000-Hz range at the beginning of the fricative noise. The formant transition from [z] into the vowel [ɚ] is level, but from [ʒ] it falls considerably. This last word, *pleasure*, also enables us to see what happens when an aspirated stop such as [p] is followed by an approximant such as [l]. Most of the [l] is voiceless, audible only by the effect it has on the [p] burst and the aspiration noise.

EXAMPLE 8.9

The last set of English consonants to consider are the lateral and central approximants, [l, ɹ, w, j]. Figure 8.11 shows these sounds in the words *led*, *red*, *wed*, *yell*. All these voiced approximants have formants not unlike those of vowels. The initial lateral in the first word has formants with center frequencies of approximately 250, 1100, and 2400 Hz (low intensity), which change abruptly in intensity at the beginning of the vowel. As we noted above, a marked change in the formant pattern is characteristic of voiced nasals and laterals. At the end of a word, as in *yell* in Figure 8.11, there may be a less marked change. A final lateral may have little or no central contact, making it not really a lateral but a back unrounded vowel. A formant in the neighborhood of 1100 or 1200 Hz is typical of most initial laterals for most speakers.

Figure 8.11 A spectrogram of *led, red, wed, yell*.

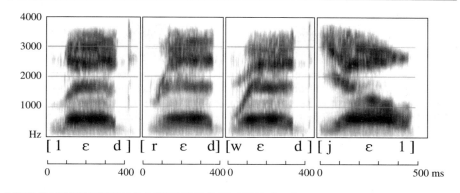

The second word in Figure 8.11 illustrates the approximant [ɹ] in *red*. The most obvious feature of this kind of [ɹ] is the low frequency of the second and third formants. The third formant in particular has a very low frequency. In this example, its origin (above the symbol [ɹ]) is around 1600 Hz. There is a great deal of similarity between *red* and the third word, *wed*, which is why young children sometimes have difficulty learning to distinguish them. The approximant [w] also starts with a low position of all three formants, but this time, it is the second formant that has the sharpest rise. The movements of the formants for [w] are like those in a movement away from a very short [u] vowel. Finally, the movements of the formants for [j], as in *yell* or *yes*, are like those in a movement away from a very short [i] vowel. Both [w] and [j] are appropriately called semivowels.

The vagueness of many of the remarks in the preceding paragraphs is meant to convey that the interpretation of speech spectrograms is often not all straightforward. The acoustic correlates of some articulatory features are summarized in Table 8.1 (on the next page). But in a book such as this, it is impossible to give a completely detailed account of the acoustics of speech. The descriptions that have been given should be regarded as rough guides rather than accounts of invariable structures that can always be seen in spectrograms. When any of the segments described above occurs in a different phonetic context, it may have a surprisingly different acoustic structure.

INTERPRETING SPECTROGRAMS

All the words illustrated in spectrograms so far were spoken in a fairly distinct way. In connected speech, as illustrated in the remainder of the spectrograms in this chapter, many of the sounds are more difficult to distinguish. Before reading the next paragraph, transcribe the segments in Figure 8.12 (on the next page), given the information that the utterance was *She came back and started again*, as spoken by the speaker who produced the vowels in Figure 8.3.

TABLE 8.1	Acoustic correlates of consonantal features. Note: These descriptions should be regarded only as rough guides. The actual acoustic correlates depend to a great extent on the particular combination of articulatory features in a sound and on the neighboring vowels.
Voiced	Vertical striations corresponding to the vibrations of the vocal folds
Bilabial	Locus of both second and third formants comparatively low
Alveolar	Locus of second formant about 1700–1800 Hz
Velar	Usually high locus of the second formant; common origin of second and third formant transitions
Retroflex	General lowering of the third and fourth formants
Stop	Gap in pattern, followed by burst of noise for voiceless stops or sharp beginning of formant structure for voiced stops
Fricative	Random noise pattern, especially in higher frequency regions, but dependent on the place of articulation
Nasal	Formant structure similar to that of vowels but with nasal formants at about 250, 2500, and 3250 Hz
Lateral	Formant structure similar to that of vowels but with formants in the neighborhood of 250, 1200, and 2400 Hz; the higher formants considerably reduced in intensity
Approximant	Formant structure similar to that in vowels, usually changing

Looking at the segments one at a time, we can see that the initial [ʃ] sound is similar to that in *shy* in Figure 8.9. Note that [s] in segment (12) has a higher frequency. The second segment, [i], has a relatively high second at about 2000 Hz (compare this with vowel [i] in Figure 8.4.) Segment (3) is the velar stop [k]. This stop is followed by a burst of aspiration—marked as segment (4)—before the onset of the vowel. The vowel in *came*, (5), is a diphthong, [eɪ], with some blurring of the lowest formant, which is associated with the nasalization of the vowel. At the end of the bilabial nasal (6), there is a short [b] closure (7) in which the voicing is just barely visible. The formant transitions after the bilabial stop at the beginning of [æ] (8) in *back* are not particularly clear indicators of

Figure 8.12 A spectrogram of *She came back and started again.*

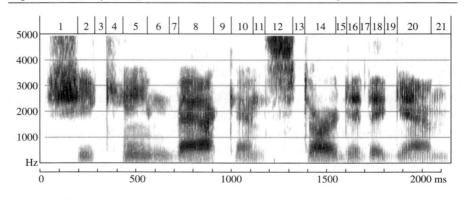

bilabial, but we might guess this place of articulation by process of elimination. On the other hand, there is no difficulty in seeing the coming together of the second and third formants before the velar stop [k] (9). There is only a short period of aspiration—not given a separate segment number—followed by a transition, the coming apart of the second and third formants before a neutral vowel, [ə] (10). This is followed by an alveolar nasal [n] (11).

The [s] (12) in *started* is followed by a short [t] (13), which is only slightly aspirated (as is normal for [t] whenever it occurs after [s] in English). The falling second formant into the vowel, [ɑ] (14), is typical of the transition from [t] into [ɑ]. The low third formant in segment (14) is associated with the *r*-coloring. Approximately the last half of the vowel is rhotacized. The very short stop in (15) has a voice bar and could be symbolized by [ɾ] in a narrow phonetic transcription. For many people, including this speaker, past tense *–ed* forms after an alveolar stop have a fairly high second formant and a low first formant. The vowel in segment (16) is probably better as [ɪ] rather than [ə]. Segment (17), like (15), is a tap [ɾ]. The vowel in segment (18) is also [ɪ]; unstressed vowels before velar consonants are often [ɪ] rather than [ə]. The velar stop [g] in (19) is marked by the coming together of the second and third formants in the vowels on either side of it. The final syllable in *again* has a fairly low vowel—formant one is about as high as it is in segment (8), the vowel [æ] in *back*. Segment (20) could be transcribed as [ɛ] or [æ]. Segment (21) is the final nasal [n].

Now you should try segmenting a more difficult utterance. Figure 8.13 shows a spectrogram of Peter Ladefoged saying, *I should have thought spectrograms were unreadable*. This phrase was spoken in a normal, but rapid, conversational style. This time, instead of marking the separate segments, we have simply placed evenly spaced lines above the spectrogram so that we can refer to particular places. Try to write a transcription below these lines. Make sure the symbols you write indicate correctly how the phrase was actually pronounced, rather than how you might say it.

EXAMPLE 8.11

When given a problem like this, it is always best to find the obvious things first. The voiceless fricatives [s] and [ʃ] stand out from other sounds, so begin by

Figure 8.13 A spectrogram of *I should have thought spectrograms were unreadable* spoken in a normal, but rapid, conversational style (British English).

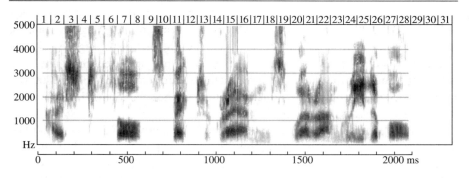

trying to find the [ʃ] in *should* and the [s] in *spectrograms*. The [ʃ] is at (3) and the [s] is between (9) and (10). You can now start at the beginning, and find the vowel [aɪ] in the first word. It is below (1) and (2), ending where the [ʃ] begins. You know that the [s] in *spectrograms* is between (9) and (10), so the vowel in *thought* must be at (7), with the [t] after it at (8). What happens before the vowel in *thought* and after the [ʃ] in *should*? Is there any voicing in any of the segments between these sounds? It seems as if the whole of the phrase *should have* was pronounced without any voicing. There must be a [t] at (4) and an [f] and a [θ] at (6). A narrow transcription of the phrase *I should have thought* is [aɪʃtf ˈθɔt].

Now go on from the [s] in *spectrograms*, bearing these points in mind. Try to transcribe *spectrograms were unreadable*, remembering that some of the sounds you might have expected to be voiced might be voiceless. When you have done this, read the next paragraph.

As you might expect, there is no aspiration after the [p] in *spectrograms*, which is between (10) and (11). The vowel [ɛ] at (11) is very short, but you can see the coming together of the second and third formants for the [k] at (12). The [t] is also at (12), and is highly aspirated, so that the following [r] is almost completely voiceless (and hence in a narrow transcription [ɹ̥]). There is virtually no voicing in the short [ə] at (13). The velar stop [g] at (14) is released into [ɹ], easily located by the lowering of the third and fourth formants. The vowel [æ] at (15–16) is followed by a long [m], with its faint formants occupying most of (17) and (18). The fricative at the end of this word, below (18–19), appears to be voiceless. It might be best, though, to transcribe it as [z̥] rather than [s] because of its lack of intensity.

One of the next most identifiable points is the drop in the third formant below (21) at the end of the word *were*, showing that on this occasion there was an [ɹ] in this word. This is normal for most speakers of British English when the next word begins with a vowel. The [w] at the beginning of this word, at (20), is distinguishable by the low second formant. The syllable [ʌn] of *unreadable* is below (22) and (23). The lowering of the third formant at (24) marks the beginning of the syllable *read*, the high vowel [i] at (25) having a low first formant and a high second formant. The very short [d] and [ə] at (25–26) are followed by a comparatively long [b] at (26–27), and the final syllabic [l̩] at (27–28) looks like a back vowel.

EXAMPLE 8.12

If you want a more difficult exercise in interpreting sound spectrograms, look at Figure 8.14 and see if you can say what it is. It is an ordinary English sentence spoken by the British English speaker who said the vowels in Figure 8.4. You will find it hard to determine the whole sentence, but some segments are quite easy. For example, what must be there when the third formant is below 2000 Hz, near (14–15)? Can you see a distinctive pattern of the second and third formants at (26)? And perhaps also at (24–25)?

At the beginning, below (1), there is a small fricative noise near 3000 Hz. Then, at (2), there is a vowel that might be [i] or [ɪ]. A sharp break in the pattern is followed at (3) by a segment with faint formants at about 250, 1300, and 2400 Hz. This break must indicate a nasal or a lateral, with a lateral being the

Figure 8.14 A spectrogram of an English sentence as described in the text.

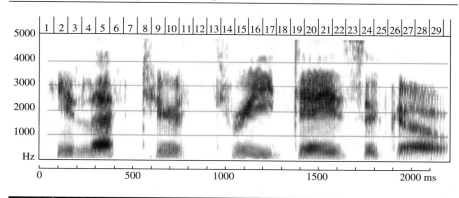

more probable here. If you look at Figure 8.3, you will see that the vowel at (5) is something like [æ] or [ε]. This is followed by a fricative at (6) that could only be [θ] or [f]. At (7), there is a voiceless stop [p], [t], or [k], with the aspiration at (8) being strong and at high frequency, making it most likely [t]. The vowel at (9) is again either [i] or [ɪ], judging by the first two formants. The second formant falls slightly in (10), indicating diphthongization.

As there seems to be a pause after (10), we can stop there for a moment and write out our possible transcription choices:

(1)	(2)	(3)	(4)	(5)	(6)	(7)	(8)	(9)	(10)
?	i	l		æ	θ	t	ʰ	ɪ	
	ɪ		n, m, ŋ	ε	f	k, p		i	

Can you make a path through these possible choices? The second syllable could be *laugh* or *laughed* or *left*, making a possible phrase *He laughed* or *He left*. What was actually said was *He left here*, but it would be very difficult to get this. You should, however, get segments such as those listed above.

Now look at the last part of the sentence in Figure 8.14, which is a bit easier. There is a fricative at (13–14) that is [θ] or [f], followed by a low third formant at (15) indicating [ɹ], and then a vowel at (16–17) in which the first formant is lower and the second formant higher than anywhere else in the sentence, making it clearly [i]. This gives us the syllable *free* or *three*. You can see a little bit of voicing near the baseline at (17–18) during what is presumably a voiced stop. The intensity of the burst, the high-frequency energy, and the level formants at the onset of the vowel all suggest that this is [d]. The vowel at (20–21) is long and almost as high (first formant low) and front (second formant high) as the preceding vowel, making it probably [eɪ]. (23) is clearly a fricative looking like [s], but, because of its lack of intensity, it may be [z] with voicing too faint to be seen. There is a very short vowel at (24), and a good rule for such vowels is to regard them as [ə]. The velar pinch indicated that the consonant at (25–26) must be a velar stop. The final long vowel at (27–29) is a diphthong, ending in a back vowel (low second formant) like [ʊ].

Putting this last part together, we have:

(13–14)	(15)	(15–16)	(17–18)	(20–21)	(23)	(24)	(25–26)	(27–29)
f	ɹ	i	d	eɪ	s	ə	g	... ʊ
θ			b		z		k	

Read these possible transcriptions and you may be able to find a path that gives you the whole sentence: *He left here—three days ago.*

Try another of these sentences on your own. Figure 8.15 is a spectrogram of the British English speaker. The utterance is a normal English sentence, containing no proper nouns. As before, many of the sounds occur in new combinations, which means that they have slightly different patterns. But if you start with the more obvious sounds and use your knowledge of possible English words, you should be able to succeed. Many readers of earlier editions of this book have already done so.

The spectrograms that have been used to illustrate this chapter so far are called wide-band spectrograms. They are very accurate in the time dimension. They show each vibration of the vocal folds as a separate vertical line and indicate the precise moment of a stop burst with a vertical spike. But they are less accurate in the frequency dimension. There are usually several component frequencies present in a single formant, all of them lumped together in one wide band on the spectrogram.

It is a fact of physics that one can know either fairly precisely when a sound occurred or, to a comparable degree of accuracy, what its frequency is. This should be intuitively clear when you recall that knowing the frequency of a sound involves observing the variations in air pressure over a period of time. This period of time has to be long enough to ensure observations of a number of repetitions of the variations in air pressure. You can either know that a pulse from the vocal folds has happened (producing the vertical voicing striation in all the spectrograms we have considered so far), or, if the piece of the sound wave

Figure 8.15 A spectrogram of an ordinary English sentence containing no names (British accent).

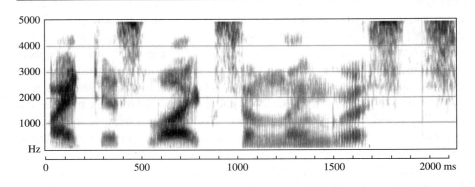

Interpreting Spectrograms 219

Figure 8.16 Wide-band (upper part of the figure) and narrow-band (lower part) spectrogram of the question *Is Pat sad, or mad?* The fifth, tenth, and fifteenth harmonics have been marked by white squares in two of the vowels.

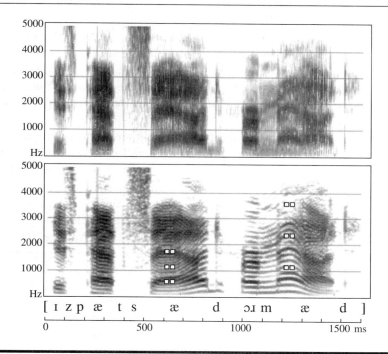

being analyzed contains two or three pulses of the vocal folds, you can tell how far apart they are and hence know the frequency.

Spectrograms that are more accurate in the frequency dimension (at the expense of accuracy in the time dimension) are called narrow-band spectrograms. Figure 8.16 shows both wide- and narrow-band spectrograms of the question *Is Pat sad, or mad?* In the wide-band spectrogram, there are sharp spikes at the release of each stop, for example, for the [d] at the end of the utterance. The spikes are smeared in the time dimension in the narrow-band spectrogram. But the frequencies that compose each formant are visible.

When the vocal folds vibrate, they produce what are called harmonics of their fundamental frequency of vibration. Harmonics are vibrations at whole-number multiples of the fundamental frequency. Thus, when the vocal folds are vibrating at 100 Hz, they produce harmonics at 200 Hz, 300 Hz, 400 Hz, and so on. In a given vowel, the particular harmonics evident are those that correspond to the resonances of the vocal tract shape occurring in that vowel. We put two small white squares in the middle of the fifth, tenth, and fifteenth harmonics in the middle of the vowels in *sad* and *mad*. The vocal folds are vibrating at about 118 Hz in *sad*, so the fifth harmonic has a frequency of

5 × 118 = 590 Hz, the tenth harmonic a frequency of 1180 Hz, and the fifteenth harmonic a frequency of 1770 Hz. The first formant in *sad* is formed by the fifth and sixth harmonics, and the principal components of the second formant are the fourteenth and fifteenth harmonics. Compare this with the vowel in *mad*, which has formants very similar to *sad*, both being examples of the / æ / phoneme. Near the beginning of the last word, the third harmonic is the principal component of the first formant, and the eighth harmonic the principal component of the second formant. As we have noted, the quality of a vowel sound depends on the frequencies of the formants. But the pitch depends on the fundamental frequency, which is determined by the rate of vibration of the vocal folds.

In women's voices, which usually have a higher pitch, the formants are sometimes more difficult to locate precisely. Figure 8.17 show spectrograms of a female speaker of American English saying the same set of vowels as those of the male speaker in Figure 8.3. Even though these spectrograms have been made with considerable care, choosing the most appropriate degree of narrowness of the spectrogram to best show the formant frequencies, the harmonics still interfere with the display of the formants. Notice, for example, the change in vowel quality in the vowel [ʊ], which appears as a series of steps as different

Figure 8.17 A spectrogram of the words *heed, hid, head, had, hod, hawed, hood, who'd* as spoken by a female speaker of American English. The locations of the first three formants are shown by arrows.

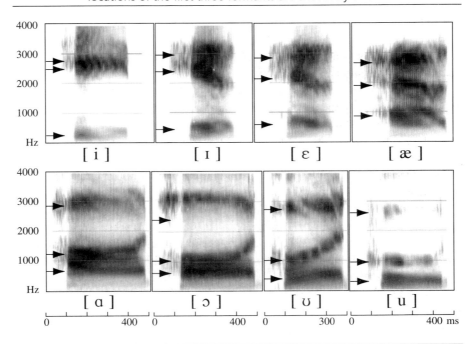

harmonics become available to make up the formant. In a narrow-band spectrogram, it is even more difficult to locate the centers of the formants when the fundamental frequency is high.

Narrow-band spectrograms are obviously useful for determining the intonation—or tone—of an utterance. One can do this by looking at the fundamental frequency itself, but when this goes from, say, 100 to 120 Hz, the frequency of the tenth harmonic will go from 1000 to 1200 Hz, which is much easier to see. The actual pitch—or, to be more exact, the fundamental frequency—at any moment will be one-tenth that of the tenth harmonic. As we saw in Chapter 5, computers can analyze speech to give a good record of the fundamental frequency (the pitch). But most fundamental frequency routines make occasional errors when the pitch is too low, or when the vocal folds are not vibrating regularly. In these cases, a narrow-band spectrographic analysis can be very useful.

We may now summarize the kinds of information that can and cannot be obtained from spectrograms. The most reliable measurements will be those of the length of the segments, for which purpose spectrograms are often even better than waveforms. Differences among vowels, nasals, and laterals can be seen on spectrograms, whereas it may be impossible to see these differences in waveforms.

Spectrograms are usually fairly reliable indicators of relative vowel quality. The frequency of the first formant certainly shows the relative vowel height quite accurately. The second formant reflects the degree of backness quite well, but there may be confusions due to variations in the degree of lip rounding.

It is also possible to tell many things about the manner of articulation from spectrograms. For example, one can usually see whether a stop has been weakened to a fricative or even to an approximant. Affrication of a stop can be seen on most occasions. Trills can be separated from flaps, and voiced from voiceless sounds. One can also observe the relative rates of movement of different articulations.

Spectrograms cannot be used to measure degrees of nasalization, nor are they much help in differentiating between adjacent places of articulation. For studying these aspects of speech, other techniques are more useful.

INDIVIDUAL DIFFERENCES

The last subject that must be dealt with in this chapter is that of differences between individual speakers. This is important for several reasons. First, we often want to know whether a particular speech pattern is typical of a speech community or whether the speaker might have some kind of idiosyncrasy. Second, when trying to measure features that are linguistically significant, one must know how to discount purely individual features. Third, now that acoustic analyses of voices are used in forensic situations, we must discuss the validity of speaker identification.

Individual variation is readily apparent when studying spectrograms. In summarizing the uses of spectrograms, we were careful to say that they showed *relative* vowel quality. It is clearly true that one can use spectrograms such as that in Figure 8.14 to tell that the speaker has a higher vowel in *three* than in the beginning

Figure 8.18 A formant chart showing some of the vowels of two speakers of Californian English. The frequency of the first formant is plotted on the ordinate (the vertical axis), and the frequency of the second formant is plotted on the abscissa (the horizontal axis).

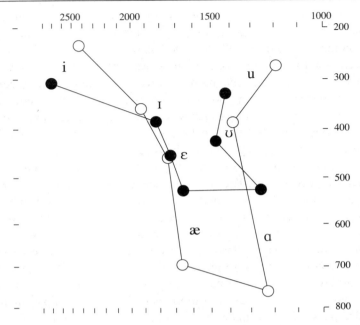

of the vowel in *here*. One can also use formant plots such as that in Figure 8.5 to show that the average American English vowel in *who'd* is farther forward than that in *hawed*. But it is not so easy to say whether the vowel in a given word as pronounced by one speaker is higher or lower than that of another speaker.

In general, when two speakers pronounce sets of vowels with the same phonetic quality, the relative positions of these vowels on a formant chart will be similar, but the absolute values of the formant frequencies will differ from speaker to speaker. Figure 8.18 shows the formants for the vowels in *heed, hid, head, had, hod, hood, who'd* as pronounced by two speakers of Californian English. The Californian English of most university students does not distinguish between *hod* and *hawed*, or between *cot* and *caught*, so it was possible to show only seven of the eight vowels in Figure 8.3. The relative positions of the vowels in each set are similar, but the absolute values are different.

No simple technique will enable one to average out the individual characteristics so that a formant plot will show only the phonetic qualities of the vowels. One way to deal with this problem is probably to regard the average frequency of the fourth formant as an indicator of the individual's head size, and then express the values of the other formants as percentages of the mean fourth formant frequency. But this possibility is not open when the fourth formant frequencies have not been reported for the sets of vowels being compared. An alternative method is to assume that each set of vowels is representative of the complete range of a speaker's vowel qualities. Then we can express the formant frequency of each vowel in terms of the total range of that formant in that speaker's voice. This method will minimize differences between extreme vowels, falsely assuming that all speakers of all languages pronounce [i, ɑ, u] in much the same way. Phoneticians do not really know how to compare acoustic data on the sounds of one individual with those of another. We cannot write a computer program that will accept any individual's vowels as input and then output a narrow phonetic transcription.

Much of the work of the applied phonetician today is concerned with computer speech technology and is directed toward improving speech-synthesis systems. The greatest challenges in the field of speech synthesis are concerned with improvements in intonation and rhythm. Synthetic speech often sounds unnatural because the intonation is too stereotyped. To get the correct pitch changes, one must know the speaker's attitude toward the world in general and to the topic under discussion in particular. In addition, the syntax of the utterance must be taken into account, as well as various higher-level pragmatic considerations, such as whether the word or a synonym of it has been used in a previous sentence. The rhythm of the sentence depends not only on all the segmental influences discussed in earlier parts of this book, but also on the particular emphasis that the speaker wishes to convey at that moment. If we are going to make synthetic speech lively and interesting, we have to develop computer programs that are very linguistically sophisticated and can also simulate human emotions.

Speech-recognition systems are largely the province of engineers, but phoneticians also play a part. For a long time, we have been able to use computers to distinguish single words, such as the digits zero through nine. More recently, several systems have been developed that can recognize limited sets of words in task-specific situations, in which the computer can structure the dialogue. For example, in an airline reservations system, the computer can ask, "Which day of the month do you wish to travel? At what time? On what airline? To what airport?" Each of these questions has only a limited set of possible answers. Computers can do all this and more, with sufficient accuracy for commercial purposes. But they cannot as yet serve as court reporters, producing an accurate written transcript of ordinary speech as spoken by people with a wide range of accents and different personal characteristics.

We will conclude this section with a few comments on speaker identification in legal proceedings. Spectrograms of a person's voice are sometimes called "voice-prints," and they are said to be as individual as fingerprints. This is a greatly exaggerated claim. If it were true, it would be very useful. Banks would be able to verify a depositor's identity over the telephone, and the police would be able to make a positive identification of criminals whose conversations had been recorded. Some individual characteristics are recorded in spectrograms. The position of the fourth and higher formants in most vowels is indicative of a speaker's voice quality rather than the linguistic aspects of the sounds. Similarly, the exact locations of the higher formants in nasals depend to a great extent on individual physiological characteristics of the speaker.

There are also a number of features observable on spectrograms that indicate a speaker's speech habits and do not depend on the speaker's language. For example, there is a great deal of individuality in the length and type of aspiration that occurs after initial voiceless stops. The rate of transition of the formants after voiced stops also varies from one individual to another. Individuals also vary considerably in their mean pitch and in the range of fundamental frequencies that they use.

Nobody knows how many individuals share similar characteristics. There are occasions when one might say that the voice on a particular recording is *probably not* the same as the voice on some other recording, and times when one might say that the voice on a recording *could* be the same as the voice on another. An expert's opinion on the probability of two voices being the same certainly has evidential value, the weight given to that evidence being for the jury to decide. But this is not the best way of reporting the results of a comparison between two voices. It is impossible to make a valid calculation of the probability of making a correct identification in any particular case, as no two cases are ever the same. There are seldom two equally good recordings of the voices in question, with both speakers talking for comparable amounts of time. The known and unknown voices may be saying the same words, but they are seldom both talking naturally, neither one being excited or worried about making a recording, and neither one bored or angry. On any pair of recordings, it's possible that the one voice is disguised or deliberately imitating the other voice. In theory, it would be possible to set up experiments that take these points and many others into account when comparing a particular pair of voices, but without elaborate prior testing, it is literally impossible to calculate the statistical probability of being right or wrong in a particular case.

The better way of reporting the results of an investigation into whether two voices are the same is in terms of the likelihood ratio, the likelihood that the two voices in question are the same as compared with the likelihood that they are different. This is a more complex statistical measure, but it does not depend on prior probabilities being known.

RECAP

This chapter outlines briefly the source/filter theory of speech production. It is interesting to call it a theory because it is now widely accepted as the explanation of speech acoustics. In the source/filter analysis of voiced sounds, the vibration of the vocal folds produces a noise source which is then filtered by the vocal tract so that some parts of the source signal are amplified and some are attenuated. If you've ever played with a graphic equalizer on a stereo system (perhaps your grandparents own one?) this concept of shaping a sound may be familiar. The acoustics of tubes, familiar from musical instruments like trombones and pipe organs, is applicable to the acoustics filter properties of the vocal tract.

The three lowest resonant frequencies of the vocal tract filter (the first three formants) uniquely specify most vowels in the languages of the world, and when you plot the first formant against the second formant the resulting vowel space pretty much is the auditory vowel space that we discussed in Chapter 4.

Consonant sounds also have source and filter characteristics. Consonant place of articulation is largely evident in the movements of formants in the vowels just before or after the consonant (the formant locus). This is almost the only information available for stop consonants, while in fricatives we also have noise during the fricative that indicates the place of articulation. The source of noise in voiceless sounds clearly can't be voicing, but is instead some form of turbulence, either in a short burst of noise at the release of a stop or in a sustained period of turbulence in a fricative. These sources, like voicing, are also shaped by the vocal tract and so differ by place of articulation. Given these basic observations, a few general acoustics correlates (Table 8.1), and some basic strategies, it is often possible to decode spectrograms well enough to guess what the utterance was. It is also possible, given knowledge of the intended utterance, and with listening and phonetic transcription, to discern a great deal about the articulatory details of an utterance by taking acoustic measurements of duration and formant frequency trajectories.

EXERCISES

(Printable versions of exercises as well as additional interactive spectrogram reading exercises are available on the website.)

A. Put a transcription of the segments in the phrase *Please pass me my book* above the waveform. Draw lines showing the boundaries between the segments.

B. The spectrogram shows the phrase *Show me a spotted hyena*. Put a transcription above it, and show the segment boundaries. In places where there are no clear boundaries (as in the first part of *hyena*), draw dashed lines.

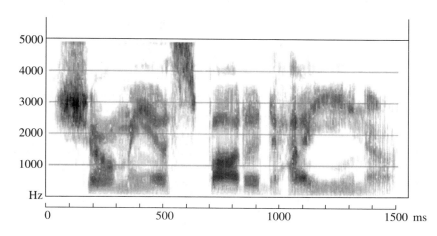

C. In the following spectrogram, the segments have been delimited, some with dashed lines because they do not have sharp boundaries. In each of the spaces above the spectrogram, write a symbol for a sound that has the same manner of articulation as that segment. Possible symbols for the first segment have been filled in as examples. A few other segments that are particularly difficult to determine have also been filled in.

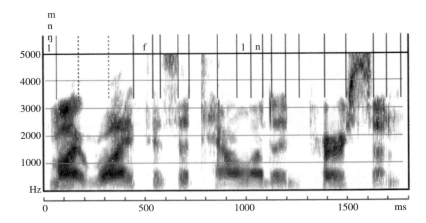

D. In Exercise C, the spectrogram is of an ordinary English sentence, containing no names, so obviously the third possibility shown for the first segment could not be correct, as no English sentence could begin with [ŋ]. Bearing in mind what sequences of sounds are possible in English, write as many words or syllables as you can. The sentence is a true statement.

E. Look at the sentence in Figure 8.15, a spectrogram for which the text is not given. Say as much as you can about the different segments.

F. Using a speech analysis program such as WaveSurfer, make spectrograms of the sound files in Web example 8.2. Measure the F1, F2, and F3 in *bird*, *hand*, *two*, and *bush*. Given these measurements, which vowels are most similar to each other? Does this way of measuring vowel similarity correspond with your auditory judgment of their similarity?

G. Using the "4L" formula that relates vocal tract length and formant frequencies [$F_n = (2n - 1) \times c/4L$], what are the formant frequencies for [ə] of a child whose vocal tract is 9 cm long?

H. Again using the same formula, calculate the resonances of a vocal tract 16 cm long when the person is breathing air $c = 35,000$ cm/s versus helium $c = 92,700$ cm/s.

I. Looking at Figure 8.2, give the perturbation theory explanation for why F2 has a low frequency in the high back rounded vowel [u]. Californian English [u] has a somewhat higher F2 than is found in other varieties of English. Some people say that the Californian [u] is "fronted," while others think of it as "unrounded." Interestingly, perturbation theory doesn't help resolve this question—why not?

9

Vowels and Vowel-Like Articulations

In previous chapters, we saw that there are three main aspects of vowel quality: (1) vowel height, which is inversely proportional to the frequency of the first formant; (2) backness, which is proportional to the difference between the frequencies of the second and first formants; and (3) the degree of lip rounding, which usually lowers both the second and the third formants. This chapter discusses these three features in greater detail and also considers some additional, less prominent, features of vowel quality.

Figure 4.2 in Chapter 4 shows the relative auditory qualities of the English vowels and diphthongs. As we mentioned at that time, the precise locations of the points in this diagram reflect acoustic measurements, not mere auditory impressions. It is, in fact, a formant chart, similar to that shown in Figure 9.1 (on page 228). Some of the acoustic measurements are the formant frequencies reported in Chapter 8. They are supplemented by measurements of the formant frequencies of the other vowels and diphthongs, all taken from published sources. (For bibliographical details, see the Notes at the back of the book.)

Most phoneticians would agree that Figure 9.1 is a fairly accurate reflection of both the way in which American English vowels have traditionally been described and the way in which listeners perceive the relative auditory qualities. During the discussion of this diagram in Chapter 4, you probably made up your own mind as to the extent to which it agrees with your perception of the relative distance between vowels. But remember that if it seems inaccurate to you, this may be because your accent is not identical to the variety of English represented in the figure.

CARDINAL VOWELS

When describing the vowels that occur on a particular occasion, one may not have access to measurements of the formant frequencies. Phoneticians who want to describe the vowels of a certain dialect or of a certain speaker often have to rely on their auditory abilities. They plot the vowels on a vowel chart, so that anybody familiar with vowel charts can see where the points are and can infer the quality of the vowels they are describing.

228 CHAPTER 9 Vowels and Vowel-Like Articulations

Figure 9.1 A combined acoustic and auditory representation of some of the vowels of American English. (Compare Figures 4.2 and 8.9.)

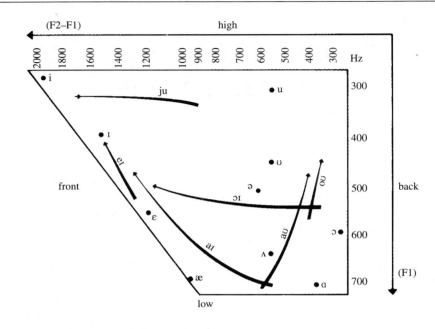

For a vowel chart to be truly interpretable, the vowels on it must be plotted with reference to certain fixed points. These points must be known to both the people originally plotting the vowels and the people who are going to interpret their descriptions. The space within a vowel chart represents a continuum of possible qualities. Before you can convey anything by saying that a certain vowel is halfway (or a third of the way) between one vowel and another, you must be certain that you and your readers share a set of auditory reference vowels. There are several ways in which known reference vowels can be provided.

In the first place, we can rely on the fact that a vowel chart shows the limits of possible vowel quality. Thus, a point in the extreme upper left corner of the chart represents a vowel with the highest and most front quality possible. If the tongue were moved higher or more forward, a palatal consonant would be produced. A vowel in the extreme lower right corner represents the lowest and most back quality possible. Further movement of the tongue would produce a pharyngeal consonant. This gives us two fixed reference points—[i] and [ɑ]. Similarly, the points in the other two corners of the diagram represent extreme acoustic qualities, though their articulatory definition is not simple.

EXAMPLE 9.1 This use of a vowel chart is quite satisfactory for the description of vowels that are near the corners of the possible vowel area. But it does not provide enough fixed points for the description of other vowels. Recognizing this problem, the

Figure 9.2 The cardinal vowels.

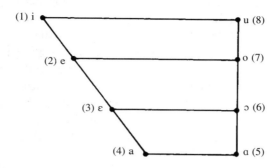

British phonetician Daniel Jones proposed a series of eight **cardinal vowels**, evenly spaced around the outside of the possible vowel area and designed to act as fixed reference points for phoneticians (see Figure 9.2 and listen to the vowels in Web example 9.1). In no case is the quality of a cardinal vowel exactly the same as that of an English vowel. It can happen that a particular language may have a vowel that is virtually identical to a cardinal vowel. Several of the vowels of a conservative form of Parisian French are very similar. But by definition, the cardinal vowels are arbitrary reference points.

Two of the cardinal vowels are defined in articulatory terms. Cardinal vowel (1) is produced with the lips spread and the tongue as high and far forward as possible without causing audible friction. It is therefore something like the vowel [i], but with a more extreme quality. The symbol for it is also [i].

The other cardinal vowel that is defined in articulatory terms is cardinal vowel (5). This vowel is made with the lips in a neutral position—neither spread nor rounded—and with the tongue as low and as far back as possible. Accordingly, it is something like some forms of the American English vowel [ɑ] as in *father, hot* or the British English vowel [ɒ] as in *hot*. The American [ɑ], however, is not usually made with the tongue as far back as possible, and the British [ɒ] usually has slight lip rounding. The symbol for cardinal vowel (5) is [ɑ].

Try to make cardinal vowels (1) and (5) in accordance with these descriptions. Remember to have your lips fully spread when saying [i]. Make sure your tongue is so close to the roof of the mouth that you would produce a voiced palatal fricative [ʝ] if you raised it any higher. Similarly, when producing [ɑ], make sure your tongue is pulled so far down and back in the mouth that you are almost producing a voiced pharyngeal fricative [ʕ] (not to be confused with a glottal stop, which is [ʔ]).

Cardinal vowels (2), (3), and (4) are defined as front vowels that form a series of auditorily equidistant steps between numbers (1) and (5). As we saw in the previous chapter, the acoustic definition of front vowels is that the distance between formant one and formant two is as great as possible. We can also specify in acoustic terms what is meant by *auditorily equidistant steps*. It implies that when these five vowels are plotted on a formant chart of the kind we have been discussing, they will be represented by points that are equal distances apart. (There are some complications in this respect that we will discuss later.)

Cardinal vowels (6), (7), and (8) are defined as vowels that continue from number (5), with the same-size steps as in the first part of the series, but are as back as possible (i.e., with as small a distance as possible between formants one and two). In order to continue with these same-size steps, the back vowels have to become not only increasingly higher but also increasingly more rounded. As a result, cardinal vowel (8) is in fact the highest, most back, most rounded possible vowel—even though it is not defined in this way.

The symbols for cardinal vowels (2), (3), and (4) are [e, ɛ, a], respectively. The symbols for cardinal vowels (6), (7), and (8) are [ɔ, o, u]. Most of these vowels have qualities something like those of the English vowels we have been symbolizing in a similar way. In accordance with the principles of the IPA, the symbols chosen for most of the English vowels are those of the nearest cardinal vowels. The major exception is the vowel in *fat*, which, following the tradition of many English-speaking phoneticians, has been symbolized by [æ] rather than [a].

The cardinal vowel system has been extensively used by phoneticians in the description of a wide variety of languages. There are, however, a number of difficulties in this respect. First, as Daniel Jones said in *An Outline of English Phonetics* (London: Heffer, 1957): "The values of the cardinal vowels cannot be learned from written descriptions; they should be learned by oral instruction from a teacher who knows them." It was for this reason that we did not suggest you try to produce a complete series of cardinal vowels immediately after reading the descriptions given above. Listen to the recordings of cardinal vowels on the book's website, and try to find someone who can listen critically to your imitations of them. With a good assistant, it is possible to learn to produce them with a fair degree of accuracy. It is also helpful to listen to a recording of yourself saying the cardinal vowels.

A second problem with the cardinal vowel system is the notion of auditory equidistance between the vowels. The traditional description of the cardinal vowels arranges them on a plot, as shown in Figure 9.2, in which the points are not equidistant. Cardinal vowels (5), (6), (7), and (8) are much closer together than (1), (2), (3), (4), and (5). This plot is somewhat in agreement with the notion that vowel height corresponds inversely to the frequency of formant one, and backness corresponds to the distance between formant two and formant one. The line on the left-hand side of the figure slants because the degree of the distance between formants one and two decreases in going from [i] to [ɑ]. It is comparatively straight on the right-hand side because the distance between the first two formants is much the same for these vowels; both formant one and formant two go steadily down from [ɑ] to [u].

Another problem with the cardinal vowel system is that there has been a great deal of confusion over whether vowels are being described in terms of tongue height or in terms of acoustic properties. Many phoneticians, and many textbooks

Figure 9.3 The highest points of the tongue as shown in a published set of x-rays of cardinal vowels. The outline of the upper surface of the vocal tract is not clear on the x-rays and is, therefore, estimated.

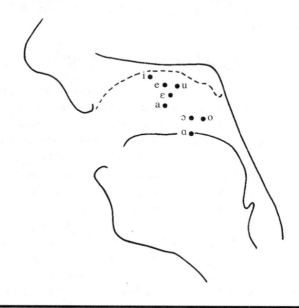

on phonetics, talk about diagrams such as Figure 9.2 as if they specified the highest point of the tongue. The distance between the points representing the back vowels is therefore said to be less because the movements of the tongue are said to be less (which is not actually true). The differences in auditory quality are presumed to be the same in both front and back vowels, despite the supposed smaller movements of the tongue in back vowels, because back vowels also have increasing lip rounding. But diagrams such as Figures 9.1 and 9.2 do not really specify the position of the highest point of the tongue. Figure 9.3 shows the relative positions of the highest point of the tongue in a set of cardinal vowels. These positions form an outline very different from that in Figure 9.2. The same point can be made by referring to Figures 1.8 and 1.9, which show the articulatory positions of some of the vowels in Figure 9.1. The position of the highest point of the tongue is not a valid indicator of vowel quality. We have tried to avoid describing vowels in terms of tongue height, using instead the term *vowel height*—meaning an auditory quality that can be specified in acoustic rather than articulatory terms.

Despite these problems, the cardinal vowel system has worked fairly successfully. It has allowed the vowels of many languages and dialects to be described with far greater precision than by any other method. The descriptions may have been said in the past to be descriptions of tongue height, but in fact, phoneticians had all along been making very accurate judgments of the frequency of the first formant and the distance between the frequencies of the second and first formants. The best way to describe vowels is by making acoustic analyses and video recordings of a group of speakers—specifying their formant frequencies and lip and jaw positions. But this is not always possible, and the ability to make auditory judgments in terms of a set of reference vowels is still a necessary skill for any phonetician.

SECONDARY CARDINAL VOWELS

The cardinal vowels have increasing degrees of lip rounding, [i] having spread lips, [ɑ] having a neutral lip position, and [u] being fully rounded. If we consider vowels to be specifiable in terms of three dimensions, this implies that the cardinal vowels fall on a plane in this three-dimensional space, as shown in Figure 9.4. Most of the vowels of English would also fall on this plane, although for many speakers of American English, [u] is a back vowel that is comparatively unrounded. As a result, F2 is comparatively high, and the location on the chart appears to be farther forward than it would be if it were rounded.

As an aid in the description of vowels with different degrees of lip rounding, there is a series of secondary cardinal vowels numbered (9) through (16). These vowels differ from the eight primary cardinal vowels in having an opposite amount of lip rounding. Cardinal vowel (9) is defined as a vowel with the same tongue position as cardinal vowel (1), but with closely rounded lips. Cardinal vowels (10) through (16) have the same tongue positions as cardinal vowels (2) through (8), but continually decreasing—instead of increasing—lip rounding. Cardinal vowel (16), therefore, is an unrounded version of cardinal vowel (8).

Figure 9.4 A three-dimensional representation of the vowel space, showing that the cardinal vowels fall on a plane that cuts across the space.

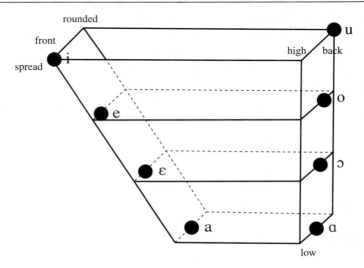

Figure 9.5 The symbols for some secondary cardinal vowels and some central vowels.

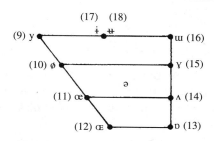

Figure 9.5 shows the symbols for these vowels, together with some additional symbols for central vowels. The symbols [ɨ] and [ʉ] are used for unrounded and rounded vowels midway between cardinal vowels (1) and (8). The symbol [ə] is not defined in terms of cardinal vowels but is used, as we have seen, for a range of mid-central vowels. In addition, note that the symbol [ʌ], which is the symbol for an unrounded cardinal vowel (6), is sometimes used for a lowered mid-central vowel.

Even if you cannot make a complete set of the primary cardinal vowels, you should try to make some of the secondary cardinal vowels. Practice rounding and unrounding your lips while saying cardinal vowel (1), so that you say [iy iy iy]. Make sure you maintain an absolutely constant tongue position and move only your lips. Next, repeat this exercise with cardinal vowel (2) or some similar vowel of the [e] type. Remember that the rounding for [ø] is not as close as that for [y]. Last, try unrounding cardinal vowel (8), producing [uɯ uɯ uɯ]. The usual difficulty here is in maintaining a sufficiently back tongue position, as most dialects of English do not have a very back variety of [u]. Note also that the secondary cardinal vowels you learn to produce by doing these exercises are arbitrary reference points and not necessarily the same as the vowels in any particular language. However, the vowels [y] and [ø] are fairly similar to the French front rounded vowels that occur in *tu* [ty] 'you' and *peu* [pø] 'small.'

Distances on an appropriately scaled acoustic vowel chart such as that in Figure 8.6 are similar to auditory distances for vowels in the plane of the cardinal vowels. But this is not so for vowels with degrees of rounding unlike those of the nearest cardinal vowels. Front vowels that are rounded or back vowels that are unrounded will be misplaced on a chart if we rely simply on acoustic criteria. The degree of rounding is an independent dimension that must be stated separately from the degree of height (the inverse of the first formant) and the degree of backness (the distance between formant two and formant one). The perspective of the vowel space in Figure 9.4 was chosen to reflect the formant frequencies of the secondary cardinal vowels as much as possible. Secondary cardinal vowel [y] will have a lower formant two, bringing it more to the right of the figure; secondary cardinal vowel [ɯ] will have a higher formant two, bringing it more to the left. But the first formant of each of these vowels is much the same as the corresponding primary cardinal vowel.

VOWELS IN OTHER ACCENTS OF ENGLISH

For those who do not know the cardinal vowels, an alternative method of describing vowels is to use as reference points the vowels of a particular dialect of a language that is known to both the person making the description and the person reading the description. This is what we have been trying to do in reference to the vowels of American English as shown in Figure 9.1. If both the person making the description and the person reading the description know what these vowels sound like, then the points in Figure 9.1 provide good reference points. When we remark, for example, that in some forms of New Zealand English, the vowel in *sacks* is similar to the American English [ɛ] vowel in *sex*, then you should be able to pronounce this word in this particular way. (You can listen to a sample of New Zealand English in the recordings for transcription in the "Extras" section of the website. Note the pronunciation of *rat*.)

Any language will serve to provide known reference points. For example, when teaching English as a second language, one might use the vowels of the first language of the students as reference points for comparison with the dialect of English that one is trying to teach. If a chart of the vowels of this language is not available, then the instructor's first step should be to make one. This will involve either comparing the vowels of this language with the vowels of some language known to the instructor for which there is a chart available, or making a recording of the vowels of the language in question and analyzing them using a program such as WaveSurfer.

There are published descriptions of the auditory quality of the vowels in a large number of languages. There are also many sets of acoustic measurements available. We can now make precise statements about many accents of English by reference to the average formant frequencies of groups of speakers. The accent of American English represented in Figure 9.1 is fairly conservative, typical perhaps of senior newscasters. The first two formants of a group of university students in California are shown in Figure 9.6. We have already noted that this accent does not contrast the vowels in *cot* and *caught*—they are both [ɑ]. Now we can see that younger Californians have a higher vowel (lower first formant) in [eɪ] than in [ɪ]. The high back vowels seem more front in that they have a higher second formant. In the case of the vowel [ʊ] as in *good*, this is largely a matter of unrounding. This vowel is often pronounced with spread lips.

Another change is going on in a number of northern cities in the United States, such as Pittsburgh and Detroit. As you can see from Figure 9.7, in this accent, [æ] has been raised (formant one has decreased) so that it is very close to [ɛ]. The back vowels have a lower second formant, making them all farther back than in Californian English. This accent does distinguish [ɑ] and [ɔ].

Vowels in Other Accents of English   235

Figure 9.6 A plot of the first two formants of the vowels of a group of Californian English speakers.

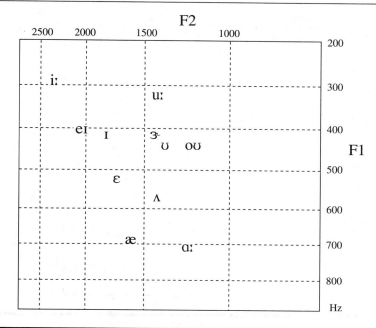

Figure 9.7 A plot of the first two formants of the vowels of northern U.S. cities English.

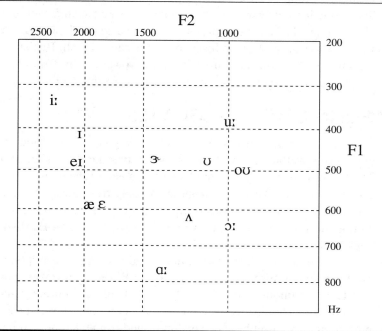

Figure 9.8 A plot of the first two formants of the vowels of BBC English.

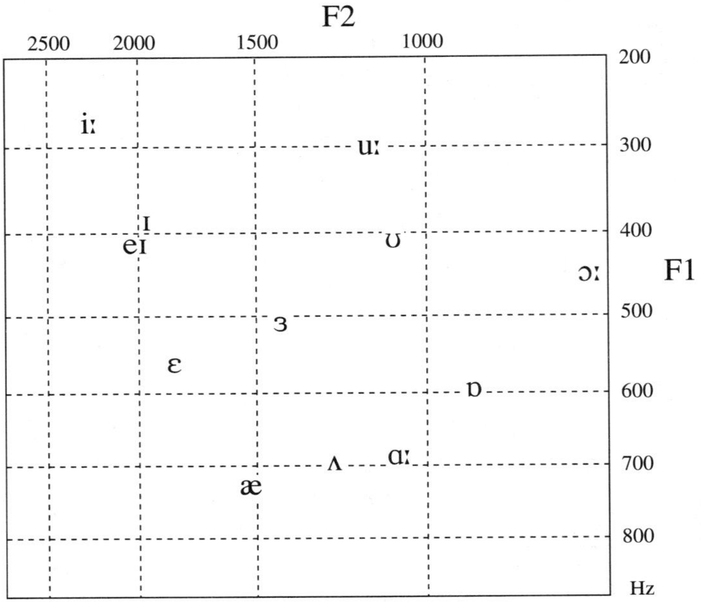

[Figure 9.8: Vowel formant plot with F2 (2500–1000 Hz) on horizontal axis and F1 (200–800 Hz) on vertical axis, showing positions of iː, ɪ, eɪ, ɛ, æ, ʌ, ɜ, ɑː, ɒ, ɔː, ʊ, uː]

Finally, among accents of English, consider the vowels in Figure 9.8, which are the mean of a group of BBC English speakers. The main feature to be noted here is the distinction between the three back vowels [ɑ] as in *father*, *cart*, [ɒ] as in *bother*, *cot*, and [ɔ] as in *author*, *caught*. Note also that [ʌ] has a very low position in comparison with most forms of American English. British English speakers distinguish the vowel [ʌ] in *cut* from the vowel [ɜ] in *curt* (which does not have any *r*-coloring) mainly by the frequency of the first formant.

VOWELS IN OTHER LANGUAGES

Next we will consider the vowels of three other languages for which acoustic measurements are available. Vowel charts for all three languages are shown in Figure 9.9. The sources for the data are listed at the end of the book.

Spanish has a very simple system, contrasting only five vowels. Note that the symbols used in broad transcriptions of Spanish are [i, e, a, o, u]. Obviously, these symbols do not have the same values in Spanish and in English, or in descriptions of cardinal vowels.

Japanese also has a set of five vowels. In a broad phonetic transcription, these might also have been transcribed [i, e, a, o, u]. But in a narrower transcription that reflects the phonetic quality of the vowels more accurately, the high back vowel could be transcribed as [ɯ], as has been done in Figure 9.9. The point representing this vowel has been distinguished from the others. It has been

Figure 9.9 The vowels of Spanish, Japanese, and Danish. Front rounded vowels and back unrounded vowels are indicated by asterisks.

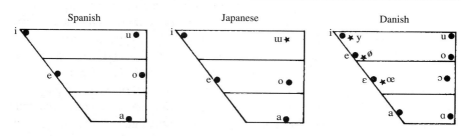

marked by an asterisk to show that this vowel does not have the lip rounding associated with the primary cardinal vowel in this area. It is not, however, really unrounded. The lips are fairly close together. In a more detailed phonetic analysis, one could say that there are two types of lip movements. In one, the corners of the lips are brought forward so that they are somewhat protruded, and in the other, they are simply narrowed vertically so that they may be said to be compressed. Note also that [e] in Japanese is slightly lower than it is in Spanish. This is the kind of small difference between vowels that is easily and conveniently expressible in terms of vowel charts.

Also shown in Figure 9.9 are the vowels of a conservative form of Danish. (Danish is changing rapidly, and young Danes have different vowel qualities.) Asterisks have been used to represent the quality of some of the Danish vowels in Figure 9.9, but in this case it is to indicate that those vowels differ from the primary cardinal vowels in the area by having more rather than less lip rounding. Danish contrasts three front rounded vowels in words such as *dyr* / dyːr / 'expensive,' *dør* / døːr / 'dies,' and *dør* (same spelling) / dœːr / 'door.' (As you can hear in the recording of these words on the website, Danish / r / is realized as a pharyngeal approximant.) All the Danish vowels shown in Figure 9.9 can occur in long or short form. The front vowels are illustrated in Table 9.1 and in Web example 9.4. The qualities of most of the short vowels are very similar to those of the long vowels, but in the case of [a, ɔ, o], the short versions are slightly lower and more centralized.

EXAMPLE 9.4

The three charts in Figure 9.9 are good examples of the way in which vowels may be described. They are in part descriptions of the relative auditory quality, in part articulatory descriptions. For the vowels in which the lip rounding is

TABLE 9.1 Contrasts in vowel length in Danish.

viːdə	hvide	'white'	vilə	vilde	'wild'	viːlə	hvile	'rest'
veːdə	hvede	'wheat'	menə	minde	'remind'	meːnə	mene	'mean'
vɛːdə	væde	'wet'	lɛsə	læsse	'load'	lɛːsə	læse	'read'
væːdə	vade	'wade'	mæsə	masse	'mass'	mæːsə	mase	'mash'

the same as that of the primary cardinal vowels, they reflect the acoustic data exactly. In these cases, they are equivalent to plots of the first formant frequency against the difference between the frequencies of the second and first formants.

Front rounded and back unrounded vowels cannot be represented on a vowel chart that assumes the degree of lip rounding is like that of the primary cardinal vowels. In describing these other vowels, the degree of lip rounding must also be specified. One way of doing this is to use asterisks rather than ordinary points. The asterisks indicate that the lip rounding is more like that of the secondary cardinal vowels than that of the primary ones. The locations of the asterisks indicate the vowel qualities in much the same way that the points indicate the qualities of the other vowels. It is as if they show what the formant frequencies would have been had the lip-rounding been like that of the primary cardinal vowels.

When we consider the actual formant frequencies of front rounded vowels and back unrounded vowels, we can see why these vowels are not quite so common in most languages. Adding lip rounding to front vowels lowers the higher formants. As a result, a high front rounded [y] sounds as if it were between [i] and [u], as we noted at the end of the preceding section when discussing Figure 9.4. Similarly, [œ], which is the front rounded vowel corresponding to [ɛ], has a lower formant two than [ɛ]. When its formants are plotted on a chart, it appears nearer the center. Conversely, removing lip-rounding from the back vowel [u] to produce [ɯ] raises formant two, so that it would also be nearer the center of a formant chart. If the vowels of a language are to be maximally distinct from one another, then the front vowels will have to be unrounded and the back vowels rounded.

One of the forces acting on languages may be called the principle of *sufficient perceptual separation*, whereby the sounds of a language are kept acoustically distinct to make it easier for the listener to distinguish one from another. As a result of this principle, in by far the majority of languages, the degree of lip rounding can be predicted from the degree of backness and, to a lesser extent, the degree of height. Front vowels are usually unrounded and back vowels are usually rounded, with the degree of rounding increasing with the degree of height. In this way, the vowels of a language are kept maximally distinct. Front rounded vowels occur in a number of well-known languages spoken in Europe, such as French, German, Dutch, and Swedish (all of which can be found on the website), but, in accordance with the notions of perceptual separation, they are not particularly common among the languages of the world.

ADVANCED TONGUE ROOT

Differences in vowel quality can usually be described in terms of variations in the degrees of height, backness, and lip rounding. But in some languages, there are differences in vowel quality that cannot be described in these terms. For example, in Akan, a West African language spoken mainly in Ghana, there are two sets of vowels, which you can hear on the website in example 9.5. They differ primarily in the size of the pharynx. In the one set, there are vowels in which the root of the

Figure 9.10 Narrow (−ATR, broken line) and wide (+ATR, solid line) vowels in Akan, a language spoken in Ghana.

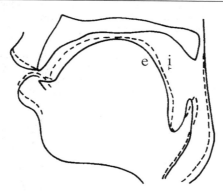

tongue is drawn forward and the larynx is lowered so that the part of the vocal tract in the pharynx is considerably enlarged. These vowels are called **advanced tongue root** (more simply, +ATR) vowels. In the other set, there are vowels in which there is no advancement of the tongue root or lowering of the larynx (−ATR vowels). Figure 9.10 shows the shape of the vocal tract in two Akan vowels that differ in this way. In the +ATR vowel [e], the whole tongue is bunched up lengthwise in comparison with the −ATR vowel, here symbolized as [i̠]. We should also note that not all speakers of Akan make a distinction between these two vowels in this way. Some seem to rely more on movements of the root of the tongue, and others more on differences in larynx height. What matters for the distinction between the two sets of vowels is that one should have a comparatively large pharyngeal cavity and the other a comparatively small one.

In English, no pairs of vowels are distinguished simply by this tongue gesture, although tongue root position varies to some extent in conjunction with vowel height. The tense high vowels [i] and [u], as in *heed* and *who'd*, have a more advanced tongue root than the lax mid-high vowels [ɪ] and [ʊ], as in *hid* and *hood*. However, the distinction between +ATR vowels and −ATR vowels is not the same as the distinction between tense and lax vowels in English, which was discussed in Chapter 4. The two sets of English vowels are divided by phonological considerations, such as the fact that tense vowels can occur in open syllables and lax vowels cannot, rather than by a particular tongue gesture or shape of the vocal tract.

RHOTACIZED VOWELS

As we saw in Chapter 4, many forms of American English have rhotacized vowels in words such as *sir, cur, bird*. We also noted that *r*-coloring can be produced in more than one way. Figure 9.11 (on page 240) shows the tongue positions of three forms of American English [ɚ]. Some speakers use one of these; others, another. As shown by the heavy black line, the gesture can involve the tongue being

Figure 9.11 Possible tongue positions for the vowel [ɚ] in American English. The tongue-tip-up post-alveolar approximant (thin black line) is the most common, followed by the bunched tongue (solid black line). The gray line indicates possible intermediate positions.

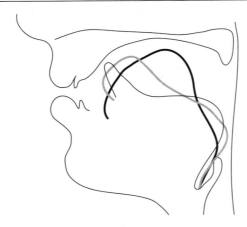

bunched up in the center of the mouth, with the tip down and pulled back from the lower teeth. An important feature of this kind of rhotic articulation is that there is also a slight narrowing of the pharyngeal cavity. A second possibility, shown by the thin black line, is a gesture in which the tip of the tongue is raised to near the back of the alveolar ridge, forming a post-alveolar approximant. This is accompanied by a narrowing of the pharyngeal cavity at a slightly higher level. The third possibility, the gray line, shows a bunched tongue configuration in which the tip of the tongue is raised. If you are a speaker a rhotic form of American English, see if you can determine which of these articulations you use. One way of getting helpful information is to insert a toothpick between the teeth while you hold the position for the vowel [ɚ]. Does the toothpick touch the upper surface of your tongue, or is your tongue tip raised so that it touches the tip or the undersurface of the blade of the tongue? Using this "toothpick test" we find that most Americans (about 60 percent) touch the underside of the tongue rather than the top—the tongue tip is raised. Ultrasound imaging suggests that relatively few speakers produce the truly retroflex [ɚ] (the thin line in Figure 9.11). Instead, the tip raised, bunched configuration (the gray line in Figure 9.11) is the most common tongue position for [ɚ] in American English. You can hear an American English speaker producing rhotacized vowels among those recorded for Chapter 2 on the website. This speaker has his tongue bunched with the tip down and (almost certainly, although we have no x-ray or other evidence) a constriction in the pharynx.

Rhotacization is an auditory quality, which, like height and backness, is most appropriately defined in acoustic terms. In a rhotacized vowel (or portion of a vowel) there is a marked lowering of the frequency of the third formant. The frequencies of the first two formants determine the vowel height and backness.

Figure 9.12 A spectrogram showing the lowering of the frequency of the third formant (and the second formant) during rhotacized sounds in a sentence in American English.

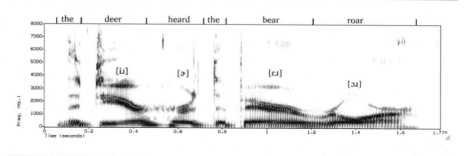

The frequency of the third formant conveys comparatively little information about either of these aspects of vowel quality. If you look back at Figure 8.3, you will see that throughout the whole series of non-rhotacized vowels, the third formant falls only slightly. But, as you can see in Figure 9.12, there is a large fall in the frequency of the third formant in words such as *deer* and *bear*, in which the ends of the vowels are considerably rhotacized in many forms of American English. Furthermore, throughout most of the word *heard*, (until the formant transitions for / d / begin) the third formant may be low, indicating that even at the beginning of the vowel, there is a rhotacized quality.

NASALIZATION

In all the vowels we have been considering in this chapter so far, the soft palate has been raised so that there is a velic closure, and air does not flow out through the nose. Vowels will be **nasalized** if the soft palate is lowered to allow part of the airstream to escape through the nose. The "tilde" diacritic [˜] may be placed over any vowel to indicate that it is nasalized. Vowels of this kind are commonly called **nasal vowels**.

Learn to produce a variety of nasalized vowels. Start by saying the low vowel [æ̃] as in *man* [mæ̃n]. Alternate a series of nasalized and non-nasalized vowels, saying [æ æ̃ æ æ̃ æ æ̃]. You should be able to feel your soft palate moving up and down when you say these vowels. Try to say a whole series of nasalized vowels [ĩ ẽ ɛ̃ ã ɑ̃ ɔ̃ õ ũ]. Alternate each of these vowels with its non-nasalized counterpart. Many languages have contrasts between nasal and oral vowels. French contrasts are illustrated in Web example 9.7.

Consonants such as [m, n, ŋ] are, of course, nasals, but they are not *nasalized*, since this term implies that part of the air goes out through the nose and part through the mouth. Contrasts between nasalized and non-nasalized consonants probably do not occur in any language, but some consonants, such as [w, j, ɹ, l], may be nasalized if they occur next to nasalized vowels. In Yoruba, the word for 'they' is [w̃ɔ̃], with the whole syllable being nasalized.

TABLE 9.2	The features of vowel quality.
Quality	Correlates
Height	Frequency of formant one
Backness	Difference between frequencies of formant two and formant one
Rhotacization	Frequency of formant three
Rounding	Lip position
ATR	Width of the pharynx
Nasalization	Position of the soft palate

SUMMARY OF VOWEL QUALITY

Table 9.2 summarizes the discussion of vowels. There are two features of vowel quality—height and backness—that are used to contrast one vowel with another in nearly every language, and there are four other features that are used less frequently. Of the six features, the first three in the table reflect auditory properties, each of which may be produced in more than one way from an articulatory point of view, and the remaining three reflect relatively invariant articulatory properties with complex acoustic correlates that differ from vowel to vowel. Thus, lip rounding generally lowers the second formant, but in the case of high front vowels, it is predominantly the third formant that is lowered; similarly, ATR and nasalization affect different formants in different vowels.

SEMIVOWELS

Without being too precise about the meaning of the terms *syllable* and *syllabic* (a matter we will discuss in the next chapter), we can say that all sounds function either as the peaks of syllables or at the syllable margins. Vowels are clearly at the peaks of syllables and are syllabic. Consonants are generally not syllabic, although some consonants such as [l] and [n] can be syllabic in words like *shuttle* [ˈʃʌtl̩] and *button* [ˈbʌʔn̩]. We can also divide sounds into those that have no obstruction in the center of the mouth, which may be called **vocoids**, and those that have an obstruction. The latter group, which will include most consonants, may be called nonvocoids. This gives us a pair of divisions that we can arrange as shown in Table 9.3.

TABLE 9.3	Sounds can be classified as vocoids or nonvocoids and as syllabic or nonsyllabic.	
	Vocoid	Nonvocoid
Syllabic	Vowels [i] [u] [a]	Syllabic cons. [n̩] [l̩]
Nonsyllabic	Semivowels [j] [w]	Consonants [p] [t] [k]

| TABLE 9.4 | Contrasts involving palatal, labial-palatal, and labial-velar approximants in French. |

Palatal		Labial-Palatal		Labial-Velar	
mjɛt	'crumb'	mɥɛt	'mute'	mwɛt	'sea gull'
lje	'tied'	lɥi	'him'	lwi	'Louis'
		ɥit	'eight'	wi	'yes'

Given this division, we can define vowels as syllabic vocoids and **semivowels** as nonsyllabic vocoids. The term *semiconsonant* is sometimes used for syllabic nonvocoids, but we will refer to them simply as syllabic consonants. Similarly, nonvocoids are sometimes called true consonants, a term that could be applicable whether they are syllabic or not.

Here we are concerned with semivowels, which are vocoids that function as the beginning or end of a syllable. When at the beginning of a syllable, a semivowel usually consists of a rapid glide from a high vowel position to that of the following vowel. The semivowels in English are [j] and [w], which are like nonsyllabic versions of the English high vowels [i] and [u], respectively. In some languages (e.g., French), there are the three high vowels [i, u, y]. In some of these languages, there is also a semivowel corresponding to the high front rounded vowel [y]. The symbol for this sound is [ɥ], an inverted letter *h*, which is intended to look a little like [y]. Examples of words contrasting the three semivowels in French are given in Table 9.4.

Earlier in this chapter, we noted that Japanese has a high unrounded vowel [ɯ]. It does not have spread lips like [i] but lips that are fairly close together, compressed vertically, with the corners neither drawn back as in a spread vowel nor pulled together as in a rounded vowel. There is a Japanese semivowel bearing the same relation to this vowel as [w] does to [u] in English. The symbol for this semivowel is [ɰ].

EXAMPLE 9.8

The gesture for a semivowel is like that for an approximant in that it can be considered to have a particular place of articulation, like other consonants. We have already noted that [j] is a palatal approximant, and [w] is a labial-velar approximant. The semivowel [ɥ] is a labial-palatal approximant. We have not discussed this place of articulation before because approximants are almost the only sounds that are made in this region. The semivowel [ɰ] is a velar approximant.

When learning to produce the distinction between the French sounds / w / and / ɥ /, note that the English / w / is between the two French sounds. It is not the same as French / w /. It is, of course, also true that / u / in English is between the two French sounds [u] and [y]. As is often the case, when a language does not have to distinguish between two possibilities, it produces a sound that is between the two. Recall, for example, the quality of English vowels before [ŋ] and before [r], where there are no oppositions between tense and lax vowels.

To produce the French sound / w / as in *oui* [wi] 'yes,' start from a high rounded vowel that is fully back, like a cardinal [u]. Glide from this vowel very rapidly to the following vowel. The result will be similar but not identical to the English word *we* [wi]. Now try to say the French sound [ɥ] as in *huit* [ɥit] 'eight.' This time, start from the secondary cardinal vowel [y] and glide rapidly to the following vowel.

It is also possible to consider the common form of English [ɹ], as in *red*, as a semivowel. In the same way that [w] may be said to be a nonsyllabic counterpart of [u], so [ɹ] as in *red* may be said to be a nonsyllabic version of the vowel in American English *fur*. From a phonetic point of view, regarding [ɹ] in *red* as a semivowel may be a valid description. But from a phonological point of view, it may not be appropriate in describing the sound patterns that occur in English.

SECONDARY ARTICULATORY GESTURES

It is appropriate to consider secondary articulations in conjunction with vowels because they can usually be described as added vowel-like articulations. Formally defined, a **secondary articulation** is a gesture with a lesser degree of closure occurring at approximately the same time as another (primary) gesture. We will consider four types of secondary articulation.

Palatalization is the addition of a high front tongue gesture, like that in [i], to another gesture. Russian and other Slavic languages have a series of palatalized consonants that contrast with their nonpalatalized counterparts. In Slavic linguistics the palatalized consonants are called *soft* and the nonpalatalized consonants (which are sometimes actually a little pharyngealized) are called *hard*. Palatalization can be symbolized by [ʲ] after a symbol. Russian words illustrating palatalized sounds are given in Table 9.5.

EXAMPLE 9.9

The terms *palatalization* and *palatalized* are sometimes used in a slightly different way from the way in which we have been using them so far. Instead of describing a secondary gesture, these terms may describe a process in which the primary gesture is changed so that it becomes more palatal. Thus, sounds are said to be palatalized if the point of articulation moves toward the palatal region in some particular circumstance. For example, the English / k / in *key* may be

TABLE 9.5 Contrasts involving palatalization in Russian.

formə	'form'	fʲərmə	'farm'
vıtʲ	'to howl'	vʲitʲ	'to weave'
sok	'juice'	sʲok	'he lashed'
zof	'call'	zʲof	'yawn'
pakt	'pact'	pʲatʲ	'five'
	'he was'	bʲil	'he stroked'
tot	'that'	tʲotʲə	'aunt'
domə	'at home'	dʲomə	'Dyoma' [nickname]
kuʃətʲ	'to eat'	kʲuvʲətkə	'dish'

said to be palatalized because, instead of the velar contact of the kind that occurs in *car* [kɑɹ], the place of articulation in *key* is changed so that it is nearer the palatal area. Similarly, palatalization is said to occur when the alveolar fricative [z] in *is* becomes a palato-alveolar fricative in *is she* [ɪʒʃi]. A further extension of the term palatalization occurs in discussions of historical sound change. In Old English, the word for *chin* was pronounced with a velar stop [k] at the beginning. The change of this sound into Modern English [tʃ] is said to be one of palatalization, due to the influence of the high front vowel. All these uses of the terms *palatalization* and *palatalized* involve descriptions of a process—something becoming something else—rather than a secondary gesture.

Velarization, the next secondary articulation to be considered, involves raising the back of the tongue. It can be considered as the addition of an [u]-like tongue position, but without the addition of the lip rounding that also occurs in [u]. We have already noted that in many forms of English, syllable final / l / sounds are velarized and may be written [ɫ].

To help you appreciate how it is possible to add vowel-like articulations to consonants, try saying each of the vowels [i, e, ə, a, ɑ, ɔ, o, u], but with the tip of your tongue on the alveolar ridge. The first of these sounds is, of course, a palatalized sound very similar to [lʲ]. The last of the series is one form of velarized [ɫ]. Make sure you can say each of these sounds before and after different vowels. Now compare palatalized and velarized versions of other sounds in syllables such as [nʲa] and [nˠa]. Remember that [nˠ] with the velarization diacritic [ˠ] is simply [n] with a superimposed unrounded nonsyllabic [u] glide (i.e., an added [ɯ] glide).

Pharyngealization is the superimposition of a narrowing of the pharynx. Since cardinal vowel (5)—[ɑ]—has been defined as the lowest, most back vowel possible without producing pharyngeal friction, pharyngealization may be considered as the superimposition of this vowel quality. One IPA diacritic for symbolizing pharyngealization is [˷], the same as for velarization. If it is necessary to distinguish between these two secondary articulations, then the IPA provides an alternative: using small raised symbols corresponding to velar and pharyngeal fricatives, representing a velarized alveolar nasal as [nˠ] and a pharyngealized alveolar nasal as [nˤ]. Marking velarization and pharyngealization in this way is also preferable when the use of the [˷] diacritic creates a symbol that is hard to decipher.

There is very little difference between velarized and pharyngealized sounds, and no language distinguishes between the two possibilities. In Arabic, there is a series of consonants that Arabic scholars call *emphatic consonants*. Some of these sounds are velarized, and some are pharyngealized. All of them can be symbolized with the IPA diacritic [˷]. (Arabic scholars often use a subscript dot [.].) There is some similarity in quality between retroflex stops and velarized or pharyngealized stops, because in all these sounds the front of the tongue is somewhat hollowed.

Labialization, the addition of lip rounding, differs from the other secondary articulations in that it can be combined with any of them. Obviously, palatalization,

TABLE 9.6	Secondary gestures.	
Phonetic Term	Brief Description	Symbols
Palatalization	Raising of the front of the tongue	sʲ lʲ dʲ
Velarization	Raising of the back of the tongue	sˠ ɫ bˠ
Pharyngealization	Retracting of the root of the tongue	sˤ ɫ bˤ
Labialization	Rounding of the lips	sʷ lʷ dʷ

velarization, and pharyngealization involve different tongue shapes that cannot occur simultaneously. But nearly all kinds of consonants can have added lip rounding, including those that already have one of the other secondary articulations. In a sense, even sounds in which the primary articulators are the lips—for example, [p, b, m]—can be said to be labialized if they are made with added rounding and protrusion of the lips. Because labialization is often accompanied by raising the back of the tongue, it is symbolized by a raised [ʷ]. In a more precise system, this might be taken to indicate a secondary articulation that we could call *labiovelarization*, but this is seldom distinguished from labialization.

In some languages (for instance, Twi and other Akan languages spoken in Ghana), labialization co-occurs with palatalization. As palatalization is equivalent to the superimposition of a gesture similar to that in [i], labialization plus palatalization is equivalent to the superimposition of a rounded [i]—that is, [y]. As we have seen, the corresponding semivowel is [ɥ]. Accordingly, these secondary articulations may be symbolized by a raised [ᶣ]. Recall the pronunciation of [ɥ] in French words such as *huit* [ɥit] 'eight.' Then try to pronounce the name of one of the dialects of Akan, Twi [tᶣi].

Table 9.6 summarizes the secondary gestures we have been discussing. As in some of the previous summary tables, the terms in Table 9.6 are not all mutually exclusive. A sound may or may not have a secondary articulation such as palatalization, velarization, or pharyngealization; it may or may not be labialized; and it may or may not be nasalized. To demonstrate this for yourself, try to make a voiced alveolar lateral [l] that is also velarized, labialized, and nasalized.

RECAP

This chapter introduces the cardinal vowels. When I (Keith Johnson) was interviewed for a postdoctoral fellowship with Peter Ladefoged at UCLA, one of his interview questions was, "Right then, so could you give us cardinal number 4." The correct answer, which gladly I was able to do, was to say [a] as it is̩ said by Daniel Jones (the book web page has recordings of him saying the cardinal vowels). The aim of this chapter is to prepare you to use the cardinal vowels to transcribe vowel sounds that you hear in languages, or speech varieties, that you seek to describe. The chapter argues for the practical utility and scientific adequacy of using the cardinal vowels as an auditory basis for vowel transcription.

With this basis, the chapter then describes vowels in different varieties of English and in other languages, giving practical guidelines on how to use cardinal vowel symbols to transcribe vowel sounds that are not quite exactly like the cardinal vowel auditory qualities. We also discuss vowel features that go beyond the features of the cardinal vowels (which are height, frontness, and rounding) such as ATR (advanced tongue root), rhotacization, and nasalization. The chapter ends by discussing the similarity between vowels and glides, which leads to a discussion of consonantal secondary articulations because they involve essentially adding a glide articulation to a consonant. The secondary articulations include palatalization (adding an [i]-like tongue position to a consonant), velarization (adding an [u]-like tongue position), pharyngealization (adding an [ɑ]-like articulation), and labialization (adding lip-rounding).

EXERCISES

(Printable versions of all the exercises are available on the website, where you will find additional interactive exercises on identifying the cardinal vowels.)

A. Look at the positions of the tongue in the English vowels shown in Figure 1.13. It has been suggested (see "Notes") that vowels can be described in terms of three measurements: (1) the area of the vocal tract at the point of maximum constriction; (2) the distance of this point from the glottis; and (3) a measure of the degree of lip opening.

  1. Which of the first two corresponds to what is traditionally called vowel height for the vowels in *heed, hid, head, had*?

  2. Which corresponds to vowel height for the vowels in *father, good, food*?

  3. Can these two measurements be used to distinguish front vowels from back vowels?

B. Another way of describing the tongue position in vowels that has been suggested (see "Notes") is to say that the tongue is in a neutral position in the vowel in *head* and that (1) the body of the tongue is higher than in its neutral position in vowels such as those in *heed, hid, good, food*; (2) the body of the tongue is more back than in its neutral position in *good, food, father*; (3) the root of the tongue is advanced in *heed, food*; and (4) the root of the tongue is pulled back so that the pharynx is more constricted than in the neutral position in *had, father*. How far do the data in Figure 1.12 support these suggestions?

C. In the seventeenth, eighteenth, and early nineteenth centuries (see "Notes"), there were said to be three sets of vowels: (1) a set exemplified by the vowels in *see, play, father* (and intermediate possibilities), which were said to be

Figure 9.13 The vowel classification used by Helmholtz (1863), with key words suggested by Ellis (1885).

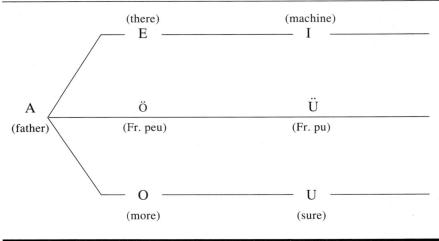

distinguished simply by the degree of jaw opening; (2) a set exemplified by the vowels in *fool, home, father* (and intermediate possibilities), which were said to be distinguished simply by the degree of lip rounding; and (3) a set exemplified by the vowels now symbolized by [y, ø] as in the French words *tu, peu* 'you, small,' which were said to be distinguished by both the degree of jaw opening and the degree of lip rounding. These notions were shown in diagrams similar to that in Figure 9.13. How do they compare with contemporary descriptions of vowels? What general type of vowel cannot be described in these terms?

D. Try to find a speaker of some language other than English. Elicit a set of minimal pairs exemplifying the vowels of this language. You will probably find it helpful to consult the pronunciation section in a dictionary or grammar of the language. Listen to the vowels and plot them on a vowel chart. (Do not attempt this exercise until you have worked through the Performance Exercises for this chapter.)

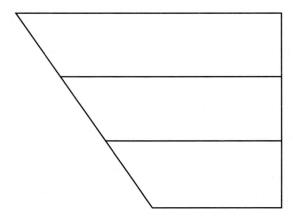

PERFORMANCE EXERCISES

The object of many of the following exercises is to get you to produce a wide variety of vowels that are not in your own language. When you can produce small differences in vowel quality, you will find it easier to hear them. Hear audio examples of these exercises on the website.

A. Say the monophthongs [i, e] corresponding to at least the first part of your vowels in *see, say*. Try to make a vowel with a quality in between [i] and [e]. Then make as many vowels as you can in a series between [i] and [e]. Finally, make a similar series going in the opposite direction—from [e] to [i].

B. Repeat this exercise with monophthongs corresponding to the following pairs of vowels in your own speech. Remember to produce each series in both directions.

[ɪ–ɛ]
[ɛ–æ]
[æ–ɑ]
[ɑ–ɔ], if occurring in your speech
[ɔ–o] or [ɑ–o]
[o–u]

C. Try moving continuously from one member of each pair to the other, slurring through all the possibilities you produced in the previous exercises. Do this in each direction.

D. For each pair of vowels, produce a vowel that is, as nearly as you can determine, halfway between the two members.

E. Repeat Exercises A, C, and D with the following pairs of vowels, which will involve producing larger adjustments in lip rounding. Remember to produce each series in both directions, and be sure you try all the different tasks suggested in Exercises A, C, and D.

[i–u]
[e–o]

F. Now repeat all the same exercises, but with no adjustments in lip rounding, using the following pairs of vowels. Go in both directions, of course.

[i–ɯ]
[e–ɤ]
[y–u]
[ø–o]

G. Practice distinguishing different central vowels. When you have learned to produce a high-central unrounded vowel [ɨ], try to produce mid- and low-central unrounded vowels, which may be symbolized [ə] and [ɜ]. Try Exercises A, C, and D with the following pairs of vowels:

[i–ə]
[ə–ɜ]

H. Produce the following nasal and oral vowels. When making the nasalized vowels, be careful to keep the same tongue position, moving only the soft palate.

[i–ĩ–i]
[e–ẽ–e]
[æ–æ̃–œ]
[ɑ–ɑ̃–ʌ]
[o–õ–o]
[u–ũ–u]

I. Now compare nasalized vowels with oral vowels that have slightly different tongue positions. Say:

[i–ĩ–ɪ–ĩ]
[e–ẽ–ɛ–ẽ]
[ɛ–ɛ̃–æ–æ̃]
[u–ũ–o–ũ]
[o–õ–ɔ–õ]

J. Make sure you can produce a variety of vowels by saying nonsense words such as those shown below, preferably to a partner who can check your pronunciation.

ˈpetuz	syˈtøt	ˈmẽnod
ˈtynob	diˈgɯd	pæˈnyt
ˈbɯgɛd	moˈpɑt	ˈdegũn
ˈnisøp	guˈdob	syˈtõn
ˈbædid	kɯˈtyp	ˈkøbẽs

K. Learn to produce diphthongs going to and from a variety of vowels. Using the vowel symbols with their values as in English, read the following, first column by column, then row by row.

iɪ	ɪi	ei	ɛi	æi	ɑi	ɔi	oi	ʊi	ui	ʌi
ie	ɪe	eɪ	ɛɪ	æɪ	ɑɪ	ɔɪ	oɪ	ʊɪ	uɛ	ʌʌ
iɛ	ɪɛ	eɛ	ɛe	æe	ɑe	ɔe	oe	ʊe	uɪ	ʌɪ
iæ	ɪæ	eæ	ɛæ	æɛ	ɑɛ	ɔɛ	oɛ	ʊɛ	uɛ	ʌɛ
iɑ	ɪɑ	eɑ	ɛɑ	æɑ	ɑæ	ɔæ	oæ	ʊæ	uæ	ʌæ
iɔ	ɪɔ	eɔ	ɛɔ	æɔ	ɑɔ	ɔɑ	oɑ	ʊɑ	uɑ	ʌɑ
io	ɪo	eo	ɛo	æo	ɑo	ɔo	oɔ	ʊɔ	uɔ	ʌɔ
iʊ	ɪʊ	eʊ	ɛʊ	æʊ	ɑʊ	ɔʊ	oʊ	ʊo	uo	ʌo
iu	ɪu	eu	ɛu	æu	ɑu	ɔu	ou	ʊu	uá	ʌá
iʌ	ɪʌ	eʌ	ɛʌ	æʌ	ɑʌ	ɔʌ	oʌ	ʊʌ	uʌ	ʌu

L. Try saying some of these diphthongs in one-, two-, and three-syllable nonsense words such as those shown below. These are good items to use in ear-training practice with a partner.

tɪɒp	'doeb'mɔid	sæo'tɑoneu
tʌep	'deub'mɑud	sɔɑ'tɛonɪʊ
tɑɔp	'dɪʊb'mʌɔd	soɛ'tæunue
tɛɑp	'doeb'moid	sɑʌ'tʌinui
toʌp	'dʊɛb'nuɛd	sɔɪ'tɪunæɑ

M. Now extend your range by including front rounded and back unrounded vowels as exemplified below.

iy	ey	ɑy	uy	yi	øi	ɯi	yø	øy	ɯy
iø	eø	ɑø	uø	ye	øe	ɯe	yɯ	øɯ	ɯø
iɯ	eɯ	ɑɯ	uɯ	yɑ	øɑ	ɯɑ	yu	øu	ɯu

N. These vowels can also be included in nonsense words such as those shown below for both performance and ear-training practice.

dɯeb	'tyæb'meyd	tɯy'neɑsʌø
diøb	'tuʊb'muød	tue'nøusʊɪ
deub	'tɔøb'mɑud	tɛɯ'noysæu
doub	'tøʊb'mɯɛd	tyɪ'nøysoɔ
dæob	'tɯɑb'miod	tɑø'nɑesɪy

O. Practice all the vowels and consonants discussed in the previous chapters in more complicated nonsense words such as the following:

ɣɑ'roti̪ɸ	ŋɔvø'd̪eŋ	jæʛɯ'ɓeɖ
be'ɟʑɛʒuð	ɢɑçy'bɪg	sy't'oʍɛk‖
ɲi'd̪yxen̪	ʂeʕɔ'pæz	ʎɛ'nøk'æx
θæ'ɴɑkɯʃ	fiʀo'ceɫ	k!iɹu'god

10

Syllables and Suprasegmental Features

Throughout this book, there have been references to the notion *syllable*, but this term has never been defined. The reason for this is simple: there is no agreed phonetic definition of a syllable. This chapter will discuss some of the theories that have been advanced and show why they are not entirely adequate. We will also consider **suprasegmental features**—those aspects of speech that involve more than single consonants or vowels. The principal suprasegmental features are stress, length, tone, and intonation. These features are independent of the categories required for describing segmental features (vowels and consonants), which involve airstream mechanisms, states of the glottis, primary and secondary articulations, and formant frequencies.

SYLLABLES

The fact that syllables are important units is illustrated by the history of writing. Many writing systems have approximately one symbol for each syllable, a well-known present-day example being Japanese. But only once in the history of humankind has anybody devised an alphabetic writing system in which syllables were systematically split into their components. About three thousand years ago, the Greeks modified the Semitic syllabary to represent consonants and vowels by separate symbols. The later Aramaic, Hebrew, Arabic, Indic, and other alphabetic writing systems can all be traced back to the principles first and last established in Greek writing. It seems that everybody finds syllables comparatively easy units to use in a writing system. But people who have not been educated in an alphabetic writing system find it much more difficult to consider syllables as being made up of **segments** (consonants and vowels).

Most syllables contain both vowels and consonants, but some, such as *eye* and *owe*, have only vowels. Many consonants can also function as syllables. Alveolar laterals and nasals (as at the ends of *button* and *bottle*) are common in English, but other nasals may occur, as in *blossom* and *bacon*, particularly in phrases such as *the blossom may fade* and *bacon goes well with eggs*, in which the following sounds aid the assimilatory process. Fricatives and stops may become syllabic in unstressed syllables as in *suppose* and *today*, which may be [s̩'poʊz] and [t̩ʰdeɪ] in a narrow transcription. People vary in their pronunciation of these words and phrases. For us, they are all syllabic consonants, but others may pronounce all the examples in this paragraph with a consonant and an associated [ə].

Although it is difficult to define what is meant by a syllable, nearly everybody can identify individual syllables. If you consider how many syllables there are in *minimization* or *suprasegmental*, you can easily count them. Each of these words has five syllables. Nevertheless, it is curiously difficult to state an objective phonetic procedure for locating the number of syllables and especially the boundaries between syllables in a word or a phrase in any language, and it is interesting that most people cannot say how many syllables there are in a phrase they have just heard without first saying that phrase themselves.

In a few cases, people disagree on how many syllables there are in a word in English. Some of these disagreements arise from dialectal differences in the way particular words are spoken. For some, the word *predatory* has three syllables because they say ['prɛdətrɪ]. Other people who pronounce it as ['prɛdətɔɹi] say that it has four syllables. Similarly, there are many words (e.g., *bottling* and *brightening*) that some people pronounce with syllabic consonants in the middle, so that they have three syllables, whereas others do not.

There are also several groups of words that people pronounce the same way that nevertheless differ in their estimates of the number of syllables. One group of words contains nasals that may or may not be counted as separate syllables. Thus, words such as *pessimism* and *mysticism* may be said to have three or four syllables, depending on whether the final [m] is considered to be syllabic. A second group contains high front vowels followed by / l /. Many people will say that *meal*, *seal*, *reel* contain two syllables, but others will consider them to have one. A third group contains words in which / r / may or may not be syllabic. Some people consider *hire*, *fire*, and *hour* to be two-syllable words, whereas others (who pronounce them in exactly the same way) do not. Similar disagreements also arise over words such as *mirror* and *error* for some American English speakers. Finally, there is disagreement over the number of syllables in a group of words that contain unstressed high vowels followed by another vowel without an intervening consonant. Examples are words such as *mediate*, *heavier*, *Neolithic*. Differences of opinion as to the number of syllables in these words may be due to differences in the way they are actually pronounced, just as in the case of *predatory* cited earlier. But, unlike *predatory*, it is often not clear if a syllable has been omitted on a particular occasion.

It is also possible that different people do different things when asked to say how many syllables there are in a word. Some people may pay more attention to the phonological structure of words than others. Thus, many people will say that *realistic* has three syllables. But others who are more sensitive to correspondences between word forms (and thus to phonological patterning) will consider it to have four syllables because it is like the word *reality*, which everybody agrees has four syllables. Similarly, *meteor* will be two syllables for some people but three syllables for those who consider it the same as the stem in *meteoric*.

Judgments on the number of syllables in words such as *hire* and *hour* may also be affected by phonological considerations. Some people distinguish between *hire* and *higher* and pronounce *hour* so that it does not end in the same way as *tower*. These people are likely to consider *hire* and *hour* to be monosyllables and *higher* and *tower* to have two syllables. But others who do not differentiate between *hire* and *higher* and who pronounce *hour* in the same way as *tower* may say that each of these words has two syllables. Thus, two speakers may pronounce *hire* in exactly the same way, but one will consider it to have one syllable, and the other two, because of the way in which they pronounce other words.

Even though there are a number of words in which there are problems in determining the number of syllables they contain, it is important to remember that there is no doubt about the number of syllables in the majority of words. Consider a random list of words from a collection of movie subtitles (the SUBTLEX database)—*bronze, medications, waif, stoical, established, thistledown, nurtured*. There is complete agreement on the number of syllables in each of these words except perhaps for the relatively more unfamiliar word *stoical*, which looks as if it could be pronounced with two syllables [stɔɪ.kəl] but is usually said with three syllables [sto.ɪ.kəl] when it is said at all.

In looking for an adequate definition of a syllable, we need to do two things. We must account for the words in which there is agreement on the number of syllables, and we must also explain why there is disagreement on some other words. One way of trying to do this is by defining the syllable in terms of the inherent sonority of each sound. The **sonority** of a sound is its loudness relative to that of other sounds with the same length, stress, and pitch. Try saying just the vowels [i, e, ɑ, o, u]. You can probably hear that the vowel [ɑ] has greater sonority (due, largely, to its being pronounced with a greater mouth opening). You can verify this fact by asking a friend to stand some distance away from you and say these vowels in a random order. You will find that it is much easier to hear the low vowel [ɑ] than the high vowels [i, u].

We saw in Chapter 8 that the loudness of a sound depends mainly on its acoustic intensity (the amount of acoustic energy present). The sonority of a sound can be estimated from measurements of the acoustic intensity of a group of sounds that have been spoken on comparable pitches and with comparable degrees of length and stress. Estimates of this kind were used for drawing the bar graph in Figure 10.1 (on page 256). As you can see, the low vowels [ɑ] and [æ] have greater sonority than the high vowels [u] and [i]. The approximant [l] has about the same sonority as the high vowel [i]. The nasals [m, n] have slightly less sonority than [i], but greater sonority than a voiced fricative such as [z]. The voiced stops and all the voiceless sounds have very little sonority.

The degrees of sonority shown in Figure 10.1 should not be regarded as exact measurements. The acoustic intensity of different sounds may vary quite

Figure 10.1 The relative sonority of a number of the sounds of English.

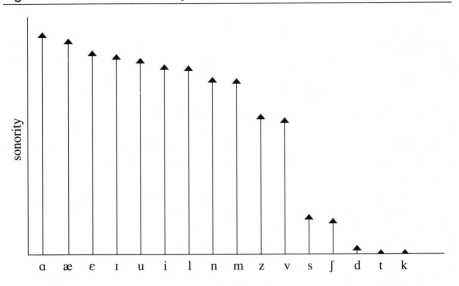

considerably for different speakers and recording setups. Thus, in a particular circumstance, one speaker may pronounce [i] with a greater sonority than [l], whereas another may not.

We can now see that one possible theory of the syllable is that peaks of syllabicity coincide with peaks of sonority. This theory would explain why people agree on the number of syllables in the majority of words. In words such as *visit, divided, condensation*, there are clear peaks of sonority. In these words, each of the syllable peaks has much more sonority than the surrounding sounds. The theory also explains why there are disagreements over words such as *prism, seal, meteor*. Different individuals may vary in the number of peaks of sonority they have in some of these words. The final [m] in *prism* might have greater sonority than the preceding [z] for some people, but not for others. Similarly, the [l] in *seal* and the second [i] in *meteor* might or might not constitute distinguishable peaks of sonority.

A sonority theory of the syllable will not, however, account for all the observed facts. It obviously fails in a word such as *spa*. This word is one syllable, but it must be said to contain two peaks of sonority. It consists of three segments, the first and last of which have greater sonority than the second. A sonority theory also fails to account for the difference in the number of syllables in the phrases *hidden aims* and *hid names*. For speakers who do not have a second vowel in *hidden*, each of these phrases may contain the same sequence of segments, namely, [hɪdneɪmz] (disregarding the pronunciation with a glottal stop favored by some speakers [hɪdnʔeɪmz]). Therefore, there is the same number of peaks of sonority. But the first phrase has three syllables, and the second has two.

There are also a number of words that many people can pronounce with or without one of the syllables. Typical of these words are *paddling, frightening, reddening*. Each of these words can be said as two syllables, with the division between them as shown by the inserted period: [ˈpæd.lɪŋ, ˈfraɪt.nɪŋ, ˈrɛd.nɪŋ]. Alternatively (still using an inserted period to show the syllable breaks), they can be said as three syllables, with a syllabic nasal or lateral in the middle: [ˈpæd.l̩.ɪŋ, ˈfraɪt.n̩.ɪŋ, rɛd.n̩.ɪŋ]. Some people claim that they make a distinction between *lightning* (in the sky) [ˈlaɪt.nɪŋ] and *lightening* (making light) [ˈlaɪt.n̩.ɪŋ] and between *codling* (a little codfish) [ˈkɑd.lɪŋ] and *coddling* (pampering) [ˈkɑd.l̩.ɪŋ]. In all these cases, a sonority theory of the syllable is inadequate. The variations in the number of syllables cannot be said to be due to variations in the number of peaks of sonority.

One way of avoiding this difficulty is to say that syllables are marked not by peaks in sonority but by peaks in **prominence**. The relative prominence of two sounds depends in part on what their relative sonority would have been if they had had the same length, stress, and pitch, but it also depends in part on their actual stress, length, and pitch. Then we can say that, for example, the [n] in *hidden aims* constitutes a peak of prominence because it has more stress or more length (or both) than the [n] in *hid names*.

The problem with this kind of definition is that one cannot state a cross-linguistically valid procedure for combining sonority, length, stress, and pitch to form prominence. Part of the problem is that the perceived prominence of sounds relies on language-specific weighting of phonetic factors such as length and sonority. And part of the problem is that what makes a sound prominent is its position in a word. There is, thus, no way in which one can measure the prominence of a sound. As a result, the notion of a peak of prominence becomes a completely subjective affair—it does not really shed any light on how one defines a syllable. A sound is prominent because it forms the peak of a syllable; it is syllabic because it is prominent.

A completely different approach is to consider syllabicity not as a property of the sounds one hears but as something produced by the speaker. A theory of this kind was put forward by the psychologist R. H. Stetson, who suggested that every syllable is initiated by a chest pulse, a contraction of the muscles of the rib cage that pushes more air out of the lungs. Stetson made numerous observations of the actions of the respiratory system. But his claims about the actions of the muscles were nearly all deductions based on his observations of the movements of the rib cage and his measurements of the pressure of the air in the lungs. Unfortunately, subsequent direct investigations of the activity of the muscles themselves have failed to confirm his theory. It is clearly untrue to say that every syllable is initiated by a chest pulse.

Still another way of considering syllables is to regard them as units of planning in speech motor control. Some research on speech planning suggests that syllable-size motor control plans are stored in a mental syllabary. The support for this view comes from various sources. Consider, for example, the errors—the slips of the tongue—that people make when talking. Perhaps one of the commonest is the interchanging of consonants, so *our dear old queen* becomes *our queer old dean*. In virtually all cases of errors involving the interchange of consonants, it is not a matter of one consonant interchanging with any other consonant. Instead, it is the case that there is an interchange between consonants in the same place in the syllable. Observations such as these are hard to explain unless we consider the syllable to be a significant unit in the production of speech. Further evidence of a similar kind is provided by descriptions of the sound patterns that occur in languages. We have seen in the earlier chapters that it is difficult to describe English or, indeed, any language without considering syllables as units. Since phonological descriptions are of speakers' phonetic plans, it makes sense that planning units like syllables would be included in phonological descriptions.

In summary, we can say that there are two types of theories attempting to define syllables. First, there are theories in which the definitions are in terms of properties of sounds, such as sonority (acoustic energy) or prominence (some combination of sonority, length, stress, and pitch). Second, there are theories based on the notion that a syllable is a unit in the organization and planning of the sounds of an utterance.

In one sense, a syllable is the smallest possible unit of speech. Every utterance must contain at least one syllable. It is convenient to talk of speech as being composed of segments such as vowels and consonants, but these segments can be observed only as aspects of syllables. A syllable can also be divided for descriptive purposes into its **onset** and **rhyme**. The rhyming part of a syllable consists of the vowel and any consonants that come after it—a fairly familiar notion. Any consonants before the rhyme form the onset of the syllable. The rhyme of a syllable can be further divided into the **nucleus**, which is the vocalic part, and the **coda**, which consists of any final consonants. Words such as *I* and *owe* consist of a single syllable that has only a rhyme, which is also the nucleus. They have neither an onset nor a coda. Words such as *splint* and *stripes* are single syllables containing onsets with three consonants and codas with two consonants.

Sometimes, it is difficult to say whether a consonant is the coda of one syllable or the onset of another. How do you divide a word such as *happy* into syllables? Some people will say it is [ˈhæ.pi]; others regard it as [ˈhæp.i]. Another solution is to consider the [p] as belonging to both syllables, and to call it **ambisyllabic**. The result of doing this would be to transcribe *happy* as [ˈhæpi] with no syllable division. Phoneticians disagree on the correct solution to this problem, and we will not discuss it further here. In speech technology, though, when a syllabification of English words is required, it is common to use an algorithm that will tend to maximize onsets rather than codas—which would prefer [ˈhæ.pi] over [ˈhæp.i] and always avoid positing ambisyllabic segments.

Languages differ considerably in the syllable structures that they permit. As we have noted, English has complex onsets and codas. Hawaiian allows no more than one consonant in an onset, and none in the coda, so every word (e.g.,

Honolulu and *Waikiki*) ends in a vowel. Standard Chinese allows only nasal consonants in the coda, producing words such as *Beijing* and *Shanghai*.

STRESS

As we discussed in Chapter 5, in English, stressed syllables in careful citation forms are often pronounced unstressed in conversational speech. This indicates that stress, as a property of English words, is to some extent only a potential for speakers to give prominence to the "stressed" syllable. This pattern, which we could call the "/ stress / as a potential for [stress]" pattern is probably true for other languages as well. Therefore, when discussing the general phonetics of stress, it is probably best to confine the discussion to the pronunciation of citation speech.

Stress is a suprasegmental feature of utterances. It applies not to individual vowels and consonants, but to whole syllables. A stressed syllable is pronounced with a greater amount of energy than an unstressed syllable and is more prominent in the flow of speech.

English and other Germanic languages make far more use of differences in stress than do most of the languages of the world. They have somewhat variable word stress so that the location of stress is not always predictable from the segmental structure of the word; for example, *(to) insult* versus *(an) insult*, or *below* versus *billow*, or *market* versus *Marquette*. In many other languages, the position of the stress is fixed in relation to the word. Czech words nearly always have the stress on the first syllable, irrespective of the number of syllables in the word. In Polish and Swahili, the stress is usually on the penultimate syllable.

Variations in the use of stress cause different languages to have different rhythms. Stress, however, is only one factor in causing rhythmic differences. Because it can appear to be a major factor, it used to be said that some languages (such as French) could be called syllable-timed languages in which syllables tend to recur at regular intervals of time. In contrast, English and other Germanic languages were called stress-timed because stresses were said to be the dominating feature of the rhythmic timing. We now know that this is not true. In contemporary French, there are often strong stresses breaking the rhythm of a sentence. In English, the rhythm of a sentence depends on several interacting factors, not just the stress. Perhaps a better way of describing stress differences among languages would be to divide languages into those that have *variable word stress* (such as English and German), those that have *fixed word stress* (such as Czech, Polish, and Swahili), and those that have *fixed phrase stress* (such as French).

In contrast to the nature of syllables, the nature of stress is fairly well understood. Stressed sounds are those on which the speaker expends more muscular energy. This usually involves pushing out more air from the lungs by contracting the muscles of the rib cage. In general, increased effort leads to increases in the perceptual salience of segments, so aspirated stops will have longer aspiration, voiceless consonants will be less likely to have voicing assimilation, and vowels will have more peripheral vowel formants so high vowels are higher and low vowels are lower, and so on. The increased perceptual salience of stressed syllables is also signaled by intonational gestures that result in more peripheral pitch, higher high tones, and lower low tones, and stress generally involves increased duration of stressed syllables.

When there is an increase in the amount of air being pushed out of the lungs, there is an increase in the loudness of the sound produced. Some books define *stress* simply in terms of loudness, but this is not a very useful definition if loudness is considered to be simply a matter of the amount of acoustic energy involved. We have already noted that some sounds have more acoustic energy than others because of factors such as the degree of mouth opening.

A much more important indication of stress is the rise in pitch, which may or may not be due to laryngeal action. You can check for yourself that an increase in the flow of air out of the lungs causes a rise in pitch even without an increase in the activity of the laryngeal muscles. Ask a friend to press against the lower part of your chest while you stand against a wall with your eyes shut. Now say a long vowel on a steady pitch and have your friend push against your chest at an unexpected moment. You will find that at the same time that there is an increase in the flow of air out of your lungs (as a result of your friend's push), there will also be an increase in the pitch of the vowel.

There is a final factor to note when discussing stress in English. We saw in Chapter 5 that a syllable in English is either stressed or not stressed. If it is stressed, it can be at the center of an intonational pitch change so that it receives a tonic accent, which might be said to raise it to a more primary level of stress. If it is unstressed, it can have a full vowel or a reduced vowel. In some views, a reduced vowel implies that there is a lower level of stress, but in the view expressed here, this is a matter not of stress but of vowel quality. We also saw that there are pairs of words, such as *(an) insult* and *(to) insult*, that differ only in stress. What happens when these words appear to lose their stress because of a heavy stress elsewhere in the sentence? Consider a pair of sentences such as '*He **needed** an increase in price*' and, with an equally strong stress on 'needed,' *He **needed** to increase the price*. Although speakers (and linguists) may have a strong impression that *(an) increase* is stressed differently from *(to) increase* in these sentences, controlled acoustic studies have failed to find any phonetic difference between them. This appears to be a case where the speaker's knowledge of the potential for a difference in the stress patterns of these words causes a phonetic hallucination.

LENGTH

The individual segments in a syllable may also vary in length. The English of the Scottish Highlands makes a length contrast between *week* [wik] and *weak* [wiːk], both having the same monophthongal vowel quality. In most varieties of

English, variations in lengths are completely allophonic. We saw, for example, that the vowel in *bad* is predictably longer than the vowel in *bat* because, other things being equal, vowels are always longer before voiced consonants than before voiceless consonants.

Many other languages make considerable use of length contrasts. Long vowels contrast with short vowels in several languages. The website language index will guide you to examples in Estonian, Finnish, Arabic, and Japanese. You can also hear Danish examples on the website. Length may be shown by [ː] placed after a symbol or by doubling the symbol.

Contrasts between long and short consonants are not as common, but they do occur. Luganda has contrasts such as [ˋkkúlà] 'treasure' and [kúlà] 'grow up.' Italian has contrasts such as *nonno* [ˈnɔnno] 'grandfather' versus *nono* [ˈnɔno] 'ninth,' and *Papa* [ˈpapa] 'Pope' versus *pappa* [ˈpappa] 'porridge, baby food'. Long consonants (or vowels) that can be analyzed as double consonants (or vowels) are called **geminates**. Italian geminates are also illustrated on the website.

The Italian geminate consonants can be compared with the contrasts between English consonants in *white tie* [waɪt.taɪ], *why tie* [waɪ.taɪ], and *white eye* [waɪt.aɪ]. The difference is that in Italian, a long consonant can occur within a single morpheme (a grammatical term for the smallest meaningful unit). But in English, geminate consonants can occur only across word boundaries, as in the previous examples, or in a word containing two morphemes, such as *unknown* [ʌnˈnoʊn] or *guileless* [ˈɡaɪlles]. Note, however, that some words that are historically two morphemes, such as *immodest,* are usually pronounced with a single consonant, [ɪˈmɑdɪst].

Probably one of the most interesting languages in its use of length is Japanese. Japanese may be analyzed in terms of the classical Greek and Latin unit called a *mora*. A mora is a unit of timing, in the sense that each mora is felt to have a "beat" that counts in the rhythmic structure of the language. The most common type of Japanese mora is formed by a consonant followed by a vowel. Japanese words such as [kakemono] 'scroll' and [sukijaki] 'beef stew' each consist of four morae of this type. Note that in the latter word, the high vowel / u / is voiceless because it occurs between two voiceless consonants, but it still is counted as a beat in the word's rhythm. Another type of mora is a vowel by itself, as in the word [i.ki] 'breath.' This word has two morae. A consonant cannot occur after a vowel within a mora, but it too can form a mora by itself. The word [nippoŋ] 'Japan' must be divided into four morae [ni.p.po.ŋ]. Although it has only two vowels, it has the same number of beats as [kakemono] or [sukijaki]. You can hear these three words in Web example 10.3.

TIMING

Languages give the impression of different modes of timing. We have noted that Japanese seems to be "mora-timed" so that speakers feel as if all morae have approximately the same duration. Similarly, linguists have classified some of the Romance languages (Spanish and French particularly) as "syllable-timed" languages because time in these languages seems to be counted in syllables rather than moras or stresses. English and German, on the other hand, seem to be timed so that the best way to count out a rhythm in these languages is in terms of the stressed syllables (as our systems of meter would tell us).

The phonetic basis for these statements about rhythm and timing in language is elusive. Perhaps the most direct and simple theory is that the units of timing in a language—what we have been calling the beats—should be regularly timed like the beats of a metronome. This type of timing is called **isochrony**. We have been suggesting that for native speakers of a mora-timed language, such as Japanese, it *feels* as if the moras are isochronous; for a speaker of a stress-timed language, such as English, it feels as if the stressed syllables are isochronous. But, of course, saying that it "feels" isochronous does not come close to reality. When researchers look at the actual timing of speech, they do not find isochrony anywhere. Perhaps the most that we can say is that IF a speaker were to try to speak in a very rhythmic way, as if performing speech almost musically or for great effect in public speaking, the speaker of a stress-timed language would aim for isochrony of stresses, the speaker of a syllable-timed language would aim for isochrony of syllables, and the speaker of a mora-timed language would aim for isochrony of moras. It may be that one consequence of this somewhat idealized psychological position for rhythm is that the strongest effect of speech timing will be seen an accumulation of evidence in the historical development of word forms over the generations. Stress-timed languages will tend to develop words with reduced unstressed syllables and clusters of consonants, while syllable-timed languages will tend to develop word forms where all the syllables have roughly equal size.

WEB
lg. index

This leads to the most successful class of measures of cross-linguistic rhythm type—measures of the segmental makeup of words. The most reliable correlates of stressed versus syllable timing (and probably also mora timing) has to do with the segmental makeup of syllables. So, although one factor that determines the perceived timing of a language is where the stresses fall, equally important are factors such as whether the language contrasts long and short vowels, whether sequences of vowels can occur, whether vowels in unstressed syllables can be reduced, and what syllabic structures are allowed (notably, whether onsets and codas can include sequences of consonants). In Hawaiian, there is never more than a single consonant between any two vowels, but in English, there can be seven, as in the phrase *texts spread* [teksts sprɛd]. In Polish, there are even more, as you can find in the many examples of Polish consonant clusters on the Polish page of the website (check the Languages index on the Extras page).

Differences in the permitted syllable structures affect the perceived timing of a language. One way of describing timing differences is to consider how much variation in length occurs within a sentence. In French, it seems as if the vowels all have a fairly similar length, whereas in English, there are short vowels interspersed with long ones. These kinds of differences can be quantified by calculating the pairwise variability index. The PVI can be applied to various units—just the vowels, the intervals between vowels (i.e., including the consonants), or other stretches of speech. It is calculated by finding the average ratio of all the adjacent units in the utterance. The procedure involves three steps, which sound more complicated than they actually are when taken one at a time. First, decide which interval is to be measured (e.g., vowel durations, or the interval between vowel onsets). Second, for each pair of adjacent intervals calculate the difference in duration and divide this difference by the mean duration of the pair. Finally, establish the average ratio of pairs. Expressed mathematically, this is

$$PVI = 100 \times \left[\sum_{k=1}^{m-1} \left| \frac{d_k - d_{k+1}}{(d_k + d_{k+1})/2} \right| /(m-1) \right]$$

where m is number of items in an utterance and d_k is the duration of the kth item. The index has been multiplied by 100 so as to avoid fractional values. The PVI gives a normalized ratio of vowel duration variability so that if all vowels are approximately equal in duration the PVI will be close to zero and if successive vowels are three times or one/third the duration of their neighbor the PVI will be 100.

The PVI for vowels has been calculated for many languages, some of which are shown in Figure 10.2 (on page 264). It is clearly greater (i.e., the variability in duration between adjacent vowels is larger) for the first four languages, Thai, Dutch, German, and English, shown in the figure with black bars. These are languages that have heavy stresses and large variations in vowel length. The final four languages, French, Japanese, Spanish, and Chinese, are shown with white bars. These languages have more constant vowel lengths. None of them have stresses on particular syllables in words. Polish, the language with the gray bar in the center of the figure, is closest to the last group of languages. Although it does stress particular syllables (the penultimate syllables of words), it does not fit into the group of languages that have strong rhythmic stresses because Polish stress is not accompanied by great variability in vowel length. We should also note that the position of Polish on this scale would have been different if the PVI had been calculated to take into account the sequences of consonants. As we have seen, Polish can have great variability in the number of consonants between vowels. Figure 10.2 also shows that there are no clear-cut distinctions in timing between languages. Insofar as the PVI is a measure of strong versus weak stress timing it seems that languages have various degrees of this feature.

You can easily calculate the PVI for a set of vowel durations by using the PVI Excel spreadsheet in Web example 10.4. This will apply the formula to any set of measurements that you paste in. The example on the spreadsheet shows the calculation for the variability in duration between adjacent vowels as discussed above, and for variability in duration between adjacent syllables (i.e., including the consonants).

Figure 10.2 Pairwise variability index for a number of languages.

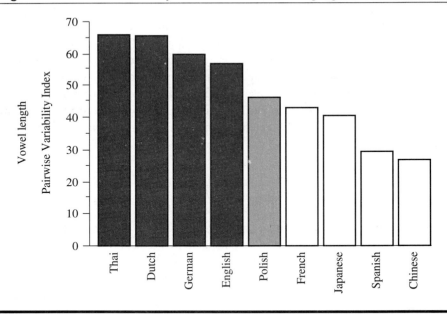

INTONATION AND TONE

The pitch of the voice is determined by several factors. The most important is the tension of the vocal folds. If the vocal folds are stretched, the pitch of the sound will go up. Altering the tension of the vocal folds is the normal way of producing most of the pitch variations that occur in speech. In addition, as we saw in the section on stress, an increase in the flow of air out of the lungs will also cause an increase in pitch, so that stressed sounds will usually have a higher pitch. Finally, variations in pitch occur in association with the variations in the position of the vocal folds in different phonation types. Thus, creaky voice usually has a low pitch as well as a particular voice quality.

Many different kinds of information can be conveyed by variation in pitch. As is the case with other aspects of speech sounds, some of this information simply indicates the personal characteristics of the speaker. The pitch of the voice usually indicates whether the speaker is male or female and, to some extent, what his or her age is. In addition, it conveys a great deal of nonlinguistic information about the speaker's emotional state—whether the person is calm or angry, or happy or sad. As yet, nobody knows if the pitch changes conveying this sort of information are universal. But it is apparent that speakers of many different languages have similar inflections when conveying similar emotional information.

EXAMPLE 10.5 There also seem to be some universal aspects to the ways in which languages use pitch differences to convey linguistic information. All languages use pitch to mark the boundaries of syntactic units. In nearly all languages, the completion of a grammatical unit, such as a normal sentence, is signaled by a falling pitch. The last syllable (or the last stressed syllable) is on a lower pitch than it would have been if it had been non-final. Conversely, incomplete utterances, such as mid-sentence clause breaks where the speaker intends to show that there is something still to come, often have a basically rising intonation. These and other intonations of English were illustrated in Web example 5.11 (which is also linked as example 10.5) and discussed in Chapter 5. There are, of course, exceptions to the two generalizations suggested earlier. In some styles of English, for example, it is possible to have a rising intonation on many sentences. But the use of a falling pitch to mark non-interrogative sentences occurs in by far the majority of utterances.

Discourse information is also conveyed by intonation in English. For example, the sentence *But, he also wrote a very long one* can be pronounced to convey that the new information is that the book is a long one, say in the context of a preceding sentence like *Peter has written a few short books*, by putting a high pitch accent on the word *long*. The same sequence of words can also be used to convey that the new information is that the book is one that Peter wrote, say in the context of a preceding sentence like *Peter read a very long book*, by placing a high pitch accent on the word *wrote*. Try saying these with the correct and incorrect accent placement to experience the importance of intonation in conveying discourse information.

In addition to syntactic and discourse functions, in many other languages pitch variations can be used to signal the meaning of a word. In Mandarin Chinese, for example, the consonant–vowel sequence [ma] pronounced with a high and level pitch means 'mother,' but the same sequence pronounced with a high falling pitch means 'scold.'

Pitch variations that affect the meaning of a word are called **tones**. In the majority of the languages in the world, the meaning of a word depends on its tone. All languages also use intonation, the use of pitch variations, to convey syntactic information. The intonation patterns form a framework for the tones in a way that we will discuss later.

The simplest kind of tone language is that in which there are only two possible tones, high and low. In many Bantu languages, such as Shona (spoken in Zimbabwe), Zulu, or Luganda, every vowel may be classified as being on a high or on a low pitch. Thus, in Shona, the sequence [kùtʃérá], meaning 'to draw water', has a low tone on the first syllable and a high tone on the second and third syllables. But when this sequence is [kùtʃèrà], with low tones on each syllable, it means 'to dig.'

Tones may be transcribed in many ways. One of the simplest systems is to mark a steady (or level) high pitch by an acute accent over the vowel [á] and a level low pitch by a grave accent [à]. Middle pitches can be left unmarked. This is the kind of transcription we have been using in the examples cited in some of the tables illustrating sounds not found in English (e.g., see contrasting clicks in Xhosa in Table 6.3 and Ewe fricatives in Table 7.1). In a language with three level tones, such as Yoruba (spoken in Nigeria), the mid tone would be left unmarked. In this way, we could transcribe a three-way opposition such as occurs in Yoruba: [ó wá] 'he comes,' [ó wa ...] 'he looked for ...,' [ó wà] 'he existed.' If the three tones included a high tone, a mid tone, and a falling tone, as is the case in Ibibio, another language spoken in Nigeria, then a circumflex accent mark (which symbolizes a conjunction of a high tone followed by a low tone) can be used, as in the Ibibio words in Web example.

Please note that the number one mistake that phonetics students make in reading IPA tone marks is to think that [á] indicates a rising tone while [à] indicates a falling tone. This is wrong: [á] indicates a level high tone in the IPA and [à] indicates a level low tone.

Speakers of English often find it hard to consider the tone as an important, meaningful part of a word. But for speakers of a tone language, a difference in tone is just as significant as a difference in consonant or vowel quality. If you are trying to say 'he looked for (something)' in Yoruba, and you say [ó wà] instead of [ó wa], it will sound just as odd as if you had said *he licked* instead of *he looked* in English.

Contrastive tones are usually marked over the vowel in a tone language. But they are often properties of the syllable as a whole. They can also occur on voiced consonants that can be regarded as syllabic. The Igbo (spoken in Nigeria) for 'I'm beautiful' is [ḿ mà ḿ má]. Occasionally, tones occur on consonants that are not normally syllabic. In the section on length in this chapter, we transcribed the Luganda word for 'treasure' as [`kkúlà], with a low tone mark before the first [k]. Obviously, the silence preceding a voiceless consonant cannot be said on a low pitch. Only voiced sounds can have a high or a low pitch. This tone was added to the transcription because it helps explain the phonological patterns of Luganda as a whole and the distribution of tones in Luganda words.

Tone languages make two slightly different uses of pitch within a word. In the examples given so far, differences in pitch have affected the lexical (dictionary) meaning of a word. But many, if not most, tone languages also use pitch differences to make changes in grammatical (morphological) meaning. Thus, in Igbo, the idea of possession—roughly the equivalent of *of* in English—may be expressed by a high tone. This high tone appears, for example, in the phrase meaning 'the jaw of a monkey.' The word for 'jaw' is [àg͡bà], with two low tones. The word for 'monkey' is [èŋwè], also with two low tones. But the phrase 'the jaw of a monkey' is [àg͡bá èŋwè], with a high tone on the second syllable of the word for 'jaw.' Thus the English word *of* can sometimes be represented simply as a high tone on a particular syllable in Igbo.

Another example of the grammatical use of tone occurs in the tense system of Edo, spoken in Nigeria, as shown in Table 10.1. In what may be called the timeless tense (indicating a habitual action), there is a low tone on both the pronoun and the verb. In what may be called the continuous tense (indicating an action in progress), there is a high tone on the pronoun, a low tone on monosyllabic verbs, and a tone going from low to high on disyllables. In the past tense, there

TABLE 10.1		The use of tone in part of the tense system of Edo.		
Tense	Monosyllabic Verbs		Disyllabic Verbs	
Timeless	ì mà	'I show'	ì hrùlè	'I run'
Continuous	í mà	'I am showing'	í hrùlé	'I am running'
Past	ì má	'I showed'	ì hrúlè	'I ran'

is a low tone on the pronoun, a high tone on monosyllabic verbs, and high to low on disyllables.

Before considering more complicated tonal systems, you should check that you can pronounce correctly all the tones that have to be pronounced in the examples cited in the previous paragraphs. You should, of course, say the high tones on a pitch in the upper part of your own pitch range, and the low tones on a pitch in the lower part. If you are working with a friend or with recordings of a speaker of a tone language, be careful *not* to imitate their exact pitches, unless they have just the same pitch range as you normally do. Contrastive tones must always be considered relative to the presumed mean pitch of the speaker. (One problem in doing fieldwork with speakers of tone languages if you have a rather deep voice is that consultants will often say that you are mispronouncing a word when you imitate them fairly exactly. To sound right, you should make a distinct effort to say the tones not in the same way as the speaker, but in your ordinary pitch range.)

The tones in many languages can be described in terms of given points within the speaker's pitch range. If the speaker is aiming at a single target pitch for a syllable, the tone can be regarded as a level tone. Luganda, Zulu, and Hausa are examples of tone languages having basically just two tones, high and low. Yoruba is an example of a tone language with three tones, high, mid, and low. (Additional contour tones do occur in Yoruba, but they can be shown to be the result of combining two of the tones within a single syllable.) The majority of tone languages have two or three tones, but languages with four or even five pitch levels do occur. Egede and Kutep (both spoken in Nigeria) have tones that can be distinguished as being top, high, mid, and low.

A transcription system using grave and acute accents is sufficient for languages that have only a single tone target within a syllable. It can incorporate languages with four tones by marking the lower of the two mid tones with a horizontal bar, [ā], and leaving the upper one unmarked. The IPA expands this range by marking "extra-high" tone with two acute accents [a̋] and "extra-low" tone with two grave accent marks [ȁ], giving a total of six possible tone levels. But this kind of system using accents is not satisfactory for languages that have more complex tones. In Mandarin Chinese, for example, there are four tones, three of which involve significant pitch movements. Tones of this kind are called **contour tones**. When making these tones, the speaker's aim is to produce a characteristic pitch movement, rather than a single target in the pitch range. In addition to Chinese, many of the languages of Southeast Asia (e.g., Thai and Vietnamese) have contour tones. It should be noted, however, that these well-known tone languages are not typical. Most of the tone languages in the world have single pitch targets, or at most just a rising or falling pitch, for each syllable.

EXAMPLE 10.7

One way of transcribing contour tones is to consider five equally spaced points within the normal pitch range of a speaker's voice: (1) low, (2) half-low, (3) middle, (4) half-high, and (5) high. We can then describe a contour tone as a movement from one of these points to another. We can represent this information graphically. If we draw a vertical line to indicate the normal range of a speaker's voice, we can plot a simplified graph of the pitch to the left of this line. In this way, we can form a letter-like symbol that represents the tone. Table 10.2 specifies the tones of Mandarin Chinese in three ways: (1) by giving each tone an arbitrary number; (2) by tone letters in column 4; and (3) by the numbers for the pitches depicted by the tone letter in column 3. The traditional numbers assigned to Mandarin tone are shown in the first column. These tones can be heard in Web example 10.7.

EXAMPLE 10.8

Other tone letters designed in the same way can be used for the description of tones in other languages. The tones of Thai are illustrated in Table 10.3 and in Web example 10.8. Note how the numbers conventionally used in specifying Thai tones do not have the same values as those conventionally used for Chinese in Table 10.2. Tone 1 in Thai is a falling tone, whereas in Standard Chinese, it is

TABLE 10.2 The tones of Mandarin Chinese.

Tone Number	Description	Pitch	Tone Letter	Example	Gloss
1	high level	55	˥	ma^{55}	'mother'
2	high rising	35	˧˥	ma^{35}	'hemp'
3	low falling-rising	214	˨˩˦	ma^{214}	'horse'
4	high falling	51	˥˩	ma^{51}	'scold'

TABLE 10.3 Tonal contrasts in Thai.

Tone Number	Description	Pitch	Tone Letter	Example	Gloss
1	low falling	21	˨˩	naa^{21}	(a nickname)
2	high falling	51	˥˩	naa^{51}	'face'
3	high rising	45	˦˥	naa^{45}	'aunt'
4	low falling-rising	214	˨˩˦	naa^{214}	'thick'
"common"	mid falling	32	˧˨	naa^{32}	'field'

a high-level tone. In Thai, there is also a fifth tone, designated the *common tone*, which is left unmarked in transcriptions.

Even in a tone language, the pitch of the voice changes continuously throughout sequences of voiced sounds. There are seldom sudden jumps from one pitch level to another. As a result, assimilations occur between tones in much the same way as they do between segments. When a high tone precedes a low tone, the low tone will usually begin with a downward pitch change. Conversely, a high tone following a low tone may begin with an upward pitch movement. Considering two adjacent tones, it is usually the first that affects the second rather than the other way around. There seems to be a tendency in the languages of the world for tone assimilations to be perseverative, the tone of one syllable hanging over into that of later syllables, rather than anticipatory, the tone of one syllable changing because it anticipates that of the syllable yet to come.

Changes of tone due to the influence of one tone on another are called **tone sandhi**. Sometimes these changes are fairly complex. For example, in Standard Chinese, the word meaning 'very' is [hao^{214}], with a falling-rising tone. But in the phrase meaning 'very cold,' it is pronounced with a high rising tone [hao^{35} leŋ^{214}]. In this way, Standard Chinese avoids having two falling-rising tones one after another. Whenever a tone 3 word is followed by another tone 3 word, the low falling-rising tone is changed into tone 2—the high rising tone. As another example of tone sandhi, we can consider what happens to compound words in Shanghai Chinese, a related but different language from Standard Chinese. The word for 'sky' is [tʰi], with a pitch fall that we could write as [51]. The word for 'earth' is [di], with a pitch rise [15]. Put together, these form the word for universe' [tʰi^{5}di^1], which has a pitch fall going from high on the first syllable to low on the second. Thus, the pitch pattern associated with the first syllable has extended over the whole compound word. This is the general rule in Shanghai Chinese for compound words beginning with a syllable that is high falling when it occurs in isolation. The word for 'symphony' is composed of the words meaning 'exchange,' 'sound,' and 'song.' When said in isolation, the first of these, [tʃiɔ^{51}], has a high falling tone [51]; the second, [ʃiã^{35}], has a mid rising tone [35]; and the last, [tʃʰioʔ^5], has a short high tone [5]. But when put together to form [tʃiɔ^{5}ʃiã^{3}tʃʰioʔ^1] 'symphony,' the first syllable is high [5], the second mid [3], and the third low [1].

As we mentioned earlier, tone languages also use intonational pitch changes. In many tone languages, ordinary statements will have a generally falling intonation, and at least some questions will have a rising intonation over part of the utterance. Doubt, anger, excitement, and many other emotional signals will be conveyed by intonations similar to those in English, the distinctive tones of individual words being superimposed on the overall patterns.

As in English, the regular intonation of a sentence often marks syntactic boundaries. In most languages, there is a downward trend of the pitch over a syntactic unit such as a sentence. This general pitch lowering is known as **declination**. However, the specific phonetic realization of declination varies from language to language. For example, in Hausa, declination involves the falling of the mean pitch level throughout the sentence. Both high tones and low tones are higher at the beginning of a sentence than they are at the end. A Hausa sentence with alternating high and low tones such as [málàm ínsù jánà bá sà námà] 'teacher their he gives them meat' may have a high tone at the end of the sentence that has about the same absolute pitch that a low tone had at the beginning of the sentence.

In other languages, the declination may take a slightly different form. Instead of both high and low tones falling, the low tones may remain at about the same level throughout the sentence so that the declination affects only the high tones. For example, in Luganda, high tones are lowered slightly whenever they are preceded by a low tone within the same sentence. This is the reason that we marked the low tone at the beginning of [`kkúlà] 'treasure,' even though it was on a voiceless consonant and could not be pronounced. We know that there must be a low tone there because the high tone in this word is slightly lower than it would have been if this (silent) low tone had not been there.

To summarize, variations in pitch are used in a number of different ways. In the first place, they convey nonlinguistic information about the speaker's emotional state and, to some extent, personal physiological characteristics. Second, in all languages, differences in pitch convey one or more kinds of linguistic information. The linguistic uses of pitch are intonation (the distinctive pitches in a phrase), which in all languages conveys information about the syntactic components of the utterance, and tone (the distinctive pitches within a word), which may convey both lexical information about the meaning of the word and the grammatical function of the word. Within tone languages, the tones can be divided into contour tones, which require the specification of a change in pitch within the syllable, and target tones, in which only a single target height needs to be specified for each syllable, the pitch changes within a syllable being regarded as simply the result of putting syllables together to form a sentence.

STRESS, TONE, AND PITCH ACCENT LANGUAGES

It is clear that Chinese is a tone language, in which the meaning of a word is affected by the pitch, and that English is not, despite the fact that we can describe certain syllables in an English sentence as having high or low tones, as we saw in Chapter 5. The "tones" in an English sentence do not affect the meaning of the individual words, although they may affect the meaning of the phrase or sentence. English has stress contrasts, such as *below* versus *billow*, but not tone contrasts.

So far, we have been considering languages to be either stress or tone languages, but this is an oversimplification. There are some languages in which a multisyllabic pitch pattern apparently plays a role in distinguishing words. Swedish has stress differences that can be described in much the same way as stress differences in English. But it also has a pitch contrast between, for example, *anden* 'the duck' and *anden* 'the ghost.' In the Stockholm dialect the word for 'the duck' has a high pitch early in the word, whereas 'the ghost' may have two pitch peaks. Swedish phoneticians describe the difference as accent 1 versus accent 2. We should note, however, that this is not really a difference in tone. The base form of the word for 'duck' is / and /; the suffix / -en / makes it 'the duck.' The word for 'ghost' is / ande / with the suffix being simply / -n /. The difference in the composition of the words accounts for the difference in pitch. Pitch may be said to play a role in showing the base forms of words in Swedish, but it does not otherwise distinguish meanings.

Scottish Gaelic spoken in the Outer Hebrides has words that differ in pitch, but again they are not really different in tone. For example, *duan* / tuan / 'song' contrasts with *dubhan* / tuan / 'hook,' the first word having a rising pitch, and the second word falling steeply at the end. Although these two words have identical sequences of segments and often have the same length, the second word is felt by speakers to have two syllables (as it did historically and still does in the orthography), and this results in the two words having different pitch patterns. There are quite a number of Scottish Gaelic words that have lost intervocalic consonants in this way, so it is possible to argue that the language is now becoming a tone language.

Japanese is a more striking case of a language that is in some ways between a tone language and a stress language. Words in Japanese have an accent on a particular syllable in much the same way that English words have one or more stresses. In Japanese, the accent is invariably realized as a high pitch, so Japanese is often called a pitch-accent language. Japanese words differ in the placement of the accent, giving rise to contrasts such as / kákiga / 'oyster,' / kakíga / 'fence,' / kakigá / 'persimmon.'

RECAP

The focus of this chapter was on the phonetic organization of language "above" the segments. We emphasized the importance of syllables in describing linguistic structure, but then went on a long discussion of how hard it is to find syllables in phonetic measurements. Defining exactly where the syllable boundaries are in a word is especially problematic—is 'alligator' [ˌæ.lɪ.ˈgeɪ.ɾɚ] or [ˌæɫ.ɪ.ˈgeɪ.ɾɚ]? Syllable "peaks" aren't terribly hard to define in terms of sonority (the relative loudness of segments). Though even in just counting the number of syllables based on sonority peaks we have complications with sequences like [sta] that have two sonority peaks (on [s] and then again on [a]) but are one syllable and sequences like [læn.l̩.ɪn] *lanolin* that have two sonority peaks but three syllables. Ultimately, it seems best to consider syllables as units of speech planning that are not directly measurable in speech movements or sound. It may be possible to come to a similar conclusion about stress (that stress is largely a unit of speech planning rather than a measureable property of utterances), though we suggested that if there were a good way to measure muscular effort during speech stress might be directly measurable. Speech timing has a similar, somewhat abstract nature. We can certainly measure the duration of speech sounds and note that in many languages length is used to distinguish words much as stop place of articulation is used to distinguish *pat* and *cat* in English. However, when it comes to defining the rhythmic pattern of a language (as syllable-timed or stress-timed), we find that timing units are not produced isochronously, no matter how it feels to speakers. Instead, an indirect measure of timing—the relative duration of adjacent vowels (roughly alternating strong-weak, versus all vowels more or less the same length) seems to be a good indication of whether a language will seem stress-timed or syllable-timed. The final suprasegmental property that we discussed is tone. We noted that some languages make use of a small tonal inventory (just contrasting high and low tones on syllables), while others may use a larger inventory of both level and contour tones. As with syllables, stress, and timing, we noted that the phonetic realization of tone varies depending on contextual factors related to tone sandhi and intonational declination. So again a simple phonetic property like pitch is not a direct correlate of linguistic tone.

It may seem frustrating to learn that such important properties of language sound systems are so phonetically indeterminate, but another way of looking at it is to suggest that this highlights a fundamentally interesting aspect of phonetics. Listeners rarely have problems using language to convey meaning, but now we know that they are using a system that is anything but a simple cipher like Morse code or typewritten letters. The physical signal that we produce as speakers and decode as listeners is complex and variable. Understanding how we succeed with such a variable code is one of the great intellectual challenges of contemporary social science.

EXERCISES

Printable versions of all the exercises are available on the website.)

A. People differ in their judgments of the number of syllables there are in the following words. Ask several people (if possible, include some children) to say these words and then tell you how many syllables there are in each of them. Try to explain, for each word, why people may differ in their judgments, even if the people you ask are all in agreement.

laboratory _____

spasm _____

oven _____

prisoner _____

million _____

merrier _____

feral _____

B. List four words for which the sonority theory of syllabicity is inadequate in accounting for the number of syllables present.

C. Make a list of ten words chosen at random from a dictionary. In how many cases is there no doubt as to the number of syllables they contain? Explain the reasons for the doubt in the case of the others.

D. Look at dictionaries or introductory textbooks on four or five foreign languages not mentioned in this chapter. Try to state whether they have variable word stress or fixed word stress, or whether stress does not seem to be a property of the word.

E. Again by looking at dictionaries or introductory textbooks, find examples of tone languages not mentioned in this chapter. For each language, try to state how many contrasting tones it has, exemplifying the distinctions between each of them with minimal pairs if possible.

F. In Luganda, many words fall into one or the other of two classes, each with a different pattern of permissible tones, as exemplified in the lists that follow.

Class I		Class II	
èkítábó	'a book'	ákásózì	'a hill'
òmúːntú	'a man'	òmùkázì	'a woman'
òlúgúːdó	'a road'	èm̀bwáː`	'a dog'
òkúwákáná	'to dispute'	òkùsálà	'to cut'

Describe the permitted sequences of tones in each class. (In fact, Class II is more complicated than is indicated by the data given here.)

G. Roughly speaking, when making a declarative statement in Luganda, the initial vowel is dropped and the tones in Class I words become as shown below.

kìtábó   'it is a book'

lùgúːdó   'it is a road'

State the rule that affects the tones in this grammatical construction.

PERFORMANCE EXERCISES

A. Practice saying nonsense words with long and short vowels. Say partially English phrases such as those shown below. Try to make the length of each vowel independent of the quality, so that [bɪb] is as long as [bib]—and independent of the following consonant, so that [bip] is as long as [bib]. The syllables are included within a phrase so that you can make sure you keep the overall rate of speech constant, but note that when the lengths are changed, these will not sound like English words.

'seɪ	'biːb	ə'gɛn
'seɪ	'bib	ə'gɛn
'seɪ	'bɪb	ə'gɛn
'seɪ	'bɪːb	ə'gɛn
'seɪ	'biːp	ə'gɛn
'seɪ	'bip	ə'gɛn
'seɪ	'bɪp	ə'gɛn
'seɪ	'bɪːp	ə'gɛn

B. Repeat Exercise A with other syllables such as those shown below. Continue using a frame such as "Say ___ again."

buːd

bud

bʊd

buːd

buːt

but

bʊt

buːt

C. Learn to differentiate between single and double, or geminate, consonants. Say:

e'pɛm	o'num	ø'zys
ep'pɛm	on'num	øz'zys
'epɛm	'onun	'øzys
'eppɛm	'onnun	'øzzys

D. Take a sentence that can be said with strong stresses recurring at roughly regular intervals, such as

'What is the 'difference in 'rhythm in 'English and 'French?

Say this sentence with as regular a rhythm as you can, while tapping on the stressed syllables. You should be able to say it slowly, then at a normal speed, and finally fast, in each case tapping out a regular rhythm. Now try saying it as a Frenchman just learning to speak English might say it, with each syllable taking about the same length of time. Make regular taps, one corresponding to each syllable throughout the sentence. Say the sentence first slowly, then at a normal speed, and then fast, continuing to tap the rhythm in this way.

E. One of the best ways to learn about suprasegmental features is to say a short sentence backward. To do this properly, you have to reverse the intonation pattern of the sentence, make the aspiration come before rather than after voiceless stops, and take into account all the variations in vowel and consonant length due to the phonetic context. If you can make a recording of yourself on a computer, you may be able to judge how successfully you can do this by playing the recording backward, so the reversed sentence should sound as if it had been said normally. Begin with a fairly easy phrase such as

Mary had a little lamb.

Then go on with a more difficult one such as

Whose fleece was white as snow.

In each case, it is best to begin by making a narrow transcription of the phrase, including the intonation pattern, and then to write this in reverse order.

F. Practice tonal contrasts by learning to say the following set of words in Ibibio, a language spoken in Nigeria. Ibibio has three tones: high [´], low [`], and falling [ˆ]. The six contrasting patterns in disyllabic words are illustrated here. (Saying these words also gives you practice in saying the labial velar [k͡p], discussed in Chapter 7.)

Tone Sequence	Example	Gloss
high followed by high	ák͡pá	'expanse of ocean'
high followed by low	ákù	'priest'
high followed by falling	ák͡pân	'square woven basket'
low followed by high	àk͡pá	'first'
low followed by low	àk͡pà	'species of ant'
low followed by falling	àk͡pâ	'rubber tree'

G. Cantonese Chinese has a different tone system from Mandarin Chinese (shown in Table 10.2). In Cantonese, there are six tones that occur on open syllables and three that occur only on syllables containing a final consonant. Say each of the following Cantonese words.

Description	Pitch	Tone Letter	Example	Gloss
high	55	˥	si	'poem'
mid	33	˧	si	'to try'
low	22	˨	si	'matter'
extra low	11	˩	si	'time'
mid rising	35	˧˥	si	'to cause'
low rising	13	˩˧	si	'city'
high	5	˥	sik	'to know'
mid	3	˧	sit	'to release'
low	2	˨	sik	'to eat'

11

Linguistic Phonetics

In this final chapter, we will review the approach to linguistic phonetics embodied in the principles of the International Phonetic Association and in a hierarchical phonetic descriptive framework that provides some basis for formal phonological theory. The chapter will then end with a prospectus of cognitive phonetic research touching on speech production and perception, and how they shape language sound systems.

Unlike the previous chapters, this chapter deals with theoretical issues in phonetics where the focus is on finding explanations for some of the kinds of observations that have been the focus of the previous chapters. There is more room for interpretation and less confirmed knowledge when it comes to this explanatory side of phonetics. You might find it interesting to ask your teacher if he or she has a different point of view about some of the things we say in this chapter.

PHONETICS OF THE COMMUNITY AND OF THE INDIVIDUAL

Linguistic phonetic descriptions of the sort that you have learned about in this book are, by and large, descriptions of the phonetics of the community. The representations that we write in IPA, and analyze in formal phonology, are intended to show the community's shared knowledge of how to say the words of a language. Shared phonetic knowledge is perceptible to other speakers (and thus to the phonetician too) and is emergent from the aggregate behavior of the group in the sense that it captures what community members accept as correct pronunciation. For example, speakers of English generally agree that voiceless stops in the onset of stressed syllables are aspirated. However, looking at a database of recorded utterances, we may find some examples where voiceless stops in stressed syllables have been pronounced without aspiration. For example, in fast speech, we may find the words *on top of* pronounced as [ə̃dapə]. Despite the fact that such a pronunciation may occur, speakers of English agree that this is not really how these words should be pronounced. Our shared phonetic competence is thus somewhat divorced from normal speech and in practice is best revealed in careful speech.

We have also, at various points in the book, noted that speakers differ in interesting ways. Indeed, there can be little doubt that the set of phonetic habits and memories that each speaker possesses is different from those of every other speaker of the language—so that no two people have exactly the same English, or French, or Japanese. Our description of the phonetics of the individual involves describing the phonetic knowledge and skills that are involved in the performance of language. As we have seen, certain aspects of the phonetics of the individual can be captured using IPA transcription, just as we describe language or dialect variation. Other aspects, though, are not as compatible with the tools of linguistic phonetic description. Analysis of the individual's phonetic knowledge has only been occasionally touched on in this book because phonetic performance involves private knowledge that is inherent in the individual's experience of language and is usually only revealed in laboratory studies. Being private, the phonetics of the individual is usually not the focus of the linguist in speech elicitation, and it is difficult to describe even with spectrograms of the person's speech. Interestingly, the phonetics of the individual is the locus of much of the explanatory power of phonetic theory, as we will see in the last sections of this chapter. In the next two sections, we will review linguistic phonetics (the phonetics of the community), and in the final sections, we will discuss three aspects of the phonetics of the individual.

THE INTERNATIONAL PHONETIC ALPHABET

One way to review the key elements of linguistic phonetic description is to consider the International Phonetic Alphabet. This is the set of symbols and diacritics that have been officially approved by the International Phonetic Association. The association publishes a chart, which is reproduced (with permission) inside the front and back covers of this book. This chart is really a number of separate charts, which have been rearranged to fit the space in this book. At the top inside the front cover, you will find the main consonant chart. Below it is a table showing the symbols for nonpulmonic consonants, and below that is the vowel chart. Inside the back cover is a list of diacritics and other symbols, and a set of symbols for suprasegmental events, such as tone, intonation, stress, and length.

In the usual arrangement of the IPA chart, the material that we have divided between the inside front and inside back covers appears on a single page, summarizing a complete theory of linguistic phonetics. The IPA chart does not try to cover all possible types of phonetic descriptions, including, for example, all the individual strategies for realizing linguistic phonological contrasts, or gradations in the degree of coarticulation between adjacent segments. Instead, it is limited to those sounds that can have linguistic significance in that they can change the meaning of a word in some language.

You should be able to understand all the terms in the consonant chart. If you have any problems, refer to the glossary at the back of the book. The symbols in this chart are arranged in such a way that if there are two items within a single cell, the one on the right is voiced. This enables the consonant chart to be taken as a three-dimensional representation of the principal features of consonants: the target of the articulatory gesture (where it is made, across the chart), the type of gesture (the manner of articulation, down the chart), and the state of the glottis (within each cell).

The consonant chart thus summarizes the major features required for describing consonants. It even shows, by the use of shaded areas, which combinations of features are judged to be impossible. Thus, it is considered that no language could have a velar trill or tap—a sound in which the back of the tongue vibrated or moved in a ballistic tap gesture against the soft palate. The blank cells on the chart—those that neither are shaded nor contain a symbol—indicate combinations of categories that are possible but have not been observed to be distinctive in any language. For example, it is perfectly possible for a language to have a voiceless retroflex lateral fricative. No symbol was provided because there was no documentation in the phonetic literature of a language containing such a sound. But it in fact occurs in Toda, a Dravidian language spoken by about a thousand people in the Nilgiri Hills in southern India. This language has a contrast between a voiced retroflex lateral approximant [ɭ] and a voiceless retroflex lateral fricative. We will consider later how this sound should be symbolized.

Some of the other blanks and shaded areas simply reflect the judgments of the phoneticians who drew up the chart. Go through each of these cells and see whether you agree with its assignment as a blank or a shaded area. For example, can you make a labiodental plosive? Some people with well-aligned teeth can make a complete stop of this kind. But, given that not everyone in a speech community will have well-aligned teeth, labiodental plosives may not be as effective in language as other plosives. As another example, could you make a pharyngeal plosive? You may be able to make a complete stop in the upper part of the pharynx, but there is no symbol for a sound of this kind because it is not used contrastively in any known language. On the whole, the makers of the chart have been fairly conservative in their addition of shading, putting it in only when it was reasonably clear that the sound could not be produced. It is quite certain that nobody could produce a voiced glottal stop (i.e., a sound in which the vocal folds were simultaneously vibrating with normal voicing and were also held tightly together) or a pharyngeal nasal in which the air was completely stopped by a closure in the pharynx but nevertheless simultaneously escaped through the nose.

When considering the status of the rows and columns on the chart, it is worth considering the placement of [h] and [ɦ]. Are these sounds really glottal fricatives? As we noted earlier, [h] usually denotes a voiceless transition into (or, in some languages, out of) a syllable. Its place of articulation depends on the adjacent sounds. There is usually very little audible friction (turbulent airflow) produced at the glottis. Also, [ɦ] is best regarded as a state of the glottis without a specific place; like [h], it is not a fricative. Both [h] and [ɦ] might have been better placed under "other symbols."

Below the consonant chart is a set of symbols for consonants made with different airstream mechanisms. The IPA recognizes three possibilities: clicks, voiced implosives, and ejectives. This does not mean that the IPA denies the existence of voiceless implosives. It means that the IPA considers them too rare to need separate symbols and would suggest using a diacritic. For example, a voiceless bilabial implosive, which occurs in only a handful of languages, can be symbolized by combining the voiceless diacritic with the voiced symbol, forming [ɓ̥]. The ejective symbol, ['], is like a diacritic in that it can be added to many different consonants, including fricatives, as exemplified by [s'].

The vowel chart implies that there are three dimensions applicable to vowels: front–back across the top of the chart, close–open on the vertical dimension, and rounding specified by the relative locations of members of pairs of vowels. Again, these are only the principal types of vowels. Other types, such as those that are nasalized or have an advanced tongue root, can be symbolized by adding diacritics.

The "other symbols" at the top left on the inside back cover represent sounds that could not be conveniently described in terms of the main sets of categories we have been considering. They include symbols for sounds with multiple places of articulation (labial velar and labial palatal) and the epiglottal sounds that occur in Arabic, Hebrew, and some of the languages of the Caucasus. These sounds would have been hard to place on the chart without adding further columns with many empty cells.

The diacritic section of the chart allows a number of additional aspects of sounds to be represented by adding a mark above or below the symbol for the principal features of the sound. Some of the diacritics correspond to the provision of additional features or dimensions applicable to many different sounds. Thus, additional states of the glottis are recognized by the provision of aspirated, breathy-voiced, and creaky-voiced diacritics. More specific features, such as particular tongue shapes, are recognized by providing diacritics for linguo-labials, dentals, apicals, and laminals. Further vowel qualities can be symbolized with many of the other diacritics.

In addition, the IPA provides for the representation of stress, length, tone, and intonation. In the characterization of stress, only three possibilities are recognized: primary stress, secondary stress, and unstressed. There are four possible lengths: long, half-long, unmarked, and extra-short. The possibilities for tone and intonation allow for five contrasting levels and numerous combinations.

The IPA does not provide a symbol for every contingency, so phoneticians have to improvise when they come across some previously unrecorded event. Let us now return to the question of how to symbolize the voiceless retroflex lateral fricative that occurs in Toda. One possibility that is always open to us is to use an asterisk, and add, after giving a consonant chart or transcription of Toda: "[*] represents a voiceless retroflex lateral fricative." Another possibility is to use the symbol for the voiced retroflex lateral approximant [ɭ] and add the diacritic [̥], which indicates that the symbol to which this diacritic has been added should be taken as representing a voiceless sound. It is sometimes difficult to add a diacritic below a symbol that itself descends below the level of the writing line. A possible solution is to put the [̥] slightly in front of the [ɭ], making [̥ɭ]. This symbol would really designate a voiceless retroflex lateral approximant, and an explanatory note would still be needed, saying "[̥ɭ] is a fricative rather than an approximant." However, this might almost be taken for granted, as no language contrasts any kind of voiceless lateral fricative with a voiceless lateral approximant made at the same place of articulation. Try saying a voiceless version of an ordinary English [l]. You will probably find that you are making a lateral [ɬ] with audible friction rather than a voiceless approximant.

The avowed aim of the IPA is to be able to symbolize all the distinctive sounds in languages. The intent is to represent by separate symbols the sounds that serve to distinguish one word from another in a language. The IPA would like to do this, as far as possible, by using ordinary letters of the roman alphabet or simple modifications of these letters. When this would mean the creation of a large number of symbols for a set of related sounds, the IPA favors the use of diacritics. This happens, for example, in the case of nasalized vowels or ejective stops.

IPA symbols can be used in a variety of ways. There is no sense in which one can speak of *the* IPA transcription of a given utterance. Many types of transcription are possible, as we saw in Chapter 2 in the discussion of English phonology. The relationship between some different types is summarized in Figure 11.1.

The first distinction is between a transcription that in some way reflects the systematic, linguistic facts of the utterance being described, as opposed to one in which the symbols are used just to provide an impressionistic record of the sounds as heard—the kind of record that might be made by a speech pathologist who has not yet found out anything about the patient, or a linguist hearing the first few words in a language that had never been transcribed before. In theory, an impressionistic transcription is one in which the symbols represent intersections of general phonetic categories.

Phoneticians very seldom make a totally impressionistic transcription. Generally, within a few minutes of starting to transcribe the utterances of a new patient or a speaker of a language with which we have not worked before, we begin to

Figure 11.1 A schematic representation of some terms used for describing different types of transcription.

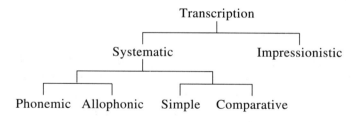

use symbols that rely on our linguistic hunches and preconceptions. We very soon stop noting small differences between repetitions of the same utterance, particularly if they are of the kind of which the speaker seems to be unaware. Virtually the only occasion when a completely impressionistic transcription is necessary is in the investigation of an infant's prelinguistic babbling.

Within the class of systematic (phonetic) transcriptions, there are two independent divisions. First, a transcription may be phonemic or allophonic. A phonemic transcription is one in which all the different words in a language are represented by the smallest possible number of different symbols. An allophonic transcription is one that uses a larger number of distinct symbols so that it can differentiate among systematic, allophonic differences in the sounds of an utterance.

As we noted when discussing the sounds of English, phonemic and allophonic transcriptions are related to each other by a set of statements that define the distributions of sounds in different phonetic environments. A phonemic transcription collapses the allophonic transcription into just those phonetic values that are contrastive in the language. The difference between these two types of transcription is simply in whether the detailed phonetic information is made explicit within the transcription itself or within the set of statements that describes the distributions of sounds in the language.

The other kind of distinction among systematic phonetic transcriptions is that between a simple and a comparative use of particular symbols. The simplest IPA symbols are those that use ordinary letters of the roman alphabet, such as [a] and [r]. More exotic letters such as [ɑ, ɒ, ɐ] and [ʀ, ɹ, ɾ] convey greater phonetic detail. A transcription using more unusual symbols is called a *comparative transcription*, on the grounds that the use of more specific symbols implicitly reflects a comparison between the general phonetic values of the simple symbols and the more precise values of the exotic symbols. In general, as we noted earlier, a broad transcription is one that is both phonemic (as opposed to allophonic) and simple (as opposed to comparative). A narrow transcription may show allophonic distinctions, or it may show more phonetic detail by using more specific symbols, or it may do both these things.

When we think about transcriptions, we can see that phonological analysis and phonetic transcriptions are inextricably intertwined—both focus on the shared phonetic knowledge of the community. It is generally recognized that phonology must rest on accurate phonetic observations. But it is equally true that most phonetic observations are made in terms of a phonological framework.

FEATURE HIERARCHY

The second way in which we will review linguistic phonetic descriptions is by considering a hierarchical organization of linguistic phonetic **features**. A feature, in this sense, is a property of a sound and may be a rather general descriptive term like "labial" or a more specific descriptive term like [bilabial]. At the most specific level, a feature may be tied to a particular articulatory maneuver or

Figure 11.2 The supraordinate features in a feature hierarchy.

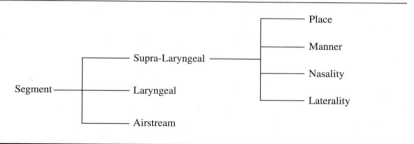

acoustic property. Thus, the feature [bilabial] indicates not only that the segment is produced at the lips but also that it involves both of them. Features may be listed in a hierarchy, with nodes in the hierarchy defining ever more specific phonetic properties.

The major phonetic dimensions of speech sounds are shown in Figure 11.2. All sounds have some Supra-Laryngeal characteristics, some Laryngeal characteristics, and some Airstream mechanism. The Supra-Laryngeal characteristics can be divided into those for Place (of articulation), Manner (of articulation), the possibility of Nasality, and the possibility of being Lateral.

A detailed specification of the Place feature is given in Figure 11.3. The first division is into the major regions of the vocal tract, giving us the five features Labial, Coronal, Dorsal, Radical, and Glottal. We used the first three of these terms in Chapter 1. Now we are adding **Radical** to apply as a cover term for [pharyngeal] and [epiglottal] articulations made with the root of the tongue. We also have a feature Glottal, with only one value, [glottal], to cover various articulations, such as [h, ʔ]. If we are to have a convenient grouping of the features

Figure 11.3 Features dominated by the feature Place.

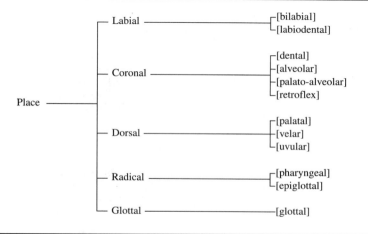

for consonants, we have to recognize that Supra-Laryngeal features must allow for the dual nature of the actions of the larynx and include Glottal as a place of articulation.

A sound may be articulated at more than one of the regions Labial, Coronal, Dorsal, Radical, and Glottal. We have described sounds such as [ɥ] that simultaneously have articulations that have feature values [labial] and [palatal], and [w], which is simultaneously [labial] and [velar]. Within the five general regions, Coronal articulations can be split into three mutually exclusive possibilities: Laminal (blade of the tongue), Apical (tip of the tongue), and Sub-Apical (the under part of the blade of the tongue). The mutually exclusive possibilities for each of these and for the other places of articulation are shown at the right of Figure 11.3. Some of these possibilities have not been discussed in this introductory textbook, but they are all needed for describing the sounds of the languages of the world.

In a simple framework, it is sufficient to consider Coronal to be a terminal feature like Labial and Dorsal, as shown in Figure 11.3. A more elaborate feature hierarchy would include the apical/laminal distinction we discussed in Chapter 7. In this way, we could deal with a wider range of languages, using the distinctions shown in Figure 11.4. The features for possible manners of articulation are shown in Figure 11.5. Four of the features we have been using—Stop, Fricative, Approximant, and Vowel (without explicitly calling them features)—can be grouped together as aspects of another feature, Aperture. This grouping reflects the fact that the four features Stop, Fricative, Approximant, and Vowel all depend on the degree of closure of the articulators. In some older feature systems, these possibilities are split into two groups, but it is now thought better to recognize that they form a continuum. The changes in the pronunciation of Peter Ladefoged's name, for example, fall on this continuum. The name is of Danish origin. Peter pronounced it [ˈlædɪfoʊɡɪd] in English, with consonants as they once were in Danish. These stops first became fricatives, which later became approximants in Danish [ˈlæːðəfoːɣəð], later [ˈlæːð̞əfoːɣəð], and now perhaps more like [ˈlæːð̞foːwð], making it apparent that there is a continuum going from

Figure 11.4 An elaboration of the feature Coronal.

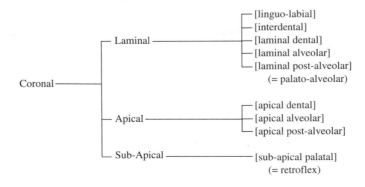

Figure 11.5 Features dominated by the feature Manner.

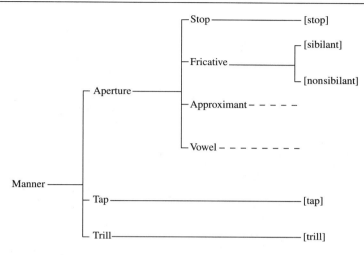

[stop] through [fricative] to [approximant]. (Note the use of the diacritic [̞], meaning *more open*, turning the fricative symbols into symbols for approximants.) The name is simply two Danish words put together, *lade*, a barn, and *foged*, something like a steward or bailiff; so Ladefoged = Barnkeeper. Spanish also has a process whereby stops first become fricatives and then approximants.

The manner category Stop has only one possible value, [stop], but Fricative has two: [sibilant] and [nonsibilant]. The possible values for Approximant and Vowel will be discussed in the next paragraph, but first we should note that there are two other Manner features, Trill and Tap, each of which has only a single possible value, respectively [trill] and [tap]. The further relationships among all the Manner features are beyond the scope of this book.

As shown in Figure 11.6 (on page 286), Approximant and Vowel dominate other features. There are five principal features, the first of which, Height, has five possible values [high], [mid-high], [mid], [mid-low], and [low]. As far as we know, no language distinguishes more than five vowel heights. Backness has only three values, [front], [center], and [back]. As we saw in Chapter 9, when discussing Japanese [ɯ], there are two kinds of Rounding: Protrusion with possible values [protruded] and [retracted], and Compression, with possible values [compressed] and [separated]. The feature Tongue Root has two possible values: [+ATR] and [−ATR]. Pharyngealized sounds may be classified as having the opposite of an advanced tongue root and are therefore [−ATR]. The feature Rhotic has only one possible value, [rhotacized].

Separate figures have not been drawn for the other two Supra-Laryngeal features, Nasality and Laterality, as each of them is itself a terminal feature. Nasality has the possible values [nasal] and [oral]; Laterality has the possible values [lateral] and [central].

Figure 11.6 Features dominated by the features Vowel and Approximant.

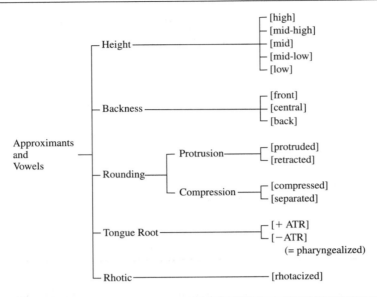

The Laryngeal possibilities, shown in Figure 11.7, involve three features. Glottal Stricture specifies how far apart the vocal folds are. Languages make use of five possibilities: [voiceless]; [breathy voice], as we saw in languages such as Hindi; [modal voice], which is the regular voicing used in every language; [creaky voice] in languages such as Hausa; and [closed], forming a glottal stop. Many in-between possibilities occur, but if we are simply providing categories for the degrees of glottal opening that are used distinctively, these five are sufficient. A separate feature, Glottal Timing, is used to specify voiceless aspirated stops and breathy voiced aspirated stops. A third feature, Glottal Movement, is also included among the Laryngeal features to allow for the specification of

Figure 11.7 Features dominated by the feature Laryngeal.

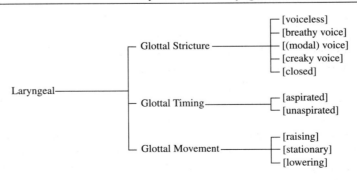

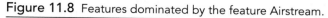

Figure 11.8 Features dominated by the feature Airstream.

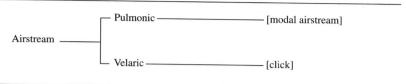

implosives and ejectives. Some books, including previous editions of this book, prefer to consider these sounds as simply involving a different airstream mechanism. This is the way we began describing them at the beginning of Chapter 6. At the end of that chapter, we included them in the summary of actions of the glottis. As pointed out there, they interact with other Laryngeal features, and are accordingly put at this point in the hierarchy.

The arrangement in Figure 11.7 leaves the Airstream feature, shown in Figure 11.8, dominating only two features, Pulmonic and Velaric. Both of these have only one value. In a more elaborate arrangement, it would be appropriate to consider whether the pulmonic airstream mechanism varied in force, but this possibility will not be considered here.

The figures in this chapter provide a hierarchical arrangement of the features required to describe nearly all the sounds of the world's languages. Try working through this hierarchy from the top down so that you get a complete specification of a variety of sounds. Table 11.1 (on page 288) gives a partial specification of a number of English segments.

A PROBLEM WITH LINGUISTIC EXPLANATIONS

We now turn to a discussion of the phonetics of the individual. Current phonetic research and theory focuses to a large extent on topics such as speech motor control, the representation of speech in memory, and the interaction of speech perception and production in language change (the topics of the next three sections), because it is in topics such as these that we find explanations for language sound patterns. For example, we have given a name to the phenomenon of "assimilation" and can describe it by saying that adjacent sounds come to share some phonetic properties. But if we restrict ourselves to the terminology and knowledge base of linguistic phonetics, we are restricted to descriptions of sound patterns and not their explanation. In fact, explanations that are restricted in this way often fall into the fallacy of **reification**—acting as if abstract things are concrete. Here's an explanation that falls into this trap: Assimilation happens because there is a tendency in pronunciation for adjacent sounds to share phonetic properties. This "explanation" is even more impressive if we state it as a formal constraint on sequences of sounds: **AGREE(x)** *Adjacent output segments have the same value of the feature x.* The problem is that the explanation is just a restatement of the description. Assimilation is when adjacent segments

TABLE 11.1 A partial feature specification of some English segments (vowels that may not occur in all accents are omitted).

Place	Labial		[bilabial]	p, b, m
			[labiodental]	f, v
	Coronal		[dental]	θ, ð
			[alveolar]	t, d, n, l, s, z
			[post-alveolar]	r
			[palato-alveolar]	ʃ, ʒ
	Dorsal		[velar]	k, g, ŋ
Aperture			[stop]	p, t, k, b, d, g, m, n
	Fricative		[sibilant]	s, ʃ, z, ʒ
			[nonsibilant]	f, θ, v, ð
	Approximant Vowel	Height	[high]	i, u
			[mid-high]	ɪ, ʊ, eɪ, oʊ
			[mid]	ə, ɜ
			[mid-low]	ɛ, ɔ
			[low]	æ, ɑ
		Backness	[front]	i, ɪ, eɪ, ɛ, æ
			[back]	ɑ, ɔ, oʊ, ʊ, u
		Rounding	[rounded]	ɔ, oʊ, ʊ, u
			[unrounded]	i, ɪ, eɪ, ɛ, æ, ɑ
Nasality			[nasal]	m, n, ŋ
			[oral]	(all others)
Laterality			[lateral]	l
			[central]	(all others)
Laryngeal	Glottal Structure		[voiceless]	p, t, k, f, θ, s, ʃ
			[(modal) voice]	(all others)

share features, so the "explanation" says nothing more than that when we look at language we see that assimilation happens. The explanation has this form: the tendency to assimilate (a cross-linguistic generalization) exists because there is a tendency to assimilate (reified as a specific "explanatory principle"). In the following sections, we look to the private phonetic knowledge of the individual for a more satisfying way to explain language sound patterns.

CONTROLLING ARTICULATORY MOVEMENTS

Underlying our linguistic description of [p], to take one simple sound as an example of speech motor control, is a dizzying array of muscular complexity involving dozens of muscles in the chest, abdomen, larynx, tongue, throat, and face. And all of these must be contracted with varying degrees of tension in specific sequence and duration of contraction. For example, in producing a lip closure movement, there are two main muscles (depressor labii inferior and incisivus inferior) that depress the lower lip, that is, pull the lower lip away from the upper lip. These muscles must relax so as not to oppose the lip closure motion of [p] too much. There are also two main muscles that when contracted will move the lower lip toward the upper lip (obicularis oris inferior, mentalis). These two must be given enough tension to overcome the tension of the lip-depressing muscles. As the formulations above "too much" and "enough tension" imply, the actual degree of tension needed for lip closure cannot be specified in absolute terms but depends on the tension of the opposing muscles. Furthermore, the tension of the cooperating muscles must be coordinated. For instance, obicularis oris inferior (OOI) and mentalis must trade off with each other so that if mentalis is not very tense for a particular [p], the OOI will compensate with greater tension.

So coordination of the four main lower lip muscles is complicated and cannot be specified with predetermined target "tension" levels because the actual degree of muscle fiber activation for raising the lower lip in [p] depends on the tension of the other lip muscles. But the situation is even more complex than this because the lower lip moves up and down as the jaw moves up and down. So the muscles that depress the jaw (geniohyoid, mylohyoid, and digastricus) must also be coordinated with the muscles that raise the jaw (masseter and temporalis). The activation of these jaw muscles depends on the tension of the lip muscles and, just as the muscles within the lower lip may trade off with each other, so also the jaw muscles may trade with the lip muscles so that in one [p], there is more jaw movement, while in another, there is more lower lip movement, and in yet a third [p], the upper lip does more work. Movement of the jaw also depends on its starting location. If the jaw is already relatively closed, such as in the utterance [ipi], there may be no need for it to move as part of the [p] production, while in [apa], the jaw-closing muscles might be quite active.

The number of free parameters (separate muscle activations) that must be controlled in speech has been called a **degrees of freedom problem** because a flat control structure in which the tension of each muscle is separately controlled presents a control problem of exceeding complexity. The solution to the degrees of freedom problem that has been achieved in the speech motor control system (and most other motor control systems, like swallowing, walking, reaching, looking, etc.), is to organize the control system hierarchically in goal-oriented **coordinative structures**.

For example, one of the **gestures** involved in saying [p] is lip closure. The coordinative structure for lip closure is illustrated in Figure 11.9. This structure

Figure 11.9 Part of the coordinative structure involved in lip closure.

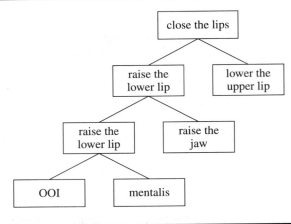

specifies an overall task "close the lips" at the top node, and subtasks such as "raise the lower lip" and "lower the upper lip" are coordinated with each other to accomplish the overall task. Some subtasks also require further reduction of the goal into smaller subtasks. For example, "raise the lower lip" is present twice in the figure—first as a specification of the absolute position of the lower lip (which is coordinated with the upper lip in accomplishing the task "close the lips") and second as a specification of the relative position of the lower lip (which is coordinated with the jaw in accomplishing the task "raise the [absolute position of] the lower lip"). The idea with coordinative structures is that each gesture is defined in terms of subtasks, and thus there is no direct control from a task like "close the lips" to the muscles. Instead, the muscles have more limited goals and the degrees of freedom problem in coordination is solved by dividing the overall task into smaller, simpler coordination problems.

One way that we know about the coordinative structures for speech is by looking at how articulators and muscles may trade off with each other. For example, when we track the locations of the upper and lower lips in a sequence of [papapapapa], we find that on some instances of [p], the lower lip may raise more than it does on other instances of [p]. In those instances where the lower lip doesn't reach as far toward the upper lip, we find that the upper lip compensates with a greater magnitude of movement toward the lower lip. Similar patterns of compensation are seen for all of the subtasks illustrated in Figure 11.9—the jaw and lower lip compensate for each other, and the OOI and mentalis compensate for each other. These patterns of compensation, or trading relations in speech, are **motor equivalences**—different motor activation patterns producing the same result.

For further simple examples of coordinative structures, we will consider the production of vowels. As you can see quite easily for yourself, it is possible to produce the same vowel with many different jaw positions. Try to say

[i] with your teeth almost together, and then with them fairly far apart. There need be very little, if any, difference in the sounds you produce. The same is true of many other vowels. In fact, it is possible to produce a complete set of English vowels with your teeth almost together or held apart by a wedge such as a small coin. Obviously, the motor activity must be very different in these two circumstances. When the teeth are held far apart, you can feel the muscles of the tongue raising it up in the jaw when you say [i]. When the teeth are close together, the raising of the jaw itself contributes greatly to the lifting of the tongue for [i]. You can also observe the results of the motor equivalence of different gestures that people use when making vowels by watching them say the words *heed*, *hid*, *head*, *had*. You will probably be able to see that some people lower the tongue by lowering the jaw as they say this series of words. But others keep the jaw comparatively steady and simply lower the tongue within the jaw.

Motor control nearly always involves considering speech production in more detail than is necessary for the description of differences in meaning and is open to much variation within and across speakers. This is why we say that speech motor control involves private phonetic knowledge. In each of the cases we have been considering, it is possible to produce the sounds in a variety of specific physiological or articulatory ways. Thus, if two [p] sounds have the same lip closure, they are linguistically equivalent, irrespective of the pattern of jaw and lip coordination used to produce the closure. Similarly, the different jaw positions in vowels will not affect the position of the highest point of the tongue or its shape relative to the upper surface of the vocal tract.

Although there is quite a bit more to speech motor control than this, we can nonetheless see how investigation of speech motor control may offer some additional insight into phonological patterns like assimilation. We are closer to an explanation of assimilation by being able to note that the production of speech is accomplished by ensembles of gestures that in essence compete for control of the muscles of the vocal tract. One segment requires that the lower lip-raising muscles be more active than the lower lip depressors, while an adjacent segment requires the opposite pattern of activation. Because muscle activations come on and off gradually over time, we have a good start toward further explaining the tendency for adjacent sounds to become like each other from patterns of gestural activation (and motor control principles generally).

MEMORY FOR SPEECH

As we have seen, the speech to which we are exposed is quite diverse. Different speakers of the same language will have somewhat different productions depending on vocal tract physiology and their own habits of speech motor coordination. We are also exposed to a variety of speech styles ranging from very careful pronunciations in various types of public speaking to the quite casual style that is typical between friends.

This "lack of phonetic invariance" has posed an important problem for phonetic theory as we try to reconcile the fact that shared phonetic knowledge can be described using IPA symbols and phonological features with the fact that the individual phonetic forms that speakers produce and hear on a daily basis span a very great range. The lack of invariance problem also has great practical significance for engineers who try to get computers to produce and recognize speech.

One way to account for phonetic variability across languages is to posit language-specific **phonetic implementation** rules. This approach assumes a universal set of phonetic features such as we find in the IPA, coupled with a language-specific set of statements to specify the phonetic targets for each phonetic feature. For example, both Navajo and Mandarin have voiceless aspirated stops, but as we saw in Chapter 6, the VOT of the Navajo aspirated stops is much longer than the VOT of the Mandarin aspirated stops. The implementation approach says that there is one feature [+ spread glottis], and that it is implemented differently in Navajo and Mandarin.

The phonetic implementation approach becomes more complicated when we try to account for stylistic pronunciation variation. Part of the complication comes from the fact that it is not plausible to assume that all languages have the same set of reduction processes mapping careful speech into casual speech. For example, as we discussed in a previous chapter, vowel devoicing in Japanese is usually described as affecting the high vowels [i] and [u] only, with a statement like "high vowels devoice between voiceless consonants." The problem is that mid vowels also devoice in Japanese—but this devoicing process is not categorical. The devoicing rule of mid vowels is something like "mid vowels devoice sometimes between voiceless consonants, with increasing probability of devoicing as speech rate increases." Devoicing is a phonetic reduction process in which contrastive phonetic information is lost or neutralized as a function of speech rate or style. And although vowel devoicing does occur in other languages (see if you get it in *potato*), it is by no means universal or uniform in character across languages. Thus, each language needs a set of phonetic implementation rules to account for stylistic variation.

The prognosis for the phonetic implementation approach becomes even more dire when we look at individual differences among speakers. Anatomical differences between speakers, whether they be large differences such as those between children and adults, or small differences related to the size and shape of the palate within an otherwise homogenous group, have an impact on speech motor control. In response to variability of this sort, the phonetic implementation approach must hope that these sources of individual phonetic variation are quite small relative to the larger—and presumably more rule-governed—sources of variation. Experience in automatic speech recognition, which is still troublingly unreliable for large-vocabulary multiple-talker systems, suggests that individual variation is a substantial problem for the implementation model.

In this section, we have been discussing phonetic variability (across languages, styles of speech, and different speakers of the same language), yet the section is entitled "memory for speech." This is because the main alternative to the phonetic

Figure 11.10 A hypothetical cloud of [u] exemplars.

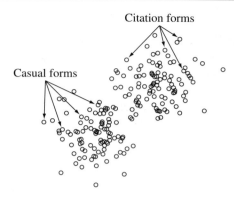

implementation approach is a theory that focuses on how experiences are encoded in memory. It is worth noting that the phonetic implementation view assumes that words are stored in memory in their most basic phonetic form, from which we calculate phonetic variation using phonetic implementation rules. Given the problems of the phonetic implementation approach, an alternative theory—that many instances of each word are stored in memory—is suggested. This **exemplar theory** of phonetics holds that variability is memorized rather than computed. Figure 11.10 illustrates a phonetic category (e.g., the vowel [u]) in this theory. The axes of the figure stand for two phonetic dimensions, perhaps F1 and F2, or alternatively, the location and degree of tongue–body constriction. Obviously, real phonetic spaces have many more dimensions than this. Rather than posit the existence of an abstract phonetic entity [u] from which each exemplar must be derived, in exemplar theory, the representation of [u] *is* the set of exemplars. By cross-classifying each exemplar as also an exemplar of citation speech or casual speech, the model also provides a representation of these speech styles. As you can see, exemplar theory relies heavily on stored exemplars that use processes of selection and storage rather than processes of transformation to define the range of variability found in speech.

Exemplar theories offer a shift in perspective on several core concepts in phonetics.

Language universal features   Broad phonetic classes (e.g., aspirated vs. unaspirated) derive from physiological constraints on speaking or hearing, but detailed phonetic definitions are arbitrary—a matter of community norms. This theory tends to disfavor cognitive universals and sees instead a role for physiological or physical universals.

Speaking styles   No one style is basic (from which others are derived), because all are stored in memory. Bidialectal speakers store two dialects, and all speakers control a range of speaking styles. Listeners may learn to recognize new varieties of speech—regional dialects or computer-mangled synthesis—by storing exemplars of them.

Generalization and productivity Interestingly, productivity—the hallmark of linguistic knowledge in the phonetic implementation approach—is the least developed aspect of exemplar theory.

Sound change The Neogrammarians (around the turn of the twentieth century) argued that sound change is phonetically gradual and operates across the whole lexicon. They conceived of this in an exemplar theory where sound change is a gradual shift of the exemplar "cloud" as new instances are added. Note that in the phonetic implementation model, phonetically gradual sound change requires two distinct yet logically independent mechanisms—change in phonetic implementation rules, then, after a big enough shift, change in a feature value.

THE BALANCE BETWEEN PHONETIC FORCES

When we consider how sounds pattern within a language, we must take into account both the speaker's point of view and the listener's point of view. Speakers often like to convey their meaning with the least possible articulatory effort. Except when they are trying to produce very clear speech, they will tend to produce utterances with a large number of assimilations, with some segments left out, and with the differences between other segments reduced to a minimum. Producing utterances in this way allows a speaker to follow a principle of **ease of articulation**. The main way to reduce articulatory effort is by using coarticulations between sounds. As a result of coarticulations, languages change. For example, in an earlier form of English, words such as *nation*, *station* contained [s] so that they were pronounced [ˈnasion] and [ˈstasion]. As a result of gesture overlap in some exemplars, the blade of the tongue became raised during the fricative in anticipation of the position needed for the following high front vowel. Thus, the [s] became [ʃ], [i] was lost, and the unstressed [o] became [ə]. (The *t* was never pronounced in English. It was introduced into the spelling by scholars who were influenced by Latin.)

Further examples are not hard to find. Coarticulations involving a change in the place of the nasal and the following stop occurred in words such as *improper* and *impossible* before these words came into English through Norman French. In words such as these, the [n] that occurs in the prefix *in-* (as in *intolerable* and *indecent*) has changed to [m]. These changes are even reflected in the spelling. There are also coarticulations involving the state of the glottis. Words such as *resist* and *result* are pronounced as [rəˈzɪst] and [rəˈzʌlt], with a voiced consonant between the two vowels. The stems in these words originally began with the voiceless consonant [s], as they still do in words such as *consist* and *consult*, in which the [s] is not intervocalic. In all these and in many similar historical changes, one or more segments are affected by adjacent segments so that there is an economy of articulation. These are historical cases of the phenomenon of assimilation, which we discussed at the beginning of Chapter 5.

Ease of articulation cannot be carried too far. Listeners need to be able to understand the meaning with the least possible effort on their part. They would therefore prefer utterances with sounds that remain constant and distinct on all occasions. Perceptually, what matters is that sounds that affect the meaning of a word should be sufficiently distinct from one another. A language must always maintain *sufficient perceptual separation*. Therefore, languages constrain speakers so that they keep words sufficiently distinct. The language makes sure that there is sufficient perceptual distance between the sounds that occur in a contrasting set, such as the vowels in stressed monosyllables (as in *beat, bit, bet, bat*, etc.).

The principle of perceptual separation does not usually result in one sound affecting an adjacent sound, as occurs with the principle of maximum ease of articulation. Instead, perceptual separation affects the set of sounds that potentially can occur at a given position in a word, such as in the position that must be occupied by a vowel in a stressed monosyllable. Articulatory processes are syntagmatic, affecting adjacent items in a sequence, whereas perceptual processes are paradigmatic, affecting the set of items that can occur in a given place in a sequence.

We have already noted some of the ways in which languages tend to maximize the perceptual separation between sounds. As we saw in Chapter 9, this tendency explains why some vowel systems are more likely to occur than others. If the vowels of a language are to be maximally distinct, the formant frequencies will be such that the vowels are as far apart as possible when plotted on a vowel chart. Consequently, there is a natural tendency in languages for vowels to be spaced at approximately equal distances and on the outside of the possible vowel area. This tendency is most evident in languages with a comparatively small number of vowels. Hundreds of languages have only five contrasting vowels (e.g., Spanish, Hausa, Japanese, and Swahili, to name four completely unrelated languages). In all these languages, the vowels are roughly evenly distributed so that there are at least two front vowels and two back vowels. No language has only five vowels unevenly distributed so that all are front vowels. But there are, of course, many languages like English that have five front vowels and an approximately similar number of back vowels.

If there is a possibility that a pair of contrasting sounds will occur in the same place within a word, then there will be a tendency for the perceptual distance between them to be increased. Conversely, whenever a language does not distinguish between two similar sounds, the actual sound produced will tend to be between the two possibilities. Thus, as we have seen, English distinguishes between voiced and voiceless stops as in *pie, buy*. But this distinction cannot occur after / s /. Consequently, the stop in *spy* is between these two possibilities (but closer to the stop in *buy*).

Other examples of this phenomenon have also been mentioned. We saw that before [ŋ], English does not distinguish between tense and lax vowels.

Consequently, the vowel that occurs in, for example, *sing* has a quality between that of [i] and [ɪ]. Similarly, there is no distinction between tense and lax vowels before [ɹ]. The vowel in *here* in most forms of American English is also intermediate between [i] and [ɪ].

The principle of maximum perceptual separation also accounts for some of the differences between languages. French has two high rounded vowels, [u] as in *tout* [t̪u] 'all,' and [y] as in *tu* [t̪y] 'you.' These two possibilities are kept distinct by one's being definitely a front vowel and the other definitely a back vowel. But English does not have this opposition. Consequently, the high rounded vowel that occurs in, for example, *who, two* varies considerably. In some dialects (e.g., most forms of American English), it is a central or back vowel, and in others (e.g., some forms of Scottish English), it is a front vowel not very different from French [y]. As far as this vowel is concerned, what matters most in English is that it should be high and rounded. Whether it is front or back is less important.

All these examples illustrate how languages maintain a balance between the requirements of the speaker and those of the listener. On the one hand, there is the pressure to make changes that would result in easier articulations from a speaker's point of view. On the other hand, there is the pressure from the listener's point of view that there should be sufficient perceptual contrast between sounds that affect the meaning of an utterance.

RECAP

This chapter, unlike other chapters in the book, delves into some of the less settled and perhaps more cutting-edge aspects of phonetics. We consider similarity structures of speech sounds by examining feature hierarchies. This provides a useful taxonomy of phonetic knowledge and also requires assumptions about the basis for judging sound similarity. The articulatory basis adopted here is compatible with many of the phonological patterns observed in the world's languages. We also consider cognitive aspects of phonetic knowledge, including patterns of speech motor control and the nature of phonetic memory. Research continues to delve into these domains, so the discussion here in terms of the hierarchical control of speech production and the exemplar basis of speech memory may be refined by future results.

PERFORMANCE EXERCISES

The material at the end of this chapter will help you review many of the sounds that have been described in previous chapters. It consists of real words in different languages. If possible, consult a native speaker on your pronunciation of these words. In any case, you should listen again to the sounds in the Web examples. Begin your review by trying to pronounce the words just on the basis of the transcription provided before you listen to them, or ask your consultant how to say them.

6.1	Lakhota	(ejectives)
6.2	Sindhi	(implosives)
6.3	Xhosa	(clicks)
6.5	Gujarati	(murmured vowels)
6.6	Thai	(stops)
6.7	Hindi	(stops)
7.1	Ewe	(bilabial and labiodental fricatives)
7.2	Malayalam	(places of articulation)
7.3	Quechua	(palatal, velar, and uvular plosives and ejectives)

Now try to say the following words.

A. Navajo

Navajo has a three-way stop contrast that will require your making voiceless, unaspirated, and ejective stops that do not occur in English. There are also several different affricates.

Voiceless Unaspirated	Voiceless Aspirated	Ejective
tota	tˣá:ʔ	t'ah
'not'	'three'	'just'
hã́títsɪ	tsʰah	ts'ah
'you will speak'	'awl'	'sagebrush'
	tɬʰah	niʃtɬ'a:
	'ointment'	'left'
tʃ í	tʃʰa:ʔ	tʃ'ah
'day'	'beaver'	'hat'
	bɪkʰá:	k'a:ʔ
	'its surface'	'arrow'

B. Zulu

Zulu has a series of clicks that are similar to those in Xhosa.

Dental	Alveolar	Alveolar lateral
kǀá:gà	kǃà:ká	kǁá:gà
'to whitewash'	'to undo'	'to put into a fix'
kǀʰa:gá	kǃʰà:kǃʰà	kǁʰá:ga
'to identify'	'to rip open'	'to link horses'
gǀò:ɓá	gǃò:ɓá	gǁò:ɓá
'to grease'	'to milk'	'to beat'
ìsì:ŋǀé	ìsì:ŋǃé	ìsì:ŋǁé:lè
(kind of spear)	'rump'	'left hand'

C. Burmese

Burmese contrasts voiced and voiceless nasals at four places of articulation.

Voiced Nasals	Voiceless Nasals
mâ̰ 'lift up'	m̥â̰ 'from'
nă 'pain'	n̥ă 'nose'
ɲă 'right'	ɲ̥ă 'considerate'
ŋâ 'fish'	ŋ̥â 'borrow'

D. Greek

Greek is one of the comparatively few languages that contrast both voiced and voiceless palatal and velar fricatives. It also has interdental fricatives.

Dental	Palatal	Velar
θiki 'box'	çɛri 'hand'	xɔma 'soil'
ðiki 'trial'	ʝɛri 'men'	ɣoma 'eraser'

E. Ewe

Ewe contrasts voiced and voiceless bilabial and labiodental fricatives both intervocalically and in clusters with [l].

Voiceless Bilabial	éɸá 'he polished'	éɸle 'he bought'
Voiceless Labiodental	éfá 'he was cold'	éflé 'he split off'
Voiced Bilabial	éβé 'Ewe' (the language)	èβló 'mushroom'
Voiced Labiodental	évé 'two'	évló 'he is evil'

F. Zulu

In addition to a complex set of clicks, Zulu has several different contrasts that involve laterals.

	Voiced Lateral Approximant	Voiced Lateral Fricative	Voiceless Lateral Fricative/Affricate
Alveolar	lá!là 'sleep'	ɮá!là 'play' [imperfect]	ɬânzá 'vomit'
Nasal+ Alveolar		ínɮàlà 'hunger'	ín͡tɬʼàn͡tɬʼà 'good luck'
Velar			k͡ʟʼîná 'be naughty'

The exercises below review vowels and semivowels. As noted in Chapter 9, the main features of vowel quality cannot be adequately described by means of written descriptions. Listen to the recordings in the Web example and, if you can, find native speakers of some of the languages listed below and try to imitate their pronunciation.

Note that the symbols do not have the same values that they have in the transcription of English.

G. French

French has twelve contrasting oral vowels. (Some speakers of French do not make all these distinctions.)

li	*lit*	'bed'
le	*les*	'the' [plural]
lɛ	*laid*	'ugly'
la	*là*	'there'
lɑ	*las*	'tired'
lɔʁ	*Lore*	(name)
lo	*lot*	'prize'
lu	*loup*	'wolf'
ly	*lu*	'read' [past participle]
lø	*le*	'the' [masc. sing.]
lœʁ	*leur*	'their'
lɛ̃	*lin*	'flax'
lɑ̃	*lent*	'slow'
lõ	*long*	'long'
lœ̃di	*lundi*	'Monday'

French also has three contrasting semivowels.

mjɛt	*miette*	'crumb'
mɥɛt	*muette*	'mute'
mwɛt	*mouette*	'sea gull'
lje	*lié*	'tied'
lɥi	*lui*	'him'
lwi	*Louis*	'Louis'
ɥit	*huit*	'eight'
wi	*oui*	'yes'

H. German

German has so-called tense and lax vowels, which differ in both length and quality. The symbol [ʏ] denotes a slightly lowered high front vowel—a rounded version of [ɪ].

biːten	*bieten*	'to offer'
beːtən	*beten*	'pray'
bɛːtən	*bäten*	'asked' [subjunctive]
baːtən	*baten*	'asked'
vyːtən	*wüten*	'to rage'
bøːtən	*böten*	'offered' [subjunctive]
buːtən	*buhten*	'booed'
boːtən	*boten*	'boats' [dative plural]
bɪtən	*bitten*	'to ask'
bɛtən	*betten*	'beds'
latən	*latten*	'bars'
bʏtən	*bütten*	'tubs'
bœtiŋən	*Böttingen*	(town name)
bʊtə	*butter*	'butter'
bɔtiç	*bottich*	'vat'
vaɪtən	*weiten*	'to widen'
bɔʏtə	*beute*	'booty'
baʊtən	*bauten*	'built'

I. Swedish

Swedish has long and short vowels; the short vowels are followed by long consonants. The symbol [ʏ] denotes a slightly lowered high front vowel—a rounded version of [ɪ]. The symbol [ɵ] denotes a more centralized high rounded vowel—a slightly lowered [ʉ].

ɹiːta	*rita*	'draw'
ɹeːta	*reta*	'tease'
ɹɛːta	*räta*	'straighten'
hæːɹ	*här*	'here'
ɹɑːta	*rata*	'refuse'
ɹoːta	*Rota*	(name of a valley)
ɹuːta	*rota*	'root'
ɹyːta	*ryta*	'roar'
ɹøːta	*ro·ta*	'rot'

hæːɹ	hör	'hear!'
ɹʉːta	ruta	'windowpane'
ɹɪtː	ritt	'ride' [noun]
ɹɛtː	rätt	'correct' [adjective]
hæɹː	herr	'Mr.'
ɹatː	ratt	'steering wheel'
ɹɔtː	rått	'raw'
ɹʊtː	rott	'rowed'
nʏtːa	nytta	'use' [noun]
ɹœtː	rött	'red'
ɹɵtː	rutt	'route'

J. Vietnamese

Vietnamese has eleven vowels, including contrasting back rounded and unrounded pairs. Tones in this exercise are marked as follows: mid-level tone is unmarked, high-rising tone has an acute accent [´].

Front	Back	
	Unrounded	**Rounded**
ti 'bureau'	tɯ 'fourth'	tu 'to drink'
te 'numb'	tɤʌ 'silk'	to 'soup bowl'
té 'to fall down'	ʌŋ 'favor'	tɔ 'large'
æŋ 'to eat'	tɑ 'we/our'	

Appendix A

Additional Material for Transcription

The full text of the story "Arthur the Rat," recorded by both British and American English speakers, is available on the website. This text was used by fieldworkers as they conducted interviews for the *Dictionary of American Regional English* (Harvard University Press). A similar story was used for recordings made by the Linguistic Survey of Scotland. Both versions are based on a much older story called "Grip, the Rat," devised for dialect studies in the nineteenth century.

The first paragraph of this story and some additional freely spoken sentences were recorded by speakers with accents typical of the following places: Alabama, Edinburgh, London, Dublin, and New Zealand. See the *Course in Phonetics* web page (Linguistics CourseMate at www.CengageBrain.com) for the audio files.

Arthur the Rat

Once there was a young rat named Arthur, who could never make up his mind. Whenever his friends asked him if he would like to go out with them, he would only answer, "I don't know." He wouldn't say "yes" or "no," either. He would always shirk making a choice.

His aunt Helen said to him, "Now, look here. No one is going to care for you if you carry on like this. You have no more mind than a blade of grass."

One rainy day, the rats heard a great noise in the loft. The pine rafters were all rotten, so that the barn was rather unsafe. At last the joists gave way and fell to the ground. The walls shook and all the rats' hair stood on end with fear and horror. "This won't do," said the captain. "I'll send out scouts to search for a new home."

Within five hours, the ten scouts came back and said, "We found a stone house where there is room and board for us all. There is a kindly horse named Nelly, a cow, a calf, and a garden with an elm tree." The rats crawled out of their little houses and stood on the floor in a long line. Just then, the old one saw Arthur. "Stop," he ordered coarsely. "You are coming, of course?"

"I'm not certain," said Arthur, undaunted. "The roof may not come down yet."

"Well," said the angry old rat, "we can't wait for you to join us. Right about face. March!"

Arthur stood and watched them hurry away. "I think I'll go tomorrow," he calmly said to himself, but then again, "I don't know; it's so nice and snug here."

That night there was a big crash. In the morning some men—with some boys and girls—rode up and looked at the barn. One of them moved a board and he saw a young rat, quite dead, half in and half out of his hole. Thus the shirker got his due.

Appendix B

Guidelines for Contributors to the *Journal of the International Phonetic Association*

Before writing a contribution to the series "Illustrations of the IPA," it is advisable to contact the journal's editors to ensure that no one else has already arranged to provide an illustration of this particular language. There is no set form for these contributions.

Every language has its own peculiarities, and it is impossible to do more than suggest guidelines so that some uniformity is maintained. In general, a submission to this section of *JIPA* should be relatively brief and not a full-fledged article on the phonetics of the language. There are usually five sections: (1) introduction, (2) consonant chart and discussion, (3) vowel chart and discussion, (4) prosodic features, (5) illustrative passage in transcription. A short list of references may also be appended. A recording of all the material (not just the final passage) should accompany the submission.

(1) The one- or two-paragraph introduction (with no section heading) should say where the language is spoken, what kind of language it is, and who the speaker on the recording is.

(2) This section should have the heading "Consonants." The chart immediately after the heading should give a set of IPA symbols for the consonantal phonological contrasts, arranged as on the official IPA chart but using only such columns and rows as are needed. The headings for columns should be chosen from the list given at the end of this paragraph, in the order shown (and with the use of capitals and parentheses as shown). If secondary articulations are listed in a separate column, that column should follow the column with no secondary articulation, as exemplified by "(Labialized Velar)" in the following list: Bilabial, Labiodental, Dental, Alveolar, Post-alveolar, Retroflex, Palatal, Velar, (Labialized Velar), Labial Velar, Uvular, Pharyngeal, Glottal.

The rows, in an order suggested by their order in the IPA chart, should be chosen from the following: Plosive, Affricate, Ejective, Ejective Affricate, Ejective Lateral, Implosive, Click, Nasal, Trill, Tap or Flap, Fricative, Lateral Fricative, Approximant, Lateral Approximant. Note that "Stop," a generic term, is not used, and the row titles are given in the singular.

The consonant chart should be followed by a list of words illustrating the consonants. These words should form as minimal a set as possible; at the very least, each consonant should be followed by the same vowel, unless the phonology makes this impossible. Each word should be given in transcription and the local orthography (if any) and should be followed by an English gloss. Following the list, there should be a paragraph or two giving a more precise account of the consonants, using diacritics where necessary, and noting significant allophones. Authors are welcome to follow a less traditional phonological format, but they should provide a traditional segmental description in addition to their own formal description.

(3) In a section headed "Vowels," vowel symbols should be placed on a conventional IPA vowel chart: 4 units across the top, 3 down the (right) side, and 2 across the bottom. Vowels should be illustrated by near minimal sets of contrasts in the same way as consonants. The vowel chart should be followed by a discussion of the precise phonetic qualities of the vowels and their principal allophones. Authors are encouraged to include formant charts showing the mean values of the frequencies of the first and second formants of a number of speakers, but this is in no way required. If a formant chart is provided it should, for preference, use a Bark scale, and have the origin at the top right, and the F1 scale double the expansion of the F2 scale.

(4) Prosodic characteristics should be presented in whatever way is appropriate for the language, in a section with a heading appropriate for the content. If there are lexical tones, they should be illustrated by minimal sets arranged in a list, in the same way as the lists illustrating consonants and vowels. Contrasting stress or pitch accents should be similarly illustrated. Prosodic features of syntactic phrases should be mentioned briefly.

(5) A transcription of a short text should be included in a section with the heading "Transcription." The preferred text is a translation of the fable of the North Wind and the Sun as reproduced below. As this passage is inappropriate for some cultures, it may be replaced in whole or in part to make it more suitable for the particular language or dialect. There is, however, some value in having the same piece for as many languages as possible, and changes should not be made unnecessarily. The transcription should use only the symbols listed in the earlier sections. It should be preceded by any necessary interpretative comments accounting for notable allophones or assimilations and should be followed by an orthographic version. A literal, phrase-by-phrase translation may be included if appropriate. Authors, even if they are speakers of the language themselves, should bear in mind that it is usually advisable to make a recording of a representative speaker first, and then transcribe that recording, rather than ask a speaker to read a passage that has already been transcribed.

> The North Wind and the Sun were disputing which was the stronger when a traveler came along, wrapped in a warm cloak. They agreed that the one who first succeeded in making the traveler take his cloak off should be considered stronger than the other. Then the North Wind blew as hard as he could, but the more he blew the more closely did the traveler fold his cloak around him; and at last the North Wind gave up the attempt. Then the Sun shined out warmly, and immediately the traveler took his cloak off. And so the North Wind was obliged to confess that the Sun was the stronger of the two.

Source: Editorial note: Illustrations of the IPA. *Journal of the International Phonetic Association*, 32 (1): 89–91 (2002). DOI http://dx.doi.org/10.1017/S0025100302000166. Reprinted with permission.

Notes

Much of the data on particular languages in this book is from Peter Ladefoged's own fieldwork, usually conducted with the invaluable assistance of other linguists who were more familiar with the languages being investigated. Many of these data have been published, with appropriate acknowledgments to the linguists who were the original sources, in Peter Ladefoged and Ian Maddieson, *Sounds of the World's Languages* (Oxford: Blackwell, 1996). Also, unless noted otherwise, the sagittal sections of the vocal tract shown in this book are based on x-ray tracings of Peter Ladefoged.

Chapter 1

The x-ray movie. The high-speed x-ray movie of Kenneth N. Stevens is included in full on the website. The original 35-mm cineradiography film was made by Sven Öhman and Kenneth Stevens at the Wenner-Gren Research Laboratory at Norrtull's Hospital, Stockholm, Sweden, as described in an abstract of a paper by Sven E. G. Öhman and Kenneth N. Stevens, "Cineradiographic Studies of Speech: Procedures and Objectives," *Journal of the Acoustical Society of America* 35, 1889 (1963), and in Kenneth N. Stevens and Sven E. G. Öhman, "Cineradiographic Studies of Speech," *Quarterly Progress and Status Report*, Speech Transmission Laboratory, KTH, Stockholm, 2/63: 9–11 (1963). The original film was described and analyzed in detail by Joseph S. Perkell in *Physiology of Speech Production: Results and Implications of a Quantitative Cineradiographic Study* (Cambridge: MIT Press, 1969).

The film was converted to DVD format and distributed at a conference at the Massachusetts Institute of Technology (MIT) in June 2004, honoring Professor Stevens, *From Sound to Sense: 50+ Years of Discoveries in Speech Communication*. The film was part of the poster *Articulatory KENematics: Revisiting the Stevens Cineradiography*, K. G. Munhall (Queen's University), M. Tiede (Haskins Laboratories), J. Perkell (Massachusetts Institute of Technology), A. Doucette (Industrial Light & Magic), and E. Vatikiotis-Bateson (University of British Columbia).

Chapter 2

The IPA. *The Handbook of the International Phonetic Association* is the definitive, authoritative source on the International Phonetic Alphabet. Every serious student of phonetics should own a copy of the handbook. Here is a link to the handbook publisher's website: http://www.langsci.ucl.ac.uk/ipa/handbook.

Chapter 3
Consonants influenced by vowels. The data for Figure 3.6 were kindly provided by Anne Vilain, Pierre Badin, and Christian Abry based on MRI data that they published in their 1998 paper "Coarticulation and Degrees of Freedom in the Elaboration of a New Articulatory Plant: Gentiane," in *Proceedings of the 5th International Conference on Spoken Language Processing* (R. H. Mannell & J. Robert-Ribes, Eds.), vol. 7, pp. 3147–3150. Sydney, Australia, December 1998, http://www.icp.inpg.fr/%7Ebadin/Vilain_Abry_Badin_ICSLP_1998.

Chapter 4
Pronouncing dictionaries. Three current dictionaries are mentioned in the text: J. Peter Roach, Jane Setter, and John Esling *English Pronouncing Dictionary*, 18th edition (Cambridge: Cambridge University Press, 2011); John C. Wells *Longman Pronunciation Dictionary*, 3rd edition (Harlow, U.K.: Pearson, 2008); and Clive Upton, William Kretzschmar, and Rafal Konopka, *Oxford Dictionary of Pronunciation for Current English* (Oxford: Oxford University Press, 2003). It should be noted that dictionaries, like most other reference works, are more often now consulted in online form rather than printed form, and publishers are adjusting, sometimes in fits, to the change.

British tongue positions in vowels. A version of these MRI images was posted by Professor John Coleman on the University of Oxford Phonetics Laboratory's website http://www.phon.ox.ac.uk/jcoleman/British_English_vowels.html, and he was kind enough to grant permission for their use in this chapter.

Bunched vs. retroflex / r /. Originals of the MRI images of bunched versus retroflex / r / in English were kindly provided by Mark Tiede. These data are discussed in Xinhui Zhou, Carol Y. Espy-Wilson, Mark Tiede, and Suzanne Boyce, "An Articulatory and Acoustic Study of 'Retroflex' and 'Bunched' American English Rhotic Sound Using Magnetic Resonance Imaging," in *Proceedings of Interspeech 2007* (Antwerp, Belgium), 54–57. Suzanne Boyce added the following information: "The images come from two different subjects sustaining / r / for 13 to 20 seconds. The instructions were to sustain the / r / as in 'pour.' We also have ultrasound data from running speech from these subjects, and the ultrasound data tell us that these subjects use similar tongue shapes during real and nonsense words—although we have some ultrasound and tagged MRI from subject 22 indicating he shows a more bunched tongue position in intervocalic / gr / context."

Lexical sets. The important British phonetician J. C. Wells suggested the use of these lexical sets in his book *Accents of English* (Cambridge University Press, 1982). The British and General American sets were discussed earlier in the chapter. The Australian set is derived from Felicity Cox and Sallyanne Palethorpe (2007). Australian English. *Journal of the International Phonetic*

Association, 37: 341–350. The Irish set was derived from Raymond Hickey's great website, the Irish English Resource Center (http://www.uni-due.de/IERC/), and his 2004 book, *A Sound Atlas of Irish English* (Berlin: Mouton de Gruyter).

English allophones. Many of the statements on English allophones in Chapter 4 are based on observations by Professor Patricia Keating (UCLA) and her students Dani Byrd, John Choi, and Edward Flemming of the TIMIT database, as well as other databases that reflect the pronunciation of a large number of American speakers of various dialects.

Voice talent. Professor Bruce Hayes (UCLA) spent many hours being the "General American" speaker.

Chapter 5
Two opposites. The illustration of vowel deletion in conversational speech was drawn from the Buckeye Corpus (http://buckeyecorpus.osu.edu/) of phonetically transcribed conversations, which is described in Mark A. Pitt, Keith Johnson, Elizabeth Hume, Scott Kiesling, and William Raymond, "The Buckeye Corpus of Conversational Speech: Labeling Conversations and a Test of Transcriber Reliability," *Speech Communication* 45 (1): 89–95 (2005).

Musical Obama. The rhythmic transcription of the first 47 seconds of Barack Obama's Iowa acceptance speech was produced by UC–Berkeley Professor Richard Rhodes using the Macintosh application Garage Band.

ToBI transcription. Mary Beckman (Ohio State University) and Sun-Ah Jun (UCLA) reviewed and corrected the intonation transcriptions presented in this chapter. The Tones and Break Indices system of transcription (of which I am only presenting the tones part here) is not as widely taught as the IPA, though all of the symbols in ToBI tone transcription could be translated into IPA tone letters and overall intonation markings (such as downstep [↓] and global rise [↗]). However, some phoneticians don't teach ToBI because there is a sense in which aspects of ToBI transcription are divorced from phonetic reality, for example, the use of H-L% to mark a tonal plateau. If there were a better transcription system for writing intonation contours we would have put that one into the book, and from our point of view a phonetic description of language that has nothing to say about intonation is incomplete.

Chapter 6
How to make a click. The sequence of articulatory events in a click noise illustrated in Figure 6.5 is based on an x-ray study reported by Anthony Traill in his 1985 book *Phonetic and Phonological Studies of !Xoo Bushman* (Quellen zur Khoisan-Forschung 5: Helmut Buske, Hamburg).

The glottis. The photographs of the glottis in Figure 6.6 were taken by John Ohala and Ralph Vanderslice. Regarding these photos, Ohala says, "Those were the vocal cords of the (recently) late Ralph Vanderslice. My job was the sort of 'macrophotography' (with my then trusty Nikon), using a telephoto lens plus an extension tube and a ring strobe (one that fits around the lens—to give even lighting). But the real technical credit is Ralph's who could tolerate an oversize mirror (about 3 cm diameter, if I recall correctly)—and he literally had to 'mount' this mirror since it was affixed to a stationary device—there was no other way for me to get good focus on each pic."

Chapter 7
Dental stops in California. The "careful palatographic study" mentioned in the discussion of dental sounds in English was done by Peter Ladefoged's student Sarah Dart in her 1991 Ph.D. dissertation "Articulatory and Acoustic Properties of Apical and Laminal Articulations," which was published as *UCLA Working Papers in Phonetics* Number 79.

Chapter 8
First campaign. The illustration of low- and high-frequency components in Figure 8.1 was drawn from the Buckeye Corpus of phonetically transcribed conversations, which is described in Mark A. Pitt, Keith Johnson, Elizabeth Hume, Scott Kiesling, and William Raymond, "The Buckeye Corpus of Conversational Speech: Labeling Conversations and a Test of Transcriber Reliability," *Speech Communication* 45 (1): 89–95 (2005).

Vowel formants. The acoustic data on the formant frequencies of vowels (Figure 8.5) are from G. E. Petersen and H. L. Barney, "Control Methods Used in a Study of the Vowels," *Journal of the Acoustical Society of America* 24, 175–184 (1956); and A. Holbrook and G. Fairbanks, "Diphthong Formants and Their Movements," *Journal of Speech and Hearing Research* 5: 38–58 (March 1962).

Bark frequency. The relation between frequency in Hz and pitch in Bark scale is given in M. R. Schroeder, B. S. Atal, and J. L. Hall, "Objective Measure of Certain Speech Signal Degradations Based on Masking Properties of Human Auditory Perception," in B. Lindblom and S. Öhman (Eds.), *Frontiers of Speech Communication Research* (New York: Academic Press, 1979), 217–229.

Chapter 9
Vowels of English. The acoustic data on the formant frequencies of vowels (Figure 9.1) are from G. E. Petersen and H. L. Barney, "Control Methods Used in a Study of the Vowels," *Journal of the Acoustical Society of America* 24: 175–84 (1956); and A. Holbrook and G. Fairbanks, "Diphthong Formants and Their Movements," *Journal of Speech and Hearing Research* 5: 38–58 (March 1962).

Tongue position in cardinal vowels. The x-rays of cardinal vowels used in Figure 9.3 were published in S. Jones, "Radiography and Pronunciation,"*British Journal of Radiology*, New Series, 3: 149–50 (1929).

Vowels of English dialects. The data for the plots of different accents of English are from R. Hagiwara (1995), "Acoustic Realizations of American / r / as Produced by Women and Men," unpublished Ph.D. dissertation, University of California, Los Angeles (Californian English); J. Hillenbrand, L. A. Getty, M. J. Clark, and K. Wheeler, "Acoustic Characteristics of American English Vowels," *Journal of the Acoustical Society of America* 97 (5): 3099–3111 (1995) (northern cities); and D. Deterding (1990), "Speaker Normalisation for Automatic Speech Recognition," unpublished Ph.D. dissertation, University of Cambridge (BBC English).

Vowels in other languages. The data on Spanish vowels are from Pierre Delattre, "Comparing the Vocalic Features of English, German, Spanish and French," *International Review of Applied Linguistics* 2: 71–97 (1964). The data on Japanese vowels are from Han Mieko, *Japanese Phonology* (Tokyo: Kenkyuusha, 1962). The data on Danish vowels are from Eli Fischer-Jørgensen, "Formant Frequencies of Long and Short Danish Vowels," in E. S. Firchow et al. (Eds.), *Studies for Einar Haugen* (The Hague: Mouton, 1972).

The tongue shape of ATR. Figure 9.10 is based on Mona Lindau's x-rays of the Akan vowels (see Mona Lindau Webb [1987], "Tongue Mechanisms in Akan and Luo." *UCLA Working Papers in Phonetics,* v. 68: 46–57).

Bunched vs. retroflex / r /. The data on American English / r / are also from Robert Hagiwara's 1995 UCLA Ph.D. dissertation.

Exercise A. The description of vowels mentioned in Exercise A is published in Kenneth N. Stevens and Arthur House, "Development of a Quantitative Description of Vowel Articulation," *Journal of the Acoustical Society of America* 27: 484–493 (1955).

Exercise B. The description mentioned in Exercise B was suggested by Morris Halle and Kenneth N. Stevens in their article, "On the Feature 'Advanced Tongue Root'" *Quarterly Progress Report.* 94: 209–215 (1969), published by the MIT Research Laboratory of Electronics. Historical descriptions of vowels mentioned in the third exercise may be found in Hermann Helmholtz, *Sensations of Tone* (New York: Dover Publications, Inc., 1954). First published in German in 1863, the fourth edition was translated by A. J. Ellis and published in English in 1885. Reprinted by New York: Dover Publications, Inc., 1954.

Chapter 10
Measuring speech timing. The PVI (pairwise variability index) was introduced by E. Grabe and E. L. Low, "Durational Variability in Speech and the Rhythm Class Hypothesis," *Papers in Laboratory Phonology*, 7 (The Hague: Mouton, 2000). If you are interested in this (most interesting) topic, be sure to also look at F. Ramus, M. Nespor, and J. Mehler, "Correlates of Linguistic Rhythm in the Speech Signal," *Cognition,* 73 (3): 265–292 (1999). The discussion of timing in this section reflects an attitude of mine (KJ) that I wrote about in my second published paper—K. Johnson and B. Sinsabaugh, "The Simplification of the Greek Vowel System," *Chicago Linguistic Society* 21: 189–198 (1985)—which was on the segmental consequences of a change in timing (from syllable-timing to stress-timing in Ancient Greek).

Chapter 11
Coordination for [p]. Figure 11.9 is based on one from Mary Beckman's great course handout titled "Notes on Speech Production." Dr. Beckman's influence on this edition of the *Course* is also evident in Chapter 5.

Neogrammarian exemplars. Many thanks to Professor Andrew Garrett for pointing out the following quotation from Hermann Paul's (1920) *Prinzipien der Sprachgeschichte* (5th ed. Halle: Niemeyer. First edition 1880, 2nd ed. 1886) in which Paul clearly outlines the connection between exemplar memory ("earlier and later production of the same utterance") and sound change:

> To understand the phenomenon we call sound change (*Lautwandel*), we must clarify the physical and psychological processes that take place in the production of an utterance: first, the motions of the speech organs . . .; second, the series of sensations by which these motions are necessarily accompanied, the articulatory sensations (*Bewegungsgefühl*) . . .; third, the acoustic sensations (*Tonempfindungen*) produced in listeners, among whom speakers themselves belong under normal circumstances. Even after the physical excitement has disappeared, an enduring psychological effect remains, representations in memory (*Erinnerungsbilder*), which are of the greatest importance for sound change. For it is these alone that connect the intrinsically separate physiological processes and bring about a causal relation between earlier and later production of the same utterance.

Glossary

Note: The explanations given in this glossary should be regarded not as formal definitions but as general guides for use in review. Bold words within the definitions have separate entries in this glossary.

advanced tongue root (ATR) Having the root of the tongue pulled forward so as to widen the pharynx (and, often, to raise the body of the tongue nearer to the roof of the mouth). Pharyngeal sounds are [–ATR], as the pharynx is narrowed.

affricate A stop followed by a homorganic fricative.

allophone A variant of a phoneme. The allophones of a phoneme form a set of sounds that (1) do not change the meaning of a word, (2) are all very similar to one another, and (3) occur in phonetic contexts different from one another—for example, syllable initial as opposed to syllable final. The differences between allophones can be stated in terms of phonological rules.

alternations Variations in words that can be described in terms of phonological rules; for example, the difference between [aɪ] and [ɪ] in *divine*, divin(ity).

alveolar An articulation involving the tip or blade of the tongue and the alveolar ridge, as in English [d] in *die*.

alveolar ridge The part of the upper surface of the mouth immediately behind the front teeth.

alveolo-palatal Post-alveolar consonant produced with significant raising of the front of the tongue toward the palate.

ambisyllabic Belonging to two syllables. A consonant such as [p] in *happy* is sometimes said to be ambisyllabic.

anticipatory coarticulation An action in which one of the speech organs that is not involved in making a particular sound moves toward its position for a subsequent sound. For example, the rounding of the lips during [s] in *swim* is due to the anticipation of the lip action required for [w].

apical An articulation involving the tip of the tongue.

approximant An articulation in which one articulator is close to another but without the tract being narrowed to such an extent that a turbulent airstream is produced. In many forms of English, / j, l, r, w / are approximants.

articulation The approach or contact of two speech organs, such as the tip of the tongue and the upper teeth.

articulator One of several parts of the vocal tract that can be used to form speech sounds.

arytenoid cartilage One of a pair of structures at the posterior ends of the vocal folds. Their movements control phonation types.

aspiration A period of voicelessness after the release of an articulation, as in English in *pie* [pʰaɪ].

assimilation The change of one sound into another making it more similar to a neighboring sound, as in the change of underlying [n] to [m] in *input* [ˈɪmpʊt] or of underlying [z] to [ʒ] in *does she* [ˈdʌʒʃi].

back (of the tongue) The part of the tongue below the soft palate.

back vowel Vowel in which the body of the tongue is in the back part of the oral cavity (mouth). The vowels [u, o, ɔ, ɑ] form a set of back reference vowels.

Bark scale A scale in which equal intervals of pitch as perceived by listeners are represented by equal distance on the scale.

bilabial An articulation involving both lips, as in English [m] in *my*.

binary feature A feature (e.g., Lateral) that can be used to classify sounds in terms of two possibilities.

breathy voice Another name for murmur; a type of phonation in which the vocal folds are only slightly apart so that they vibrate while allowing a high rate of airflow through the glottis, as in Hindi [$b^ɦ$].

broad transcription A transcription that does not show a great deal of phonetic detail; often a simple phonemic transcription.

cardinal vowels A set of reference vowels first defined by Daniel Jones. The vowels of any language can be described by stating their relationships to the cardinal vowels.

citation form The form a word has when it is cited or pronounced in isolation.

click A stop made with an ingressive velaric airstream, such as Zulu [ǁ].

closed syllable A syllable with a consonant at the end, as the first syllables in English *magpie*, *pantry*, *completion*.

coarticulation The overlapping of adjacent articulations.

coda The consonants occurring after the vowel in a syllable.

contour tone A tone in a language, such as Chinese, that must be specified as a gliding movement within the pitch range.

coordinative structure The functional organization of a group of muscles into a hierarchical structure of goal-oriented control units that accomplish subtasks of a phonetic task like closing the lips.

coronal A term for sounds articulated with the tip or blade of the tongue raised toward the teeth or the alveolar ridge (or, sometimes, the hard palate), such as [θ, s, t].

creaky voice See **laryngealization**.

declination Gradual falling of intonational pitch over the course of an utterance.

degrees of freedom problem In speech motor control, the control problem caused by needing to control a great number of independent muscles. See **coordinative structure**.

dental Refers to sounds made with the tongue touching the teeth.

diacritic Small added mark that can be used to distinguish different values of a symbol. For example, the addition of [˜] distinguishes a velarized from a nonvelarized sound, as in [ɫ] as opposed to [l].

diphthong A vowel in which there is a change in quality during a single syllable, as in English [aɪ] in *high*.

dorsal Describing a sound articulated with the back of the tongue.

dorsum The back of the tongue.

downdrift The tendency for the pitch to fall throughout an intonational phrase.

downstep Optional lowering of a high pitch accent or high tone after a similar high pitch accent or high tone.

ease of articulation A phonetic force that impacts linguistic sound systems so that patterns that are easier to produce are more likely than difficult patterns.

ejective A stop made with an egressive glottalic airstream, such as Hausa [k'].

epenthesis The insertion of one or more sounds in the middle of a word, such as the pronunciation of *sense* as [sɛnts].

exemplar theory The idea that phonetic categories are represented in the mind as a set of all of the examples of the category that the speaker has produced and/or heard.

feature A phonetic property of a sound. Some features like Coronal are fairly general, while others like Laminal Dental are more specific.

filter In acoustic phonetics, a filter is an acoustic tube that enhances some frequency components of a sound source while decreasing the amplitudes of other components.

flap An articulation in which one articulator, usually the tongue tip, is drawn back and then allowed to strike against another articulator in returning to its rest position.

formant A resonating frequency of the air in the vocal tract. Vowels are characterized by three formants.

frequency The rate of oscillation in air pressure in a periodic sound wave.

fricative Narrowing of the distance between two articulators so that the airstream is partially obstructed and a turbulent airflow is produced, as in English [z] in *zoo*.

front vowel Vowel in which the body of the tongue is in the front part of the oral cavity (mouth). The vowels [i, e, ɛ, a] form a set of front reference vowels.

full A full, unreduced form of a word is a production that exhibits all or most of the phonetic information that is present in a citation production.

geminate Adjacent segments that are the same, such as the two consonants in the middle of Italian *folla* ['folla] 'crowd.'

gesture Abstract representation of the motor control plans for linguistically significant vocal tract actions. See also **coordinative structure**.

glottal An articulation involving the glottis, as [ʔ] in many forms of English *button* ['bʌʔn̩].

glottal stop (glottal "catch") A stop sound produced by pressing the vocal folds tightly together.

glottalic airstream mechanism Movement of pharynx air by the action of the glottis. Ejectives and implosives are produced with a glottalic airstream mechanism.

glottis The space between the vocal folds.

hard palate The bony structure that forms the roof of the front part of the mouth.

homorganic Made with the same place of articulation. The sounds [d] and [n], as in English *hand*, are homorganic.

implosive A stop made with an ingressive glottalic airstream, such as Sindhi [ɓ].

impressionistic transcription A transcription in which the symbols indicate only the general phonetic value of the sounds.

intensity The amount of acoustic energy in a sound.

interdental Articulated with the tongue between the upper and lower teeth. Many speakers of American English use an interdental articulation in words such as *thick, thin*.

intonation The pattern of pitch changes that occur during a phrase, which may be a complete sentence.

intonational phrase The part of an utterance over which a particular intonation pattern extends. There may be one or more tone groups in an English sentence.

labial An articulation involving one or both lips, such as [f, v, m].

labial velar (labiovelar) An articulation involving simultaneous action of the back of the tongue forming a velar closure and the lips forming a bilabial closure.

labialization A secondary articulation in which lip rounding is added to a sound, as in English [ʃ].

labiodental An articulation involving the lower lip and the upper front teeth.

laminal An articulation made with the blade of the tongue.

laryngeal The region of the vocal tract at the glottis in which consonantal articulations such as [h, ʔ] are made.

laryngealization Another name for **creaky voice**; a type of phonation in which the arytenoid cartilages hold the posterior end of the vocal folds together so that they can vibrate only at the other end, as in Hausa [ɓ].

lateral An articulation in which the airstream flows over the sides of the tongue, as in English [l] in *leaf*.

lateral plosion The release of a plosive by lowering the sides of the tongue, as at the end of the word *saddle*.

lax A term with no specific phonetic correlates, used when dividing vowels into classes on phonological grounds. In English, the lax vowels are those that can occur in monosyllables closed by [ŋ], such as *sing, length, hang, long, hung*.

length The linguistic use of physical duration to distinguish words. See **geminate**.

lexical sets Key words illustrating the main sets of lexical items that share a vowel; used to compare vowel pronunciation across varieties of English.

linguo-labial Articulated with the tongue near or contacting the upper lip.

lip rounding The action of bringing the corners of the lips toward one another so that the mouth opening is reduced.

liquid A cover term for laterals and various forms of *r*-sounds.

locus The apparent point of origin of the formants for each place of articulation.

loudness The auditory property of a sound that enables a listener to place it on a scale going from soft to loud without considering the acoustic properties, such as the intensity of the sound.

mid-sagittal section A view of the midline vocal tract as if the head was cut down the middle from the forehead to the chin.

monophthong A vowel in which there is no appreciable change in quality during a syllable, as in English [ɑ] in *father*. Compare *diphthong*.

motor equivalence Production of one sound by two different gestures of the vocal organs.

multivalued feature A feature such as Height that can be used to classify sounds in terms of more than two possibilities.

murmur Another name for **breathy voice**; a type of phonation in which the vocal folds are only slightly apart so that they vibrate while allowing a high rate of airflow through the glottis, as in Hindi [bʱ].

narrow transcription A transcription that shows phonetic details (such as, in English, aspiration, length, etc.) by using a wide variety of symbols and, in many cases, diacritics.

nasal A sound in which the soft palate is lowered so that there is no velic closure and air may go out through the nose, as in English [m] in *my*.

nasalization Lowering of the soft palate during a sound in which air is going out through the mouth, as in the vowel [æ̃] between nasals in English *man*.

nasal plosion The release of a plosive by lowering the soft palate so that air escapes through the nose, as at the end of the word *hidden*.

nasal stop A complete stoppage of the oral cavity so that the airstream passes only through the nose. Usually, nasal stops are simply called **nasals**.

nasal vowel A vowel in which part of the airstream passes out through the nose.

nucleus The center of a syllable, usually just the vowel.

obstruent A fricative, stop, or affricate.

onset A consonant that occurs before the vowel in a syllable.

open syllable A syllable without a consonant at the end, as the first syllables in English *beehive*, *bylaw*, *sawing*.

oral stop Complete stoppage of both the oral and nasal cavities, as in [b, d, g].

palatal An articulation involving the front of the tongue and the hard palate, as in English [j] in *you*.

palatalization A secondary articulation in which the front of the tongue is raised toward the hard palate, as in the so-called soft sounds in Russian.

palato-alveolar An articulation between the tongue blade and the back of the alveolar ridge.

palatography A technique for showing articulatory contact. In one form, the tongue is covered with a marking medium, and then, after a word has been articulated, it is possible to observe where the medium has been transferred onto the roof of the mouth.

perseverative coarticulation The persistence of an aspect of the articulation of one sound into the following sound, for example, the laryngealization of a vowel after a glottal stop.

pharyngeal An articulation involving the root of the tongue and the back wall of the pharynx, as in the Arabic [ʕ].

pharyngealization A secondary articulation in which the root of the tongue is drawn back so that the pharynx is narrowed, as in some so-called emphatic consonants in Arabic.

phonation Vibration of the vocal folds in voicing.

phoneme The smallest distinctive unit in the structure of a given language. See also **allophone**.

phonetic implementation Accounting for phonetic variability by writing rules that show the relationship between abstract phonological representations and cross-linguistic, dialectal, or individual variants.

phonology The description of the systems and patterns of sounds that occur in a language.

pitch The auditory property of a sound corresponding to a musical note that enables a listener to place it on a scale going from low to high.

plosive A stop made with a pulmonic airstream mechanism, such as in English [p] or [b].

post-alveolar A sound produced with constriction between the alveolar ridge and the palate.

prominence The extent to which a sound stands out from others because of some combination of its sonority, length, stress, and pitch.

pulmonic airstream mechanism The movement of lung air by the respiratory muscles. Most sounds are produced with a pulmonic airstream mechanism.

***r*-colored** Vowels that are essentially some form of a syllabic rhotic approximant [ɻ].

radical An articulation made with the root of the tongue.

reduced A reduced form of a word is a production that exhibits significant deviation from a citation production, including reduced vowels and deleted segments.

reduced vowel A vowel that is pronounced with a noncontrasting centralized quality, although in the underlying form of a word it is part of a full set of contrasts. The second vowel in *emphasis* is a reduced form of the vowel / æ /, as in *emphatic*.

reification A logical fallacy in which explanatory force is attributed to the observation to be explained. For example, this explanation falls into this fallacy: Assimilation tends to happen in language because there is a universal constraint on phonologies called AGREE(x) that requires that adjacent segments have the same value of the feature *x*.

release burst A burst of noise produced when a stop consonant is released.

retroflex An articulation involving the tip of the tongue and the back part of the alveolar ridge. Some speakers of English have retroflex approximants in *rye* and *err*. Retroflex stops occur in Hindi and other languages spoken in India.

rhotacization The auditory property known as *r*-coloring that results from the lowering of the third formant.

rhotic A form of English in which / r / can occur after a vowel and within a syllable in words such as *car*, *bird*, *early*. Most forms of Midwestern American English are rhotic, whereas most forms of English spoken in the southern part of England are nonrhotic.

rhyme The vowel (nucleus) and any consonants occurring after the vowel in a syllable.

roll See **trill**.

rounded A sound with added lip rounding.

secondary articulation An additional constriction that is at a different place of articulation from that in the primary articulation. The English alveolar lateral at the end of a syllable, as in *eel*, is often made with the back of the tongue raised, and thus has the secondary articulation of velarization.

segment A unit of sound of the size of a consonant or vowel.

semivowel A sound articulated in the same way as a vowel, but not forming a syllable on its own, as in [w] in *we*.

sibilant A speech sound in which there is high-amplitude, turbulent noise, as in English [s] and [ʃ] in *sip* and *ship*.

soft palate The soft, movable part of the palate at the back of the mouth.

sonority The loudness of a sound relative to that of other sounds with the same length, stress, and pitch.

source In acoustic phonetics, a sound source that is subsequently filtered by the vocal tract. Voicing, frication, and burst noises are the main sound sources in human speech.

spectrogram A graphic representation of sounds in terms of their component frequencies, in which time is shown on the horizontal axis, frequency on the vertical axis, and the intensity of each frequency at each moment in time by the darkness of the mark.

stop Complete closure of two articulators. This term usually implies an oral stop—that is, complete closure of two articulators and a velic closure, as in English [b] in *buy*. But nasals, as in English [m] in *my*, can also be considered stops.

stress The use of extra respiratory energy during a syllable.

strong form The form in which a word is pronounced when it is stressed. This term is usually applied only to words that normally occur unstressed and with a weak form, such as *to*, *a*.

suprasegmental Phonetic feature such as stress, length, tone, and intonation, which is not a property of single consonants or vowels.

syllable A unit of speech for which there is no satisfactory definition. Syllables seem to be necessary units in the mental organization and production of utterances.

systematic phonetic transcription A transcription that shows all the phonetic details that are part of the language and can be stated in terms of phonological rules.

tap A rapid movement of the tip of the tongue upward to contact the roof of the mouth, then returning to the floor of the mouth along the same path.

target position An idealized articulatory position that can be used as a reference point in describing how a speaker produces utterances.

tense A term with no specific phonetic correlates, used when dividing vowels into classes on phonological grounds. In English, the tense vowels are those that can occur in stressed open syllables such as *bee*, *bay*, *bah*, *saw*, *low*, *boo*, *buy*, *bough*, *boy*, and *cue*.

ToBI A system for transcribing the intonation of utterances in terms of a sequence of pitch accents—H(igh) and L(ow) and combinations—on stressed syllables, intonational phrases, and boundaries, together with a set of break indices indicating the degree of connection between adjacent words ranging from 1 (close connection) to 4 (maximum break).

tone A pitch that conveys part of the meaning of a word. In Chinese, for example, [ma] pronounced with a high level tone means 'mother,' and with a high falling tone means 'scold.'

tone sandhi A change of tone due to the influence of neighboring tones.

tonic accent See **tonic syllable**.

tonic syllable The syllable within a tone group that stands out because it carries the major pitch change.

trill An articulation in which one articulator is held loosely near another so that the flow of air between them sets them in motion, alternately sucking them together and blowing them apart. In some forms of Scottish English, [r] in *rip* is trilled.

unrounded See **rounded**.

uvular An articulation involving the back of the tongue and the uvula, as in French [ʁ] in *rouge* [ʁuʒ].

velar Describes an articulation that involves the back of the tongue and the velum, or the soft palate, as in English [g] in *guy*.

velar pinch A visual pattern often seen on spectrograms of velar sounds. The F2 and F3 are quite close to each other.

velaric airstream mechanism Movement of mouth air by action of the tongue. Clicks are produced with a velaric airstream mechanism.

velarization A secondary articulation in which the back of the tongue is raised toward the soft palate. In many forms of English, syllable final [ɫ] as in *hill* is strongly velarized.

velic Involving the upper surface of the velum, or soft palate, and the pharynx. A *velic closure* prevents air from escaping through the nose.

velum The soft, movable part of the palate at the back of the mouth.

vocal tract The air passages above the vocal folds. The vocal tract consists of the oral tract and the nasal tract.

vocoid A sound with no obstruction in the center of the mouth. Vowels and semivowels are vocoids.

voice bar A dark area near the baseline in a spectrogram, indicating voicing during a consonant.

voice onset time The moment at which the voicing starts relative to the release of a closure.

voiced Having vibrations of the vocal folds during an articulation, as in English [m] in *me*. In a partially voiced sound, vocal fold vibrations occur during only part of the articulation, as often in English [d] in *die*.

voiceless Pronounced without vibrations of the vocal folds, as in English [s] in *see*.

vowel quality The timbre of a vowel caused almost entirely by the frequencies of the vowel formants (see **formant**).

weak form The unstressed form of any word, such as *but* and *as*, that does not maintain its full form when it occurs in conversational speech.

Further Reading

Phonetics has been studied for many centuries. This list is limited to some of the more important books that have been published in the last forty or fifty years. Of course, many important findings have appeared in journals rather than in books. If you want to keep up to date in the subject, try looking at the following journals: *Journal of the International Phonetic Association*, *Journal of Phonetics*, *Journal of Speech and Hearing Research*, *Language and Speech*, and *Phonetica*, as well as more specialized journals in other fields, such as acoustics (notably the *Journal of the Acoustical Society of America*), linguistics, speech pathology, and particular language areas. And, of course, check the websites of professional linguistics organizations.

Phonetic Dictionaries

Jones, Daniel, James Hartman, Jane Setter, and Peter Roach. *English Pronouncing Dictionary* (18th edition). Cambridge: Cambridge University Press, 2011.

Wells, John. *Longman Pronunciation Dictionary* (3rd edition). Harlow: Pearson ESL, 2008.

Both these dictionaries are great reference books that all students of phonetics should consult.

Upton, Clive, William Kretzschmar, and Rafal Konopka. *Oxford Dictionary of Pronunciation for Current English*. New York: Oxford University Press, 2003. This is a comparatively new dictionary described by the publisher as "a unique survey of how English is really spoken in the twenty-first century."

Kenyon, J. S., and T. A. Knott (1953) *A Pronouncing Dictionary of American English* (2nd edition). Springfield, MA: Merriam Webster. Kenyon and Knott is a standard reference on American English pronunciation, though at this point many of the pronunciations are a bit antiquated. Knott's "How the dictionary determines what pronunciations to use" (*Quarterly Journal of Speech*, 21, 1–10) is an entertaining companion to the dictionary.

General Books on Phonetics

Abercrombie, David. *Elements of General Phonetics*. New York: Aldine, 1967. A classic book on a number of the most important concepts in phonetics. It is very easy to read and a good introduction to the topics selected, but it is somewhat limited in scope.

Ball, Martin, and Nicole Müller. *Phonetics for Communication Disorders*. LEA. 2005. A comprehensive textbook "that equips the communication disorders student to deal with the wide range of speech types that will be encountered in a clinic."

Catford, John C. *Fundamental Problems in Phonetics*. Bloomington: University of Indiana Press, 1977. Not a beginner's book, but a good account of the phonation types and aerodynamic processes involved in speech production.

Celce-Murcia, Marianne, Donna Brinton, and Janet Goodwin. *Teaching Pronunciation: A Coursebook and Reference Guide* (2nd edition). Cambridge: Cambridge University Press, 2010. A good phonetics book for ESL teachers.

Clark, John, Colin Yallop, and Janet Fletcher. *An Introduction to Phonetics and Phonology* (3rd edition). Oxford: Wiley-Blackwell, 2007. Covers much the same ground as here but more specifically aimed at linguists.

Hardcastle, William, and John Laver. *The Handbook of Phonetic Sciences*. Oxford: Blackwell, 1997. A comprehensive book containing chapters by leading authorities on all aspects of phonetics.

International Phonetic Association. *The Handbook of the International Phonetic Association*. Cambridge: Cambridge University Press, 1999. A reference book that every student of phonetics should own.

Johnson, Keith. *Acoustic and Auditory Phonetics* (3rd edition). Oxford: Wiley-Blackwell, 2011. A comprehensive introduction to acoustic phonetics, the acoustic theory of speech production, and auditory response to speech sounds.

Ladefoged, Peter, and Sandra Ferrari Disner. *Vowels and Consonants* (3rd edition). Oxford: Wiley-Blackwell, 2011. A shorter, simpler, more casual introduction to phonetics than this book.

———. *Elements of Acoustic Phonetics* (2nd edition). Chicago: University of Chicago Press, 1996. A basic account of just those aspects of acoustics that are relevant for students of phonetics.

———. *Phonetic Data Analysis: An Introduction to Fieldwork and Instrumental Techniques*. Oxford: Wiley-Blackwell, 2003. This is intended to be a how-to book—how to do phonetic fieldwork, how to make phonetic analyses.

Ladefoged, Peter, and Ian Maddieson. *Sounds of the World's Languages*. Oxford: Wiley-Blackwell, 1996. An attempt to give a comprehensive account of all the different sounds that have been reported in the world's languages.

Laver, John. *Principles of Phonetics*. Cambridge: Cambridge University Press, 1994. An extensive overview of the field.

Maddieson, Ian. *Patterns of Sounds*. Cambridge: Cambridge University Press, 1984. A survey of the sound systems of more than 300 languages, providing a basis for a description of a number of universal phonetic tendencies.

Pickett, J. M. *The Acoustics of Speech Communication: Fundamentals, Speech Perception Theory, and Technology*. Boston: Allyn and Bacon, 1999. This book goes further than other introductory books on acoustic phonetics, discussing several aspects of speech perception and speech technology.

Pike, Kenneth. *Phonetics: A Critical Account of Phonetic Theory, and a Technique for the Practical Description of Sounds*. Ann Arbor: University of Michigan Press, 1943. This is a classic book for advanced students.

Pullum, Geoffrey, and William Ladusaw. *Phonetic Symbol Guide* (2nd edition). Chicago: University of Chicago Press, 1996. An invaluable reference book describing a wide variety of phonetic symbols, including all the symbols of the IPA.

Roach, Peter. *English Phonetics and Phonology: A Practical Course* (4th edition). Cambridge, UK: Cambridge University Press, 2000. A good book for those especially interested in English.

Stevens, Kenneth. *Acoustic Phonetics.* Cambridge, MA: MIT Press, 1999. Clearly the leading technical book, describing everything that is known about the acoustics of speech.

Zemlin, Willard. *Speech and Hearing Science, Anatomy and Physiology* (4th edition). Englewood Cliffs: Prentice-Hall, 1998. A good account of the anatomy and physiology of the vocal organs.

Useful Websites

The IPA. The home page of the International Phonetics Association http://www.langsci.ucl.ac.uk/ipa/ has many very helpful links, including links to sound files illustrating the IPA and links to free and professional IPA fonts, as well as information about how to join the IPA and get the IPA journal.

Speech analysis software. We can recommend some free acoustic analysis software tools for waveform editing, spectral analysis, and more.

Wavesurfer: http://sourceforge.net/projects/wavesurfer/
Praat: http://www.fon.hum.uva.nl/praat/
Audacity: http://audacity.sourceforge.net/

Phonetics on YouTube. Keith Johnson maintains (and would welcome suggested additions to) a YouTube channel with links to phonetics-related movies, ranging from physics lectures to drunken amateur laryngoscopy: http://www.youtube.com/user/keithjohnsonberkeley.

Index

Note: Terms in **bold** also appear in the Glossary.

Acoustic and Auditory Phonetics (Johnson), 6, 200
Acoustic phonetics, 197–226
   acoustic analysis, 203–208
   consonants, 19, 208–214
   individual differences, 221–224
   overview, 6
   perturbation theory, 202–203
   source/filter theory, 197–200
   spectrograms interpretation, 213–221
   tube models, 200–201
Acoustics
   analysis, 203–208
   articulation and, 2–34
   of consonants, 19, 208–214
   correlates, 213, 242
   intensity, 204, 207, 210, 216–217, 255–256
Advanced tongue root (ATR), 238–239
Affricates, 18, 71, 175, 180, 184
African language, 184, 190, 238
Airstream process, 144–171
   features, 282–287
   glottis actions, 156–159, 164–165
   mechanisms, 144–155
   overview, 5–6
   voice onset time (VOT), 159–164
Akan language, 238
Aleut language, 181
Allophones, 48–49, 61, 76–80, 107–109, 180–181
Allophonic transcriptions, 281–282
Alternations, 117, 118, 120, 121
Alveolar lateral approximants, 189
Alveolar ridge, 10, 11, 13, 14
Alveolars, 13, 36, 76, 78, 175, 179
Alveolar stops, 78, 79, 175, 215
Alveolo-palatals, 179
Ambisyllabic, 258

American English
   alveolar nasal, 78
   approximants, 72–73
   back vowel, 232
   bilabial gestures, 174
   consonant sounds, 37–38, 40
   coronal and nasal stops, 68–69
   dental fricatives, 175
   dictionaries for, 90
   diphthongs, 96–99
   glottal stops, 66, 67, 118
   intonational phrase, 126–131, 265
   lateral plosion, 68
   nasal plosion, 184
   post-alveolar sounds, 179
   regional differences, 42, 43, 69, 93, 96, 98, 101–102, 234–235
   rhotacization, 99–101, 239–241
   semivowels, 243–244
   spectrogram of, 204–205, 209, 220
   stress in, 259–260
   taps and flaps, 187
   timing, 262–263, 272
   tones, 265
   velarization, 73
   velar stops and nasals, 180
   vowel sounds, 41–44, 95–97, 203, 234
American Newscaster English, 101
Amplitude, 8–9
Anticipatory coarticulation, 74
Aperture, 284, 288
Apical sounds, 178, 280, 284
Approximants, 17, 72–73, 116, 188–190, 279–281, 284–287
Arabic language, 39, 181–182, 245, 253, 261
Aramaic language, 253
Articulation. *See also* **Coarticulation**
   acoustics and, 2–34
   central, 189–191

Articulation (*Continued*)
  of consonants, 15–18, 173–182
  controlling, 289–291
  coronal, 12, 13, 68–69, 283–284
  dorsal, 12, 180, 283–284
  ease of, 294
  formant frequencies and, 206–207
  glottal, 283, 286
  labial, 12, 282–284
  manners of, 15–19, 60, 191–192
  places of, 46, 174, 175, 178–181
  radical, 283
  secondary, 71, 244–246
  structures of, 12–13
  of vowel sounds, 20–22
Articulators, 10, 12
Articulatory gestures, 10–14, 183–191, 289–291
Articulatory process, 5–6
Arytenoid cartilages, 156–157
Aspiration, 61, 154, 160, 163
Assimilation, 119, 284–285, 287–288, 291
ATR. *See* **Advanced tongue root**
Auditory vowel space, 93–95
Australian aboriginal language, 179
Austronesian languages, 174

Back (of the tongue), 10, 12, 14, 45, 60, 152–153, 180, 245–246
Backness, 22, 227, 230, 233, 238, 240, 242, 285
Back vowels, 21–22, 91, 94, 96, 109, 232
Bantu languages, 265
Bark scale, 207
Bilabial gestures, 12, 174–175, 176, 182, 183, 187, 282–283
Break index, 136–137
Breathy voice, 157–158, 162
British English. *See also* Cockney English
  approximants, 72–73
  consonant sounds, 40
  dental fricatives, 175
  dictionaries for, 90
  diphthongs, 96–99
  glottal stops, 66, 67
  intonation, 126–134
  lateral plosion, 68
  rhotacization, 99–101
  spectrogram of, 205–206, 215, 218
  vowel sounds, 41–42, 44, 95–97, 236
Broad transcription, 35, 50
Burmese language, 185

Californian English, 222, 234–235
Canadian English, 69, 98
Cantonese language, 48
Cardinal vowels, 227–232
Central articulation, 189–191
Centre for Speech Technology (CTT), 204
Chadic languages, 158
Chaga language, 190
Charts
  consonants, 45–47, 51, 183, 279–280
  vowels, 45–47, 51, 228–229, 232–233, 280
Chinese language, 179, 259, 263, 268, 269, 270. *See also* Mandarin Chinese
Citation form, 35, 115–119
Clicks, 152–155
Closed-class words, 117
Closed syllables, 106
Coarticulation, 74–75, 294
Cockney English, 40, 66, 98, 102, 184, 211. *See also* British English
Coda, 258
Coleman, John, 91
Connected speech, 116
  citation speech compared to, 35, 117
  intonation, 126–134
  sentence rhythm, 124–126
  stress in, 121–124
Consecutive stops, 77
Consonants, 60–87, 173–196, 243
  acoustics of, 19, 208–214
  affricates, 71
  alveolar, 175
  approximants, 72–73
  articulations of, 15–18, 173–182
  charts, 45–47, 51, 183, 279–280
  coda, 258
  diacritics, 50, 80–81
  emphatic, 245
  flaps, 186–189
  fricatives, 69–71, 185
  homorganic, 68, 79
  laterals, 189–191
  liquid, 78
  nasals, 71–72, 108, 185–186, 210, 213–214, 241
  overlapping gestures, 73–76
  places of obstruction, 12–14
  stops, 61–70, 76–77, 183–185
  taps, 186–189
  transcription of, 37–40
  trills, 186–189
  waveforms of, 19–20

Consonant sounds
　American English, 37–38, 40
　British English, 40
Continuation rise, 127–129, 132, 134
Contour tone, 129–130, 133, 267–268
Coordinative structures, 289
Coronal articulations, 12, 13, 68–69, 283–284
Creaky voice, 24, 158, 164. *See also* **Laryngealization**
CTT (Centre for Speech Technology), 204
Czech language, 188, 259

Danish language, 237, 261, 284–285
Declination, 269–270
Degrees of freedom problem, 289
Dentals, 12–13, 81, 147, 152–154, 175, 178, 280
Devoicing, 292
Diacritics, 50, 80–81
Dictionaries, 89–90
Diphthongs, 44, 96–99, 211
Dorsal articulations, 12, 180, 283–284
Dorsum, 180
Downdrift, 137
Downstep, 135, 137, 138
Dravidian language, 175
Dutch language, 39, 238, 263–264

Ease of articulation, 294
Edo language, 266–267
Egede language, 267
Ejectives, 146–148, 155, 164–165
Emphatic consonants, 245
English Pronouncing Dictionary (EPD 18), 89, 90
Epenthesis, 79–80
Epiglottal sounds, 181–182, 280, 283
Epiglottis, 11
Eskimo language, 181
Esling, John, 89
Estonian language, 261
Estuary English, 66, 102
Ewe language, 174, 175, 182, 265
Exemplar theory, 293

Falling contour, 129–130
Features, 282–287
Filter, 198–199, 204
Finnish language, 39, 261
Fixed phrase stress, 259
Fixed word stress, 259

Flaps, 18, 186–189
Formants
　acoustic analysis, 203–208
　articulations and, 206–207
　consonants, 208–213
　individual differences, 221–224
　overview, 6, 24
　perturbation theory, 202–203
　source/filter theory, 197–200
　spectrograms interpretation, 213–221
　tube models, 200–201
　of vowels, 24
French language, 39
　allophones, 180–181
　alveolar consonants, 175
　laminal sounds, 178
　overlapping gestures, 74
　palatal nasals, 180
　perceptual separation, 295–296
　places of articulation, 175, 178–181
　stress in, 259, 263
　timing, 262
　trills, 188
　uvular sounds, 180–181, 188
　VOT (voice onset time), 161–162
　vowels, 238, 243–244
Frequency, 7–8, 25. *See also* Acoustic phonetics
Fricatives
　acoustic correlates, 242
　apertures and, 284, 288
　bilabial, 174, 175
　consonants, 69–71, 185
　dental, 175
　labiodental, 174–175
　mechanism of, 17
　palatal, 180
　palato-alveolar, 178–179
　retroflex, 175–177
　sibilant, 185
　stops and, 69–71
　symbols for, 179
　velar, 180
Front vowels, 20–21, 73, 80
Full vowels, 118, 122–124

Gaelic languages, 162, 271
Geminates, 261
German language, 39, 43–44, 179, 183, 184, 262
　affricates, 175
　rounded vowels, 238

German language (*Continued*)
  stress, 259, 263
  velar fricatives, 180
  voiceless palatal fricatives, 180
Gestural targets, 73–76
Gestures, 2–4
  articulatory, 10–14, 183–191, 289–291
  bilabial, 12, 174–175, 176, 182, 183, 187, 282–283
  interdental, 13
  labiodental, 12, 174–175, 183, 279
  overlapping, 73–76, 108, 109, 294
  palatal, 14, 176, 179–180
  palato-alveolar, 14, 177–179, 288
  post-alveolar, 14, 179
  retroflex, 13–14, 99, 175–177, 179, 279–281
  secondary articulation, 71, 244–246
  velar, 14, 80, 145, 147–148, 164, 180–182, 213, 287–288
Glottal articulations, 283, 286
Glottalic airstream mechanism, 145
Glottal stops, 18, 40, 65–67, 77, 118, 156–159, 164–165
Glottis, 144–149, 151, 156–159, 164–165
Greek language, 253, 261
Gujarati language, 157–158

Hard palate, 10
Hausa language, 145–146, 158, 164, 187, 270
Hawaiian language, 258–259, 262
Hebrew language, 181–182, 253
Height of vowels, 21–22, 24, 74, 91, 99, 227, 230–231, 233, 238–239, 242, 285
Helmholtz, Hermann, 201
High plus downstepped high, 135
Hindi language, 157, 162–163, 176, 178
Homorganic consonants, 68, 79
Hungarian language, 180

Ibibio language, 266
Icelandic language, 186
Igbo language, 155, 266
Implosives, 148–151, 155, 164–165
Impressionistic transcription, 51
India, language of, 157–158, 175, 177
Intensity, 204, 207, 210, 216–217, 255–256
Interdental gestures, 13
International Phonetic Alphabet (IPA), 15, 38–40, 51, 90, 245, 267, 278–282

International Phonetic Association, 38, 277, 278
Intonation, 264–270
  in connected speech, 126–134
  defined, 25–26
  rising and falling contour, 129–130, 133
  ToBI system, 135–138
  tone and, 264–265
  tonic syllables, 122, 123, 127–129, 133
Intonational phrase, 126–131, 265
IPA. *See* International Phonetic Alphabet
Isochrony, 262
Italian language, 42–43, 65, 161–162, 179, 180, 190, 261

Japanese language, 190, 236–237, 243, 253
  mora-timed, 261–262
  stress in, 263, 271
  tone, 270
  vowels, 292
Johnson, Keith, 6, 151, 200, 246
Jones, Daniel, 89–90, 229, 246

Kele language, 188
Khoisan languages, 155
Konopka, Rafal, 90
Kretzschmar, William, 90
Kutep language, 267

Labial articulations, 12, 282–284
Labialization, 71, 245–246
Labial velars (labiovelars), 182
Labiodental gestures, 12, 174–175, 183, 279
Labiovelars. *See* Labial velars
Lakhota language, 146–148, 151, 180
Laminal sounds, 178, 280, 284
Laryngeal characteristics, 286–287
Laryngealization, 158–159
Larynx, 5
Lateral plosion, 68
Laterals, 17–18, 175, 189–191, 210, 212, 283–284
Lax vowels, 105–107
Length, 199, 260–261
Length vocal tract, 198–200
Length, segmental, 260–261
Lexical sets, 101–103
Linguistic phonetics, 277–301
  of community and individual, 277–278
  controlling articulatory movements, 289–291

explanations problems, 287–288
feature hierarchy, 282–287
IPA, 278–282
memory for speech, 291–294
phonetic forces balance, 294–296
Linguo-labials, 174
Lip movements, 289
Lip rounding, 22, 71, 74–75, 206, 208, 221, 232–233
Liquid consonants, 78
Locus, 209, 211, 214
Longman Pronunciation Dictionary (LPD 3) (Wells), 89–90
Loudness, 7
LPD 3. *See Longman Pronunciation Dictionary*
Luganda language, 261, 265, 266, 270

Malayalam language, 175, 176, 177, 178, 188, 190
Mandarin Chinese, 265, 267, 268, 292
Manner of articulation, 285. *See also* **Articulation**
Margi language, 189
Mid-sagittal section, 12
Mid-Waghi language, 190
Midwestern English. *See* American English
Modal voice, 157–158, 165
Monophthongs, 95, 98, 102
Mora-timed language, 261–263
Motor control, 289–291
Motor equivalences, 290
Murmur, 154, 157–158, 162, 165

Nama language, 153, 155
Narrow-band spectrograms, 221
Narrow transcription, 50
Nasalization, 241, 285
Nasal plosion, 66–67, 184
Nasals, 184
  acoustic correlates, 213
  consonants, 71–72, 108, 185–186, 210, 213–214, 241
  features, 282–285
  palatal, 180
  in spectrograms, 116
  syllabic, 71–72, 77
  symbols for, 183
  velar, 145–147, 152, 182
  voiceless, 185
Nasal stop, 15–16
Nasal tract, 5

Nasal vowel, 107, 108, 241
Native American languages, 146, 181
Navajo language, 159–162, 184, 190, 292
Neogrammarians, 294
Newton, Isaac, 24
New Zealand English, 234
Norwegian language, 39
Nuclear pitch accent, 135
Nucleus, 258

Obama, Barack, 125
Obicularis oris inferior (OOI), 289
Obstruents, 70, 77, 145
Onset, 258
OOI (obicularis oris inferior), 289
Open syllables, 106
Oral stop, 15
Oral tract, 5
Oro-nasal process, 5–6, 15
An Outline of English Phonetics (Jones), 230
Overlapping gestures, 73–76, 108, 109, 294
Overtone pitches, 23, 197–198, 201
Owerri dialect, 155
Oxford Dictionary of Pronunciation for Current English (Upton/Kretzchmar/Konopka), 90, 98

Pairwise variability index (PVI), 263
Palatal gestures, 14, 176, 179–180
Palatalization, 244–245
Palato-alveolar gestures, 14, 177–179, 288
Perceptual separation, 238, 295–296
Perturbation theory, 202–203
Pharyngealization, 245
Pharyngeal sounds, 181–182, 285
Pharynx, 4, 5, 10, 11
Phonation process, 5–6
Phonemes, 41–43, 72
Phonemic transcriptions, 37, 282
Phonetic implementation, 292
Phonetics
  acoustic, 6, 19, 197–226
  linguistic, 277–301
Phonetic transcription, 35–57, 282
Phonetic variability, 292–293
Phonetic vowel qualities, 102
Phonology, 35–57, 281–282
Phrase accent, 136
Pitch, 7, 25, 126, 264–265
  accent, nuclear, 135
  overtone, 23, 197–198, 201
  velar, 209

Plosives, 15, 145
Polish language, 179, 259, 262
Polysyllabic word, 124
Post-alveolar gestures, 14, 179
Prominence, 257
Pulmonic airstream mechanism, 144–145, 153, 155
PVI (pairwise variability index), 263

Quality
  of sounds, 7
  vowel, 91–93, 198, 242
Quechua language, 181

Radical articulations, 283
r-**colored** vowels, 99–100
Reduced, 115
Reduced vowels, 104–105, 108, 115, 122
Reification, 287
Release burst, 146
Retroflex gestures, 13–14, 99, 175–177, 179, 279–281
Rhotacization, 99–101, 239–241, 285
Rhotic vowels, 99–101
Rhyme, 258
Rising contour, 129–130, 133
Roach, Peter, 89
Roll. *See* **Trill**
Rounded vowels, 22, 238, 243–244, 288, 296
Russell, G. Oscar, 208
Russian language, 39, 184, 244–245

Scottish English, 187
Scottish Highlands, 260–261
Secondary articulation, 71, 244–246
Secondary cardinal vowels, 232–234
Segments, 253
Semiconsonant, 243
Semitic languages, 181–182, 253
Semivowels, 242–244
Sentence rhythm, 124–126
Setter, Jane, 89
Shona language, 265
Sibilants, 17, 185, 285, 288
Sindhi language, 148–150, 159–160, 162–163, 176, 180
Slavic language, 244
Slips of the tongue, 258
Soft palate, 10
Sonority, 255–256

Sounds
  apical, 178, 280, 284
  consonant sounds, 37–38, 40
  epiglottal, 181–182, 280, 283
  laminal, 178, 280, 284
  pharyngeal, 181–182, 285
  quality of, 7
  Sub-Apical, 284
  uvular, 180–181, 188
  voiced, 4, 19, 61, 69–73, 77, 147–149, 156–157, 175, 185
  voiceless, 4, 19, 61, 69–73, 76–77, 147–149, 156–157, 175, 180, 185
  vowel, 20–22, 41–44, 95–97, 203, 234, 236
Sound waves, 6–10
Source/filter theory, 197–200
Spanish, 39, 161–162, 191, 236–237, 262, 263
  palatal nasals, 180
  trill and tap, 187
  vowels, 42–43
Speaker identification, 221, 223
Speaking styles, 293–294
Spectrograms, 8–9, 115, 241
  of American English, 204–205, 209, 220
  of British English, 205–206, 215, 218
  individual differences, 221–224
  interpretation, 213–221
  of Lakhota language, 147
  of Malayalam language, 178
  narrow-band, 221
  nasals, stops, vowels in, 116
  of trills, 186
  wide-band, 218, 219
Speech
  connected, 35, 116–117, 121–134
  memory for, 291–294
  motor control, 289–291
  planning, 257, 271
  synthetic, 201, 223
Standard American Newscaster English, 90, 95
Standard BBC English, 90, 101–102
Stetson, R. H., 257
Stops. *See also* Ejectives; Plosives; Retroflex gestures
  acoustic correlates, 213
  alveolar, 78, 79, 175, 215
  aperture, 284, 288
  consecutive, 77

consonants, 61–70, 76–77, 183–185
dental, 175, 178
fricatives and, 69–71
glottal, 18, 40, 65–67, 77, 118, 156–159, 164–165
nasal, 15–16
oral, 15
release burst, 146
in spectrograms, 116
symbols for, 183
types of, 15–16
velar, 80, 145, 147–148, 164, 180–182
Stress, 121–124, 259–260, 263, 271
Stressed syllables, 25, 99, 102, 105, 259–260
Stress-timed language, 259
Strong form of words, 117
Structures
of articulations, 12–13
coordinative, 289
Sub-Apical sounds, 284
Supra-Laryngeal characteristics, 283–285
Suprasegmentals, 24–26, 253–276
Swahili language, 37, 184, 259
Swedish language, 39, 238, 270–271
Syllabic nasals, 71–72, 77
Syllables, 263–276
closed, 106
definition of, 242
intonation and tone, 264–270
length, 260–261
onset and rhyme, 258
open, 106
prominence, 257
segments of, 263
sonority, 255–256
stress, 25, 99, 102, 105, 259–260
timing, 261–263, 272
tonic, 122, 123, 127–129, 133
unstressed, 99, 104–105
Symbols, 38–41, 45–48, 179, 183
Synthetic speech, 201, 223
Systematic phonetic transcription, 282

Tamil language, 187
Taps, 18, 50, 78–79, 186–189, 279, 285
Target position, 134–138
Tense vowels, 105–107
Thai language, 161–162, 164, 268–269
Timing, 261–263, 272
Titan language, 188
ToBI system, 135–138

Toda language, 188, 190, 279, 280
Tone and break indices, 135
Tones, 264–270
Tone sandhi, 269
Tongue, 2, 5, 10, 11, 94–95, 283–285.
See also **Back (of the tongue)**
Tonic accent. *See* **Tonic syllables**
Tonic syllables, 122, 123, 127–129, 133
Transcriptions
allophonic, 281–282
broad, 35, 50
of consonants, 37–40
dictionaries, 89–90
impressionistic, 51
narrow, 50
phonemic, 37, 282
phonetic, 35–57
systematic phonetic, 282
of vowels, 41–45, 89–90
Trills, 18, 39, 186–189, 285
Tube models, 200–201

Unrounded vowels. *See* **Rounded** vowels
Unstressed syllables, 99, 104–105
Upton, Clive, 90
Uvula, 10–11
Uvular sounds, 180–181, 188

Vanuatu language, 174
Variable word stress, 259
Velar gestures
acoustic correlates, 213
defined, 14
features, 287–288
fricatives, 180
labial, 182
stops, 80, 145, 147–148, 164, 180–182
Velaric airstream mechanism, 152–153
Velarization, 73, 245
Velar nasals, 145–147, 152, 182
Velar pitch, 209
Velic closure, 10
Velum, 10–11
V'enen Taut language, 174
Vietnamese language, 149, 151, 268
Vocal folds, 4, 7, 198–201, 205, 214, 218–221
Vocal tracts, 4–5, 10–13, 198–202, 205, 208, 219
Vocoids, 242
Voice bar, 209

Voiced sounds, 19
    approximants, 72–73
    defined, 4
    fricatives, 69–71, 185
    glottis state in, 147–149, 156–157
    laterals, 175
    stop consonants, 61, 70, 77
Voiceless sounds, 19
    approximants, 72–73
    fricatives, 69–71
    glottis state in, 147–149, 156–157
    laterals, 175
    nasals, 185
    palatal fricatives, 180
    stop consonants, 61, 70, 76–77
    voiced sounds compared to, 4
Voice onset time (VOT), 159–164
Vowels, 42–43, 89–114, 227–251
    acoustic analysis, 203–208
    allophones, 107–109
    American and British, 95–97
    apertures and, 284, 288
    approximants, 284–287
    ATR (advanced tongue root), 238–239
    auditory space, 93–95
    back, 21–22, 91, 94, 96, 109, 232
    backness, 22, 227, 230, 233, 238, 240, 242, 285
    cardinal, 227–232
    charts, 45–47, 51, 228–229, 232–233, 280
    coordinative structures, 289
    in creaky voice, 24
    diphthongs, 97–99
    formants of, 24
    French language, 238, 243–244
    front, 20–21, 73, 80
    full, 118, 122–124
    height, 21–22, 24, 74, 91, 99, 227, 230–231, 233, 238–239, 242, 285
    individual differences, 221–224
    lexical sets, 101–103
    lip rounding, 22, 71, 74–75, 206, 208, 221, 232–233
    nasal, 107, 108, 241
    nasalization, 241, 285
    in other English accents, 234–236
    in other languages, 236–238
    perturbation theory, 202–203
    PVI (pairwise variability index) of, 263
    r-colored, 99–100
    reduced, 104–105, 108, 115, 122
    rhotacization, 99–101, 239–241, 285
    rhotic, 99–101
    rounded, 22, 238, 243–244, 288, 296
    secondary articulatory gestures, 71, 244–246
    secondary cardinal, 232–234
    semivowels, 242–244
    source/filter theory, 197–200
    in spectrograms, 116
    tense, 105–107
    tense and lax sets, 105–107
    transcription of, 41–45, 89–90
    tube models, 200–201
    unstressed syllables, 99, 104–105
Vowel sounds
    American English, 41–44, 95–97, 203, 234
    articulation of, 20–22
    British English, 41–42, 44, 95–97, 236

Waveforms, 7–8, 19–20, 25, 62, 63, 64
WaveSurfer, 63, 71, 204, 234
Weak form of words, 117
Wells, John, 89–90, 102
Welsh language, 190
Wide-band spectrograms, 218, 219
Willis, Robert, 201

Xhosa, 154–155, 265
!Xóõ language, 153, 155

Yoruba language, 182, 241, 266

Zulu language, 154–155, 164, 189–190, 265